THE RED TRIANGLE

A HISTORY OF
ANTI-MASONRY

THE RED TRIANGLE

A HISTORY OF ANTI-MASONRY

ROBERT L.D. COOPER

Red Triangle
A History of Anti-Masonry
Robert L. D. Cooper

First published 2011

ISBN 978 0 085318 332 7

Published by Lewis Masonic
an imprint of Ian Allan Publishing Ltd, Hersham, Surrey KT12 4RG.
Printed in England by CPI Mackays Ltd, Chatham, Kent ME5 8TD.

Code: A3

Visit the Lewis Masonic website a www.lewismasonic.com

Distributed in the United States of America and Canada by
BookMasters Distribution Services

Picture Credits
All images copyright Robert L. D. Cooper with the exception of
concentration camp badges (copyright free); David McLetchie
cartoon, copyright Frank Boyle; Masonic Monkey, copyright The
Daily Express. Not to be reproduced without permission. All rights
reserved.

Front cover design: Lisa Dynan

CONTENTS

ACKNOWLEDGEMENTS

I always find this most difficult to write. I am sure that many authors also experience the same difficulty. The reason, certainly so far as I am concerned, is that I focus on writing the text and in the process occasionally forget to record those who assisted me in my research.

As is always the case in preparing a publication many people have helped in a variety of ways. Lindsay Anderson, Crown Office and Procurator Fiscal Service (Edinburgh, Scotland), for her assistance in explaining the manner in which the criminal justice system operates in Scotland; Stephen Walton of the Imperial War Museum for his help in gaining access to Masonophobic material relating to the Nazi regime; Lorna Black, of the Scottish National Library, for her assistance in locating some obscure publications; Yasha Beresiner, Past Master of Lodge Quatuor Coronati, No.2076 for his help in obtaining a variety of Masonophobic illustrations. Other members of that Lodge, of which I am proud to be a full member, include: John Acaster; James Daniel; Roeinton Khambatta; David Peabody; Aubrey Newman; John Wade and last but not at all least Brent Morris, who have all encouraged me in my various endeavours.

Richard Gan, Editor of *The Square* magazine, for not only his encouragement but also his helpful comments when reading the initial drafts.

All the staff at Freemasons' Hall, the home of the Grand Lodge of Scotland, indulged me when occasional moodiness overtook me. The Grand Secretary, David M. Begg, has not only been an encouragement but has also been very understanding as to the need to have time to research and prepare a work such as this. Those members of staff who have assisted (whether they know it or not!) are: Dawn Oliff; Maureen Hazel; George Preston; Clark Wilson; Derek Elms; Jim Noble and volunteer assistant Rodger Bullard.

Hugh Young, Past Grand Master of the Grand Lodge of Alberta, for his humorous and insightful observations on what, for many Freemasons, can be a rather dark subject.

Finally, I would record my grateful thanks to the publisher, Lewis Masonic, for once again indulging a 'difficult-to-deal-with' author especially in respect of allowing the inclusion of an extensive bibliography and several appendices. They were also very understanding in respect of several domestic difficulties that contributed to the long delay in the production of the final text. It has been a pleasure to deal with such a professional publishing house.

INTRODUCTION

We condemn the evils of prejudice, discrimination and racism.
We value a free, tolerant, and democratic society
(From: the United Nations Statement of Commitment)

On Wednesday, 13 March 1996 at 09.30 am Thomas Hamilton (1952 –1996) entered Dunblane Primary School and proceeded to the gymnasium where primary class 1/13 had assembled and was waiting to begin. Stopping at the entrance he fired a 9mm Browning pistol killing the class teacher (Mrs Mayor) and one pupil and wounding another teacher (Mrs Harrild) and numerous children. Hamilton then walked to the opposite (east) side of the gym where a group of children lay disabled on the floor. He 'stood over them and fired at point blank range'.[1] Moving to the south east side of the gym he fired indiscriminately in various directions both inside and outside the gym. Opening the fire escape door he fired 9 rounds into the class room occupied by primary 7. Hamilton then re-entered the gym firing more shots. He then dropped the Browning pistol and took up a .357 Smith and Wesson revolver. He placed the muzzle in his mouth pointing upwards and fired. Death was instantaneous. All this death and injury was inflicted within 3 – 4 minutes between 9.35 am and 9.40 am.

The mass murder of 16 children and one teacher together with the wounding of further 14 children and three teachers shocked the people of Scotland and engendered emotions of shock, horror and sympathy across the world. Those feelings were shared by Freemasons both at home and abroad. In the immediate aftermath of all such terrible events there is always one main question: why? When there is no answer forthcoming, especially if not quickly, speculation rather than fact becomes dominant. In respect of the Dunblane shootings the Scottish Press soon provided the world with an answer.

On 22 March 1996, less than ten days after the mass murder of 16 children and their teacher, the following article was published in *The Scotsman* newspaper:[2] [3]

'Secret brotherhood which protects its own
"The Freemasons of Britain are strongly protective of their fellow Masons. They rarely punish brethren who break the criminal law of

the land…", Martin Short, author of a best-selling investigation into Freemasonry, last night told *The Scotsman*.

"Scotland is a place where one Mason looks after another," said Mr Short. "If Thomas Hamilton was one of the brethren it's pretty bad news for the Masons because one is inclined to assume he may well have received favours." They would not allow one of their own brethren to be exposed to public ridicule and would do everything to avoid his membership being known.

Short, whose book *Inside the Brotherhood: Further Secrets of the Freemasons* was first published in 1989, referred to a local government ombudsman's decision in Hamilton's favour in 1983. The ombudsman overturned a decision by [the] Central Regional Council to end his lease of Dunblane High School premises for his boys' club, the Dunblane Rover Group.

"The fact that he managed to bamboozle the ombudsman suggests that the ombudsman was bombarded by letters," said Mr Short. "If he managed to convince the ombudsman that he was OK, you can be pretty sure that his lodge would have felt at least equally strongly. The Masons in the lodge would not have wanted to think ill of him and would therefore have tried to protect him from all-comers."

Social pressures make it difficult for an honest Mason to complain about criminal or immoral conduct by his brothers, said Mr Short. In fact, it would be the complainant, not the wrongdoers, who faced ostracism and probable exclusion from the lodge.

Mr Short said Masonry was an organisation of men only who voluntarily swear mutual aid and to guard each other's secrets: it has its own strict rules, inquiry systems, punishments and courts of appeal. He said that when it became known he was researching his book he lost count of the brethren who cautioned him to "watch out" or "take care".

Mr Short went on: "One man whose evidence sent a fellow Mason to jail told me of his fears during that trial and the extreme precautions he had taken to stay alive. He advised me to do the same."

Mr Short's 711-page book lists some of the reasons why he was inclined to take the advice seriously. It also lists some of the bizarre initiation ceremonies of Masonry. Mr Short, for example, describes a Masonic lodge in Lincolnshire where a candidate Mason is lowered into a trap below the temple floor on the Friday before full moon to confront a female skeleton as a symbol of mortality.

Several traditional crafts and professions are bastions of Freemasonry, Mr Short argues.

In his book he points to the example of the Metropolitan Police where, in 1987, he identified one assistant commissioner, two deputy assistant commissioners, 12 commanders, 23 chief superintendents, ten superintendents and seven chief inspectors as members of a single Masonic lodge.

Mr Short argues that Freemasonry extends into local government, the armed services, industry and the intelligence services to an extent which would astonish non-Masons. He says 100,000, or one in 14 of Scotland's working population, are Freemasons.'[4] [5]

When I read this I could not believe the words printed on a page of one of Scotland's most important broadsheets. I was in turn shocked, dismayed and disgusted. Like the Kennedy assassination and the 9/11 attack on the twin towers in New York City I can clearly recall where I was and what I was doing when I first heard of those events.[6] I can also recall with great clarity where I was and what I was doing when I first heard the news of the Dunblane shootings. For the purpose of this book I also recall when I first read the above article in *The Scotsman*. On both occasions I was working in the Library at Freemasons' Hall, 96 George Street, Edinburgh.[7] On the day of the shootings the then Grand Secretary burst into the room, obviously greatly distressed, and told me what had just been reported by BBC Radio Scotland.[8] This was a tragedy not only for parents and relatives, school and citizens of Dunblane but for the whole nation. Grand Secretary's distress was increased by facts of which I was then unaware and which I shall detail later (See Chapter 5). On the morning of Friday, 22 March I was again at my post in the Library at Freemasons' Hall when Grand Secretary quietly entered the room and handed me a copy of *The Scotsman* newspaper folded open to show the article produced in full above. He left without saying a word.

I have chosen 1996, therefore, as a starting point for this examination of the *contemporary* history of Masonophobia in Scotland because it is noticeable that it was from that year that the public examination of Freemasonry took on a hard, indeed nasty, edge. Prior to 1996 Freemasonry certainly had been the recipient of adverse publicity but it was often more of the tongue-in-cheek kind, poking fun at what was considered to be odd – the rolled up trouser leg, for example.[9] It is not therefore the intention to examine the period immediately before 1996 as part of the examination of contemporary Masonophobia except where necessary to draw comparisons.[10] I am sure that given the implication of Scottish Freemasonry in the mass-murder of innocent children (and one of their teachers) it will be understood why this is a turning point.

How could an ancient and honourable Scottish fraternity, which has been in recorded existence since 1491, become the subject of such a sustained campaign of vitriolic hate?[11] This is the subject of this book. However, that must be qualified somewhat in that I am not approaching this subject from a political or religious perspective (although I shall make observations on both) but rather from an historical viewpoint. This is simply because there is a duty upon me as a Freemason not to engage in matters of politics or religion. This is the prime, self imposed, rule of all Freemasons. This book is therefore about the history of Masonophobia with a focus, latterly, on events in Scotland. Why Scotland? one might ask. Scotland is a small country and is considered by many to be the home of Freemasonry. Thus together with the fact that material examined is limited as a consequence of the size of the population it seems an ideal place to focus on Masonophobia which would be more difficult in a larger country such as England with its greatly more numerous media outlets.[12] Whether the Scottish experience can be extrapolated to other countries is not a major aim but I shall make occasional reference to events in England in respect of contemporary history as they inevitably had an impact in Scotland although the reverse is not so often the case.

Because I am an historian and also happen to be a Freemason my answer to a friend's question 'What possessed you to even think of writing a book about anti-Masonry? was simply that I had been at the centre of the momentous events during the 1990s as they related to Scottish Freemasonry.[13] My friend's question made me realise that, although I wanted to record the more recent history of Freemasonry in Scotland, to do so would be deficient as it could only reveal a small part of a very large picture. The idea was born therefore to try and give an account of anti-Masonry from an historical perspective. From that starting point I had no idea of the nature of the task on which I embarked. As shall be seen this project, initially intended to begin from 1996, eventually proved to be a major undertaking. I therefore must immediately thank my publishers, Lewis Masonic, for their forbearance in placing their trust in a project which, like me, they had no possible idea of where it would lead not least the time and costs involved. They have done me proud.

Organising answers to the question 'why did I write this book?' falls into several categories. First and foremost I wished, as a Freemason who is honoured to have worked for the Grand Lodge of Scotland throughout the 1990s to the present time, to record events as seen from the point of view of a Freemason. During a period when Freemasonry was under merciless attack and scrutiny by all branches of the media I was conscious that I was in the middle of 'history in the making'. I kept notes, read and clipped newspapers, was interviewed on television, radio and by the print media. This was where the 'Masonic' interest arose.[14]

I was active in the middle of a period that saw animosity towards Freemasonry rise to the very surface of Scottish society where it remained over a period of years and when there was all sorts of talk of 'taking action' against Freemasons to the extent that the new Scottish Parliament enacted rules against its citizens who happened to be Freemasons. I heard no voices in our defence and our voices were not allowed to be heard. This caused me to ask if this was a new phenomenon. How could such a long established minority be so quickly and brutally turned upon by the very society of which they were citizens? What is more how could this occur without any possibility of a defence? The question was therefore when had attacks on Freemasonry first occurred and what was their cause and nature? As a Masonic historian I was generally aware Freemasonry had been subjected to a variety of attacks over a substantial period of its existence but had not examined this as a separate subject. I also knew that Freemasonry usually managed to mount a defence against its attackers whether successful or not. An examination of the defence of Freemasonry might also be revealing. However, this period (the 1990s) of Scottish history saw the denial of any such defence and I came to realise that modern anti-Masonry had changed into something quite different, something more vicious, strident, unforgiving and inflexible. Anti-Masonry was no longer the same as being 'anti-smoking' or 'anti-car', it had turned into Masonophobia.[15] This process had been seen to happen to other minority groups such as homosexuals, the disabled, and religious groups such as those of the Muslim faith.

Zealots, particularly in a country as small as Scotland, stand out for all to see and some of their public pronouncements will be provided here in order that some kind of context can be given. I was ashamed, as a Scot, to witness on a regular basis extending over a period of years attack after attack, innuendo after innuendo, falsehood after falsehood being repeated again and again against Freemasonry.[16] As the 'historian' of Scottish Freemasonry I offered my comments, opinions, facts and even exhibited medieval documents to demonstrate that Freemasonry was as Scottish as whisky or haggis![17] This attempt to defend the Scottish Craft largely failed. Facts relating to the history and heritage of Scottish Freemasonry and its contribution to numerous aspects of Scottish society counted for little when sensationalism dominated the media. Sensible discussion was not possible (or even suggested). As a consequence some of the vilest accusations that can be levelled against a human being were levelled against Freemasons. Almost without exception these were published in the public domain and can therefore be made available here.

'Justice', I thought would come to the aid of the small minority which had existed, if not originated, in this land of stone – called Scotland – and which had existed since medieval times. Justice is blind, so it is said, and during the 1990s, so far as Freemasonry was concerned, justice was neither blind nor mute but used its senses to aim at a specific target.

Accused of all sorts of crimes during the 1990s, including mass murder, paedophilia, gross corruption, blackmail and the perverting of the course of justice, Freemasonry came to be seen in the most appalling light possible to imagine. Here I offer an alternative view of Freemasonry and it is right and proper that I remind everyone that these are my views and my views alone. It is one of the curiosities of Freemasonry that no one Freemason, or even a group of Freemasons, can speak for all of Freemasonry.[18] [19]

Chance would have it that I became the custodian of some of the most important documents relating to the period before modern Freemasonry came into existence in the early 18th century.[20] The possession of these documents has been generally regarded as unimportant and this is hardly surprising given the terrible press Freemasonry has received during the recent past.[21] There are honourable exceptions such as Professor Emeritus David Stevenson of the University of St Andrews.

Incredibly, Scottish academia has paid little or no attention to the work of Prof. Stevenson, who has revealed a fascinating aspect of Scottish history worthy of much further exploration. His reward for this seminal work has been to be treated, at best, as an academic oddity and at worst as some kind of *agent provocateur* for the worldwide conspiracy that 'everyone knows' Freemasonry is trying to put into effect.[22]

Niceties such as 'balance' ceased to exist within the Scottish media when it came to Freemasonry. At one time, if there was something unpleasant or simply 'not nice' to be reported about a person, group or company (for example) the decent thing to do was to allow them equal (or nearly equal) space in which to defend themselves.

Given the events of the 1990s, I especially noted that after 1996 this situation ceased to apply almost completely with regard to Scottish Freemasonry, and I would go so far as to suggest, but cannot in any way substantiate the suggestion, that Scottish Freemasonry was systematically and deliberately denied that 'right' (or at least the ability) by certain parts of the Scottish media. However, this assumes that rights (be they statutory, democratic or otherwise) apply to *all* minorities including Freemasonry. As we shall see minorities are treated differently at different times under different religious and political regimes. Of all minorities Freemasonry is the one that seems to be considered 'available' as a primary target at any particular time, in any particular place for any particular purpose. It would appear that it is no longer politically correct to attack minorities – Freemasonry being the exception and this will be explored in further detail later.

Incredibly, to me at least, the allegations and accusations made against Scottish Freemasonry were not countered in any way. Politicians even publicly denied that they were Freemasons and the few that admitted a connection with the Order said that they had been but were no longer involved.[23] Others said that they had made a stupid mistake or had joined when they were young and impressionable; in other words, when the word 'Freemasonry' was mentioned politicians in Scotland ran for cover. None attempted to defend their constituents.

Lively responses by the Grand Lodge of Scotland to the media failed because, as an ancient and honourable society, it was playing by gentlemanly rules. As we shall see the media were not. The Grand Lodge of Scotland decided to place 'briefing notes' in a new magazine – the *Holyrood Magazine*.[24] This was in an attempt to inform the new political class that had come into being following the vote for devolution in 1997, followed by the establishment of the devolved Parliament in 1999, to the effect that Freemasonry was, and had been, part of the Scottish social fabric for hundreds of years.[25] These briefing notes attempted to show the usefulness of Freemasonry to Scottish society by, among other things, providing retirement homes and encouraging 'Masonic tourism'. The reaction to these briefing notes was, as we shall see, entirely negative. *The Scotsman* placed news about Freemasonry on the front page for the first time in decades, not in order to be complimentary to Freemasonry but to claim that Freemasons were attempting to recruit members of the Scottish Parliament.

Memories, such as I have, and information from numerous notes, newspaper cuttings, TV video recordings form the basis of this book which, to begin with, deals with the recent experience of Freemasonry in Scotland (especially during the 1990s). However, I shall explain the subject as dispassionately as possible as an historian is trained to do. I can only hope that the recent past sees the end of modern Masonophobia.

I am quite sure that some will ask why this is 'all being raked up again' especially as adverse comment on Freemasonry is now, thankfully, relatively rare.[26] The answer is simple. Before memories fade, my notes get lost, other material is scattered and there is no one left to bear witness to what occurred from a Masonic point of view I believe that it is important that some kind of a record of the experiences I lived through as a Freemason ought to be recorded in a small attempt to counter-balance current Masonophobic perceptions.

On beginning research for this book it quickly became clear that the scope would have to be restricted. North America, which has suffered more than its fair share of Masonophobia, has had to be, reluctantly, omitted from any detailed discussion. The same reason meant that a number of specific events have not been considered. Examples are the P2 Lodge affair and the attacks in Australia by the Anglican Church.[27]

I cannot, therefore, presume to suggest that this is a comprehensive account of the subject. In fact the reverse is true. This book is merely an introduction and possibly a poor one at that but the attempt seemed to me to be worthwhile.

As always I must emphasise that the contents of this book have been gathered, collated and analysed by me and me alone. The opinions and contents contained herein are mine and mine alone and are most certainly *not* the views of my employer, The Grand Lodge of Antient Free and Accepted Masons of Scotland, or any other branch of Freemasonry with which I am associated.[28]

In preparing this work I must confess my shock as to the extent to which Freemasonry has been subjected to repeated attacks and not merely those of the recent past. This book is an attempt to provide a short insight to the history of Masonophobia. I can but hope that this work, such as it is, will serve as a warning and a reminder to everyone, not only Freemasons, that the veneer of civilisation is thin indeed.

CHAPTER 1

THE EARLY HISTORY OF
FREEMASONRY

'Equality is the soul of liberty; there is, in fact, no liberty without it.'
Frances Wright (1795–1852)

It is often said that the origins of Freemasonry are obscure but there is a considerable amount of published material which strongly suggests that this is not so. I am thinking in particular of the seminal work of David Stevenson which examined exhaustively early material (including lodge records) from the 15th to 17th centuries.[29] However, it is important to provide a brief, and therefore limited, history of the origins and development of Freemasonry as it occurred in Scotland.

In Scottish burghs the major trades or crafts were organised into Incorporations.[30] These Incorporations allowed the important trades a limited amount of political representation in the government of a town. Although never powerful enough to have complete control over any Scottish town they did, at least, have a voice in the way any particular town ran its affairs. The cost of this limited political power was that certain responsibilities were placed on the Incorporation and thereby the authorities exercised considerable control over what the Incorporations could and could not do. For example they were expected to ensure that boys entering the trade served a minimum apprenticeship period (typically 7 years); that they set and control wage rates and that they ensure that the members conformed to the moral and spiritual mores of the time. Interestingly they were responsible for looking after a particular part of the burgh church and as all trades had their own Patron Saint this would usually be an aisle dedicated to that saint. The Hammermen of Edinburgh, for example, were responsible for the upkeep of the aisle of St. Eloi [Eligius] (?–d.362) in the church of St. Giles.[31] In the same way the masons (stonemasons) were elevated to the status of an Incorporation in 1475 and they were made responsible for the aisle dedicated to St. John the Evangelist in the same church.[32] Incorporations were engaged in religious activities, each of them taking part on various Saints' Feast Days and most of them had a particular mystery play which they enacted on the Feast Day of their Patron Saint (although this is not always the case) and other religious festivals such as Corpus Christi. All incorporated trades had rules and regulations and a form of ceremony for the admission of a new member into the craft.[33] Incorporations may legitimately be viewed as a form of proto-Trade Union.[34] They also seem to have had secrets which were restricted to members of the craft concerned. For example, a Master of the Dundee Incorporation of Hammermen was expelled during 1653-4 for revealing the secrets of the Incorporation to the 'English Commander'.[35]

However, the main difference between the craft of the mason and the other burgh trades was that they, and they alone, had a separate organisation which 'shadowed' the Incorporation. That parallel organisation was the lodge. Exactly why stonemasons felt it necessary to have an additional, and secret, group is not known but it is not unreasonable to suggest that because the Incorporation of Wrights and Masons included men who were not stonemasons it was not appropriate for the secrets of the stonemasons to be revealed at a meeting of the Incorporation.[36]

The lodge is usually considered to be a hut or other small outhouse in which the stonemasons working at a particular place could store their working tools when not in use. However, there is a reference dated 1491 which indicates that the lodge (a place) was used for more than simply storing tools and was large enough for 'recreational' purposes. This reference is contained within Edinburgh Town Council minutes and lays down the working hours to be adopted by stonemasons then working at the church of St. Giles. This reference is significant because it shows that the lodge was more than just a tool store. It is reproduced as Appendix 1.[37]

Below are the dates various Edinburgh crafts were granted a Seal of Cause by the Town Council officially forming them into Incorporations:

Craft	Date of Incorporation
Cordiners (Shoemakers)	28 July 1449
Skinners	12 January 1450
Furriers	2 December 1474
Masons and wrights (Carpenters)	14 October 1475
Wobsters (Weavers)	31 January 1476
Hammermen (Blacksmiths etc.)	2 May 1483
Fleshers (Butchers)	11 April 1490
Surgeons (originally Surgeons and Barbers)	1 July 1505
Tailors	26 August 1500
Candlemakers	5 September 1517
Baxters (Bakers)	20 March 1522
Bonnetmakers and Dyers	31 March 1530
Goldsmiths	20 August 1586

Unlike England the Reformation was a thoroughly religious Reformation.[38] In England Guilds of Merchants and Craftsmen were swept away but in Scotland they remained intact and many continue to function to this day in various cities in Scotland.[39] Although the Scottish Reformation did not sweep away the same institutions as in England it nevertheless had a major impact on the lives of all Scots. Although Incorporations remained in existence the nature of their involvement changed. Gone were the elaborate and highly ritualised mystery plays and other activities of the pre-Reformation church, which were replaced by a much plainer form of religious observance. Incorporations were subject to the same close scrutiny by the new Protestant church as every other institution. The loss of a holiday with all the revelry associated with it must have been keenly felt by many – and included other 'festivals' frowned on by the new church, such as Gowk's Day (All Fools' Day) on 1 April. Because Incorporations were public bodies their activities were open to scrutiny and after the Reformation their functions changed in that they no longer had such a prominent place in religious activities and it is likely that any esoteric knowledge communicated at meetings of the Incorporation was suppressed as being superstitious and from an era before the Reformed church came into being. Only masons had another dimension and that was one that was not public – the lodge.[40]

Because Scotland has the oldest Lodge records in the world many accept that Freemasonry began in that country and developed from the Lodges of Scottish stonemasons which are first mentioned in 1491.[41] The earliest records are those of Lodge Aitcheson's Haven (see Plate 1) and which commence on 9 January 1599. That lodge was declared Dormant (that is, it had ceased to exist) by the Grand Lodge of Scotland in 1856. The oldest records of a lodge which remains in existence are those of The Lodge of Edinburgh (Mary's Chapel), No. 1. The first entry in the Minute Book is dated 31 July 1599 and those records are continuous to the present. However, there were certainly other lodges in existence in Scotland at this time. For example Mother Kilwinning was certainly in existence in 1599 as it is on record that in December of that year the lodge sent a representative to Edinburgh to seek an audience with the King.

Elias Ashmole (1617–1692) who joined a lodge in Warrington, Cheshire, in 1646 is usually claimed as the first 'Speculative' Freemason (that is someone who is not a stonemason but who joins a lodge as a 'gentleman Mason').[42] Unfortunately, the actual records of the lodge and therefore details of his initiation are lost, if they ever existed, and all that remains is a short entry in his personal diary as proof of the event:

'1646
Oct: 16 4 H 30' P.M., I was made a Free Mason
At Warrington in Lancashire with Coll: Henry
Mainwaring, of Karincham in Cheshire. The
Names of those that were then of the Lodge, Mr.
Rich: Sankey, Henry Littler, John Ellam, Rich:
Ellam & Hugh Brewer.'
Page 303 of Ashmole's Diary.[43]

This does not take account of what was taking place in Scotland at that time and earlier. It ought to be borne in mind that Scotland was a separate country with its own parliament, different legal system, culture, customs, religion, currency and national institutions. It was united with England only in the person of the Scottish king, James VI (1567–1625, b.1566) who became James I of Britain in 1603. These two separate countries, while existing on the same land mass, developed two distinctly different forms for Freemasonry the effects of which remain with us today especially in terms of social composition and methods of governance.

The differences within Freemasonry as it existed in the two countries help to describe how Freemasonry exists in different parts of the world. This is important because few people appreciate that Freemasonry is not identical all over the world. A subsidiary but important argument is the claim that only men who were not stonemasons (but who joined a lodge made up of working or operative stonemasons) could be considered Freemasons in the modern sense. The form of Freemasonry established in England in 1717 had little, if anything, to do with the working craft of stonemasons. Thus purely 'Speculative Freemasonry'[44] began in that year. This has the effect of disposing of all the Scottish evidence prior to 1717.[45] This point is important enough for me to consider from another viewpoint. Stonemasons were employed during the working day to build a church or a castle etc. However, once the working day was finished, they attended a lodge where no physical work was undertaken.[46] (see Appendix 1) According to this argument if he is a working stonemason during the day he cannot be considered to be what is now known as a 'Speculative Freemason' whilst in a lodge. In Scotland records maintained and often still owned by the lodges concerned show that non-stonemasons joined stonemasons' lodges and, unlike Elias Ashmole, continued to attend the lodge after they had been admitted. For example, in 1634 William, Lord Alexander, and his younger brother Anthony Alexander and Sir Alexander Strachan were made Entered Apprentices and then Fellow Crafts at the same meeting in The Lodge of Edinburgh.[47]

In the following decade several more non-stonemasons joined Scottish stonemasons' lodges including Sir Robert Moray (1608–1673) first president of the Royal Society (founded 1660), who was admitted to the lodge of Edinburgh in 1641 together with Alexander Hamilton, general of artillery.[48]

There was clearly considerable activity in Scotland (some of which is recorded in surviving lodge Minute books and other records) prior to Elias Ashmole joining the lodge at Warrington in 1646.[49] Almost inevitably once non-stonemasons were admitted to stonemasons' lodges word began to circulate that these lodges possessed and transmitted secrets. Throughout the 17th century this secret knowledge is referred to as the Mason Word. The first known reference occurs in 1637, just a few years after the first non-stonemasons were admitted to a lodge and is in the form of an accusation against John Stewart, Earl of Traquair, (c.1600–1659) when he was Lord High Treasurer suggesting that he was in possession of the Mason Word. This is probably the first use of anti-Freemasonry for political purposes.[50]

The next reference is contained within the poem: *'The muses of threnodie, or, mirthfull mournings on the death of Master Gall.'*[51]

The part of interest here is:

'Thus *Gall* assured me it would be so,
And my good *Genius* truly doth it know:
For what we do presage is not in grosse,
For we be brethren of the *Rosie Crosse*;
We have the *Mason Word* and second sight,
Things for to come we can foretell aright.'[52]

Although the exact meaning of the above is obscure there are sinister overtones, as with the accusation against Traquair mentioned above, but this might be a literary device rather than accurate. However, the fact remains that stonemasons' secret knowledge had begun to 'leak out' and that attracted the attention of a number of people. The extreme Presbyterian 'Kirk Party' dominated the religious climate of the time and they believed that the civil war and the poverty and disruption it caused throughout Scotland was a consequence of God's wrath. They became preoccupied with finding all possible causes for offending God and it was in this climate that discussions about the Mason Word took place. In 1649 some members of the General Assembly of the Church of Scotland wanted to know more about the Mason Word and asked the presbyteries to investigate and report back to the Assembly. If any did so there is no record of their responses and no record of any subsequent discussion on the issue.[53] That debate ensured that there was a heightened interest in the Mason Word and what the implications of possessing it might be. James Ainslie (c.1608–1702) had been selected in January 1652 to be a Minister by the Kirk Session of Minto, Roxburghshire, but when his suitability for the position came to be examined it was alleged that he was in possession of the Mason Word (that is, he had been admitted to a lodge and was therefore a Freemason). This indicates that interest in the Mason Word lingered long after the matter had been debated at national level. The Presbytery seeking a new Minister was Jedburgh and it decided to seek advice on the issue from the neighbouring Presbyteries of Selkirk and Kelso. The responses by the Presbyteries remain extant and that of Kelso dated 24 February 1652 is as follows:

'Anent [about or concerning] a young mans having the maissounes word whither he myt [might] be admitted to the ministrie:
'that to their judgement ther is neither sinne [sin] nor scandale in that word because in the purest tymes of this kirke maisons having that word have been ministers, that maisons and men having that word are daylie admitted to the ordinances [of the church].'[54]

The Presbytery of Selkirk's advice was more guarded and recommended that the issue be referred to the Synod (a gathering of local Presbyteries) and this was duly done. The Jedburgh Presbytery met on 3 November 1652 to consider Ainslie's application and although a great deal of time was taken discussing his suitability and his qualifications there was no mention of the Mason Word. Ainslie was appointed Minister of the Parish of Minto soon after.

Here then is the first investigation as to whether Freemasonry was (is) compatible with Christianity, specifically the extreme Protestant Covenanting form, and the answer was resoundingly positive. The significance of this is even clearer because of the fact that one of the first known Freemasons (as opposed to a stonemason) was later admitted a Minister of the Church of Scotland. As many members and Ministers of that church (and others) continued to become Freemasons, either before or after they took up their Ministry, the implication is that something had changed and that that change was fairly recent. This aspect will be further discussed in the conclusion.

Although I consider the case of Ainslie to be most important in this brief exploration of Masonophobia there are other references which add to our understanding of how the Mason Word was perceived. Once again I find myself indebted to David Stevenson for revealing these details. Sir Thomas Urquhart of Cromarty was a bitter and outspoken critic of the Presbyterian Church and in a book published in London in 1653 he comments that he knew of a man who, because he possessed the Mason Word, could summon another mason from a distance without speaking or making any sign. The point he was making was that some people (members of the Church of Scotland) attributed something sinister or unnatural to the Mason Word because they could not explain it. In mocking them he suggests that their lack of understanding leads them into superstition.

Another early, but significant, reference to the Mason Word and religion occurs in 1664 in a sermon given by William Guthrie. The relevant extract from the sermon is:

'I cannot compare it better to you nor [than] to that they call the Masson-Word; there is a signe among the Massons that they call the Masson-Word; I wot not what it is but they say one of them cannot be in that dress [position] but another will take him up to be a man of th[a]t same trade. I cannot tell you what passeth betwixt Christ and his people [followers], but there is some sign th[a]t he giveth them th[a] will evermore know him, be in what dress he will.'[55]

Guthrie is here discussing the relationship between Christ and his followers. He uses the Mason Word as an analogy for how Christ's followers will 'evermore know him [Christ]' regardless of their situation. It is known that Guthrie was an ardent Presbyterian and had resisted the restoration of episcopacy and had been removed as a Parish Minister as a consequence. Guthrie sees nothing wrong with the Mason Word nor with its use between masons and goes so far as to use it as a means of illustrating the relationship of Christ with his followers. This reference to Christ in the same breath as Freemasonry is unusual in that, for once, it is positive. The implications of this and the impact of subsequent perceptions of Freemasonry will be discussed later. Guthrie would have been well aware that the Mason Word (that is, Freemasonry) did not refer to the New Testament and is probably why he found no fault with Freemasonry. Guthrie's use of Freemasonry was to make a religious point and was not intended to compare Freemasonry to religion.

Arguably the most famous reference to the Mason Word comes to us from an account of a conversation between Robert Kirk, Minister in

Aberfoyle, and Dr Edward Stillingfleet, in London on 6 October 1689. Kirk believed that the Mason Word and Second Sight came from the same milieu, no doubt because he was an avid student of Scottish folklore and alleged supernatural events. Stillingfleet on the contrary saw both the Mason Word (the existence of which Kirk seems to have revealed to Stillingfleet) and Second Sight as sinful. Kirk argued that these might be yet-to-be-explained phenomena whilst Stillingfleet was adamant that knowledge of them was sinister and sinful thus highlighting Sir Thomas Urquhart of Cromarty's earlier opinion on the same subject (see above). Kirk appears to have known the meaning of the Mason Word, and have investigated further after 1689, for in 1691 he wrote:

> 'The Mason-Word who tho some make a Misterie [mystery] of it, will not conceal a little of what I know; it's like a Rabbinical tradition in a way of comment on Iachin and Boaz the two pillars erected in Solomon's Temple; with an addition of som secret signe delivered from hand to hand, by which they know, and become familiar one with another.'

Kirk knew some of what the Mason Word meant and because it contained references to Solomon's Temple he described it as a 'Rabbinical tradition' but dismissed it as a mere mystery. Kirk therefore did not consider the Mason Word to be sinister because it had the clear purpose of one tradesman identifying himself to another even although they might not know each other personally.[56]

The interest in the Mason Word comes from two diverse points of view. One was the older religious view of the world in which inexplicable things may be the result of the supernatural (and therefore require no further explanation) and the other the rational, 'scientific', view which argues that because something cannot presently be explained does not mean that there is no explanation. This debate between Rationalists and the Religious (for want of a better means of describing the debate which continues to this day) was by no means restricted to the Mason Word which, in fact, was a minuscule aspect of that debate, and thus we find that the possibility of miracles had been dismissed by Protestants soon after the Reformation. Even previously unassailable biblical miracles were being challenged at this time.[57] The astronomer Edmund Halley (1656–1742) argued that the biblical Flood had a scientific explanation.[58]

Jews had been expelled from England (although not Scotland) in 1290 and were not permitted to return until 1656 when Oliver Cromwell granted them limited rights. It was not until 1858 that the ban on their holding public office was removed. The Puritanism of the period was 'impregnated with idea, language, argument and history all borrowed from Jewish antiquity and sacred books'.[59] The arrival of people of an older faith inevitably created even more interest in their theology, ritual and symbolism etc., especially given that their principal holy books (the Torah, Neviim and Ketuvim) are contained within the Christian Old Testament. This was also manifest by the surge in interest in matters concerning the Tabernacle and King Solomon's Temple (KST).[60] (See Plate 2) In this situation of heightened awareness of all matters and things relating to the Jewish faith and the correlation of references in the Old Testament to that faith it is unsurprising that interest in the Mason Word and its references to KST attracted attention. Although Kirk drew attention to the Mason Word and had correctly interpreted some of what it meant he also demonstrated that it was not simply a word but also incorporated a secret grip. What he did not appreciate was that it represented an entire initiatory system – something substantiated a few years later by the Edinburgh Register House (ERH) MS of 1696.[61] This manuscript describes the method of the admission of a prentice (apprentice) into a lodge as well as the (similar) process of him later becoming a fellow of [the] craft. There were only these two ceremonies (now know as 'degrees') at this time.[62] The third, or Master Masons', degree was not invented until the 1720s soon after the Grand Lodge of England had been created. Even that 'new' Masonic degree was not complete invention because it took parts of the existing stonemasons' Fellow Craft ceremony and inserted them into the new third degree.

There are a few pre-Reformation references to lodges but these are scant. More numerous and detailed records from lodges after 1599/60 show that there is a gap of approximately 100 years where little is known of lodge activity. For example a lodge was built within the precincts of Holyrood Abbey in 1529 specifically for the use of masons. This seems to have been a substantial building in its own right with approximately 12 masons engaged in its erection.[63] Another, albeit post-Reformation lodge was built within Edinburgh Castle in 1576 but whether this was of the size of the one at the church of St. Giles (1491) is not known.[64] What is known is that the Lodge of Edinburgh's records commence in 1599 and that was the direct consequence of the actions of one man now known as the father of modern Freemasonry. This man, William Schaw of Sauchie (c.1550-1602), reorganised the pre-existing, casual and informal 'organisation' of stonemason's lodges in Scotland that existed in the 16th and 15th centuries.

In 1583 Schaw was appointed the King's Master of Works to King James VI of Scotland (1568–1625, b. 1566). The latter became James I of Great Britain in 1603 when he ascended the English throne following the death of his cousin Elizabeth I (1558–1603, b. 1533). As master of works Schaw was responsible for looking after all the properties owned by the Crown as well as building any new ones as and when required. This meant that he was in daily contact with the craftsmen who built, maintained and repaired such structures – stonemasons. Records remain in existence showing Schaw making payments to stonemasons for work that he had arranged to be done on various buildings in Scotland. However, our interest in him lies not with his undoubted abilities as a diplomat and civil servant but due to his dealings with the stonemasons of Scotland. In 1598 and again in 1599 he drew up what are now known as the Schaw Statutes. The documents were sent to every known stonemasons' lodge in Scotland and these laid down the rules and regulations that they were all expected to follow from that point onwards.

On reading the Schaw Statutes it is immediately obvious that they contain a great deal of practical advice and instruction regarding the trade of stonemasonry, including internal administration such as the conditions for the employment of apprentices, the use of working tools and other matters relating to the trade. What is most curious is that Schaw addressed the statutes to lodges and not Incorporations. From the content of the statutes it would, initially, seem obvious that the Incorporation ought to have been the body to which the statutes were sent. The fact that they were not means that there was another reason other than simply providing stonemasons with instructions about 'health and safety' etc. That brings us to the nature of the lodges themselves. The statutes contain some clues as to what Schaw was trying to achieve. The very first injunction to the stonemasons, contained in the first of the statutes reads as follows:

> 'First that they observe and keep all the good ordinance as set down as before concerning the privileges of the craft by their predecessors of good memory, and especially that they be true to one another and live charitably together as becomes sworn brethren and companions of craft.' (Trans)

This tells us that these stonemasons had 'good ordinances' from before Schaw's involvement. It also reveals that stonemasons bound themselves together by means of an oath or obligation and this is understood to mean that they should act according to these 'good ordinances' and their oath. Such an instruction has very little to do with working practices and indicates that it was, to Schaw at least, of prime importance. Most importantly it informs us that Schaw did not invent lodges nor did he invent the oath (and associated ceremonies?) that stonemasons took to look after one another. All of this was already in existence by the time he wrote the Statutes. This would mean that Schaw did not invent lodges or their ceremonials but formalised an existing but casual association of stonemasons' lodges then in existence throughout Scotland.

This raises the interesting question of why he would be so interested in the activities of stonemasons and their lodges. The lodge members were after all his social inferiors and were obliged to do as he directed. Of course he may have simply been, in true civil service style, attempting to make the workforce more efficient. That still does not explain the details contained within the Statutes (such as that referred to above) that suggest an ulterior motive for the statutes in the first place.

As we have seen, the Schaw Statutes were sent to all lodges in Scotland but they provoked a strong reaction from one lodge in particular – Kilwinning. This lodge, situated in Ayrshire near the coast sent one Archibald Barclay to Edinburgh, where he was received by William Schaw and members of the lodge of Edinburgh on 27 and 28 December 1599. This meeting resulted in the Second Schaw Statutes and the contents reveal why Barclay had been sent to Edinburgh on behalf of the lodge at Kilwinning.

The first item of the Second Statutes deals with the method of electing the warden of the lodge of Kilwinning and states that the results of the election must be notified to 'the general warden', that is, Schaw himself. He is making it clear to the stonemasons of Scotland exactly who is in charge. Early in these Statutes the matter of the precedence of lodges is raised and may well have been the main complaint that the lodge of Kilwinning asked Barclay to take up on their behalf. The fact that Schaw had previously designated, in the First Statutes, that the lodge of Edinburgh was the Head Lodge of Scotland placed them in a quandary for it is unlikely that he was aware of the existence of the Kilwinning Lodge or more precisely their claim to be older than the Lodge of Edinburgh and he was placed in the invidious position of upsetting one Lodge or the other regardless of what he decided. For that reason he avoided the issue head-on, describing the Lodge as the second Lodge of Scotland and Edinburgh as being the first and principal Lodge in Scotland.

The ulterior motive seems to be revealed within the second statutes which are as follows:

' ...that the warden of the Lodge of Kilwinning, being the second
Lodge in Scotland, shall take trial of the Art of memory and science
thereof, of every fellow of craft and every apprentice according to
each of their vocations; and in case that they have lost any point
thereof given to them [that they are] to pay the penalty as follows
for their slothfulness, there is, each fellow of craft 20 shillings each
apprentice 10 shillings and that to be paid to the box for the
common good yearly and that conformed to the common use and
practice of the common lodges of this realm [of Scotland].' (Trans)

Here lodges are being instructed to 'take trial' [test] of the Art of
Memory and science thereof' of all the members of the lodge annually. In
other words they are being asked to remember 'something' but
unfortunately the 'something' is not explained. However, as there would
be little point in conducting an annual test of members on something that
was common knowledge to the rest of the population it suggests that
what was being tested was a body of knowledge known to stonemasons
alone. In other words it would appear that they were being tested as to
what was later referred to as the Mason Word. The question as to why
an annual memory test had to be implemented together with a series of
fines for each point failure must be due to the fact that the majority of
stonemasons were illiterate. Had they been able to read and write there
would have been no need to memorise 'something.' In addition, it is
obviously not short or simple as the system of fines relates to *any point*
of failure clearly indicating that there are numerous points that the
members of the lodge have to memorise. To reinforce the annual memory
test Schaw, clearly understanding the psyche of his fellow countrymen,
instituted a series of fines in order that the lodge members memorise
whatever it was he wished them to impress on their minds. What was to
be remembered is not just a word or a handshake as there would be no
need for detailed instructions such as these. It follows therefore that there
was something substantial to be memorised and that it is, I would argue,
the ceremonial as detailed in the Edinburgh Registered House MS (and
others) and to which Robert Kirk alluded in 1689 (see above).[65]

Schaw's lasting legacy was to formalise a pre-existing and probably
very lax system of stonemasons' lodges, and initiations in them, by
forcing the members of lodges to memorise all their previous 'good
ordinances' which in all likelihood included the signs, grips and other
esoteric knowledge as revealed in the first written rituals of 100 years
later. In doing this he instigated a system which subsequently developed
into modern Freemasonry. This is known as the Transition Theory and it

is manifest in the written record of Scottish lodges from the time of Schaw until the late 19th century when the last of the Scottish stonemasons' lodges finally joined the new Grand Lodge and Masonic system in 1891.[66]

We have seen that there were some slight references to stonemasons' lodges prior to the Reformation and when we are aware that William Schaw was a Roman Catholic as well as being interested in Hermeticism and other esoteric schools, we can but wonder whether he was attempting to ensure that a remnant of the pre-Reformation church survived in a Protestant environment?[67] The fact that the lodges were, at least, semi-secret and that the Mason Word was not religious may well have ensured that the religious authorities (assuming that they were even aware of lodges and their ceremonials) had no interest in them and their activities.

Throughout the 17th century awareness of the existence of the Mason Word increases as evidenced by the appearance of manuscript descriptions of the stonemasons' ceremonies.[68] This is, perhaps, suggestive of more non-stonemasons joining lodges who did not have the same motivation to keep the lodge activities as secret as previously. An example of this comes from the Lodge of Aberdeen, in existence from at least 1670, where only about 20% of the members were stonemasons and where, for the first time, a lodge makes mention in its records of the existence of the Mason Word. Towards the end of the 17th and at the beginning of the 18th centuries the general awareness of the Mason Word (which seems to have been a particularly Scottish phrase) accelerates – again evidenced by more manuscripts and references especially in England.[69] Perhaps more significantly the first known entirely Speculative Lodge, that is one with no connection to stonemasons or stonemasonry, was founded in 1702 in the hamlet of Haughfoot in the Scottish borders.[70]

For stonemasons the creation of the first biblical stone building was immensely important and it was here that the relevance of King Solomon's Temple was found. Imagine the pride of knowing that their predecessors had created such a masterpiece and furthermore that the Master Mason who designed it was reputed to have been taught (and initiated?) by the undisputed masters of architecture, the ancient Egyptians. The imagery of King Solomon's Temple is still an important part of modern Masonic ritual and learning but there are other mysterious elements in ceremonies and symbolism that may have equally important lessons.

In 1717 the Grand Lodge of England was founded and with it came a time of radical change for Freemasonry. The political system of Britain also experienced an upheaval – the Scottish and English parliaments being united in 1707. Although there is documented evidence that Freemasonry existing before 1700, it was only in 1717 that truly organised or regular Freemasonry was born with the establishment of the first Grand Lodge. Four London Lodges (there may have been more but they are now unknown) gathered together at the Goose and Gridiron ale house, near to St Paul's Cathedral and decided that Grand Lodge be formed.[71] The reason for doing so was in order to hold an annual dinner that all the London Lodges could attend. To facilitate the arrangements a gentleman by the name of Anthony Sayer (?–c.1742) was elected and given the title of Grand Master.

When, in 1721, the Duke of Montagu (1690–1749) was Grand Master, the Grand Lodge had clearly evolved into a regulatory body for Lodges initially in London but soon for all of England. Quarterly (business) meetings were arranged, two of which coincided with the spring and autumn equinoxes and two with the summer and winter solstices. St John's Day – June 24 – therefore became important enough for St John to be adopted as the patron saint of Freemasonry. The assumption was made that this dated back to pre-1717 Freemasonry and of a link to the Guilds of Operative Masons.[72] The main effect of the creation of the Grand Lodge was that Freemasonry was given a public face for the first time. Prior to the annual installation of the new Grand Master, Freemasons would process from the home of the incoming Grand Master to the place where the Installation Meeting was to take place. 'The Brethren would march two by two dressed in their aprons and jewels and carrying the emblems, symbols and banners of the Craft, followed by the nobility in their carriages...' [73]

Compare this with operative lodges of highly trained, but illiterate, stonemasons. To identify themselves to each other and distinguish them from untrained stonemasons (cowans) a system of passwords and hand-grips was devised.[74] This identified one as being either prentice (apprentice), fellow of craft or master mason. This was their equivalent to our use today of trade union membership cards! In time these stonemasons' lodges admitted a few non-practising members who eventually took over many such lodges.[75] There is considerable debate as to what at this early stage constitutes a modern or 'Speculative' Freemason. Two examples will serve to illustrate this ongoing debate. In 1641 Sir Robert Moray (1608–1673) was the first non-stonemason to be initiated into a lodge on English soil. Briefly, the facts are that he was Quartermaster General to the Scottish Covenanting army that besieged

Newcastle Upon Tyne that year. Some members of The Lodge of Edinburgh were part of that army, probably in the capacity of pioneers, and on 20 May 1641 initiated not only Moray but also the General of Artillery, Alexander Hamilton. The initiations were reported on the members' return to Edinburgh and the details duly entered into the lodge Minute Book. Moray was not a stonemason but joined a stonemasons' lodge. Another early recorded initiation occurred in 1646 when Elias Ashmole (1617–1692), an antiquarian, was made a Freemason in a lodge at his father-in-law's house in Warrington, England. Apparently, there were no stonemasons present. This lodge appears to have been an 'occasional' lodge and whether the form of initiation was the same as that which occurred in the permanent Scottish lodges is open to doubt.

Quarterly feasts, or perhaps a revival of them, seemed to have appealed to men of high social position. The early 1700s saw a considerable increase in convivial social meetings usually in the clubs and coffee shops of the time. The unique social and moral club that was Freemasonry attracted such men and comprised the members of the four lodges who came together to the Goose and Gridiron ale house on 24 June 1717 as a precursor to forming the Grand Lodge of England. This unification of Lodges caused a separation between operative or working masons and 'speculative' Masons ('speculative' referred to their speculation as to the meaning of the stonemasons' rituals, working tools, and symbolism). Henceforth lodges no longer were required to be made up of both stone masons and non-Masons, which had been the case from at least the 1660s whereby it was stipulated that a lodge must properly consist of at least five accepted brothers and a minimum of one who was an active Master of the trade.[76] In the *Constitutions* published in 1723 this separation of operative lodges from speculative Lodges is not specifically referred to but can be inferred from the statement that a Lodge can only be deemed to be 'regular' if under the jurisdiction of a Grand Lodge, or specifically the directorate of the Grand Master or his deputies. As proof of this a certificate would then be provided and the Lodge details recorded by Grand Lodges concerned. Regular freemasonry was a resounding success and by 1730 there were seventy lodges affiliated to the new Grand Lodge. The era of 'Grand Lodge Freemasonry' had begun. That did not mean that only this kind of Lodges existed as there were 'irregular' Lodges but 'regular' Freemasons were not to become involved with them.

Needless to say the sudden appearance in public of a previously unknown body oddly dressed and carrying unusual objects attracted a lot of interest and comment. The decision to 'go public' in this manner obviously reflects the pride and pleasure that Freemasons obtained from their membership. Unfortunately, there were many that did not see them in that light and soon Freemasonry was the subject of press ridicule. They were even mimicked by the Order of Scald Miserable Masons who also held processions caricaturing Masonic processions.[77] The Freemason persevered but finally, in 1747, the Grand Lodge forbade any public processions of Freemasons except with special permission. As we shall see later, ridicule is one of the uses made by those who are prejudiced or simply jealous of an individual or group.

The first written 'history' of Freemasonry was provided by the Reverend James Anderson (*c.*1680–1739) in *The Constitutions of the Free-Masons* (1723). He was a native of Aberdeen and importantly his father had been at various times Master and Secretary of the Lodge of Aberdeen.[78] Anderson together with John Theophilus Desaguliers (1683–1744) and his influential friends led the revival (as they saw it) of Freemasonry. Anderson was a Presbyterian preacher who had qualified at Marischal College (founded 1593 and now part of the University of Aberdeen), who arrived in London sometime in 1709, where he became Presbyterian Minister of a chapel in Swallow Street. He was therefore a Dissenter in that he was not in accord with the established Church of England. That he was a Freemason is not in doubt as it is known that he was a member of Horn Lodge but whether he had become a member of a Lodge before leaving for London has not been established.

It is however in the annals of Freemasonry that Anderson achieved lasting fame for he was commissioned by the new Grand Lodge to 'digest the old Gothic Constitutions in a new and better method' which resulted in *The Constitutions of the Free-Masons* published in 1723. (see Plate 3) This contains much of interest to the (Masonic) historian and it can tell us, at this very early period, as to the thinking of those responsible for founding the Grand Lodge. For example what did they believe the ethos of the new organisation to be? The ideals of this new, or revived, form of Freemasonry were not dogmatic in either politics or religion; it was utilitarian and pacifist and encouraged social integration. This latter point is often overlooked and is something to which I shall return in the conclusion. Together these points also mean that tolerance was at the heart of the 'new' organisation and this too shall be discussed later. The *Constitutions* state that discussion of state politics and religion were forbidden; brethren must have no involvement in civil plots and allegiance was to the Crown and government. These 'new' noble ideals created an exciting time for all involved; proposed members being initiated into an entirely new organization – one that was free of the main causes of dispute and often violence – politics and religion. The *Constitutions* were enlightened but skirted round matters such as those of religion and politics. The First Charge instructs the Mason 'to obey the moral Law and if he rightly understands the Art, he will never be a stupid atheist, nor an irreligious Libertine'. It proceeds to explain that, although in previous ages Masons had to follow their country's religion, in (1723) it was only necessary to 'oblige them to that Religion in which all Men agree, leaving their particular Opinions to themselves'.

This suggests that as long as members were 'good men and true' it mattered not as to their denomination or persuasion. They were now at liberty to converse and socialize with others, whom they may previously have been distanced from, before the *Centre of Union* of Freemasonry. Without stating what the 'religion in which all Men agree' was, it avoided and rather adroitly sidestepped any religious divides. So long as Freemasons remained good and honest men, personal religious and political beliefs were irrelevant. The Freemasons' ethos actively encouraged them all to be as good and honourable as possible. Thus was a solution to the confusion created by the innumerable reading and debating societies, clubs, political parties and various religious sects. Freemasons were able, perhaps for the first time to avoid the usual social divisions as these were henceforth to be left outside the Lodge.

This idea of a *Centre of Union* was a new and powerful one.[79] The concept that men of all religious and social persuasions could now meet together in an attempt to further their moral and spiritual attitudes was as revolutionary as it was novel. On offer was a process by which men could rise above base things by they *themselves* utilising the principles of religious, political and social tolerance with the aim of ushering in a more tolerant and humane world. Hindsight, it is said, is a great thing and with that benefit perhaps we can now understand why so many individuals and groups have attacked Freemasonry. James Anderson, John T. Desaguliers, and those surrounding them in the early days of Grand Lodge, seem to have been attempting to create a society without divisions and therefore a world where, potentially, all men could work for near perfection without need of the intervention of religious or political intermediaries. On reflection this concept would have been at least a concern to religious leaders and politicians. The suggestion it might be possible to create a very much better world through an individual's own efforts was bound to worry those whose avowed profession and livelihood was to do exactly the same thing.

Anderson published the *New Constitutions* in 1738 under the authority of the Grand Lodge of England, making the forceful observation: ' ...avoid Politics and Religion... our politics is merely to be honest and our Religion the Law of Nature and to love God above all things, and our Neighbour as ourself; this is the true, primitive, catholic and Universal Religion, agreed to be so in all times and Ages'.

Those who were suspicious of the new organisation could easily have been convinced that Freemasonry was a (new) religion as a matter of 'self-defence' despite the fact that it was the ethos of Freemasonry, one which allowed every Mason to feel and aspire to be of a high moral standing themselves no matter their particular faith – at that time principally Christian and Jew.[80] This was made plain by its avowed intent not to exclude anyone provided they complied with the basis of Freemasonry:

Be a free man
Of mature age (18–25 years old depending on the Grand Lodge concerned)
Be of good morals and sound reputation
Have a belief in a Supreme Being

A recent historian observed:

'The author of the constitution assumed that Freemasons had belonged to various religions in the past, and so Freemasons could belong to any religion, including the Jewish, at present as well.'[81]

This is a crucial point for, as we shall see, one of the frequent accusations made against Freemasonry is that it deliberately excludes certain Christian denominations.

The transition from stonemasonry to the new Grand Lodge system and the origins of the Craft (as it was increasingly being called) were greatly influenced by the lessons handed down by previous generations. Initially those unfamiliar with the principles of Freemasonry, the symbolism of the stonemason's working tools and the allegorical nature of the ritual together with other associated practices might consider Freemasonry rather odd. However, the separation of operative and speculative Lodges meant that original tenets of the stonemasons were no longer restricted to that small group.

To those with any interest in Freemasonry it is clear that there is more to it than just a superficial social and moral asociation. Masonic rituals (essentially morality plays) are designed to inspire the members using symbolism which goes far beyond simple analogy. Freemasonry has been described as being a 'peculiar system of morality veiled in allegory and illustrated by symbols' but this is descriptive and not analytical. It is however a good starting point.

Much of Lodge ritual and symbolism is centred on King Solomon's Temple and was elaborated during the 18th and early 19th centuries. The earliest rituals merely mentioned KST but later elaborations focused on parts of it, for example the two pillars which stood outside the entrance to the Temple. The now famous (and oft ridiculed) rolling up of the trouser leg in Masonic ritual is figuratively interpreted by some Freemasons as representing one of those pillars. Although there was a great deal of elaboration there was also some pure invention, the most important being the creation of a third ceremony – the modern Master Masons' degree. The stonemasons and the modern speculative Freemasons that followed them used the Old Testament for their own purposes. This is a matter of prime importance and shall be discussed more fully in Chapter 5.

As many non-Masons know little or nothing about the origin and history of Freemasonry its rituals and symbolism are often considered to be at least arcane and often bizarre and outlandish. What is not understood and is perceived as strange is liable to ridicule. The 'rolled up trouser leg' is much parodied but importantly no one seems to want to know what this means. Perhaps a straightforward explanation would deprive non-Masons of a great visual 'gag' which is simply too good to let go so there is a pressing desire not to know the truth. This is however something of a digression at this stage.

Those with Masonophobic tendencies often refer to the oaths taken by Freemasons during the course of taking the three degrees in a Masonic Lodge.[82] These oaths have attracted considerable comment and so the next chapter begins with a discussion and explanation of oaths.

CHAPTER 2

THE EARLY HISTORY OF
MASONOPHOBIA

*'We should not look back unless it is to derive useful lessons
from past errors, and for the purpose of profiting by
dearly bought experience.'*
George Washington (1732–1799)

On the Taking of Oaths

'The possible objection that taking oaths might foster fellowship
and group identity within a group, and render others "outsiders"
should be considered, precisely because fellowship and group
identity are produced in such circumstances. By retaining the vital
sacred and moral elements, traditional within Freemasonry, such a
situation may be celebrated, and any objection overcome with full
confidence. Freemasonry is, after all, a brotherhood of Masons, not
of general society, which is in any event, the intended ultimate
beneficiary of our Masonic endeavours.'[83]

This quote serves to succinctly explain why Freemasons take an oath.
It is the Masonic oaths (or 'obligations' as they are more commonly
known within Freemasonry) taken in private that attract criticism from
non-Masons whilst at the same time ignoring the avowed aim of
Freemasonry to try and improve society in general. But we are perhaps
getting ahead of ourselves. Oaths have existed for a very long time. They
were, and under certain circumstances remain, essential. In earlier times,
social mores, laws and even general 'good behaviour' were by no means
as easily enforced as today.[84] Oaths of fealty to a feudal lord, wedding
vows, the Hippocratic Oath and 'swearing on the Bible' were all common
methods of reinforcing society's need to standardise people's behaviour.
Some applied to particular groups such as doctors and other covered the
entire population. Other oaths were designed for a specific purpose such
as confirming a bargain.[85] It was simply not sufficient to allow someone
to say, 'Okay, I'll do that.' A harder edge was needed and that was often
the embarrassment experienced by individuals when they broke their
word which had been given in the form of an oath. Such individuals
would be seen to be hypocrites and their word was not to be trusted.[86]
Today this is a relatively mild stigma to bear but in the past it was the

first powerful step in the process of trying to make people conform to certain standards.

An oath from 1504 serves to demonstrate the antiquity of oaths. This example is that of an apprentice entering a guild in 1504.

'Ye shall swear that ye shall be true unto our liege Lord, the King, and to his heirs, Kings. Also ye shall swear that well and truly to your power ye shall serve your Master during the term of your apprenticeship. And ye shall hold and perform the covenants in your indenture of apprenticeship contained. Also ye shall hold steadfastly, secretly and for counsel all and every the lawful ordinances, whatsoever they may be, to the Craft or occupation of the Mercery belonging, and, as much as in you is, every of them ye shall observe hold and keep, and not to break, discover, open or shew any of them to any person but unto the fellowship of the Mercery is here according to this oath sworn. And that ye shall not depart out and from the said fellowship for to serve, not to be accompanied with any manner of person of any other company, fellowship, occupation or craft, whereby any prejudice, hurt, or harm may grow or be unto the fellowship of the Mercery, or any of the secrets thereof thereby to be discovered or known, So help you God, and all Saints, and by this book.'

Guilds such as the Mercers (those who deal in luxury fabrics such as silk) whose apprenticeship oath of 1504 is given above existed considerably earlier.[87] [88] The guild oath tells us several things, not least the instruction that the apprentice must keep secret all things relating to Mercery. The responsibilities adopted by the apprentice in taking this oath are reinforced by an imprecation to God and all the Saints and a book – surely a reference to the Bible.

An oath applicable to a group, and the words it contains, serves two functions. Firstly, it assists in binding the group together in 'common cause' and secondly it provides a 'membership card'. This is an important point to which we shall return in a later chapter.

The situation regarding guilds in England compared with Incorporations in Scotland is now well understood. In England the decline of the guilds began when Henry VIII (1509–1547; b. 1491) during the last year of his reign took from them all their ecclesiastical property leaving them subscriptions from their members as their only income.[89] Edward VI (1547–1553, b. 1537) finished what Henry had begun by seizing the payments made by Guilds to the church for a variety of religious functions.[90] The loss of this major function of English guilds disheartened nearly all and they slowly faded away although a very few lingered awhile with no clear purpose.

In Scotland the Reformation was different in nature from that instigated by Henry VIII in England where it was grounded in political and dynastic matters. In Scotland the Reformation was religious through and through.[91] As in England, Scottish Incorporations lost the religious dimension of their activities. This was simply due to the fact that the Roman Church was replaced 'root and branch' by the new Protestant Church and so the need for Incorporations to take part in religious activities such as paying for priests to say masses for deceased members etc. ceased almost immediately. However, Incorporations did not fade away as in England but devoted the additional time and money gained by the removal of the old faith to promoting and protecting the rights and welfare of their members.

As has already been explained Scotland was chosen for this study because its size is 'manageable' for our purposes.[92] That said, Scotland has its own peculiarities one of which is the complexities of church organisation, schisms, disagreements and disruptions. It is not within the scope of this work to explain the history of the churches in Scotland. There is however one point that is particularly relevant to the discussion regarding oaths.

The Burgess Oath was a sworn declaration taken by citizens of various towns in Scotland principally Edinburgh, Glasgow and Perth. In 1745 the Burgess Oath caused a division within the Associate Presbytery (itself a schismatic body formed in 1733 by elements of the established Church of Scotland) leading those who were against the Burgess Oath to form the General Associate Synod in 1747. Minutiae such as this might seem tiresome, especially today, but it was certainly most important at the time. This was so for several reasons. Burgesses were inhabitants of a Scottish burgh who qualified for the right to vote for municipal officers. In addition only they could engage in commerce or belong to a trade Incorporation (similar to an English guild).[93] Before discussing why the Burgess Oath was of such importance the wording of the oath might usefully be provided here:

'Here I protest, before God, that I confess and allow with my heart the true RELIGION, presently professed within this Realm, and authorised by the Laws thereof. I shall abide thereat, and defend the same to my Life's end, renouncing the Roman Religion called Papistry. I shall be leal [loyal] and true to our Sovereign Lord the

KING'S MAJESTY, and to the Provost [Mayor] and Baillies of this Burgh. I shall obey the Officers thereof, fortify, maintain and defend them in the execution of their Office, with my body and goods. I shall not colour unfreeman's [someone who is not a Burgess] goods under colour of my own. In all taxations, I shall willingly bear my part thereof, as I am commanded thereto by the Magistrates. I shall not purchase nor use exemptions to be free thereof renouncing the benefit of the same for ever. I shall do nothing hurtful to the Liberties & common well of this Burgh. I shall not brew nor cause brew, any malt but such as is grinded at the Town's milns [mills], and shall grind no other corns, except wheat, pease, rye and beans, but at the same allenarly [solitarily]. And how oft as I shall happen to break any part of this oath, I oblige me to pay to the common affairs of this Burgh the sum of One hundred pounds Scots money, and shall remain in ward while [in custody until] the same be paid. So help me God.

I shall give the best council I can, and conceal the council shown to me. I shall not consent to dispose the common goods of the Burgh, but for ane common cause, and ane common profit. I shall make concord, where there discord is, to the utmost of my power. In all lienations and neighbourhoods, I shall give my leal and true judgement, but price, prayer, or reward. So help me God.'[94] [95]

The wording of this oath raises several important matters. First and foremost from the point of view of the anti-Burghers only people who professed the true religion of this realm could become burgesses. In other words they could not because the 'true' religion, that is the established religion, was the Church of Scotland.[96] Edinburgh, Glasgow and Perth were the three places where support for the General Associate Synod (the anti-Burghers) was strongest. Refusal to take the oath would have meant that they could do no business or work at an incorporated trade in such burghs.[97] The fact that the oath specifically excluded Roman Catholics was unlikely to cause them concern. Much of the oath is concerned with maintaining the status quo, ensuring that the burgh received all the taxes due to it and that the burgess will behave in accordance with predetermined social norms – see the discussion above. More interesting is the fact that the oath binds the new Burgess to secrecy to 'conceal the council shown to me.' As this part of the oath is contained in that part dealing with the conduct of Burgh business it seems that the Burgess was committed to keeping that business secret.

The brothers Ebenezer (1680–1754) and Ralph (1685–1752) Erskine were two of the leading lights of the Associate Presbytery (Burghers) who did not believe that it was against their religious faith to take the Burgess Oath. Many commentators suggest that they adopted a theological stance and remained steadfast in that view despite many of their colleagues, and indeed friends, taking an opposing view.[98] There may, however, be another reason why they adopted this attitude. Both had become members of a 'secret society' known as the Free Gardeners, Ralph in 1720 and Ebenezer in 1721. Both would of necessity have had to take an oath to keep secret the esoteric knowledge of the Free Gardeners. It is likely that they would have taken more than one oath as there were several ceremonies involved in becoming a full member. It is interesting, in passing, that many of Ebenezer's sermons after becoming a Free Gardener contained horticultural references.[99] The reason for mentioning the Free Gardeners at this early stage is to indicate that although they were similar in nature to Free Masonry (later Freemasonry) they did not attract the same attention even although they had all the same elements (oaths, privacy, regalia and ritual). In short Freemasonry became the main target for all sorts of sundry groups whereas others rarely attracted the same attention.[100]

Oaths such as those quoted above have specific intentions, binding the group together etc., but there is one overriding function applicable to all oaths and that is to provide a sense of dignity and solemnity to the event concerned such as marriage, becoming a Guild Brother or a Member of Parliament. To add sanctity the deity or saints (or both) were also often invoked. In total, an oath was intended to be so powerful as to leave an indelible impression on the mind of the oath-taker to the extent that even although the person might not recall the exact words used, the ceremony would never be forgotten. As we have seen, such oaths have a pedigree of many hundreds of years and throughout that time were not considered objectionable.

Why then are there so many Masonophobic opinions cast around today and for our purposes why is the Masonic obligation specifically targeted for extreme opprobrium? This aspect of Freemasonry is usually referred to in graphic terms: the use of 'blood curling oaths', of being 'buried at the high water mark' and 'being fed to the birds' and other equally evocative references. The fact that such references are symbolic, although not treated as such by the detractor of Freemasonry, is something to which I shall return later. I now turn to the anti-Burghers (the General Associate Synod) and their subsequent activities regarding the Burgess Oath. The debate was frequently acrimonious and both

Burghers and anti-Burghers published numerous defences of their point of view, including six pamphlets by Ralph Erskine.[101] This now admittedly obscure debate only involves Freemasonry in that the anti-Burghers, in search of ammunition, claimed that the oaths of the Freemasons were equally pernicious. The anti-Burghers' stance against the Burgess Oath was in effect an attack on the establishment and the established church. If it could be shown that other oaths, and not those used by those in authority, were *bad* then the argument against oaths in general would be greatly strengthened. Freemasonry provided an ideal vehicle for that purpose. On Thursday, 7 March 1745 the Associate Presbytery held a meeting in Stirling at which the Masons Oath was debated. The subsequent disagreement, known as the *Breach*, led to the formation of the anti-Burghers. This is the crux of many of those who attack Freemasonry on pseudo-religious grounds.[102] Although today Freemasons, and their official institutions, shy away from commenting on matters relating to religion, during the 18th century they were not so reticent. The anti-Burghers continued to campaign against the Burgess Oath and the subject cropped up in a number of places in succeeding years. In 1757 the matter was given a public airing in the press (the *Scots Magazine*, August 1757) and a spirited defence of Freemasonry appeared soon after in the *Edinburgh Magazine*, October 1757.[103] It ought perhaps to be mentioned that at this time there was no 'official' organ of Scottish Freemasonry. The affairs of Lodges and Grand Lodge were recorded in their internal Minute Books and other records but there was no Year Book, magazine or web site! Occasionally matters relating to Freemasonry appeared in the press but assessing its volume and impact is beyond the scope of the present work. The only publicly available material devoted entirely to Freemasonry was known as Pocket Companions and as the term suggests was of a size to be carried in one's pocket. There was no apparent logic to the time of their publication, appearing in random years. It is suspected that as they were a commercial venture and much of the content remained similar in each edition, publication was determined by the amount of sales and, occasionally, by the amount of fresh material.

It is of passing interest that Brother Robert Burns (1759–1796) was a burgher and could hardly have been otherwise, given that he had taken several Masonic oaths as well as at least six Burgess Oaths (Dumfries; Dumbarton; Jedburgh; Linlithgow; Lochmaben and Sanquhar).[104]

EUROPE

At about the time that this theological debate erupted in Scotland matters involving religion and Freemasonry became an issue in Europe. As explained before it is not easy to compare matters concerning Freemasonry in Scotland with those occurring elsewhere especially where different political and religious regimes existed. However, the point of this book is to discuss Masonophobia rather than the differences between European countries although such differences obviously would have an effect.

As discussed in the preceding chapter it is now generally accepted that modern Freemasonry began in Scotland during the very late 16th century and then spread to England.[105] [106] From there Freemasonry transferred to Europe, initially via France, although there are some indications that Freemasonry appeared in Scandinavia at about the same time.

Although many places in Europe banned, or at least sought to ban, Freemasonry the different political and religious character of these places meant that there was no specific conspiracy against Freemasonry. However, the establishments (religious or political) of these areas shared one thing in common – the desire to maintain the status quo and this meant controlling the activities of the people. Freemasonry was not within any existing political or religious system and was a new introduction to the social milieu of European society. The reaction was different from place to place but the aim was the same – to remove Freemasonry from society. The reason for this aim was the same – it was beyond the control of those in power.

Although Freemasonry originated in Britain, a Protestant country, Freemasonry was viewed quite differently in Europe. In Britain, especially after the establishment of the Grand Lodge of England Freemasonry was subject to ridicule rather than persecution. More virulent attacks such as that discussed above involved relatively minor groups debating an obscure issue between themselves – at least initially.

Andrew M. Ramsay (c.1688–1743), a Presbyterian Ayrshire man, arrived in France while serving in the Duke of Marlborough's army.[107] Whilst there Ramsay became acquainted with the Archbishop of Cambrai, François Fénelon (1651–1715) and under his influence Ramsay converted to Roman Catholicism during 1710.[108] Ramsay was enamoured with the doctrine of Quietism as practised by Fénelon. The church in France took a great deal of interest in the activities of its members especially in relation to religious matters. In March 1737 Ramsay was due to deliver an oration at a meeting of the Grand Lodge of France where he now held the position of Grand Orator. In accordance with normal practice he sent a copy of his proposed oration to André-Hercule de Fleury (1653–1743) by whom it was rejected. This is significant because Fleury was not only a Cardinal (and had been Bishop of Fréjus) but also Prime Minister of France.[109] A rejection by a person of such importance would normally have put a stop to Ramsay's intended oration (now commonly known as *Ramsay's Oration*). However, Ramsay seemed to have strongly believed that Freemasonry could become a useful adjunct to the church especially in France. Although Fleury did not provide any reasons for his rejection Ramsay thought he knew what Fleury's objections were and so re-wrote the *Oration* accordingly. Again Fleury rejected the *Oration* returning it to Ramsay with a simple annotation: 'The King does not wish it.' This ended Ramsay's involvement with Freemasonry. Whether the *Oration* was ever actually delivered is in doubt but copies of it remain in existence.[110] Delivered or not, they exerted an enormous influence on the development of Freemasonry in France and subsequently across Europe. Ramsay's *Oration* claimed that the origins of Freemasonry had nothing to do with the stonemasons of Scotland but had been (re)created by crusaders fighting in the Holy Land and who on their return to Europe continued to meet in the Lodges they had formed in Outremer.[111] Although extremely interesting it is not within the scope of this book to discuss in detail Ramsay's work but rather to consider why the church was so hostile towards the *Oration*.

In the first place we should bear in mind that the *Oration* was to be given by a Freemason to an audience of Freemasons. The contents of the *Oration* do not appear to contain anything truly objectionable to the church and therefore it may well have been the circumstances under which it was to be given, and the people involved, that were seen to be the problem.

What Ramsay could not have known was that the church was already turning against Freemasonry. Whilst Ramsay was busy writing and re-writing his *Oration* arrangements were being made in Italy to hold a *Sacra Congregatio Inquisitionis* (Congregation of the Holy Inquisition) in Florence. This was duly held on Thursday, 25 July 1737 and there was apparently only one item on the agenda – Freemasonry. Under the presidency of Clement XII (1730–1740, b. 1652) the conference was attended by leaders of three paper chancelleries: Cardinals Ottoboni, Spinola and Zondadari, together with the Inquisitor of the Holy Officium.

The decision of this secret meeting of the Holy Inquisition was not immediately made known. However in 1737 a Berlin newspaper, *Vossische Zeitung* reported a communication from Lombardi [Lombardy].[112] The report stated that legal action had been taken against the followers of Luis Molina (1535–1600) and his doctrine of Quietism. Significantly, Freemasonry was claimed to be linked to this system of religious belief. Whether this was a deliberate attempt to link two problem groups together in order to deal with both is not known but if so it would have provided the church with a theological basis for proceeding against Freemasonry. There is no evidence that Freemasonry had adopted this obscure doctrine but when it is remembered that Fénelon and Ramsay were Quietists and that Ramsay was a known Freemason then one can perhaps see why this erroneous link was made by the church.[113]

Arrangements for this secret conference, where no one was present to defend Freemasonry, may well have been known to Cardinal Fleury but as the decision of the Holy Inquisition was not at that time public knowledge (apart from the leak in *Vossische Zeitung*) Fleury could not have explained the facts to Ramsay. The papal decree ('*Eminenti Apostolatus Specula*') against Freemasonry was issued a year later, on 28 April 1738, by Clement XII and it is reproduced in full below:

'**CLEMENT, BISHOP**, Servant of the Servants of God to all the faithful, Salutation, and Apostolic Benediction.

Since the divine clemency has placed Us, Whose merits are not equal to the task, in the high watch-tower of the Apostolate with the duty of pastoral care confided to Us, We have turned Our attention, as far as it has been granted Us from on high, with unceasing care to those things through which the integrity of Orthodox Religion is kept from errors and vices by preventing their entry, and by which the dangers of disturbance in the most troubled times are repelled from the whole Catholic World.

Now it has come to Our ears, and common gossip has made clear, that certain Societies, Companies, Assemblies, Meetings, Congregations or Conventicles called in the popular tongue Liberi Muratori or Francs Massons or by other names according to the various languages, are spreading far and wide and daily growing in strength; and men of any Religion or sect, satisfied with the appearance of natural probity, are joined together, according to their laws and the statutes laid down for them, by a strict and unbreakable bond which obliges them, both by an oath upon the Holy Bible and by a host of grievous punishment, to an inviolable silence about all that they do in secret together. But it is in the nature of crime to betray itself and to show itself by its attendant clamour. Thus these aforesaid Societies or Conventicles have caused in the minds of the faithful the greatest suspicion, and all prudent and upright men have passed the same judgment on them as being depraved and perverted. For if they were not doing evil they would not have so great a hatred of the light. Indeed, this rumour has grown to such proportions that in several countries these societies have been forbidden by the civil authorities as being against the public security, and for some time past have appeared to be prudently eliminated.

Therefore, bearing in mind the great harm which is often caused by such Societies or Conventicles not only to the peace of the temporal state but also to the well-being of souls, and realizing that they do not hold by either civil or canonical sanctions; and since We are taught by the divine word that it is the part of faithful servant and of the master of the Lord's household to watch day and night lest such men as these break into the household like thieves, and like foxes seek to destroy the vineyard; in fact, to prevent the hearts of the simple being perverted, and the innocent secretly wounded by their arrows, and to block that broad road which could be opened to the uncorrected commission of sin and for the other just and reasonable motives known to Us; We therefore, having taken counsel of some of Our Venerable Brothers among the Cardinals of the Holy Roman Church, and also of Our own accord and with certain knowledge and mature deliberations, with the plenitude of the Apostolic power do hereby determine and have decreed that these same Societies, Companies, Assemblies, Meetings, Congregations, or Conventicles of Liberi Muratori or Francs Massons, or whatever other name they may go by, are to be condemned and prohibited, and by Our present Constitution, valid for ever, We do condemn and prohibit them.

Wherefore We command most strictly and in virtue of holy obedience, all the faithful of whatever state, grade, condition, order, dignity or pre-eminence, whether clerical or lay, secular or regular, even those who are entitled to specific and individual mention, that none, under any pretext or for any reason, shall dare or presume to enter, propagate or support these aforesaid societies of Liberi Muratori or Francs Massons, or however else they are called, or to receive them in their houses or dwellings or to hide them, be enrolled among them, joined to them, be present with them, give power or permission for them to meet elsewhere, to help them in any way, to give them in any way advice, encouragement or support either openly or in secret, directly or indirectly, on their own or through others; nor are they to urge others or tell them, incite or persuade them to be enrolled in such societies or to be counted among their number, or to be present or to assist them in any way; but they must stay completely clear of such Societies, Companies, Assemblies, Meetings, Congregations or Conventicles, under pain of excommunication for all the above mentioned people, which is incurred by the very deed without any declaration being required, and from which no one can obtain the benefit of absolution, other than at the hour of death, except through Ourselves or the Roman Pontiff of the time.

Moreover, We desire and command that both Bishops and prelates, and other local ordinaries, as well as inquisitors for heresy, shall investigate and proceed against transgressors of whatever state, grade, condition, order, dignity or pre-eminence they may be; and they are to pursue and punish them with condign penalties as being most suspect of heresy. To each and all of these We give and grant the free faculty of calling upon the aid of the secular arm, should the need arise, for investigating and proceeding against those same transgressors and for pursuing and punishing them with condign penalties.

Given at Rome, at Santa Maria Maggiore, in the year 1738 of Our Lord.'

This pronouncement against Freemasonry reveals a considerable amount of the reasoning behind the church's suspicions regarding Freemasonry. First and foremost the church's main complaint is the alleged secrecy that surrounds Lodge meetings. The wording of this document was formulated in a secret meeting of the Inquisition in Florence in 1737 but the Holy Office seems to argue that their secret meetings are acceptable but private meetings of Freemasons are not! In fact the document goes so far as to suggest if the Lodges were doing nothing evil then there was no need for secrecy and therefore *because* the meetings were secret the Lodge members must be up to no good![114] The only hint of a theological basis for the decision is that Freemasons are suspected of heresy but as there are no details even a theologian can offer no explanation for this suggestion.

The Jacobite Lodge of Rome pre-existed the Grand Lodge of Scotland (1736) and held no Charter from any other Grand Lodge. The Lodge had several eminent members such as the Fifth Earl of Seton and Wintoun (c.1679–1749) and the portrait painter, Allan Ramsay (1713–1784).

With the publication of the *Eminenti Apostolatus Specula* in 1738 the members of the Lodge followed the instructions contained in *The Constitutions of the Free-Masons* (1723) which state:

'A Mason is a peaceable Subject to the Civil Powers, wherever he resides or works, and is never to be concerned in Plots and Conspiracies against the Peace and Welfare of the Nation, nor to behave himself undutifully to inferior magistrates; for as Masonry hath been always injured by War, Bloodshed and Confusion, so ancient Kings and Princes have been much disposed to encourage the Craftsmen, because of their Peaceableness and Loyalty.'

Immediately on publication of the *Eminenti Apostolatus Specula*, the Jacobite Lodge of Rome dissolved itself never to meet again. This is probably the most powerful indication that could be given to the 'authorities' (of whatever type) that Freemasonry posed no threat to church or state but despite this it was not perceived in that way. The Minute Book of The Jacobite Lodge of Rome is now the property of the Grand Lodge of Scotland.

In order to reinforce the power of Clement's edict Cardinal Firrao (1670–1744) issued a proclamation (see below) which eliminated all possible loopholes some might use to avoid Clement's Bull. If anything, Firrao's proclamation is not merely 'over the top' but might be described as brutal and vicious. The full text is as follows.

Proclamation
Joseph Cardinal Firrao, of the Title of St. Thomas in Parione, and of the sacred Roman College Cardinal Priest:

WHEREAS his Holiness of our Lord Pope Clement XII happily reigning, in his Bull of the 28th April last, beginning In eminenti, condemned, under pain of Excommunication reserved to himself, certain Companies, Societies, and Meetings under the title of Free-Masons more proper to be called Conventicles, which under the pretext of Civil Association, admit men of any Sect and Religion, with a strict tie of secrecy confirmed by oath on the sacred bible, as to all that is transacted or done in said meetings, and Conventicles; And whereas such Societies, Meetings and Conventicles are not only suspected of occult Heresy but even dangerous to public peace, and safety of the Ecclesiastical State; since if they did not contain Matters contrary to the orthodox Faith, to the state and to the Peace of the Commonwealth, so many and strict ties of Secrecy would not be required, as it is wisely taken notice of in the aforesaid Bull; and it being the will of the Holiness of our said Lord, that such Societies, Meetings and Conventicles totally cease and be dissolved, and that they who are not constrained by the fears of Censures be curbed at least by temporal Punishment.

THEREFORE it is the express order of his Holiness, by this Edict to prohibit all Persons, of any Sex, State or Condition soever, whether Ecclesiastical, Secular, or Regular, of whatever Rank or Dignity, though ordinary or extraordinary privileged, even such as require special mention to be made of them, comprehending the four Legations of Bologna, Ferrara, Romagna Urbino, and the city and Dukedom of Benevento, and it is hereby forbidden that in any place under the said Societies, or Assemblies of Free-Masons, or under any title or Cloak whatsoever, or even be present at such Meetings and Assemblies, under Pain of death and Confiscation of their Effects, to be irremissibly incurred without Hope of Grace.

IT is likewise prohibited as above, to any Person whomsoever to incite or tempt any one to associate with any such Societies, Meetings or Assemblies, or to advise, aid, or abet to the like Purpose the said Meetings or Assemblies, under the penalties above mentioned; and they who shall furnish or provide a House, or any other Place for such Meetings or Conventicles to be held, though under pretext of Loan, Hire, or any other Contract soever, are hereby condemned, over and above the aforesaid Penalities, to have the House, or Houses, or other Places where such Meetings or Conventicles shall be utterly erased and demolished: and it is his Holiness's Will, that to incur the above mentioned Penalty of Demolition any common conjectures, hints or presumptions, may and shall suffice for a presumption of knowledge in the Landlords of such Houses and Places, without admission of any excuse whatever.

AND because it is the express will of our said Lord, that such Meetings, Societies and Conventicles do cease as pernicious and suspect of Heresy and Sedition, and be utterly dissolved; His Holiness does hereby strictly order that any Persons, as above, who shall have notice for the future of the holding of the said Meetings, Assemblies, and Conventicles, or who shall be solicited to associate with the same, or are in any manner accomplices or partakers with them, be obliged under the fine of a thousand crowns in Gold, beside other grievous corporal Punishment, the Galleys not to be excepted, to be inflicted at pleasure, to denounce them to his Eminence, or to the Chief Magistrate of the ordinary Tribunal of the Cities and other Places in which the Offence shall have been committed, contrary to this Edict; with Promise and Assurance to such Denouncers or Informers, that they shall be kept inviolably secret and safe and shall further obtain grace and immunity, not withstanding any Penalty they themselves may or shall have incurred.

AND that no one may excuse himself from the obligation of informing under borrowed Pretext of personal Secret, or the most sacred Oath, or other stricter tie, by order of His said Holiness, Notice is hereby given to all, that such Obligation of personal Secret, or any sort of oath in criminal Matters, and already condemned under Pain of Excommunication, as above, neither holds nor binds in any manner, being null, void, and of no effect.

IT is our will that the present Proclamation, when affixed in the usual places in Rome, do oblige and bind Rome and its District, and from the term of twenty days after, the whole Ecclesiastical State, comprehending even the Legations and cities of Bologna, Ferrara, and Benevento, in the same manner as if they had been personally notified to each of them. Given in Rome this 14th day of January 1739.

Joseph Cardinal Firrao
Jerome de Bardi, Secretary
(Rome: from the printing office of the Reverend Apostolic Chamber, 1739).

Members of the church are instructed, in great detail, to give no assistance whatsoever to Freemasons under pain of excommunication. Officers of the church of whatever rank are to take action against any and all Freemasons as being suspected of heresy. This seems to reflect the fears of those in positions of power and authority who cannot tolerate not knowing what their 'subjects' might be saying or doing and is something to which I shall also return. In this scenario the alleged secrecy of Freemasonry is interpreted to mean a potential lack of control and therefore a lack of power. This argument is applied by the church to Freemasonry and not to other voluntary organisations or to businesses, governments, political parties and charities, etc. and strongly suggests that those organisations can legitimately hold secret meetings whereas Freemasonry cannot. Treating Freemasonry in this manner implies that the Order is illegitimate.

At this time rumours that Freemasonry had spread undetected (the secrecy angle yet again) throughout much of Europe had induced several countries to ban Freemasonry before and after the Papal Bull of 1738.

This is an important point on two counts. Firstly, it shows that the Roman Church could claim that it was not the first to take action against Freemasonry but secondly, and more importantly, it confirms that action against Freemasonry was based on rumour and suspicion and not fact.[115] However, the argument in Clement's proclamation that other countries first took action against Freemasonry is disingenuous in that only Holland had in 1735 moved against Freemasonry prior to 1738. Countries which took anti-Masonic action were as follows:

Holland	1735
France	1737
Sweden	1738
Geneva	1738
Zurich	1740
Berne	1745

Other European countries took steps to curtail or control Freemasonry throughout the 18th century, the severity of which varied in accordance with the perception of the threat posed by Freemasonry.

As with the example of the attacks on Freemasonry regarding the Burgess Oath by a small religious group in Scotland we find a similar situation in respect of wider attacks by religious groups in Europe. Interestingly these attacks and the response of Freemasons were reported in considerable detail in Britain. As with the Burgess Oath, which was detailed in Pocket Companions of 1761 and 1764, the European attacks on Freemasonry were reported in the Pocket Companion published in 1754.[116] [117] The argument made against Freemasonry is again provided in detail. The Papal Bull of Clement XII (see above) is given in full as is the proclamation of Joseph Cardinal Firrao of 1739 (see above). Unlike the Burgess Oath the Bull and Proclamation were not a matter restricted to one country but applied to many in Europe. Where one localised condemnation of Freemasonry attracted attention only in a limited area a Papal Bull caught the attention of a much larger number of people. The Pocket Companion of 1754 published in London included a section the title of which is given in full (See Plate 4):

'An APOLOGY for the Free and Accepted MASONS Occasioned by their PERSECUTION in the CANTON of BERNE, with the Present STATE of MASONRY in Germany, Italy, France, Flanders and Holland. Translated from the French, by a Brother.'

This is a fairly substantial piece of writing and includes Pope Clement's Bull and Cardinal Firrao's proclamation both of which have already been reproduced above.

There are several quite remarkable aspects of the inclusion of this section in the Pocket Companion. The Bull and Proclamation are reproduced in full and are then discussed. As an example of even-handedness I doubt that this has ever been improved upon in any Masonic publication. Not only are those attacking Freemasonry freely provided with a vehicle with which to state their case, it is reproduced in a publication designed to be read by the very people being attacked – Freemasons. It is also to be noted that this is a European Masonic response, although to what extent it represents the opinions of all Freemasons in Europe is unknown. However, as the original tract was printed in Frankfurt in 1748, published in French and translated into English before being published in London, it suggests that reaction was strong. Also mentioned are Italy, Flanders and Holland, which suggests that it had considerable distribution if not support. The date of the original printing, 1748, is also of importance, coming so soon after Freemasonry had been banned in the Canton of Berne which, because it is specifically mentioned in the title, was almost certainly the catalyst that led to its publication as the edict of Berne is also provided in full. It is the examination of these Bulls, Proclamations and Edicts and especially the arguments against them that provide an enormous insight into not only what the enemies of Freemasonry thought but also the grounds on which Freemasons defended themselves.

As has been suggested above there were numerous reasons for attacks on Freemasonry. The above mentioned papal proclamation is notable for the total absence of theological objections. Rather the objection was that Lodge meetings were private and that the church had no knowledge or control over what its members might be doing whilst in their Lodges. This meant that where the Catholic Church held sway this view prevailed in those countries. One exception was in France – see below. It cannot be emphasised enough that attacks on Freemasonry were based on rumour, suspicion and innuendo and not fact. The above proclamation is an example of the end product of acting on perception rather than fact. It had the unfortunate effect that it was accepted from a very early period that Freemasonry did not need to be considered on the basis of facts but on prejudice and suspicion. This attitude, established more than 250 years ago, continues to be applied to the Order today. Falsehoods or the sin of omission can be used to perpetuate a particular view of Freemasonry. For example the opinion held by many people is that Freemasonry refuses to admit those of the Catholic faith. This is quite incorrect as this is a prohibition imposed by the church by way of Bulls etc. such as that of 1738.

Within the church a rumour arose that the Bull issued by Clement XII would lapse when he died. In order to dispense with this misapprehension in 1751 Benedict XIV (1740–1758, b.1675) promulgated the '*Providas Romanorum*', an Apostolic constitution which reaffirmed the '*Eminenti Apostolatus Specula*' of 1738. It specifically repeated the *possible* Masonic threat against church and state, the use of oaths, and secrecy. It further condemned Freemasonry on the grounds of its perceived religious indifferentism and naturalism.[118] [119] It would appear that there was a sudden realisation that the Bull and Edict of 1738 contained no theological arguments against Freemasonry.[120] A theological basis was therefore added in order to *retrospectively* provide a specifically religious objection to Freemasonry. This is of crucial importance as without a theological basis the church had no reason to condemn Freemasonry as it did not fall within its orbit of legitimate commentary. This retrospective 'rescue' of the initial gives the lie that Freemasonry is a religion and was only later claimed to be so in order to justify the earlier condemnation. More importantly religious indifferentism can only be applied to a religion not a secular society such as the Boy Scouts. Thus because a denomination of one religion has decided that Freemasonry is a religion it can be condemned on religious grounds. Yet the treatment accorded Freemasonry is not applied, or certainly not with the same vigour, to other religions.[121]

In terms of geography the '*Providas Romanorum*' refers to a threat against the Church and State at a time when what is now Italy was a mixture of kingdoms, duchies, republics and the Papal States. The creation of the Unified Kingdom of Italy began in 1861 and was completed in 1870 when France withdrew from the Papal States.[122] The present Republic of Italy was formed in 1946. The various papal decrees therefore applied not only to the church across the globe but also to a specific geographic area across the centre of the Italian peninsula. They had little effect in places such as Britain and France. Without engaging in a religious debate I can safely say that an observer reading the documents of 1738 and 1751 would come to the conclusion that the church did not quite understand the true nature of Freemasonry and erred on the side of caution (from its point of view) in instructing members of the church not to become Freemasons.

Before the Unified Kingdom of Italy came into being during the mid 19th century the Papal States comprised most of the modern Italian regions of Lazio, Marche, Romagna and Umbria, with Rome as the capital. In this area papal decrees were law and implemented by the civil government. Outside the Papal States papal decrees were promulgated, or not, by the civil governments of the countries to whom the decrees were sent. Therefore, the *'Eminenti Apostolatus Specula'* of 1738 was acted upon by King Augustus III of Poland (1734–1763; b. 1696) by prohibiting Freemasonry. However in other countries, such as Britain, the decree had no effect.

In 1751 Benedict XIV's Bull *'Providas Romanorum'* was even more strident in denouncing Freemasonry and anyone involved with the Order. If we have any doubts that this was more than mere rhetoric we can turn to at least one specific example. Guiseppe 'Joseph' Balsamo (alias Count Alessandro Cagliostro, 1743–1795) arrived in Rome in 1789. He was a Freemason and had created a 'higher' level of Freemasonry that he called the Egyptian Rite. Soon after his arrival in Rome he proceeded to form a Lodge and in 1791 was arrested and interrogated by the Inquisition who had got wind of his Masonic activities. It will be remembered that being a Freemason was a capital offence within the Papal States and after 15 months of interrogation Cagliostro was condemned to death for being a Freemason. The sentence was commuted, at the last minute, to life imprisonment. Cagliostro would have preferred to have been burned at the stake but instead he endured four years of misery before dying in a papal prison. The life of Cagliostro as been well detailed elsewhere.[123] When news of his arrest reached Britain an account of his life and activities was translated and published. The anonymous translator in the brief introduction made the following observation:

'Whatever motive may have influenced the court of Rome, it will be a lasting reproach on the reign of Pius VI [1775–1799; b. 1717] to have detained, tried, and inflicted the punishment on a man, against whom he could only prove the crime – of being a Freemason!'[124]

As we shall see, there were very serious accusations soon to be made against Freemasons but this seems to have been part of a cumulative process. For example a Masonophobic campaign was launched in Germany in the Cathedral Church at Aix-la-Chapelle by the priests Peter Schuff and Ludwig Greinemann. Although the campaign did not gain any particular momentum it was indicative of the sporadic attacks on Freemasonry during the latter part of the 18th century. In this instance it is the content of one of the anti-Masonic sermons that attracts our attention:

'The Jews who crucified the Saviour [Jesus Christ] were Freemasons, that Pilate and Herod were Wardens in a [Masonic]

Lodge. Judas had been admitted a Mason in a Synagogue before he betrayed Christ, and when he gave back the thirty pieces of silver before setting out to hang himself, he did nothing more than pay the fee for initiation into the Order [of Freemasons].'[125]

Sermons such as these caused the civil authorities to ban Freemasons from meeting for their own safety. It was not until the same authorities, in an effort to restore order, forbade the priests from preaching such sermons or else be refused permission to collect alms that order was restored.[126]

However, it is not the deliberate attacks, distressing as they must have been to the Freemasons of that time and place, that are of major interest. Rather the content of the sermons indicates that at this early stage links were being made between Freemasons and Jews. The latter had long suffered the accusation of being 'Christ's killers' but here Freemasons too are being accused of the same crime. This 'linkage' resembles the earlier suggestion that Freemasons were also Quietists (see above). The terms Jew and Freemason are being used interchangeably and although the statement that Pontius Pilate, King Herod and Judas Iscariot were all Freemasons and that Pilate and Herod held office in a Masonic Lodge is ridiculous, it was a portent of what was to follow.

It has been claimed that the French Revolution of 1789 was orchestrated by Freemasons acting as a group. This is one of the earliest conspiracy theories to be laid at the door of Freemasonry and comes from two almost simultaneous sources. In 1797 Abbé Augustin Barruel (1741–1820) published, in French, a four-volume work entitled *Memoires pour servir a l'histoire du Jacobinisme* and in that same year published the first two volumes in English: *Memoirs illustrating the history of Jacobinism*. Also in that same year John Robison (1739–1805) who claimed to be a Freemason and to have been initiated in Lodge La Parfaite Intelligence in Liège during 1770, published a book: *Proofs of a conspiracy against all the religions and governments of Europe: carried on in the secret meetings of Free Masons, Illuminati, and reading societies* which he had taken almost two years to prepare. Barruel hurriedly published volumes three and four of his work the following year. The works of Barruel and Robison have been discussed extensively elsewhere and details are therefore not repeated here.[127] Both authors implicated Freemasons in the French Revolution. Barruel was a Jesuit and had fled to Britain to escape the revolution. He may therefore have had an ulterior motive for making such a claim.[128] Robison's motives are even more obscure, taking great pains to point out that Freemasonry in Britain was quite different from that which he experienced when visiting Lodges in Europe.[129] Neither author makes clear their motives for writing their books but both contain huge amounts of unverified speculation, propaganda and factual error.[130]

There is no doubt that individual Freemasons took part in the French Revolution but to suggest that they *all* acted as a Masonic group is quite incorrect. However, Barruel's specific allegations and Robison's more diffuse opinion that a European revolution led by Freemasons (in alliance with others) was imminent ensured that Freemasonry (or at least European Freemasonry) became the subject of close scrutiny. Barruel in particular was convinced that the revolution had been caused by anti-Catholic 'secret societies', specifically Freemasonry. His views became widespread as his book was translated from French into English, Polish, Italian, Spanish and Russian. This made him a very rich man.

In the aftermath of the French Revolution (1789) the British authorities became concerned that the revolution might cross the channel. The Revolutionary French Government declared war on Britain in 1793 and the French offered assistance to any who would 'revolt against a tyrant'. All sorts of associations, clubs and groups were considered to be potential breeding grounds for revolution. Some of these suspicions proved correct and in order to suppress any revolutionary activities the British government introduced legislation to curb the gathering of potential revolutionary groups. Some of these were easily identifiable: the United Irishmen; the Society of the Friends of the People; the United Scotsmen; the Society for Constitutional Information and the London Corresponding Society are a few examples. The United Irishmen is a case in point. It went underground in 1794 and it adopted many of the trappings of Freemasonry.[131] This served two purposes: the swearing of ritual oaths reinforced the bond between the members and provided a private means of identifying each other.[132] On the arrest of their leaders they rose in open rebellion in 1798, but were defeated before French forces could land.[133]

However, there were many other groups that were not identifiable for their radical aims but might have been subverted for such a purpose. The British government therefore decided that a system to regulate all potentially subversive groups and associations was required. As has already been discussed above, an oath can help greatly in binding individuals together. When the government acquired copies of some of these oaths a number were found to be explicitly seditious. There was a lot of variation however and as some oaths stated the intention to 'overthrow the present government by force if necessary' or to 'assist the

French in case of invasion' (both from United Irishmen oaths) the proposed legislation had to have a wide scope.[134]

The Unlawful Oaths Act (1797) was drawn up to counter the revolutionary threat of various groups (and vindicated in the eyes of the authorities by the rebellion of the United Irishmen in the following year). The preamble of the act read:

> 'wicked and evil deposed persons have of late attempted to seduce persons serving in his majesty's forces by sea and land and others of his Majesty's subjects from their duty in allegiance to his Majesty and to incite them to acts of mutiny and sedition and have endeavoured to give effect to their wicked and traitorous proceedings by imposing upon the persons whom they have attempted to seduce the pretended obligations of oaths unlawfully administered.'[135]

The act even anticipated that people might be forced to take such an oath against their will and the legislation permitted such people to escape the effects of the law provided they reported their coercion within four days. In Ireland landowners were required to make their tenants take an oath that they would not take an oath against the government! These are all indications of the paranoia that gripped the nation.

The turmoil and fear that existed in Britain following the mutinies and open rebellion was further exacerbated by the publications of Barruel and Robison who were widely read and went to multiple editions.

At first glance Freemasonry must have seemed an obvious target for the government. Meetings were held behind closed doors, non-members could not attend, oaths were involved, Freemasons held divergent political views and no one knew who the members were. The mere fact that these facts about Freemasonry were known, and that the Order had been in existence for almost 100 years, whereas actual seditious societies were not, tempered attitudes towards Freemasonry.[136] However, the authorities remained gravely concerned and as the war progressed badly for the British, decided that the 'enemy within' required more stern treatment. In 1799 The Unlawful Societies Act was introduced and it was this legislation that would have an impact upon Freemasonry.

The first section of the Act named the groups that were the subject of the legislation: the United Irishmen; the United Scotsmen; the United Englishmen; the United Britons; the London Corresponding Society etc. These were described:

> 'as being unlawful combinations and confederacies against the government of our Sovereign Lord the King and against the peace

and security of his Majesty's liege subjects'.

At this early stage the Act does not appear to involve Freemasonry and the following section also seems to relate to the above mentioned groups. However, a careful reading of the section belies this:

'All and every of the said societies, and also every other society now established or hereafter to be established, the members whereof shall, according to the rules thereof or to any provision or agreement for that purpose, be required or admitted to take an oath or engagement which shall be an unlawful oath or engagement within the intent and meaning of the Unlawful Oaths Act, 1797, or to take an oath not required or authorised by law; and every society the members whereof shall take, subscribe or assent to any test or declaration not required by law or not authorised in manner hereinafter mentioned and every society of which the names of members or any of them shall be kept secret from society at large, or which shall heave any committee or select body so chosen or appointed that the members constituting the same shall not be known by the society at large to be members of any such committee or select body, or shall have any president, treasurer, secretary, delegate or other officer, so chosen or appointed that the election or appointment of such persons to such offices shall not be known to the society at large, or of which the names of the members and of all presidents, treasurer, secretaries, delegates and other officers, shall not be entered in a book or books to be kept for that purpose, and to be open to the inspection of all the members of such society; and every society which shall be composed of different divisions or branches or of different parts acting in any manner separately or distinct from each other, or of which any part shall have any separate or distinct president, secretary or treasurer, delegate or other officer for such part, shall be deemed and taken to be unlawful combinations and confederances; every person who shall directly or indirectly maintain correspondence or intercourse with such society or who shall by contribution of money or otherwise aid, abet or support such society or any members or officers thereof, shall be deemed guilty of unlawful combination and confederacy.'

Although the first section of the Act made it clear who the target groups were, those drafting the legislation omitted to make that clear throughout the remainder of the Act. However, the following words are important.

'or to take an oath not required or authorised by law; and every society the members whereof shall take, subscribe or assent to any test or declaration not required by law or not authorised in manner hereinafter mentioned...'

This meant that Masonic Obligations would become Unlawful Oaths because they were neither required by law nor were they authorised in the *manner* laid down by the Act. The absence of any reference to what groups, societies and associations this applied to ensured that Freemasonry fell into the orbit of this part of the Act and would have effectively made Masonic meetings illegal.

This was quickly recognised by the Grand Lodges of Scotland and England and William Pitt 'the younger' (1759–1806) was prevailed upon to introduce certain exemptions applicable to Freemasonry. These exemptions applied to Grand Lodges and those independent Lodges in Scotland (Mother Kilwinning, Lodge St. John Glasgow and Lodge St. John Melrose) but also added new responsibilities.[137] [138] The deliberations of the Grand Lodge of Scotland are recorded in its Minute Books and although another fascinating piece of Masonic history, need not be detailed further here except to point out that even during a period of war, rebellion and mutiny Freemasonry was not considered to be a threat to British society.

Although that was the view of the authorities the inclusion of Freemasonry in the debate ensured that from the beginning of the 19th century the Craft was dogged by unwarranted controversy. Barruel and Robison's books had implanted in the minds of many that Freemasons acting in concert had been responsible for the French Revolution. At the start of the revolution the Grand Lodge of France had 88 Lodges in Paris with 43 scattered throughout the rest of the country. The Grand Orient of France had 67 Lodges in Paris and a further 468 Lodges throughout the country and French colonies.[139] The facts fly in the face of this allegation. Most of the members of the Parisian Lodges were aristocrats and the Grand Master of the Grand Orient was no less a personage than the Duc d'Orléans! Despite renouncing the Order and adopting the name Citoien Égalité (Equality) in an attempt to demonstrate his conversion to the new regime he was executed nevertheless. Most of the Lodges in Paris were sacked and most of their number executed in their hundreds.[140] [141] In addition Lodges outside Paris did not entirely escape attention. For example:

'As from today, the city's four Masonic Lodges are going to have to shut up shop. Despite the constant patriotism they have displayed. The deputy Mallarmé, who came from Paris on a mission to put Lodges on a list of "monuments to fanaticism" that he is responsible for destroying. The Toulouse brothers had hoped for better treatment from a Lodge brother. But Mallarmé, although himself a Mason, was unable to resist pressure from the city's lower classes; they have pointed out to him that such associations are against the law.'[142]

Despite the facts, Freemasonry had been implicated in a major conspiracy – to take over Europe (if not the world) and the French Revolution was merely the first step. In the immediate aftermath of the books by Barruel and Robison Freemasonry was the only 'organisation' bent on creating a New World Order. The 19th century would see that change and the resultant 'super-conspiracy' would begin and develop into that which exists today. In Barruel's writings he mentioned the Jews only in passing and maintained that the Freemasons and only the Freemasons had been responsible for the French Revolution. Barruel was aggressive in his claims that the French Revolution was a Masonic conspiracy and his voluminous letter writing defending that position did much to spread and support this idea. In 1806 Barruel received a letter from 'Florence' ostensibly from an army officer by the name J. B. Simonini. In the process of congratulating Barruel he explained that Barruel knew only part of the Masonic plot to take over Europe. Simonini revealed that while in Piedmont he met some Jews who had become separated from Jewish faith and culture at a very early age. These Piedmontese Jews welcomed him with open arms and entrusted him with secrets relating to Jewish European activities. He was shown large sums of gold and silver used to reward those who would join the cause and if he was prepared to do so would receive some of these riches. More importantly arrangements would be made to have him promoted to a general. However, his side of the bargain was to become a Freemason. This was necessary because Freemasonry (and the Illuminati) had been founded by Jews and they were in control of both organisations. They were merely a continuation of the Mani and the Old Man of the Mountain (the Assassins), also founded by Jews.[143] Simonini was even more surprised to learn that Jews were disguising themselves as Christians and had infiltrated the highest level of the Roman Catholic Church where they had more than 800 members in Italy and were employing the same tactics in other countries. Even more shocking was the plan to ensure that a Jew would soon be made Pope. The French Revolution had resulted in Jews receiving full civil rights and they were determined to gain the same rights across Europe by whatever means necessary. The 'fact' that Jews had benefited from the French Revolution, instigated by Freemasons, proved that they were in league to the extent that they were one and the same. Although Barruel attempted to contact Simonini he was unsuccessful. Barruel's reaction to the contents of the letter was to dismiss them because he believed that to make it public could cause the wholesale massacre of Jews.

The same year Barruel had received the letter from the mysterious Simonini, Napoleon summoned leading Jews to a meeting in Paris. This he called an 'Assembly of the Great Sanhedrin' after the supreme court of Jewish antiquity. This had the unfortunate effect of suggesting that there had been some kind of continuous Jewish council from ancient times to the present day. Those who could not understand why the *ancien régime* had been destroyed by the revolution were now being provided with clues. Napoleon, if not a Jew himself, was far too accommodating toward them. Napoleon's purpose in gathering together leading French Jews was far more prosaic. Although the revolution had guaranteed the French people Liberty, Fraternity and Equality, Napoleon wanted to be sure that certain groups, in this case the Jews, would adopt the new regime's aims and purpose.[144] Barruel, although not making the Simonini letter public, did not hesitate to circulate it in the highest circles of French society. This 'need' by some, to have an explanation for an apparently inexplicable event is something to which I shall return later.

The Simonini letter is the first to link Freemasons and Jews together in a conspiracy (the previous claims that they killed Christ not withstanding). The letter had, however, little impact at the time but it did cause Barruel to rethink his belief that Freemasons alone were responsible for the French revolution. He consulted Pius VII (1800–1823; b. 1742) as to the contents of the letter, who suggested that all the indications were that they were accurate.[145] Towards the end of his life he spoke at length with Father P. Grival, the conversations being recorded sometime later. Simonini's letter and Pope Pius VII's opinions seem to have caused Barruel to greatly expand his conspiracy theory to include Assassins, Jews, Mani, and Freemasons, the latter being the main agents of the Jews. Barruel, although not making Simonini's letter public, passed copies to Joseph Fouché, chief of police, and Cardinal Fesch and claimed credit for the abrupt ending of Napoleon's meeting, without any conclusions being agreed, with the Great Sanhedrin. In the view of many here lies part, if not the whole, of the origins of the *Protocols of the Elders of Zion.*[146]

Exactly why Barruel's conspiracy disappears for approximately 40 years is not clear. Perhaps the absence of Barruel and his pugilistic style was sufficient for it to fall from interest. Conspiracies, like myths, have a tendency never to completely die but are revived in a reformed manner.[147]

Attacks on Freemasonry were becoming quite normal and those of the church reveal that the reasons were being refined over time. In 1814 Pope Pius VII issued an edict which condemned Freemasonry and the Carbonari, claiming that both were considered dangerous to the State and Church. This linking of two disparate groups considered dangerous to the church and then condemning both may have been a pattern or tactic established as early as 75 years previously. It seems that Freemasonry was an easy target for lumping together with undesirable groups as time and circumstances directed. The Carbonari was a secret society initially based in and around Naples, Italy.[148] It was republican and anti-clerical and its main aim was a liberal, unified Italy. It was superficially similar to Freemasonry, having taken numerous parts of its ritual and symbols. This suggests a reason why they were considered to be the same but at the same time demonstrates a lack of understanding of the true nature of Freemasonry. In 1821 the Pope promulgated another Bull against Freemasonry and the Carbonari: *'Ecclesiam a Jesu Christo'*, further reinforcing not only the idea that the two groups were inextricably linked but that Freemasonry was a secret society against the Church and State. By 1831 the attempted revolts by the Carbonari had been crushed and its members executed or exiled.[149] It is to be noted that there was no mention on this occasion of Quietism but more importantly this Bull added a political dimension.[150] A series of Bulls about Freemasonry followed. Briefly these were:

13 March 1825, Pope Leo XII (1823–1829; b.1760) decreed in his Bull, *'Quo graviora mala'*, which forbade 'forever the secret societies which are against the Church'. This Bull also continued to associate Freemasonry with the Carbonari and describes Freemasonry as a 'sect' which is an interesting choice of words.

On 24 March 1829, Pope Pius VIII (1829–1830; b.1761) issued an encyclical *'Traditi humilitati'*;[151]

On 15 August 1832, Pope Gregory XVI (1831–1846; b.1765) proclaimed his encyclical *'Miravi vos'*.

Pope Pius IX (1846–1878; b.1792) – issued several edicts against Freemasonry, such as *'Qui Pluribus'* (9 August 1846). In his *'Allocution*

Multiplices Inter' (25 November 1865) it was stated:[152]

' ...this perverse society of men, called Freemasons... is neither
defeated nor overthrown in front of whose door lie many insurgent
movements, many incitements to wars which have set fire to all of
Europe.'

The '*Apostolicae Sedis*' (12 November 1869) is along similar lines as
is the '*Etsi Multa*' of 21 November 1873. Pius IX proclaimed a total of
eight encyclicals and allocutions against Freemasonry during his long
reign.

From these Bulls and encyclicals a continuing process of refining, and
elaborating, the case against Freemasonry can be clearly identified.

Freemasons did not simply ignore such attacks but as there is no single
Masonic 'head office' and given the self-imposed rule of not becoming
involved in religion or politics such responses were personal and
sporadic. One example will serve to illustrate this point. Johann K.
Bluntschli (1808–1881) was a Swiss-born jurist and politician. He
became a professor at the University of Heidelberg and in 1865 published
an open letter refuting Pope Pius IX's accusations against Freemasonry.
Bluntschli was Master of Lodge Ruprecht zu den fünf Rosen, Heidelberg,
and wrote the letter in that capacity. In rejecting the Pope's allegations
Bluntschli said:

' ... The Brotherhood of Freemasons is a society of free men, who
observe the laws of the country, but, because it is not an ecclesiastic
institution, and for this reason does not belong to any Church, it is
not a subject of the Church authority. For this reason, the Papal
condemnation has no power over the Brotherhood.'

This neatly encapsulates several strands of thought discussed here.
Bluntschli wrote as Master of his Lodge but was not speaking for all
members of the Lodge and certainly was not speaking for all Freemasons.
This is a concept that many non-Masons seem unable, or are unwilling,
to accept. Bluntschli also repeats the fact that Freemasonry is not a
religion and draws the logical conclusion that the church therefore has
no power or authority over Freemasonry. He further reiterates that
Freemasonry is a 'society of free men, who observe the laws of the
country' and therefore Freemasons are law abiding and members of the
Order are not subject to the church. Despite this simple and clearly stated
reason why Freemasonry is not a religion, many religious groups

consider it to be so.

The Year of Revolutions, 1848, saw upheavals in several parts of Europe particularly Germany, France, some Italian States, the Hapsburg Empire (Hungary), Poland and Switzerland.[153] The reasons for these revolutions were numerous. Famine (1846 and 1847), plague, political awareness (and agitation), and republicanism all played a part.[154] [155] Marxist ideas were beginning to permeate society and the rise in 'individual determinism' began to undermine the Christian beliefs that had underpinned the Enlightenment. Marx analysed human society in *The Communist Manifesto* (1848) and came to the conclusion that a revolution would destroy capitalism and replace it with a different economic order. Later Darwin, after *The Origin of Species* (1859) was published, argued from a scientific point of view that humans were the result of natural selection not of divine creation. Each in their very different ways were hammer blows against existing religious belief, especially in the West.[156] [157]

At the time no specific causes could be identified for the revolutions, social unrest and general upheaval. This point, the desire, in fact the desperate *need*, for an explanation for the apparently unexplainable was felt by many and was actively sought. The reasons underlying events usually only become clear after a lapse of time. In the intervening period imagination, assumption and perception dominate. This is a theme which will be more fully explored later.

Eduard E. Eckert (?–1866), a German Protestant lawyer and essayist in Dresden, Saxony, writing in the immediate aftermath of the 'Year of Revolutions', the effects of which he probably had personally experienced, published *Freemasonry in its True Significance* (1851).[158] [159] This book was also translated into French. In addition to a number of smaller works, mainly pamphlets, in 1855 he published another book under the title '*The Temple of Solomon*'. These books revived Barruel's conspiracy: that Freemasonry was responsible for all the recent revolutions (echoing Barruel's claim that the French Revolution was only the start of a European upheaval) but added a new twist. Freemasons were no longer simply organising revolutionary movements but were actively creating the conditions that made revolutions possible. In particular he accused Freemasonry of causing moral degradation, religious turmoil and economic chaos as preliminaries to revolution. When the time was right, that is when chaos reigned, Freemasons launched the revolution. In this Eckert closely follows Barruel in accusing Freemasons of being the sole agents responsible for the revolution albeit adding that they also engineered suitable conditions. Eckert linked

Freemasonry and Judaism as co-conspirators. The history of that alleged link is in itself very interesting and is something to which I shall return.

The *Historisch-politische Blätter* (Historical and Political Notes for Catholic Germany) for 1862 carried an article allegedly written by a Freemason.[160] It was entitled *Daumer on the Freemasons* but was, due to elementary errors about the Craft, clearly not written by a Freemason. It was an anonymous spoof written to discredit Freemasonry.[161] Eight pages in one of the most prominent conservative Catholic periodicals in Germany ensured that it was widely read.[162] The content of the article is important because, along with the Protestant Eckert, for the first time it is alleged that there was a link between the conspiracy theories of Barruel and Robison and actual events – the aforementioned revolutions.

Much more important is the fact that Jews are introduced to the conspiracy for the first time. Jews are said to be increasingly influential in Prussia and have formed an association which has all the appearance of being Masonic, the aim of which is the subversion of all European states. Jews, and their Masonic 'association', were directed by 'unknown superiors' nearly all of whom were said to be Jews. The main guiding hand was a Grand Master: Henry John Temple, 3rd Viscount Palmerston (1784–1865) who was in British government office from 1807 until his death. His support, tacit and otherwise, for many of the revolutions sweeping Europe was based on his firm belief in national self-determination and the need for the introduction of constitutional liberties. These characteristics were more than sufficient for the author of the article in *Historisch-politische Blätter* to conclude that Palmerston was not simply a Freemason but a Grand Master.[163]

Goedsche's novel *Biarritz* (1868) appeared just at the point in time when Jews were indeed seeking complete emancipation and the novel must have had some impact within the more conservative elements of the new Germany. However, it is the more specific use made of this novel that is of interest to us here. There is clear evidence that Goedsche used a French political tract entitled *The Dialogue in Hell between Machiavelli and Montesquieu* published by Maurice Joly (1829–1878) although Goedsche's Jewish cemetery scene was his.[164]

Until this point the situation was relatively straightforward, but was beginning to be elaborated. Freemasons were regarded with suspicion because of their oath-taking and emphasis on privacy. Despite the British government exonerating the Order at a time of war and national crises European authorities were not so liberal. The work of Barruel and Robison ensured that the basis of an alleged Europe-wide conspiracy was kept alive long after the immediate danger had passed. The revolutionary upheavals of the mid-19th century seemed to confirm Barruel and Robison's prediction of a Europe-wide revolution orchestrated by Freemasonry. With the alleged collusion of European Jews the conspiracy became all the more potent. With hindsight what is surprising is that people who experienced or observed these tumultuous events unquestioningly accepted unsubstantiated opinions as to their causes.

Modern Germany is a relatively recent creation. A convention met in Vienna in 1814 after the defeat of Napoleon with the intention of reorganising Europe. The Holy Roman Empire was renamed the German Confederation and comprised 39 states (35 principalities and four independent cities) under Austrian leadership. Although an improvement the next structure ensured that numerous points of contention were included not least of which was the pre-eminence given to Austria. During the 1830s as industrialisation progressed, the fragmented nature of the confederation was seen as a major hindrance to further expansion. In March 1848 a revolution caused the German National Assembly to draw up a German constitution. King Frederick William IV of Prussia (1840–1861; b. 1795) declined the title of Emperor and the princes of the confederation used force to suppress the revolution and the proposed new constitution. Consequently, the German Confederation was restored in 1850.

Eduard E. Eckert's *Freemasonry in its True Significance* and *The Temple of Solomon*, the article in *Historisch-politische Blätter* (1862) and Hermann Goedsche's *Biarritz* (1868) all came together at a time when European society was undergoing intense scrutiny and political debate. Eckert also produced a magazine entitled *Magazin der Beweisführung für Verurteilung des Freimaurer Ordens* (Magazine Stating the Case for the Condemnation of the Order of Freemasons) which was used by Count Franz von Kuefstein (1841–1918) to convince the Austrian Minister of Police (Kempen von Fichtenstamm, 1793–1863) that Freemasonry was dangerous and incompatible with the law of the land.

Despite the clamour against Freemasonry in Germany (which included Austria) at this time one dramatic event served to calm things, at least temporarily. King Frederick William IV of Prussia applied to be initiated into Freemasonry. He intimated this publicly and made his own personal arrangements to travel by train to Solingen, going directly from the railway station to the Lodge room for his initiation. Needless to say this dramatic and public demonstration of a ruler's support for an organisation that had been the butt of so many attacks led to confusion. Frederick William vigorously defended the Order and his principal observation, one that he made repeatedly, was that the Order was attacked on the basis of heresy, presumption and ill judged perception. His written defence of the order was frequent, eloquent and insightful. For example:

'I give you my solemn word as a Prince of Prussia that Prussian Freemasonry indulges in no misuse. Now in all truth, why should members of the clergy not be Freemasons?'

And

'A man's Christian religion does not change when he becomes a Mason; in Masonry it rests on the same foundation as that which you accept; how can one priest persecute another in face of such truths?'[165]

Unfortunately, Frederick William IV suffered a stroke that left him incapacitated until his death in 1861 when he was succeeded by his brother William I (1861–1888; b. 1797). In 1862 William I appointed Otto von Bismarck Prime Minister of Prussia (1815–1898) who oversaw the unification of Germany, becoming Chancellor of the North German Confederation in 1867.

In 1870 France declared war on Prussia (part of the German Confederation) over a dispute regarding the succession to the Spanish throne. France surrendered in January 1871 and the German Empire under Chancellor Bismarck was created which comprised 25 states but excluded Austria. The German Empire began a process of standardisation and the economy advanced. Bismarck, however, pursued policies intended to neutralise potential enemies, in particular the Roman Catholic Church and its political arm, the Catholic Centre Party. At the other end of the political spectrum, the Socialist Workers' Party was outlawed. He introduced a social security system which he hoped would win over the working classes to supporting the consolidation of the new German Empire.[166]

German Jews had been emancipated in 1867 but most areas of public service remained closed to them. With the creation of the German Empire in 1871 nearly all the prohibitions against Jews in German were removed. The emergence of a united Germany was so recent however that the creation of laws did not cause an immediate change in attitudes. It was just prior to the creation of the German Empire that the novel entitled '*Biarritz*' by Hermann Goedsche (1815–1878) was published in

1868. One of the chapters detailed the meeting of representatives of each of the twelve tribes of Israel in a Jewish cemetery in Prague. This annual gathering was to report on the progress of the subversion of Europe and make plans for the forthcoming year. The task that each tribe had was extremely detailed. For example, Reuben was to ensnare rulers and governments in enormous debt, Naphtali was to campaign for Jews to be allowed into government positions and Manasseh was to seize control of the press. Goedsche blatantly plagiarised the work of Maurice Joly entitled *The Dialogue in Hell Between Machiavelli and Montesquieu*. This was a political tract attacking the political aspirations of Napoleon III (1808–1873) to rule the world. Ironically Joly's work itself plagiarised another author by the name Eugène Sue. His book *The Mysteries of the People* had, as its main plot, a conspiracy that the Jesuits (not Napoleon) were intent on creating a New World Order. Neither Joly nor Sue implicated Freemasons or Jews in these political, fictional, conspiracies but that was soon to change.

The Protocols of the Elders of Zion (of which more later) have a direct descent from Goedsche's novel and other material mentioned earlier in this chapter. How the *Protocols* implicated Freemasonry in some of the most depraved actions carried out by human beings will be discussed in the following chapter.

In Britain meantime Freemasonry was not escaping unnoticed. Much of what was written about Freemasonry across Europe was in the form of 'exposures', the first of which was by Samuel Pritchard in 1730 and Britain too had versions of these. Arguably more restrained, we discover *The Realities of Freemasonry* by Mrs Blake (actually one Edith Osbourne) published in 1879.[167] The book was not so much an attack on Freemasonry as an attempt to understand it but is often tinged with ridicule and mockery. However, the authoress did some research quoting from many sources and making comparisons with other 'secret' societies. The ritual and the words and handshakes etc. are provided in full in order to place them in the same context that Freemasons make use of them. The last paragraph sums up the author's attitude:

'We do not deny that the Masonic tie of brotherhood may occasionally be useful – though we doubt if, in any civilized land, honesty, straightforwardness, and politeness will not prove at least as useful passports as any number of secret grips and signs; but in many cases, it is to be feared, the plea of Masonic fraternity is employed as a cloak for jobbery, and an excuse for the unfair promotion of a brother Mason to the detriment of some more worthy man who happens to be uninitiated.'

How wonderfully English in tone but it cannot disguise the belief that Freemasonry employs jealously preferential treatment, suspicion, subterfuge and unfairness. It is this *perception* of Freemasonry that is important and is something that will be examined in the concluding chapter. It is noticed that throughout the compilation of this work many of those who write disparagingly about Freemasonry do so under a pseudonym themselves, a 'sleight of hand' similar to that directed at Freemasonry.[168] Ultimately Mrs Blake's book served to stir once again the debate surrounding Freemasonry and created public comment but its lasting legacy is that it forms part of a very long chain of innuendo and suspicion of which Freemasonry has never managed to free itself.

There remains a further episode that is indicative of the deliberate abuse of Freemasonry in political and religious matters. Many non-Masons may be surprised to learn that Freemasons are not permitted to engage in political or religious activities *as Freemasons*. Of course all individual Freemasons can hold political and religious views which are quite often different from their fellow Freemasons. They cannot, however, express those views within Masonic Lodges nor can they do so as *a Freemason* in any public or private capacity. Freemasonry, as an organisation, is therefore apolitical and non-religious. The reason for this 'self imposed' rule is that these subjects above all others are the most liable to cause dissention, argument and even violence. By disallowing them as topics for discussion Masonic Lodges attempt to create a place of harmony where men of all creeds, colours, faiths, social background and status can meet together without animosity. To digress momentarily, this gives the lie to Freemasonry being responsible for the French Revolution as to have such a hugely disparate membership unite for a single monumental political purpose would have been impossible.

However, towards the end of the 19th century French Freemasons united to promote the implementation of policies that would, in their view, be for the greater good. For many this was a natural extension of Masonic philosophy – putting thought into action. This was different from counties such as Britain where individual thought remained at that level and that 'Freemasonry' did not act as a group. This may well be one of the points that Robison was trying to make when differentiating between British and continental Freemasonry. There may well be a measure of a 'self-fulfilling prophecy' at play here. The more Masonophobes attacked Freemasonry for acting as a group (such as causing the French Revolution) groups could adopt the actions that they were accused of, especially if thought to be beneficial.

In France Jews enjoyed a level of acceptance and integration that they could only aspire to in other countries – including Germany. This was a consequence of the French Revolution (see above) and subsequently reinforced by Napoleon. Captain Alfred Dreyfus (1859–1935) was convicted of treason (by means of espionage) in November 1894. He was specifically found guilty of passing French military secrets to the German Embassy in Paris. His sentence was life imprisonment on Devil's Island off the coast of French Guiana. Dreyfus was a Jew. Whilst suffering in solitary confinement on Devil's Island new evidence came to light showing that Dreyfus was not guilty.[169] Conservative elements in the French army decided that the case should not be reopened in order to preserve the honour and dignity of the army and its judicial system. They were supported in this by the conservative political establishment. In order to counter the rumours that Dreyfus was innocent French Military Intelligence forged documents to support the original conviction. Doubts about Dreyfus's guilt began to spread and Émile Zola's (1840–1902) famous open letter, *J'Accuse…!* addressed to the French President and published in the newspaper *L'Aurore* on 13 January, meant that the issue could no longer be ignored. The effect was to polarise French society. On one side were the army, church, some elements of the press and the right-wing government, all of whom fervently believed that the suffering of one individual was a sacrifice worth making to maintain the honour of the French nation and its institutions. Those who campaigned for the release of Dreyfus included luminaries such as Émile Zola; Victor Hugo (1802–1885); Georges Clemenceau (1841–1929) and Ernest Renan (1823–1892). None of these were Freemasons but it was noticed that a large number supporting the release of Dreyfus were Freemasons. As has been mentioned, Freemasonry normally does not act in the political or religious sphere consciously as a group with an end result in mind. However, France has on occasions provided the 'exception that proved the rule'. The Dreyfus Affair is a case in point. The Grand Orient of France facilitated meetings of Freemasons who saw the imprisonment of Dreyfus as a gross miscarriage of justice.[170] [171] Facilitating meetings with an obvious political outcome was seen to be 'sailing close to the wind' by the Grand Lodges of Britain, which had by this time withdrawn recognition from the Grand Orient.[172] Because of this, Dreyfus supporters came to be seen as being Freemasons who were left-wing (because the opposition was right-wing!). Once again we see the process of observation leading to an assumption – that 'Freemasonry' was attempting to use the Dreyfus affair to overthrow the government. In other words Freemasonry was attempting to create the conditions necessary for a revolution to take place and then to put it into effect. This view chimes well with predictions of Barruel etc. but sadly it had much more profound and deadly consequences as we shall see in the following chapter. One of the long-term effects was the politicisation of Freemasonry in some parts of Europe. In the eyes of many, in France at least, Freemasonry is perceived to be a socialist organisation whereas, in complete contradiction, it is considered in other countries to be right-wing and part of the establishment. The reason for this contradiction, dependent on the politics of the country concerned, is yet another theme to which I shall turn later.

Alfred Dreyfus was formally exonerated in 1906 and reinstated in the army, being promoted to the rank of Major. Although retired he volunteered and served during World War 1. It would be a mistake to believe that Dreyfus was the victim of an anti-Jewish plot. As mentioned earlier, Jews enjoyed complete emancipation and many served in the French army before, during and after the 'Dreyfus Affair'. It would have another effect and that was to supply those who held Masonophic and anti-Semitic views with the motive to continue to do so. Despite France being one of the most liberal countries in its treatment of Jews and Freemasons, that does not mean that it was totally benign. Anti-Semitic and Masonophobic (explicit and implicit) propaganda was openly available in print and in public speeches. This was a tactic used by the reactionaries whose aim was to overthrow the Republic and restore the pre-Revolutionary *ancien régime* that had been supposedly destroyed by Freemasonry. There was inevitably a reaction to the perception that Freemasonry was involved in this conspiracy. In 1902 (that is before Dreyfus was exonerated) more than 80,000 people signed a petition calling on the government to declare Freemasonry in France to be proscribed. The petition was received and debated but was not pursued, no doubt due in part that Dreyfus was by now known to be innocent but formalities had yet to be completed.

The perception of a Masonic conspiracy introduced at the end of the 18th century, developed into a Judaic/Masonic conspiracy and was continuously elaborated up to the time of the Dreyfus Affair and beyond. This brief overview of the origin and progress of a Masonic conspiracy in France must end here – at least for the moment.

Theodor Fritsch (1852–1933) was a German anti-Semite whose views found a receptive audience in Germany during the late 19th and early 20th centuries amongst those who were disillusioned by rapid industrialisation and consequential urbanisation. This process also highlighted the decline in romantic notions of a German agrarian past. Although we have seen above that Germany during the late 19th century was relatively peaceful regarding attitudes towards Freemasonry the fallout from the Dreyfus Affair had an impact on German opinion and coincided with Fritsch's publication of *The Handbook of the Jewish Question (Antisemites' Catechism)*, which caught the imagination of many. The book came into being as a direct consequence of an appeal to the public published in the known anti-Semitic newspaper *Deutsche Reform* (German Reform) in November 1884 for a handy, pocket sized guide with a wealth of information on the Jewish Question.[173] This was published under the name Thomas Frey, one of Fritsch's known aliases. The book was hugely popular, the first edition selling out in the week after publication. In the tenth edition (1891) Fritsch revealed his authorship and throughout the lifetime of the book added to the content in nearly every edition. The 25th edition, published in 1891 was expanded to 411 pages. In total 49 editions were published, the last in 1944, and more than 335,000 copies were printed. The use of the word Catechism shows the nature of the work and probably why it was so popular. Written in an 'all the questions and answers you ever wanted to know about the Jews' style, it could be picked up and read at a moment's notice. Fritsch was clever enough to include statements by many famous anti-Semites such as Eugen Dühring (1833–1921); Arthur Schopenhauer (1788–1860); Richard Wagner (1813–1883) and Heinrich von Treitschke (1834–1896), as well as a host of lesser known intellectuals interspersed with his own fictitious commentators on Jewish manners, customs and history. One of his inspired inclusions was the use of anti-Semitic material allegedly in circulation from the time of Cicero (*c.*106 BC–*c.* 43 BC) the implication being that one of the Roman Empire's greatest philosophers knew the 'truth' about the Jews before the son of God, Jesus Christ (a Jew), had been sent to save the world.

The influence of Fritsch's work cannot be underestimated. The period over which his work continued to be published, the number of editions and the influence that it had on those who were seeking *the* cause for not only the demise of the German 'Volk' but also the collapse of the German Empire ought not to be minimised. When one is aware that Fritsch was but one man competing in a market to supply anti-Semitic material to the general public it shows how people of the time were receptive to not only reading but paying for such material.

So far as Fritsch was concerned the Aryan race was superior to all others and the 'obvious' stagnation, if not actual degradation, of that superiority was a result of unknown causes. The clear, visual, rapid industrialisation and urbanisation could be seen by him and many others but the cause of this dramatic shift in German society was not understood. One possible solution, or 'antidote', was the return to romantic notions of the past contained within the essence of the 'Volk' but that was believed to be being restricted at every turn by the Jews and their main functionaries – the Freemasons. Again we see here the impulse for people to find a cause or reason for events they cannot understand or control.

In 1890 during the years following Fritsch's publication of *The Handbook of the Jewish Question (Antisemites' Catechism)* there were about 200 political parties in Germany which had, to a greater or lesser degree, an anti-Semitic element included in their agenda. Fritsch recognised this general theme and attempted to unite them in a single political organisation. The sheer number of the diverse groupings led to failure but the anti-Semitic and therefore by default, anti-Masonic, attitudes were brought further into the sphere of public discussion. This heightened debate led Fritsch, and by now many others (such as Otto Böckel (1859–1923), to argue that it would be beneficial for Germans not to associate with Jews (and therefore their alleged lackeys the Freemasons.[174]

As shall be explored in the following chapter Fritsch's ideas had a great influence on Hitler and the nascent National Socialist Party (the Nazis) especially after World War 1. (see Plate 5).

In conclusion I repeat, as I have elsewhere in this book, that I have no doubt that I shall be accused of being a 'defendant of the Jews', of being a 'Zionist', 'a pro-Semite' etc. but such barbs miss the point entirely. Those who have been judged by recent history to have been anti-Semitic have been, by and large also to have been Masonophobic. When anti-Semitic and anti-Masonic (I prefer Masonophobic) terms are used interchangeably by those on whose work I comment, it is difficult, if not impossible, for me to differentiate between the two. This is another point to be more fully explored in the conclusion.

CHAPTER 3

CREATING MODERN MASONOPHOBIA

'Man's inhumanity to man
Makes countless thousands mourn!'
Robert Burns (1759-1796)

As was seen in the preceding chapter Fritsch's book *The Handbook of the Jewish Question (Antisemites' Catechism)* sold in large numbers prior to World War 1. In 1902 he also founded an anti-Semitic journal – *The Hammer: Journal of the German Way*. He further developed this by forming local groups which he called 'Hammer Alliances' and together with Willibald Hentschel (1858–1945) he formed the German Renewal Community which was intended to re-create their vision of a pre-industrial romantic pastoral Germany. Hammer Alliances sprung up all over Germany and Austria: Berlin; Breslau; Charlottenburg; Danzig; Duisburg; Frankfurt; Hamburg; Nuremberg; Stettin and Vienna, to name but a few. As well as selling Fritsch's publications they gave public readings and lectures and helped promote the German Renewal Community. It was not primarily a political organisation but sought a return to a past 'golden age' which had been lost because of the activities of non-Germans – Jews and to a lesser extent their stooges, the Freemasons. Whilst not therefore overtly political the dissemination of their anti-Semitic and Masonophobic views ensured that these were always available for public consumption.

Although Fritsch and his associates were important other events were taking place which, although not overshadowing the German Renewal Community certainly complemented it and much more importantly supplied it with powerful material.

In the previous chapter we touched on the *Protocols of the Elders of Zion* (hereinafter known as the *Protocols*) the kernel of which was contained in Hermann Goedsche's novel *Biarritz* (1868) in which a chapter described the annual meeting of the leaders of the 12 tribes of Israel, at which it reviewed the progress of the Jewish European-wide conspiracy and plans to progress it over the following 12 months (see Chapter 2, page 65).

The impact of the *Protocols* cannot be underestimated and still reverberates today. A close examination of the *Protocols* is therefore essential for our understanding of subsequent events particularly in relation to Freemasonry.

Although the idea of a 'Jewish Council' dedicated to the overthrow of all European states and religions began as a single chapter in a work of fiction it soon reappeared as an 'authentic' document. The chapter was reproduced as a small pamphlet in St. Petersburg, Russia, during 1872. The pamphlet acquired 'authenticity' because although it admitted that it was taken from a work of fiction it claimed it was based on fact. In other words the publisher claimed that Goedsche used the truth to improve his fictional work. However, even this convoluted reasoning was soon dropped and in 1876 the pamphlet was reprinted, as fact, under the title *In the Jewish Cemetery in Czech Prague*. Reprints appeared during the 1880s in Odessa, Prague and France. Those responsible adopted specific tactics. Goedsche's novel had been published under the pseudonym Sir John Retcliffe and the French edition of the pamphlet (*Le Contemporain*) was allegedly a 'flyer' to promote a forthcoming book by Sir John Readclif under the title *Annuals for the Political and Historical Events of the Last Ten Years*. The book was never published but the pamphlet continued to be printed and was included by Fritsch in his *The Handbook of the Jewish Question (Antisemites' Catechism)* first published in 1887 and which remained in print until 1944. However, the pamphlet, widely circulated although it was, still had not metamorphosed into the *Protocols*. In a newspaper published in Odessa the pamphlet was described as a speech made by a Rabbi to a secret gathering of the Sanhedrin.[175] [176] The speech was again authenticated by attributing it to Sir John Readclif.[177]

The *Protocols*, incorporating the fictional conspiratorial meeting in a Jewish cemetery, first appeared as a serial in the Saint Petersburg newspaper *Znamya* (The Banner) during August and September 1903 by Pavel Krushevan (1860–1909). However, it seems that the *Protocols* were manufactured by another journalist, Matvei Golovinski (1865–1920) who under the direction of Pyotr Ivanovich Rachkovsky (1853–1910) was chief of the Imperial Russian secret service and based in Paris. The previous chapter detailed the synthesis of Joly's and Sue's work and Goedsche's plagiarism of them. The reason for their further plagiarism and elaboration at the very end of the 19th century by the Russian establishment seems due to concerns that Tsar Nicholas II (1868–1918) was intent on extending political and social reforms commenced by his predecessor.

Once the Russian Revolution began in 1905, however, the use of this forgery changed. The same group, now part of the White movement, disseminated the document during their 18-year fight against the Bolsheviks in an attempt to link the Red Army, which had a few Jews in its leadership, to the fictitious Jewish conspiracy.

Although the 18th century saw the beginning of Masonophobia which accelerated throughout that century culminating in the likes of the works of Barruel and Robison, the 19th century brought no respite. Indeed the works of Barruel, in particular, continued to be sold well into the 19th century (he died in 1820) with other authors continuing to refine their conspiracy theories concerning Freemasonry – as has been seen above and in the previous chapter. These theories continued to be repeated and were incorporated into the *Protocols* and other anti-Semitic and Masonophobic works. This later aspect is the main focus of this chapter.

In the years leading up to the First World War the nature of anti-Semitism changed, especially in Germany. Whereas previously anti-Semitism had a religious basis (as 'Christ's killers' etc.) this had been adapted into a racially based attack. The Jew was now seen as racially debased and although the idea of the 'perfidious Jew' continued before and during the war the idea of a 'perfidious Freemason' did not come into being until the war had commenced and was not in common circulation until after the war was over. And, as we shall see, there was for this a particular reason. This anti-Semitic but not yet Masonophobic campaign was taken up by a huge range of societies, clubs, leagues etc. prior to the war. In light of this, that so many German Jews joined the military is, to say the least, surprising.

The main anti-Semitic publications were *Auf Vorposten,* which was the mouthpiece of *Verband gegen die Ueberhebung des Judentums* (The League Against Jewish Arrogance), and the *Hammer* (founded 1902), the official publication of the *Hammerbund* (Hammer League). The former publication was edited by Ludwig M. von Hausen (1851–1926) and the latter by Theodor Fritsch (1852–1933). Their activities have been discussed in part in the previous chapter but their involvement in events of the early 20th century are no less important. When Italy entered the war in 1915 against Germany this was completely unexpected as Italy had been allied with the German and Austro-Hungarian Empires as part of the Triple Alliance created in 1882.[178] This sudden development required an explanation and blaming the Jews, although that continued, could not be easily and quickly adapted to suit this 'unnatural' occurrence. Something else must lie behind the Italians turning on their friends and Freemasonry was made to fill that role. The campaign against Freemasonry began with attacks on *Weltfreimaurere* (World Freemasonry) and it was argued that this international organisation was in reality run by Jews who had not therefore been identified as manipulating the Italians. This is another example of the use of Freemasonry for cynical political purposes. It also accorded perfectly with the claims of Eduard Emil Eckert that Freemasons were the 'hidden hand' creating the necessary conditions for war and revolution. (See Chapter 2, page 61.) It had happened before and it would happen again. As the war progressed the 'link' between world Freemasonry and world Jewry became more and more attractive not only to these conspiracy theorists but numerous others. These diatribes against Freemasonry by such magazines (leaflets and pamphlets were also printed and distributed) might not have had any significant impact (the circulation seems to have been quite modest) if not for one major event. On 19 July 1918 Prince Otto Salm-Horstmar (1867–1941) gave a speech in the *Herrenhaus* (The Upper House of the Prussian Diet) in which he stated that Freemasonry was an instrument of International Revolution and that Leon Trotsky (1879–1940) and Vladimir Lenin (1870–1924) were members of French Lodges. (Plate 6)[179] The German press gave the speech enormous coverage and by the time the war ended a few short months later (11 November 1918) large parts of the German population had been exposed to the details of the alleged world Judaeo-Masonic conspiracy. This was very quickly reinforced by the publication of *Welt Freimaurerei, Weltrevolution, Weltrepublik* (World Freemasonry, World Revolution, World Republic – Munich 1919) by Dr Friedrich Wichtl (1872–1922). Gottfried zur Beek (actually Ludwig M. von Hausen) quickly capitalised on a growing market with the publication of *Die Geheimnisse der Weisen von Zion* (The Protocols of the Elders of Zion). His introduction is entitled *Das Entschleierte Judentum* (Judaism Unveiled) and its contents are very reminiscent of the same kind of excuse used by generations of anti-Masons who want to 'expose' Freemasonry for the benefit of the unwary.[180] General Erich von Ludendorff (1865–1937) approached the subject in a very similar manner.[181] His booklet (96 pages) *Vernichtung der Freimaurerei durch Enthüllung ihrer Geheimnisse* (Annihilation of Freemasonry through the revelation of its secrets – Munich 1927) became a bestseller. As a small indication of Ludendorff's beliefs regarding Freemasonry a few of his comments are repeated below:

'The Secret of Freemasonry is the Jew. A man of any racial affinity, particularly a German, ought to recognize this fact.'

'This World Freemasonry had made propaganda for the World

War, and now prevents the establishment of truth about this war by means of Judaizing this our Universe.'

'Rulers, Sovereigns were chosen Protectors, and then had to suffer.' 'Emperor William II and the Czar of Russia were not Freemasons, and for this reason both lost their throne.'

'Freemasons are influential officials in the German government. Streseman is a Mason. Freemasonry is a sticky, glutinous, invisible substance penetrating everything.'

The large number of patriotic German Jewish World War 1 veterans caused an ideological problem for the Nazis' anti-Semitic policies. The solution was to adopt an incremental approach, only applying their racial policies to this group gradually and surreptitiously. Such was the power of the *Protocols* that regardless of the readily available evidence that Jews and Freemasons (and other groups which later came to be considered as enemies of the Nazi state) were as patriotic as any other Germans the *Protocols* were accepted as fact.[182]

In *Mein Kampf* (My Struggle) Hitler made it clear that he considered Freemasonry to be the main organ of an international Jewish conspiracy to create a 'New World order'.[183] Jews were the 'head' and Freemasonry the 'body' but initially the Nazi party did not consider them separately. Had they done so that would have logically led them to consider 'cutting off the head of the snake' as an immediate and effective way of eliminating the supposed threat. That they did not perceive the 'problem' in this way demonstrates that Nazi ideology was initially poorly developed.[184] Their rhetoric reveals that that they conflated Freemasonry and Judaism. From an early stage those seeking a scapegoat for Germany's defeat, and who decided that Jews and Freemasons were responsible, considered them to be one and the same. This view was repeated not only by Hitler but was being promoted by Wichtl, Hausen and Ludendorff. The latter was, of course the military genius who, as Chief of Staff, almost led Germany to victory in 1914.[185] His desire to deflect blame for defeat from himself (and the rest of the military hierarchy) seems to have fuelled his incessant accusations that Freemasons and Jews were to blame for 'stabbing Germany in the back', leading to defeat by underhand means.

Hitler appears to have taken on board or shared Ludendorff's ideas. The continuing effect of the Dreyfus affair together with the *Protocols of the Elders of Zion* on Hitler, the fledgling Nazi Party and the German population in general should not be underestimated. However, the question must be asked why did anti-Semitic and Masonophobic attitudes find such fertile ground in post First World War Germany and why was it not restricted solely to the fledgling National Socialist party? Most historians now agree that the civilian population had been kept in the dark as to the real military situation and the defeat of the German army came as a complete shock. Given the extent of the catastrophe, combined with the normal human reaction of the avoidance of blame, there was little desire on the part of either the government or the governed to accept that defeat was a result of military failure. That being the case there was only one viable alternative and that was that Germany had been 'stabbed in the back'. Ludendorff, as one of the supreme military leaders, may well be considered a prime example of that attitude – a widespread disbelief that German military might had been defeated by force of arms alone. As *The Protocols of the Learned Elders of Zion* 'proved', at least to those who wished to believe so, the New World Order was being orchestrated by a Jewish-Masonic conspiracy. This was a convenient and acceptable explanation to many in Germany but it also ought to be borne in mind that this anti-Semitic and Masonophobic attitude was not the sole preserve of Europe and Russia.

To some extent this view also prevailed for a time in Britain but was one the victors, it did not need a reason to explain why Germany had been defeated. The so-called Jewish-Masonic conspiracy therefore carried far less weight than within the defeated nations. It was, in effect, not needed. Yet if the world was under such an enormous threat the question must be asked why did the winning democracies (in particular) not accept that such a conspiracy existed? The answer appears to be simply that the idea of such a conspiracy was 'wheeled out' whenever required by those unable to accept unpalatable facts – a matter to be further considered in the conclusion. To make matters even clearer, certainly in Britain at least, the main supporting text of the alleged Judaeo-Masonic world conspiracy – *The Protocols of the Learned Elders of Zion* – was exposed as a forgery.

The Protocols had been published in London in 1920 under the title *The Jewish Peril* (with sub-title: *Protocols of the Learned Elders of Zion*) translated by the journalist Victor E. Marsden (1866–1920). Prior to that publication, part of *The Protocols* was serialised in the newspaper *The Morning Post* over a three-week period from Monday, 12 July to Friday, 30 July 1920. Because this was one of the most widely read versions of *The Protocols* in English it is of prime importance in understanding how the Judaeo-Masonic world conspiracy spread throughout the English speaking western world and consequently how it was central to the subsequent shaping of Masonophobia.[186] It makes numerous specific references to Freemasons and their alleged activities. For these reasons those parts of *The Protocols* as published in *The Morning Post* are reproduced in full as Appendix 2.

The Morning Post achieved a great deal of attention, not to say notoriety, by running this series. Some of the paper's journalists subsequently expanded the series into a booklet entitled *The Jewish Peril* (also published in 1920) and later the same year an expanded volume of 269 pages was published under the title *The Cause of World Unrest*.[187] Another newspaper *The Times* mounted a major investigation and in August 1921 the journalist Philip P. Graves (1876–1953), exposed *The Jewish Peril* to be a forgery.[188] Despite Graves' demolition of *The Protocols* as a hoax and a forgery, those who wished to maintain a prejudice despite facts would, as we shall see, continue to *believe* regardless.

THE AFTERMATH OF WORLD WAR 1

When the Weimar Republic was established after the abdication of Kaiser Wilhelm II (1859–1941) the belief that Germany had been 'stabbed in the back' (*Dolchstosslegende*) by Jews and Freemasons was given its most acceptable and refined form with the publication of *World Freemasonry – World Revolution – World Republic* by Friedrich Wichtl in 1919. Facing protestations that Freemasons, and their Order, were as patriotic as any other institution in Germany, it laboured under the double difficulty that it was not originally a German organisation (its origins clearly lay in Britain – one of the democratic nations that had 'won' the war) and that Freemasonry in Germany was fragmented and so rarely spoke with one 'voice' at and not at the same time. Unlike Britain, and many other countries, where Grand Lodges governed Freemasonry throughout a specific geographic area, the situation in Germany was different. By 1929 there were nine Grand Lodges in Germany.[189] Whilst some restricted themselves to particular area(s) others did not and there was considerable geographic overlapping. Curiously, despite the relentless attacks on Freemasonry and its alleged part in a world-wide Judaeo-Masonic conspiracy, membership actually increased substantially in the years immediately after World War 1. Although there was undoubtedly an element of banding together in the face of poverty, economic and political turmoil, the increasing numbers of Freemasons and Masonic Lodges never reached the critical mass to represent a single unified force within German society – partly due to the fragmentation previously mentioned.[190]

There was one further factor that caused confusion for Masons and non-Masons alike and that was due to the different ethos of the different Grand Lodges and other Masonic organisations. The 'Old Prussian Grand Lodges' were nationalistic and specifically *excluded* Jews from membership. These Grand Lodges might, inadequately, be described as being establishment, right-wing, organisations. Other Grand Lodges have been described as being 'Humanist' Grand Lodges whose membership was drawn more from the liberal middle classes and who, in the main, held left of centre political views.[191] These more liberal Grand Lodges admitted Jews. One of the curiosities of Freemasonry is the fact that, once a member, there are few restrictions on visiting other Lodges, in other countries or under other Grand Lodges. Therefore a Jew who became a member of a German humanist Grand Lodge would be permitted to attend a Lodge of the Old Prussian Grand Lodges![192] However, a few Lodges never became overtly political (as in France and Spain) and so did not become involved with, for example, the labour movement. However, this did not stop debates taking place within Lodges as to what their purpose was in the existing political and economic climate. In general the humanist Grand Lodges maintained a neutral, apolitical, stance at a time when German society was becoming increasingly polarised. The Old Prussian Grand Lodges viewed this as a weakness and one which was unpatriotic. These Grand Lodges, particularly the *Gross Nationalmutterloge zu den drei Weltkugeln*, began soon after 1926 to consider removing Jewish and Old Testament references from their rituals. This was no doubt a reaction to the increasingly strident propaganda attacks on Jews and Freemasonry and the desire to differentiate themselves from the humanist Grand Lodges. These moves were given further impetus by Ludendorff's *The Annihilation of Freemasonry Through the Revelation of Its Secrets* in 1927, wherein his Masonophobic beliefs are laid bare.[193] [194] In this Ludendorff contended that the Masonic rituals were nothing other than a mechanism to turn ordinary Germans into pseudo-Jews for their nefarious use in the world-wide Judaeo-Masonic conspiracy. However, Ludendorff's publication had the opposite effect from that intended. The nine Grand Lodges united and on 15 September 1927 issued a joint declaration condemning Ludendorff's claims. This was the one and only occasion that German Freemasonry presented a united front to the attacks being made upon it.[195]

The previously mentioned Theodor Fritsch whose earlier work *The Handbook of the Jewish Question* (see above) had done so much to influence the early leaders of what was to become the National Socialist

Party published his best known book *The Riddle of the Jew's Success* in English in 1927 using the name F. Roderich-Stoltheim.[196] This book reinforced the idea that Germany had been the victim of a 'stab in the back' but importantly it laid out how it had been achieved – a conspiracy by Jews and Freemasons who had become central to nearly every aspect of German society, owning banks and major businesses, and taking over the medical profession. Because they were not 'real' Germans their faith and way of life had diminished Germany to the extent that it was no longer populated by people who understood what it meant to be German.

At the very time the western democracies debunked *The Protocols of the Learned Elders of Zion,* which was the basis on which the alleged Judaeo-Masonic 'New World Order' was supposedly being created, the defeated nations, in particular Germany, were actively promoting that 'plot' which had been responsible for that country's defeat.[197] So powerful, repetitive and indeed attractive (as opposed to, for many, the unpalatable truth) was this explanation for the military defeat of Germany that it became incorporated into the ideology of what was to become the NS party (NSDAP) which allowed Hitler to seize power in 1933.[198]

Count Ernst zu Reventlow (1869–1943) read the debunking articles of Graves (see above) and within a week wrote in a German publication an article supporting the claims of another exponent of the world Judaeo-Masonic conspiracy theory – Lesley Fry (1882–1970). In the course of doing so he rebutted Graves' exposure of *The Protocols* as a hoax. Fry had previously published an article claiming that she had identified the author of *The Protocols* as a prominent Jew – Asher Zvi Hirsch Ginsberg (or Ginzberg) (1856–1927).[199] [200] In 1923 Reventlow was sued in the German courts and in the cold, hard light of the facts, rather than prejudice and conjecture, admitted that his views were incorrect, thus absolving Jews and Freemasonry of a world conspiracy.[201] Unfortunately, that successful court case did very little to subdue the advance of the idea of a Judaeo-Masonic conspiracy. It is of paramount importance, in my view, to appreciate that this case, which was heard in a German court, took place within a few years of defeat of the German military. The effect of the court judgment would, by any measure, negate the conspiracy theory but it proved, sadly, not to be the case.

It ought to be remembered that the Ginsberg vs Reventlow case took place at a time of extreme agitation and anxiety to find a creditable cause for Germany's defeat. The facts of the case were irrelevant – the tide of public opinion, media and politics was consolidating in favour of the conspiracy theorists.

The idea that a Judaeo-Masonic conspiracy (and therefore the 'stab in the back' claim) was rejected by the victorious nations but was widely accepted in the defeated nations had an effect on later events that is rarely mentioned. During World War 2 the Allies came to realise that the military defeat of Germany and its allies had not led to those nations accepting the cause of their defeat. The Allies resolved on two things: unconditional surrender and occupation of all of Germany. This was deemed necessary in order that no one could be misled by another 'stab in the back' explanation for military defeat. This time the cause was to be laid at the feet of those responsible. It may be of some small comfort to Freemasons and Jews that their alleged conspiracy played a small part in the defeat of Germany and ushering in the modern world including the closer co-operation between European nations.

'Unlike at the end of the First World War, the victorious powers would this time invade and fully occupy Germany. In the eyes of some the lack of occupation in 1918, and therefore the lack of a visible manifestation of military defeat, encouraged former German soldiers in the belief that they had been stabbed in the back by weak politicians – a belief that the Nazis had exploited.'[202]

As we have seen from the above example, from an early stage within Germany, Masonophobic rhetoric and activity was not restricted to printed works such as those of Ludendorff, Hitler etc. An example of their manifest attitudes are also to be found in speeches:

'What cause finally had brought America into the war [WW1] against Germany? With the outbreak of the world war which Judah had desired so passionately and for so long all of the large Jewish firms of the U.S. began supplying ammunitions...

Could the Freemasons perhaps stop the war? – this most noble of philanthropic institutions which foretold the good fortune of the people louder than anyone and which at the same time was principal leader in promoting the war. Who after all are the Freemasons? You have to distinguish two grades. To the lower grade in Germany belong the ordinary citizens who through the clap-trap which is served up to them can feel themselves to be somebodies, but the responsible authorities are those many sided folk who can stand any climate, those 300 RATHENAUS who all know each other, who guide the history of the world over the heads of Kings and Presidents, those who will undertake any office without a scruple,

who know how brutally to enslave all peoples – once more the Jews.' (see Plate 7)
Excerpt from a speech delivered by Hitler in Munich on 13 April 1923.

During 1931 Nazi party officials were provided with a 'Guide and Instructional Letter' that stated, 'The natural hostility of the peasant against the Jews, and his hostility against the Freemason as a servant of the Jew, must be worked up to a frenzy.'[203]

Before Hitler came to power in 1933 Masonophobic and anti-Semitic propaganda was not restricted to these groups *as groups* but also to individual members who had been identified. There are numerous examples, only some of which can be detailed here, but they are more than sufficient to demonstrate that Freemasons were not accidentally caught up in the Holocaust but had been targeted as individuals and as a group long before 1933. Gustav Stresemann (1878–1929) was a German liberal politician and statesman who served as Chancellor and Foreign Minister during the Weimar Republic. He was co-laureate of the Nobel Peace Prize in 1926. In 1923 he had become a Freemason in Lodge Friedrich der Grosse (Frederick the Great) which was a Daughter Lodge of *Grosse Nationalmutterloge zu den drei Weltkugeln*. In 1926, in Switzerland, he gave a speech regarding Germany's admission to the League of Nations. He arguably used Masonic allusions:

'The divine builder of the earth has not created mankind as a uniform whole. He gave the peoples different bloodstreams, he gave them their mother tongue as a shrine for their souls, he gave them countries with different kinds of nature for a home. But it cannot be the intent of a divine world order that mankind use their national best performances against each other and set back the collective development of culture again and again.'[204]

As a Scottish Freemason I am not convinced that these words are entirely Masonic but that may be due to my ignorance of European Masonic parlance of the time. Be that as it may, those with Masonophobic views used the contents to harangue Stresemann for the 'obvious' Masonic elements in his speech. Even if these words are not Masonic it is easy to see way they would infuriate Nazi Party members and ultra-nationalist groups. Reference to a 'divine world order' was at best unfortunate. Stresemann was 'exposed' as a Freemason and accused of using secret words and signs during his speech to communicate with fellow Masonic conspirators. Although Stresemann defended himself his Grand Lodge gave him little support hoping instead that the issue would quietly disappear. He died of a stroke in 1929 and Stresemann's tomb at the Luisenstädtischer Friedhof Cemetery, Berlin, has a number of Masonic allusions.

In 1932 Adolf Eichmann (1906–1962) joined the Nazi party in Austria and became a member of the SS at the end of that year. Along with thousands of other Nazi party members he moved to Germany soon after Hitler came to power in 1933 in the belief that they would soon be returned to Austria to topple the Dollfuss regime.[205] The attempt to overthrow Dollfuss in July 1934 was a failure and Eichmann's SS regiment, the Austrian Legion, was stood down and was employed in helping fellow countrymen who were also in the same situation as him and who, like him, had no wish to return home. Bored, he heard that the *Sicherheitsdienst* (SD) 'security service' was in search of recruits and went to the Munich office to apply. This was the intelligence and security service of the Nazi party and SS, run by Reinhard Heydrich (1904–1942) who had been invited in August 1931 by Heinrich Himmler (1900–1945) to form an internal intelligence service.[206] The SD was therefore an organisation with a limited but increasingly important remit of identifying enemies of the party. This was but one of several intelligence, espionage and counter-espionage agencies formed by the various Nazi leaders and other branches of the regime. The significant point is that Hitler wanted his 'own' intelligence service, and as he trusted Himmler he delegated that task to him. Himmler recruited Heydrich to create a secret service within the Nazi party which reported directly only to the Nazi hierarchy. For that reason it had to be ideologically pure, adhering strictly to Nazi ideology, where other agencies could not be trusted in the same way. For example Admiral Wilhelm Canaris (1887-1945) ran a counterintelligence department (the *Abwehr*) of the High Command of the German armed forces.[207]

Himmler and Heydrich created an intelligence agency based on the ideology of the Nazi party and that ideology dictated that there were certain implacable enemies including Marxists, socialists, as well as Jews and Freemasons.[208] The intelligence service thus created by Himmler and Heydrich was essentially to watch and identify these 'racial and ideological enemies' but not (at that time) to effect solutions to deal with these 'problem groups'. This meant that Adolf Eichmann was first given the task of creating a card index of all known Freemasons and their organisations.[209] Other sections of the SD obtained detailed information about other undesirables such as pacifists, Marxists and Jews. As one erudite historian of the Holocaust put it:

'Himmler saw the prime task of the merged police and SS as "the internal defence of the people in one of the greatest struggles of human history." For Werner Best [1903–1989], Heydrich's deputy, the police were a "fighting formation", existing to root out all symptoms of disease and germs of destructions that threatened the "political health of the nation." Alongside the prime racial victims, the Jews and foremost political enemies, Communists and Socialists, the Freemasons (a secret society held in deep suspicion for its alleged international power network and links with Jews engaged in world conspiracy).'[210]

That the Nazis made the distinction between Jews as a racial enemy of the German people and Freemasons as ideological (political) enemies is extremely important. One of the reasons why Freemasons are not identified as a group targeted by the Nazis is because they were frequently referred to in the same breath: 'Jews and Freemasons'. However, although the linkage of the two groups existed in the warped belief system of Nazism, the bases of considering them to be enemies of the [Nazi] state were different. Jews were enemies because of their racial 'contamination' of the Aryan Volk but Freemasons were dangerous primarily because of their ideas, their ideology. I shall return to this most important point in the concluding chapter.

Gregor Schwartz-Bostunitsch (1883–?) was Eichmann's first superior. He was a White Russian and anti-Semite and a self-proclaimed expert on Freemasonry, Jews, and Bolshevism.[211] He was in charge of the largest department within the SD which included the museum, library and an archive (including the card index on which Eichmann was assisting in compiling). The card index of German Freemasons eventually totalled 200,000 entries.[212]

Schwartz-Bostunitch perceived, the Masonic effect to be of paramount importance in the work of the SD. After working on the card index system, Eichmann was transferred to the museum where he catalogued Masonic artefacts.[213] He also prepared a Masonophobic exhibition in order to educate members of the SS as to the seriousness of the threat posed by Freemasonry. This proved to be an extremely popular exhibit and VIP visits were made by Hermann Goering (1893–1946), Heinrich Luitpold Himmler (1900–1945) and Ernst Kaltenbrunner (1903–1946). Eichmann's office was within the museum which was named the 'St John's Room' the significance of which will not escape Freemasons.[214]

One visitor to the Masonic museum was Baron Leopold Edler von Mildenstein (1902–?) who noted Eichmann's efficiency and diligence.

Mildenstein had been charged by Heydrich to organise an office devoted specifically to dealing with the 'Jewish question'. He recruited Eichmann, who was delighted to move from a boring and repetitive job. Therefore, the main organiser of the extermination of German Jews, and later Jews in countries occupied by Germany, did not apply his 'talents' to Freemasonry. That said, Eichmann 'cut his teeth' in identifying, cataloguing and explaining Freemasons as enemies of the Nazi state. An organisational chart of the SD during the time Eichmann was working in the Masonic Department is provided as Appendix 3. The consequences of his work, although left to others to complete, were several. Firstly, he established the bureaucratic method of identifying enemies of the state which was adopted throughout Germany and occupied Europe and secondly, his transfer to dealing with the 'Jewish problem' meant that the best Nazi organisational mind was not applied to Freemasonry but was transferred to 'dealing' with those of the Jewish faith. At first glance this would appear to have been a backward step for Eichmann as the Masonic department had a staff of 15 to deal with 'Masonic enemies' whereas he transferred to a department dealing with the 'Jewish problem' of just two full-time staff although that did not long remain the position. This demonstrates that Freemasonry was a primary target of the Nazi regime even before the 'Jewish problem' was considered.

This is a key turning point in the development of Nazi ideology. The Nazis had previously considered both as one and the same. Only after gaining power did the Nazi regime decide that Jews were the main problem and not Freemasons and diverted resources from the latter to the former but even then did not do so immediately. The consequences of the transfer of focus from dealing with the 'Masonic problem' to that of the 'Jewish problem' is now well known. Adolf Eichmann became responsible for implementing the Final Solution, and in fact organised and acted as secretary to the Wannsee Conference, 20 January 1942, which formally laid out the policy and methods of mass extermination of European Jews and other 'undesirable groups'. Had Eichmann remained at his post within the Masonic department of the SD one can but wonder what the results might have been.

By focusing on one individual, Eichmann, we can gain some insight to the Masonophobic attitudes in Nazi ideology but it is essential to appreciate that he did not instigate policy. He merely implemented it and his subsequent career has been amply investigated.[215] That said, this brief examination of his involvement with the Masonic department of the SD reveals that there was a shift in the regime's understanding of the 'problem'. Previously Freemasonry was seen as the main organisation subverted and used by Jews in the creation of a 'new world order' and that view, however grossly inaccurate, meant that Freemasons were viewed as a mortal enemy of National Socialism and therefore the entire German nation. That view remained for as long as the Third Reich existed and lingers to this day.[216] It was soon appreciated that instead of attacking the body – Freemasonry – the state required to cut off the head of the snake – the Jews.[217] (See Plate 8) The card index of all Freemasons, commenced and partly completed by Eichmann, also revealed that numerically Freemasons were a very small part of the population and so it was logical to turn towards the numerically bigger 'problem' of the Jews. This numerical difference continued to be revealed as Germany conquered and occupied numerous European nations.

As we have seen, the Nazi regime devoted a huge amount of time and effort to the identification of Freemasons and their various organisations. That Freemasons suffered as a consequence of being identified is not in doubt. In Germany the level of suffering varied according to the needs of the regime. Their attitude to Freemasons in the countries they conquered was much more malicious and deadly. However, before we leave the situation of Freemasons in Germany there is still much to tell.

Hjalmar Schacht (1877–1970) is an example of the flexible attitude towards some German Freemasons. He was deputy director from 1908 to 1915 of the Dresdner Bank and it was during this time that he became a Freemason. In December 1923 he was appointed president of the Reichsbank following his successful ending of the disastrous hyper-inflation and setting up of the new, stable, Rentenmark. He resigned from his position at the Reichsbank in March 1930 due to his disillusionment with the Weimar Government. After Hitler took power Schacht was re-appointed Chairman of the Reichsbank but subsequently had major problems with various aspect of Nazi policy, and made a public speech against the treatment of the Jews in 1935, specifically targeting Julius Streicher (1885–1946), the founder and publisher of the violently anti-Semitic and Masonophobic *Der Stürmer* newspaper. That summer had seen 'staged rampages and economic boycotts [against the Jews]' and Schacht was initially able to delay the 'Aryanisation' of the German economy.[218] He resigned his posts as Minister of Economics and Plenipotentiary General for the War Economy. Hitler retained him as Minister without Portfolio from 1937 to 1943. As Schacht realised that Hitler was bent on war he actively engaged with the resistance but was extremely careful to cover his tracks. He was arrested on 21 July 1944 the day after the unsuccessful July Plot, on suspicion of involvement. Despite there being no proof, merely suspicion, against him he was sent to Ravensbrück concentration camp, then Flossenbürg and Dachau. Schacht was known to be a Freemason and was often mocked accordingly. However, his usefulness to the regime cancelled any ideological quibbles. He was tried at the Nuremberg Tribunal in 1946 but declared his innocence. Extracts from the Nuremberg Tribunal transcripts are interesting:

'Schacht, in response to Dr Dix (Prosecution) 'May I say a few words here about my background and spiritual upbringing? My father, throughout his life, adhered to democratic ideals. He was a Freemason. He was a cosmopolitan. I had, and I still have, numerous relatives on my mother's side in Denmark and on my father's side in the United States, and to this day I am on friendly terms with them. I grew up among these ideas and I have never departed from these basic conceptions of Freemasonry and democracy and humanitarian and cosmopolitan ideals. Later I always remained in very close contact with foreign countries. I travelled much, and with the exception of Ireland and Finland there is no country in Europe which I have not visited. I know Asia down to India, Ceylon, and Burma. I went to North America frequently, and just before the Second World War broke out I intended to travel to South America.'[219]

And

'Dr Dix (Prosecution) calls witness Wilhelm Vocke to the stand: 'May I ask your Lordship this? Of course I can still put questions about the treatment of the Jews by Schacht. I personally think that this chapter has been dealt with so exhaustively that it is not necessary for this witness to give us more examples of the attitude of Schacht. I would only ask to be permitted to put the same question concerning Freemasons, because nothing has been stated about that [turning to the witness]. Do you know anything about the treatment of Freemasons or the attitude of Schacht to Freemasons? Vocke, Yes. The Party demanded that the Freemasons should be eliminated from the Civil Service. Schacht said: "I refuse to let anyone tell me what to do. Everybody knows that I myself am a Freemason; how can I take action against officials simply because they belong to the Order of Freemasons?" As long as Schacht was in office he kept Freemasons in office and promoted them.'[220]

Schacht was acquitted on all charges although not to everyone's agreement. Robert H. Jackson (1892–1954), the chief United States prosecutor at the Nuremberg Trials, was outraged at the final decision vindicating Schacht.[221] However, the tribunal stated that 'rearmament of itself is not criminal under the Charter... To be a crime against Peace under Article 6 of the Charter it must be shown that Schacht carried out his rearmament as part of the Nazi plans to wage aggressive wars.' The judges went on to note that as a result of Schacht's dismissal from the presidency of the Reichsbank in 1939, the case against him was based only on whether Schacht had been aware of the government's plans prior to his dismissal from the presidency of the Reichsbank. The trial judges asserted that there was not enough evidence to come to such a conclusion, and Schacht was therefore acquitted.[222] Schacht lost all of his important posts prior to the outbreak of war. He had also maintained contact with dissidents, for example, Hans Bernd Gisevius (1904–1974) during the war and, most tellingly, had spent almost a year at the end of the war in various concentration camps. This together with the fact that he never joined the NSDAP (Nazi Party) or any of its associated branches and shared very little of their ideology was sufficient proof of his innocence.

One of the explanations offered for Freemasons not being identified as a group that suffered during the Holocaust is that they were usually also members of another target group. This reasoning means that a Jewish Freemason was a victim because he was a Jew not because he was a Freemason. Whilst this argument initially seems sound it does not take into account those Freemasons who had no other known affiliation and that the Nazi apparatus had not identified any such 'dual membership' and it was for this reason that a card index existed for Freemasons (*not* Freemasons and Jews, or Freemasons and Trade Unionists etc.). (See Appendix 3). This argument also takes no account of German efficiency in such matters. Dual membership was designated by a combination of signs. A Freemason would wear a red triangle (point down) and if he also happened to be a Jew the red triangle would be overlaid on a yellow triangle (point up) forming a six-pointed star. In a similar way a homosexual who was a Jew would have a pink triangle (point down) overlaid on a yellow triangle (point up) again forming a six-pointed star. For illustrative examples see Plate 9. Those making this argument fall into the trap of suggesting, by implication, that on the 'scale of victimisation' a Freemason is not as 'important' as a Jew.

As an example of this 'dualism of victimisation' I cite Carl von Ossietzky (1889–1938) who was a radical German pacifist. In 1933 he published details of how Germany was breaking the terms of the Versailles Treaty by re-equipping the German air force and having pilots trained in the Soviet Union. Shortly after the Reichstag Fire (27 February

1933) the Reichstag Fire Decree was signed by Hindenburg. Surprisingly, von Ossietzky did not flee Germany and was arrested (28 February 1933) and tried for high treason and espionage. He was sent to Esterwegen Concentration Camp. In 1935 he was awarded the Nobel Peace Prize but the authorities refused to release him from the concentration camp to travel to Sweden (1936) to collect the prize. In May 1936 he was transferred to the police hospital in Berlin suffering from tuberculosis and died, still in custody, on 4 May 1938 as a consequence of his lack of treatment and abuse whilst in the camp. Ossietzky was a member of the Masonic Union of the Rising Sun which was considered to be an irregular Masonic body. However, the fact remains that the Nazi regime was not interested in the internal machinations of Freemasonry, be it 'regular' or 'irregular' – to them they were all Freemasons.

In June 1930, approximately 600 members separated from the Masonic Alliance of the Rising Sun and were recognised by the Grand Lodge of France. On 26 July 1930, in Hamburg, they founded the Symbolic Grand Lodge of Germany. Its first Grand Master was Brother Leopold Muffelmann (1881–1934) who had originally joined Humanitas Lodge in Berlin. His proposer was Hjalmar Schacht the Nazi Minister of Trade and Commerce (see above). From October 1930 to March 1933, the Symbolic Grand Lodge published a monthly magazine under the title *Die alten Pflichten* (The Old Charges). In the November 1931 issue Muffelmann wrote:

'The present aim of true Freemasonry is to fight against Bolshevism, Fascism and National Socialism. In spite of all contradictions, Freemasonry stays here side by side with the Roman Catholic Church as fighter for individual freedom, for humanity and mankind. The fight has begun. The common defence of the Western civilization is at stake'.

In the February 1932 issue, he wrote:

'Discussions within the Symbolic Grand Lodge of Germany resulted in a completely unanimous position against National Socialism. National Socialism is the enemy of Freemasonry. Freemasonry fights and must fight against National Socialism.' [223]

At this late stage it appears that at least one Grand Master was aware of the approaching danger but it was too late. In the March 1933 issue of *Die alten Pflichten*, the last German edition, the Symbolic Grand

Lodge announced that on 28 March it had resolved to become dormant.[224] On his return from a trip to London, 5 September 1933, Brother Muffelmann was arrested by the Gestapo and brutally interrogated for four weeks, after which he was detained in Sonnenburg concentration camp together with Brother Fritz Bensch, his successor, and Brother Raoul Koner, another close associate, who were both arrested on 28 August. All three were set free in November, due to the direct intervention of Brother John H. Cowles, the then Grand Commander of the Ancient and Accepted Scottish Rite, Southern Jurisdiction (of the United States) with the German government. Fritz Bensch was taken prisoner by the Russians and died in Berlin, 28 August 1945. Raoul Koner would die on 29 March 1977. In April 1934 Muffelmann went to Palestine to assist in setting up the Symbolic Grand Lodge of Germany in Exile.[225] Against all advice Muffelmann returned to Germany where he was arrested and died as a consequence of Gestapo mistreatment on 24 August 1934.

Other Grand Lodges tried to appease Hitler after his seizure of power. They attempted to convince the new regime that Freemasonry was not incompatable with Nazi ideology. On 7 April 1934 Hermann Goering, Interior Minister of Prussia, held an interview with Grand Master von Heeringen of the *Grosse Landesloge der Freimaurer von Deutschland*, and told him there was no place for Freemasonry in Nazi Germany. In other words if the Grand Lodges would not voluntarily dissolve themselves the state would do it for them – and all that entailed. A law was passed that day which changed the Grand Lodge to the German Christian Order of the Grail of the Knights Templar. The law included the statement that in so changing the Grand Lodge it ceased to be a Masonic body. The *Grosse Nationalmutterloge zu den drei Weltkugeln* learned of this law three or four days later and to forestall the authorities taking similar action against it immediately decided to voluntarily conform with that law by renaming itself *Nationaler Christlicher Orden Friedrich der Grosse* (The National Christian Order of Frederick the Great). The Christian Orders hoped that by changing their rituals and removing all Hebrew references they would be allowed to continue to exist.[226] This process also meant that Jewish members could no longer participate.

Almost immediately after the Nazis gained power Jews and their property were attacked, destroyed or stolen, mainly by Stormtroopers or SA. Masonic property was also attacked and vandalised and many Lodges were declared as being hostile to the state following the *Reichstagsbrandverordnung* (the Reichstag Fire Decree) and were forcibly closed.[227] The attempts to change the basis of Freemasonry as mentioned above, seem to have been partly to preserve the assets of the Grand Lodges and their Daughter Lodges. However, this ploy was ultimately unsuccessful as, despite a 'cat and mouse' game with the Reich's Department of the Interior, the Grand Masters of the three Old Prussian Grand Lodges were forced to meet with the Gestapo on 22 March 1935.[228] They were informed that the Grand Lodges would be dissolved by the state if they did not do so voluntarily. They opted for the latter and organised Freemasonry in Germany ceased to exist. The 'reorganised' Christian Orders, the last attempt to preserve Masonic assets (and presumably some form of organisation that might be revived in the future), were dissolved by Frick in May 1935.

Another law had been passed on 7 April 1933 which also had an impact on Freemasonry. This was the *Berufs Beamtentum Gesetz* (Civil Service Law). This law introduced the Nazi ideas of racial purity and political conformity into all aspects of public service:

Law for the Restoration of the Professional Civil Service

No. 1

1) To restore a national professional civil service and to simplify administration, civil servants may be dismissed from office in accordance with the following regulations, even where there would be no grounds for such action under the prevailing Law.

2) For the purposes of this Law the following are to be considered civil servants: direct and indirect officials of the Reich, direct and indirect officials of the Laender, officials of Local Councils, and of Federations of Local Councils, officials of Public Corporations as well as of Institutions and Enterprises of equivalent status...The provisions will apply also to officials of Social Insurance organisations having the status of civil servants...

No. 2

1) Civil servants who have entered the service since November 9, 1918, without possessing the required or customary educational background or other qualifications are to be dismissed from the service. Their previous salaries will continue to be paid for a period of three months following their dismissal.

2) They will have no claim to temporary pensions, full pensions or survivors' benefits, nor to retain designation of rank or titles, or to wear uniforms or emblems...

No. 3

1) Civil servants who are not of Aryan descent are to be retired (No. 8 ff.); if they are honorary officials, they are to be dismissed from their official status.

2) Section 1 does not apply to civil servants in office from August 1, 1914, who fought at the Front for the German Reich or its Allies in the World War, or whose fathers or sons fell in the World War. Other exceptions may be permitted by the Reich Minister of the Interior in coordination with the Minister concerned or with the highest authorities with respect to civil servants working abroad.

No. 4

1) Civil servants whose previous political activities afford no assurance that they will at all times give their fullest support to the national State can be dismissed from the service...

Reich Chancellor
Adolf Hitler
Reich Minister of Interior
Frick
Reich Minister of Finance
Graf Schwerin von Krosigk

Reichsgesetzblatt, I, 1933, p. 175

The loose interpretation of this law meant that as Freemasons were, according to Nazi ideology, Jews (or at the very least 'artificial' Jews), the law was applicable to them. Where this interpretation was not used most Freemasons lost their employment under item 4:1:

'Civil servants whose previous political activities afford no assurance that they will at all times give their fullest support to the national State can be dismissed from the service.'

Although many 'ordinary' Freemasons lost their jobs or were demoted those that apparently suffered most, as we have seen, tended to be prominent and/or active Freemasons.[229] [230] Exact figures are likely never to be available because of the confusing guidance issued regarding the employment of former Freemasons and different local interpretations of that guidance. Wilhelm Frick (1877–1946), the main architect of the above law, not only ensured that Freemasons were dismissed or demoted but also that Nazi favourites benefited accordingly.[231]

As might be expected, soon after Hitler's seizure of power, many of the German population thought that it would be wise to publicly align themselves in some way with the new regime. Large numbers attempted to join the Nazi Party (NSDAP) itself whilst others tried to become members of associated groups.[232] The *Untersuchung und Schlichtungs-Ausschuss (Reich-Uschla)* was an internal body created by Hitler to settle internal disputes and vet applications for membership of the various branches of the NSDAP.[233] The Law for the Restoration of the Professional Civil Service (see above) accelerated the process as Freemasons, and other victim groups, sought to prove their *bona fides* to the new regime. However, the Uschla, in examining all membership applications, were to concentrate their main efforts on identifying 'Jews, Freemasons, Communists and Socialist saboteurs, and others whose "personal relations" prevented them from unconditionally subordinating themselves to the NSDAP'.[234] The Reich-Uschla's reach extended to the local level with courts. In January 1934 these local courts were instructed to 'ban from entering (or remaining in) the party any persons with ties to such organisations as Freemason Lodges and their "*successor groups*" ' (my emphasis).[235] The fate of Freemasonry, in any shape or form, had been decided even while 'negotiations' were still taking place (see above).[236] At the Nuremberg Rally in September 1934 an assembly of the OPG (as the Reich-Uschla was now called) was convened and Walter Buch (1883–1949) in summing up gave the command that in the future work of the OPG all his subordinates deal 'above all with the race question and in the Freemason question, they rule without compassion and according to the conscience of the German people'. [237]

The Nazis believed that many events could only be explained by the existence of the 'hidden hand' that was Freemasonry. One incident will suffice to throw this into sharp relief. King Edward VIII abdicated on 11 December 1936 as a consequence of opposition to the intended marriage between the king and the twice divorced American socialite Mrs Wallis W. Simpson (1896–1986). Hitler perceived this as having been engineered by those hostile to him and Germany (Hitler still had hopes of an accommodation with Britain). Nazi Foreign Minister Ulrich F. W. J. von Ribbentrop (1893–1946) cultivated Hitler in that opinion and asserted that the king was pro-German and anti-Jewish. Ribbentrop asserted that Edward VIII had abdicated as a result of 'an anti-German conspiracy organised by Jews, Freemasons and powerful political lobbies'.[238] Clearly neither Hitler nor Ribbentrop were aware that King Edward VIII was an active Freemason and that his brother, George VI

(1895–1952) had been Installed as Grand Master Mason of the Grand Lodge of Scotland less than two weeks before the abdication.[239] (See Plate 10) This is another example of the 'use' of Freemasonry for political ends and will, as said before, be considered in more detail in the conclusion.

As we shall see, Freemasons in Germany did not suffer quite the same systematic persecution as those in occupied countries. This appears to have been due to several reasons. The administrative system being created to identify 'problem' groups was not fully developed until after Masonic bodies had been dissolved. Secondly, many Freemasons were integrated into the state's administrative system and their removal was disruptive.[240] Where they were in positions of power and/or influence they were removed or demoted and even then if an individual was considered too important to the state he could remain in place. The example of Schacht (see above) is a case in point. However, the shift in focus by the SD from the Masonic to the Jewish 'problem' probably had the effect of dramatically slowing down the process.[241] Although the SD's attention turned increasingly from Freemasonry and other small groups deemed to be in opposition to the German Nazi ideals of the 'Volk' they were not forgotten and the bureaucracy designed by the likes of Eichmann to deal with problem groups was adopted in occupied countries.[242]

Once the war began in 1939 the German establishment realised that it required every resource to engage in Total War and attention given to Freemasons in Germany waned but the propaganda war continued:

'World power and world stock exchanges, world fleets and a world church are not enough to hinder the victory of ethnicity. They can only mock the doctrine of human equality, silence the doctrine of humanity. The right to be a people is the sacred affirmation of billions. Whatever dark powers strive for world domination (among them World Jewry and World Freemasonry), ethnicity will defeat them all! The victory of ethnicity is certain wherever blood awakes. As the Irish tortured the English, so will people rise up everywhere. How many ethnic groups in Europe want justice and peace? Comrades, the world is waiting for us! We must march forward from our own ethnic victory to proclaim one people, one Reich, one Führer! We must bring true peace to the peoples, opposing a world of enemies to bring forth a victory of ethnic freedom!'[243]

It is not possible in a work of this size to examine what happened to Freemasons in every country occupied by Germany. In fact there has been very little research into this aspect of World War 2 and this chapter is therefore a tentative introduction to the subject. There is some information available regarding the situation in Czechoslovakia, France, Spain and Holland and this will have to suffice as an indication as to what may have happened in other countries.

This book cannot pretend to be based on original sources. It must therefore be considered as an introduction to the subject and one which is based almost entirely on secondary sources. It is my fervent wish that this brief and inadequate introduction to Masonophobia might stimulate others to investigate this phenomenon further.[244]

The lack of readily available primary sources, in Britain, regarding the Holocaust has of necessity meant that I have relied heavily on the work of others and give thanks to them for their work which is important and insightful. However, their work does not focus on Freemasonry as one of the groups selected for 'special treatment' by the Nazi regime. I have therefore endeavoured to pull together a huge and diverse range of references to Freemasonry and in that sense I trust that this work will be considered to be original.

One of the main problems in researching this book is that a great deal of material regarding the Holocaust is accessible and where it relates to Freemasonry is scant.[245] In light of that, this chapter seeks to firstly outline the general history of Nazism, and to a lesser extent that of Nazi ideology, and secondly to provide some hard and fast examples of that persecution by focusing on some of the countries involved.[246] The first of these relates to the institutionalised persecution of Freemasonry as an organisation.[247]

The Nazis had their Masonophobic perceptions of Freemasonry reinforced because Freemasonry made considerable use of 'Jewish' symbols and imagery including, of course, King Solomon's Temple in Jerusalem. However, they did not understand, and probably would not have cared, that the use of these symbols and imagery was not based on religion but on the myth-making of the Scottish stonemasons several centuries earlier (see page 23). Further reinforcement of their perceptions of Freemasonry was due not only to the admission of Jews, but to other 'racially impure' people becoming Freemasons (for example, black people – see Plate 11) and this 'mixing' of blood could not be tolerated.

As so little research has been done regarding the fate of Freemasons under the Nazi and Fascist regimes this chapter can only relate some examples which demonstrate that Freemasons were persecuted during the Holocaust. These examples are indicative of a common approach adopted by those regions. Having discussed the situation within Nazi

Germany I now turn to examples of the persecution of Freemasons in occupied countries and begin with Holland.

Holland

Klaus Barbie joined the SDP in 1935 but had been working for the SS in his home town of Trier (east of the Luxembourg/German border) as an informer (a 'V man') for at least two years.[248] In September he was summoned to Berlin and was interviewed by Reinhard Heydrich, 'as the creator of the SD (in 1931)' at its headquarters at the Wilhelmstrasse 102. He impressed Heydrich sufficiently enough to be appointed to Amt II (Department 2) in the SD-HAUPTAMT where he served for a year (this department was charged with combating 'opposition' groups) and was then transferred to the sub section Amt II/2 (later raised to a department in its own right: Amt III) under Prof Reinhard Höhn (1904–2000).[249] Barbie completed his training in 1936 and was posted to Düsseldorf in the Rhineland and given charge of the city's branch of Amt II, sections 122 and 123 which were devoted to dealing with political groups of the centre and those of the right (and who were therefore potentially opponents of the Nazi Party). In late 1938 Barbie was called up for three months compulsory military service and so did not participate in Kristallnacht (Crystal Night, 9–10 November 1938), nor could he be drafted in to the Einsatzkommando (Operational Commando) who followed in the footsteps of the German forces occupying the Sudetenland. On 1 September 1939 German forces invaded Poland and on 3 September the United Kingdom, Australia and New Zealand declared war on Germany. The 'Phoney War' ended on 10 May 1940 with German forces invading Holland and Belgium and on 19 May 1940 Barbie joined the Einsatzkommando already at work in Holland rooting out political and ideological enemies of the Nazi regime – including Freemasons.

Barbie arrived in Holland pre-assigned to Adolf Eichmann's Amt IV/B-4 which extended its genocidal arm into Holland. This department (Amt) was responsible for the identification, roundup and elimination of Jews and Freemasons. Barbie's SD department employed the same methods developed to deal with the Judaeo-Masonic 'problem' in Germany.

There is no doubt that the countries occupied by Germany felt the full weight of what was a well-refined system of identification and dealing with 'problem' groups. Those of the Jewish faith suffered most severely. The first trains to transport Dutch Jews to their deaths at Sobibor or Auschwitz departed in July 1942.[250] By this time Barbie had left Holland for France where he continued his work to rid the French nation of people involved in the Judaeo-Masonic conspiracy against Germany and the world. His activities in the French town of Lyon earned him the epithet the Butcher of Lyon. Details of his persecution of French Freemasons are not investigated here. However he was instrumental in putting in place the system that sent so many to their deaths.[251]

As has previously been stated, Freemasons, as victims of the Holocaust, were numerically small in comparison with other groups, such as Jews, Poles and others. That Freemasons as a group were persecuted during the Holocaust is now beyond doubt. Those responsible for ensuring that the genocidal crimes of Nazism and Fascism (and more modern occurrences such as in Rwanda in 1994) are never forgotten decline to accept that Freemasonry was a 'victim group' in its own right. The argument used to support this view is that individual Freemasons were merely caught up in the Holocaust because they were also members of other target groups such as Jews, homosexuals, trade unionists, members of an opposition party, etc. In other words Freemasons were not sent to the gas chambers because they were Freemasons but because they were identified as being members of another group considered to be dangerous to the Fascist and Nazi regimes. This argument fails to address why such regimes expended a great deal of time and effort in identifying and rounding up Freemasons, as Freemasons. Why so much Masonophobic propaganda was directed at them *as a group* and why their property was confiscated by the Nazi regime is not addressed.[252] When specific examples of the detention, torture and murder of individual Freemasons who had no such 'double affiliation' are provided the argument for not acknowledging this is shown to be spurious. Of as much concern is the fact that much of the information contained here regarding the persecution of Freemasons is publically available. After all I have located and used some of it here. Why this material is not used elsewhere is a legitimate question that goes to the heart of the purpose of this book and will be discussed in detail in the conclusion.[253]

General Hermannus Van Torgeren (?–1941) had served in the Dutch army in the East Indies but after his retirement and return to Holland he became involved in Dutch Freemasonry and rose to become Grand Master of the Grand Lodge of the Netherlands (now the Grand East of the Netherlands). Van Torgeren was therefore a prime target for Barbie and his superior, Adolf Eichmann. From the outset of the German occupation of Holland Van Torgeren had to report every day to the German authorities. In late 1940 Dutch Freemasonry was officially banned by the occupying Germans but Freemasons continued to gather under the guise of 'coffee mornings' in a variety of hotels in Amsterdam (there seems to have been similar Masonic activity elsewhere but for obvious reasons this is not well documented). It was at these meetings that Van Torgeren attended to organise a resistance movement. On 10 October 1940 the early arrivals at one such coffee morning in a hotel in the Leidseplein, Amsterdam, were arrested. Van Torgeren was immediately informed of these first arrests and arranged to intercept other Freemasons on their way to the meeting. A Freemason who happened to be near the home of Van Torgeren witnessed his arrest on 11 October 1940. He recognised those involved: Hauptscharführer Johan Peter Kalb and Obersturmführer Klaus Barbie. Van Torgeren was ill with kidney disease which worsened during his captivity. His family were only permitted to visit him once every two weeks and his daughter Charlotte recalled that her father once warned her, 'Be careful of Barbie' he is the nastiest and cleverest of the lot.' During March 1941 he informed his daughters Charlotte and Jacoba that he was to be deported to Germany. It is not known if he was tortured but this seems likely as it was standard practice and given Barbie's recorded sadistic pleasure in doing so. Van Torgeren was put aboard an unheated freight car and transported to Sachsenhausen concentration camp. He did not last a week and died after three days in freezing winter conditions. His last message to his daughters was a note thrown from the train: 'Last greetings from native soil. Life is hope and hope this life. Your old boy.' Barbie telephoned Charlotte Van Torgeren who was summoned to the SD headquarters on 1 April 1941. Barbie informed her that her father had died of an infection of both ears and had been cremated. She was asked for the equivalent of $50.00 for the return of her father's ashes.[254] The choice of date may have been Barbie's idea of a sick joke. The story of this brave Freemason does not end with his death as a victim of the Holocaust. As Grand Master he had withdrawn all the funds of the Dutch Freemasons from the Grand Lodge bank accounts before they could be seized by the invading Germans. The money was used to set up the Dutch resistance newspaper, the *Vrij Nederland* (Free Netherland). Jacoba Van Torgeren was a courier for the resistance group known as Group 2000 and she used 600,000 guilders of Masonic funds to purchase arms for the group.

Brother Jacques H. Tas, Chief of Police for Rotterdam, employed his skills as a fingerprint expert to forge passports for the Dutch underground and after having forged hundreds of passports he was captured and committed to Vught concentration camp where he perished.[255]

How many other Dutch Freemasons shared the same fate as their Grand Master, and the 'ordinary' Brother Tas, is not known given the lack of research into this aspect of the Holocaust. However, the fact of his arrest and subsequent death in Sachsenhausen concentration camp and the recorded arrest of other Freemasons suggest that there were many. In 1939 there were about 6,000 Masons in the Netherlands; in 1945 only 2,000 had survived.[256] Another aspect of Freemasons' victimisation in the Holocaust which is rarely mentioned is the seizure of their property. This was the normal practice of the Nazi regime which confiscated assets of groups which had been designated as enemies of the state. Van Torgeren had arranged for the monetary assets of Dutch Freemasonry to be secured but there was little that could be done to prevent the confiscation of physical assets such as buildings, furniture, regalia, works of art etc. Reich Commissioner Arthur Seyss-Inquart (1892–1946) facilitated the looting of Masonic Lodges and the theft of Masonic property by Rosenberg and the hunting and capture of Freemasons by Eichmann and Barbie. Much of the looted material was used to stage Masonophobic exhibitions and indeed the Nazis went so far as to produce an illustrated book, in Dutch, 'to prove that Freemasonry was a Jewish organisation'. [257] (see Plate 12). 'In 1940 all the property of the Freemasonry Lodges was confiscated and taken away to Germany. It included the well-known Klossiana Library.'[258] That for which no use could be found was destroyed or recycled.[259]

The Nazi regime justified the seizure of property as it was to be used for study purposes in order to better understand the nature of the groups which were a 'problem' to the state. Although some of this material was used for 'educational' purposes (Masonophobic exhibitions, books and other propaganda) the main motive was simply theft. The prosecution highlighted both the propaganda and looting during the course of the Nuremberg Trial:

'First of all, we are going to show a very short extract from a very specialised film directed against Freemasonry which was composed by the Germans in the manner explained in the brief. The film itself is of little interest, but it contains pictures illustrating the crude campaign of lies in which the Germans indulged in France.

'As it is a very short film [entitled *Hidden Forces*] and will be shown very rapidly – we cannot slow down on account of technical difficulties – I should like before showing it to draw attention to the Tribunal the two kinds of pictures which will follow at one another with the transition: First you will see a map of the world. This map will be rapidly covered by a colour indicating the influence of the Jews and the Freemasons, except for two victorious islands, the Nazi-fascist bloc in Europe, on the one hand, and Japan on the other.

'We give this picture to show that degree of crude simplicity arrived at by Nazi propaganda and how it submitted to the people the most stupid and misleading formulas.

'An even worse example of calumny follows the portrait of President Roosevelt with the heading, "Brother Roosevelt Wants War."[260]

And,

'If I mention the Defendant Goering, it is because a third document proves that this defendant gave the operation his full support, inviting all the organisations of the Party, the State, and the Army to afford the fullest possible support and assistance to Reichsleiter Rosenberg and his collaborator Utikal, whom Rosenberg himself had appointed Chief of the Einsatzstab on 1 April 1941. This is the order of 1 May 1941, which we produced under our Exhibit Number RF-1406 (Document Number 1614-PS). If we examine the text of this decree carefully we cannot fail to be struck by the first paragraph. The Tribunal will surely allow me to reread it rapidly:

'"The struggle against the Jews, the Freemasons, and other ideologically opposed forces allied to them, is a most urgent task of National Socialism during the war."

'Thus, it was enough for one to have a philosophy of life different from that described as the Nazi *Weltanschauung*, to be exposed to the danger of seeing one's cultural property seized and transferred to Germany. But the Tribunal will surely remember from the documents already presented to it, that not only cultural property was involved, but that anything with any kind of value was taken away'.[261]

The purpose of Rosenberg's organisation (*Einsatzstab Reichsleiter Rosenberg*) was to loot and confiscate cultural treasures from all over Europe and bring them to Germany and although initially this was limited to retrieving Jewish and Masonic material it soon developed into a 'grab all' machine. In order to demonstrate the extent of the organised looting of Masonic Lodges in The Netherlands a translation of a report by *Oberbereichsleiter* (senior zone commander) Schimmer for *Einsatzstab Reichsleiter Rosenberg* in September 1940 is reproduced in Appendix 4.

France

At the fall of France the premises of the Grand Orient, Grand Lodge of France and the National Grand Lodge were occupied by the military (14 June 1940) and the various Grand Lodges were dissolved. The area of France captured by German forces remained under their occupation. The remainder of the country became known as Vichy France under Marshal Philippe Pétain (1856–1951).[262] The Vichy Government signed an armistice with Germany on 22 June and this was ratified on 10 July by the Vichy Chamber of Deputies and Senate. Pétain immediately dissolved the Grand Lodges in Vichy and removed all known Freemasons from command positions. Almost immediately Pétain, who had assumed near absolute power, issued a host of laws, one of which banned so-called secret societies. Twelve months later in a speech, 'Address to the French People', the following paragraph was included:

> ....'The troops of the old regime are legion. I rank among them without exception all who place their personal interests ahead of the permanent interests of the State – Freemasonry, political parties deprived of clientele but thirsting for a comeback, officials attached to an order of which they were beneficiaries and masters – or those who have subordinated the interests of the Fatherland to foreign interests.'

Pétain was carefully following Hitler's ideas and Nazi ideology (could he do otherwise?) but as previously discussed, allegations of a belief in Judaeo-Masonic world conspiracy had existed within France from the previous century, the Dreyfuss Affair being a prime example. Pétain was therefore not only making use of existing prejudice within France but he was also addressing Frenchmen in Europe and elsewhere. Apparently this was done to curry favour with the Nazi regime.

Bernard Fäy (1893–1978) was a writer on Franco-American affairs. He attended the University of Harvard, USA, and wrote papers on George Washington and Benjamin Franklin. His connections with American intellectuals gained him access to French intellectual circles on his return in the early 1930s. In 1935 he published a book *La Franc-Maçonnerie au XVIIIe siècle* (Revolution and Freemasonry 1680–1800) which 'proved' that Freemasons were responsible for the French Revolution of 1789. Fäy's work had little supporting evidence for this contention. He based his conspiratorial allegations on the fact that George Washington and Benjamin Franklin (and some others associated with them) were Freemasons. American Freemasons have generally accepted Fäy's claims uncritically to the extent they have been quoted as a source of pride that Freemasonry had replaced a corrupt system of government, with a form of democratic government. As is well known the relationship between these two countries was indeed close and therefore the lack of criticism is understandable. Fäy managed to keep his anti-Masonic activities hidden until after the war when it was revealed that he was a Nazi informant paid to betray Freemasons to the Gestapo. He was also in the pay of a 'newspaper' which regularly provided details on collaborators.[263] Fäy and his partner, Geuydan de Roussel, kept a detailed journal of their activities on behalf of the Gestapo covering the period 1940–1944. This journal was later used as evidence.

Following Pétain's speeches, which more or less outlined who was considered to be 'for or against' the regime, many sought to inform on others in the hope that the new 'establishment' would consider them favourably. Fäy and Roussel decided to do just that by providing information about Freemasons. Perhaps, because they were homosexuals, they were fearful of discovery and so sought to divert attention. Fäy was also a regular supporter and protector of two lesbians, Gertrude Stein and Alice B. Toklas, both of whom were Jews.[264]

The names of more than 170,000 men suspected of being Freemasons were recorded on a filing card system used by the Gestapo in France. That is an enormous number for a very few people to have gathered unless they relied (over a four/five year period) on a network of informants. The official records show that of those listed in the card index 60,000 men were actually investigated as being 'potential' Freemasons. Of this number more than 7,000 were imprisoned. The records are not precise as to numbers, places of imprisonment or the exact nature of the offence for which these 7,000+ Freemasons were incarcerated.[265] Of those Freemasons 989 (these are precise official figures) were sent to concentration camps. There is no readily available information as to the charges, convictions, conditions of confinement, length of sentence or access (if any) to legal counsel. What is known is that exactly 549 Freemasons were executed simply because they had been identified as being Freemasons.

After the war Bernard Fäy was arrested and charged with collaboration with the Nazis. His defence was:

'I was glad to have in my hands the instrument capable of renovating the country. My mission was to organise a service for the detection of the Freemasons and Masonic archives. To be successful in the work, I was obliged to have relations with the Germans, especially as they had an organisation parallel to ours.'

The twisted logic here is that because he was 'renovating' a country ruined by Freemasons, he had to have 'relations' with the Germans. Therefore his collaboration was the fault of Freemasons, not his! Another example of how Freemasonry has been used to justify almost anything.

Italy

Italy under the Fascist regime of Benito Mussolini (1883–1945) did not link Jews with Freemasonry as had happened in Germany. The Fascist regime, however, didn't believe that Freemasonry and Fascism were compatible and in 1924 the Fascist Council required that all Freemasons who were also Fascists must resign their membership of the Craft. Fascists were no longer permitted to become Freemasons. On hearing of this decision Grand Orient announced that Fascist Freemasons could resign as such an action would be 'in accord with the love of country which is taught in the lodge'.[266] Many Masons then resigned but a campaign of violence began against Freemasons and their property. Grand Master Domizio Torrigiani (1876–1932) appealed to Mussolini to intervene and stop the violence. The response was a declaration in August 1924 that all Fascists must disclose the names of Masons not in sympathy with the Fascist government. Torrigiani was exiled on the island of Lipari.[267] Hundreds of his fellow Freemasons soon joined him there. That same year, General Luigi Cappello (1859–1941), a prominent Fascist who had at one time served as Deputy Grand Master of the Grande Oriente of Italy, resigned from the Fascist party rather than leave Freemasonry. Within a year he was arrested on concocted charges of being involved in a conspiracy to assassinate Mussolini and was sentenced to thirty years in prison but was released in 1936. In 1925 Mussolini dissolved all Italian Freemasonry. The campaign against Freemasonry escalated to the point where in 1926 all Masonic property was seized by the state and numerous Freemasons were imprisoned and many assassinated. In January 1926 the government appropriated the Grand Orient building, which had already been looted.[268] During the period 1925-1927 Mussolini's Blackshirts looted the homes of well known Masons in Milan, Florence and other cities, and murdered at least 100 of them.

Czechoslovakia

The efforts of the Czechoslovakian government directed towards a peaceful symbiosis of the peoples of this country, had been paralleled by the co-operation of the two Grand Lodges. The mutual visits, practised heretofore, have developed into joint meetings of Lodges of both Jurisdictions, Lodge of the National Grand Lodge of Czechoslovakia in a body taking part in meetings of Lodges of the Grand Lodge *Lessing zu den drei Ringen* and vice versa.[269]

From the statement we can see that Czechoslovakia had Grand Lodges within its national boundaries – the Grand Lodge *Lessing zu den drei Ringen* which was largely Jewish and German-speaking, and the National Grand Lodge of Czechoslovakia, which used the Czech language. Both were considered regular by other Grand Lodges and were on good terms with each other. The Munich agreement of 29 September 1938 (to which the Czechoslovakian government was not invited) granted the Sudetenland to Germany. Czechoslovakia lost 70% of power production and 70% of iron and steel manufacturing. More ominously the Skoda manufacturing complex came under direct German control. Skoda subsequently produced tanks, artillery and other weapons for the German war machine. The Munich agreement was engineered by Neville Chamberlain (1869–1940), the British Prime Minister who, after signing the agreement adopted an additional resolution in Britain and Germany to resolve other disputes peacefully, declared 'Peace in our time'. Six months later Germany invaded the remainder of Czechoslovakia and within a year the Second World War had begun following Germany's invasion of Poland (1 September 1939). Immediately after the Munich agreement a decree was issued dissolving the Grand Lodge *Lessing zu den drei Ringen*. Their property, assets and more importantly their membership records were seized. Because those concerned were ethnic Germans and absorbed into the German Reich it is not clear how these Czechoslovakian German Freemasons were treated. Much more is known of the members of the National Grand Lodge after Germany annexed the remainder of Czechoslovakia. When the German forces entered the country in March 1939 they were already in possession of the names of between 3,000 and 4,000 Freemasons. These names had no doubt been gathered from the records of the Grand Lodge *Lessing zu den drei Ringen* which would have contained references to many Freemasons who were members of the National Grand Lodge. These Freemasons were quickly arrested, many of whom were sent to concentration camps. Dr J. Sedmík, Grand Secretary for Foreign Relations, and Dr O. Hlavat, member of the Grand Council, were tortured for two years and then killed. Brother Jin Syllaba, Professor of Pathology, was imprisoned in Terezin Concentration Camp. He was one of the few Czech Freemasons to survive.[270] Less than 5% of all Freemasons escaped, some finding exile in England where they formed a Grand Lodge Comenius in Exile. The President, Brother Dr Eduard Benes (1884–1948), was a Freemason belonging to the National Grand Lodge and was one of those able to escape and led the Czechoslovakian government in exile.

The National Grand Lodge returned to Czechoslovakia in 1947 when it was reconstituted. The following year the Communist Party seized power and Freemasonry was again suppressed. The Grand Lodge *Lessing zu den drei Ringen* was never revived. The National Grand Lodge undertook an assessment of the effect of the German occupation and in 1947 published an official report in which it recorded that many Czechoslovakian Freemasons had fallen victim to Nazi persecution and estimated that at least 34% of the total membership had been sent to concentration camps and that more than half of that total had been tortured and executed. The exact figures are unlikely ever to be known but a conservative estimate of 1000 Freemasons put to death because of their membership of the Order is not unreasonable. The Grand Lodge also noted that just 200 had been able to escape to Britain, France and the United States. Most of those in France were able to join their brothers in Britain in 1940 after the German invasion of France.

What little can be gleaned from the treatment of Freemasons in Czechoslovakia reinforces the earlier opinion that Freemasons in occupied countries received harsher treatment than their Brothers in Germany. As well as gleaning from well known sources such as the Nuremberg Tribunal Transcripts some Freemasons have compiled lists of material relating to the persecution of Freemasons during the Holocaust and World War 2.[271] There is a considerable amount of little known evidence.

Allan Roberts' reference to the persecution of the Freemasons in Germany during the Nazi regime ('Masonic myths', February 1990) proved particularly revelatory.

'I was at Mauthausen Concentration Camp in Austria during 1944-45. I was 19-20 years of age and was not then a Freemason. I did not know what the *Freimaurer* were, but I saw that these persons were being punished even more than I was.[272]

'I remember that the Freimaurer were made to stand facing a wall, for a whole day. I remember that I felt sorry for them, and I once tried to give a piece of bread to one. I was caught and whipped 25 times for trying to be charitable.

'America has been good to me, and I thank God for my blessings.'
Sydney Newman, Cherry Hill, New Jersey, United States of America[273]

Here we have eyewitness testimony, by a Jew, of the treatment of Freemasons in a concentration camp. This kind of evidence is presented only as an example that Freemasons were treated in the same way (in this case apparently worse) as other 'problem' groups.[274] Finding such information and where it leads indicates to me that this book really must be read as an introduction to Masonophobia and that much is still to be revealed.[275] Although I have explained that it is not possible to research the persecution of Freemasons in every country it is clear that it has occurred nearly everywhere at some time or another – even in places where Freemasonry (in the normal sense of the word) did not exist! Even in Japan the government tried to stir up attacks against Freemasonry. The Japanese delegate to the Weltdienst congress in 1938, Fujivara, said,

'Judaeo-Masonry is forcing the Chinese to turn China into a spearhead for an attack on Japan, and thereby forcing Japan to defend herself against this threat. Japan is at war not with China but with Freemasonry, represented by General Chiang-Kai-shek, the successor of his master, the Freemason Sun-Yat-Sen.'[276]

According to this, the Japanese government justified its war on China because Jews and Freemasons were conspiring to precipitate China into attacking Japan. In other words the Japanese were forced to be the aggressors to forestall what they knew was coming – a Judaeo-Masonic plot to invade their country.[277]

Serbia
Following World War 1 allegations were made that Freemasons where responsible for the assassination of Archduke Franz Ferdinand (1863-1914) – the event which caused the outbreak of the war. Ludendorff (see above) made this accusation a number of times, especially in his book entitled *Cause of War*.[278] [279] He was so strident that the Grand Lodge of Yugoslavia issued a statement denying that any Freemasons were involved in the conspiracy to assassinate the Archduke. The Yugoslavian government suppressed Ludendorff's book.

Prince Paul of Yugoslavia (1893–1976), as Regent of Yugoslavia, signed the Tripartite Pact of the Axis Powers on 25 March 1941 in an attempt to keep the country out of the war. However, there was domestic opposition and King Peter II (1923–1970) staged a *coup d'état* on 27

March 1941 in opposition to the Tripartite Pact. On 6 April Germany attacked Yugoslavia which was forced to surrender on 17 April.[280] The reason for including Yugoslavia in this brief survey of some of the occupied countries is because it provides some dramatic Masonophobic material which is 'hard evidence'. (See Plate 8) The circumstances which led to the creation of this material are worth relating. In July there was a popular uprising and the occupying Germans forces were given emergency powers to suppress the partisans.[281] A puppet Serbian state was created under the leadership of Milan Nedic (1877–1946) and he undertook a campaign against Jews and Freemasons which was funded by the German Nazi regime. There were approximately 22 Lodges in Yugoslavia at the outbreak of war with a total of about 900 members. Six of these Lodges were in Belgrade and had slightly more than 200 members. Freemasonry was proscribed soon after the surrender and all property and other assets were confiscated. A full list of members was discovered and Freemasons in public service were dismissed from their employment. It is recorded that two university professors were shot and many others sent to concentration camps, because of their membership of the Order.[282] The absence of the membership records and the sheer scale of the killing that took place means that Freemasons who were murdered simply because they were Freemasons is tiny by comparison but I am not engaging in a 'numbers game' here, merely reinforcing the fact that Freemasons were one of the target groups in yet another area occupied by Nazi forces.[283] [284] Nedic followed the path directed by the Nazi occupiers – Jews, Freemasons and other 'enemy' groups were to be identified and eliminated. As in Germany and elsewhere the process was the same and Nedic's Serbia provides a micro example of that process, part of which was to win over the civilian population, to make them believe that these target groups were not 'real' Serbians but were undermining the social and economic structure of the country. A major component was the use of propaganda and the Serbian experience has left colourful and detailed examples of non-German anti-Masonic propaganda material.

Much of this Serbian material comes from an anti-Semitic and Masonophobic exhibition held in Belgrade, 22 October 1941–19 January 1942. It used Masonic property stolen from Yugoslavian Lodges. In order to encourage visitors to the exhibition a number of posters were produced. Many of the poster captions mention Freemasonry. For example:

'Come and see the anti-masonic exhibition. The Jewish dream of being the power of the world is now disappearing under the attack from finally awakened nationalism.'

'His weapons: democracy, masonry, captalism and communism.'[285]

After the exhibition was over the Serbian 'government' issued commemorative postage stamps to remind the population of the ongoing struggle against these problem groups. (See Plate 8)

The exhibition was modelled on previously staged 'The Eternal Jew' exhibitions in Munich and Vienna between 1937 and 1939 and these together with the propaganda used to promote them can tell a considerable amount above the motivation behind Masonophobic attitudes of that time – attitudes which continue to exist today. This aspect will be further explored in the conclusion.

Spain

Even less is generally known about what happened to Freemasons under Francisco Franco's (1892–1975) regime following the Spanish Civil War (1936–1939) but that he persecuted Freemasons is known.[286] Discrimination against Freemasonry became state policy when on 1 March 1940 a new law was published in the Official State Bulletin: 'For the repression of communism, freemasonry, and other movements which foment ideas against religion, the motherland and social harmony.' The Spanish dictator banned Freemasonry, Communism and other so-called 'secret societies' on the grounds that Freemasonry was the cause of the fall of the Spanish Empire in the 19th century. It was further alleged Freemasons were responsible for the Spanish Civil War. All this is reminiscent of the claim of almost 140 year previously that Freemasons were the cause of the French Revolution (1789). In Spain history allegedly repeated itself.

The law proscribing Freemasonry contained a number of interesting points which help shed some light on the thinking behind the law. These are reproduced below.

Article No 1: Constitutes a felony to be a communist, or to belong to a masonic lodge or any other secret society.

Article No 2: As these organisations are now banned by the effects of this decree, all monies and properties are to be confiscated immediately.

Article No 3: Any advertisement to exhort the principles or pretended benefits of masonry or communism, or anything against the Religion of the Motherland, will be penalised according to this law.

Article No 4: To be considered a mason, will be those who had been initiated into masonry and had not been expelled from the

Order, or not broken altogether their relationship with the organisation. It would also be considered a mason those expelled from the Order with the apparent reason to protect the member from the objects of this law.

Article No 5: From the date of this publication, masons and communists, as defined in article No 4 above, will be liable to be imprisoned with a 'minor jail offence', a minimum of 12 years and one day, but this situation could be aggravated by the 'Aggravated Circumstances' as explained in Article No 6.

Article No 6: 'Aggravated Circumstances' is to have obtained any of the Degrees from the 18th to the 33rd inclusive, having taken part in any Annual Communications or being part of any Committee or Board of the Grand Orient [Lodge] of Spain, which would indicate the great confidence of the Order entrusted upon the member.

Article No 7: Any mason or communist, who belongs to either organisation, must notify the Government of his affiliation within two months of the date of this law.

Article No 8: Without prejudice to other penalties as per article No 5, and those who have not a reasonable excuse to be absolved, will be separated immediately and indefinitely from Government jobs, Public or Official Corporations, managerial and advisory positions in private enterprise companies, as well as any other job in which any kind of confidence is entrusted upon them. This law will cover this employment situation in perpetuity. It will be considered attenuating circumstances providing information to the authorities about the persons who had performed the initiation into masonry, their superiors, or any other person involved in masonry or any other item of information that will be of benefit in the carrying of this law.

Signed: General Francisco Franco
March, 1940.

Article 1 makes it illegal for anyone to be a communist or a member of a Masonic Lodge. The wording is a reflection of the muddled Nazi belief in a Bolshevik-Judaeo-Masonic world revolution transferred to a Spanish context. The second article is very revealing in its logic which explains that now that Masonic Lodges no longer exist 'all monies and properties are to be confiscated immediately' by the state. Although the Franco regime perceived Freemasonry to be an ideological enemy the regime also had an eye on Masonic property and assets. The law is very comprehensive in terms of the regime's attitude towards Freemasonry.

Not only is the Order banned but so too are any attempts to promote the Order or its alleged aims as this would be against the 'Religion of the Motherland'.

To deal with Freemasonry in Spain the law specified who was considered to be a Freemason – essentially anyone who had been initiated in a Masonic Lodge and who had not been expelled. Even then the state reserved to itself the right to decide if those who had been expelled had been so as a means to avoid the effects of the law! In other words the authorities would decide who was a Freemason and who was not.

Having made Freemasonry illegal, confiscated its property and decided who was to be considered to be a Freemason all that remained was specifying the punishment. Those who had been initiated and had progressed no further were considered to have committed a relatively minor offence and were only to be imprisoned for 12 years! Freemasons who had attained any of the grades between the 18th and 33rd, or who had attended an Annual Communication of Grand Lodge, or had served on any Grand Lodge Committee or Board of the Grand Orient would be guilty of 'Aggravated Circumstances' because that 'would indicate the great confidence of the Order entrusted upon the member'. There is no indication what term of imprisonment a Freemason guilty of 'Aggravated Circumstances' could expect but given the severity in respect of a minor offence it was likely to be heavy.

Freemasons are given a short time in which to report to the authorities and all those who have no reason to be absolved from the crime of being a Freemason are to be dismissed from any 'Government jobs, Public or Official Corporations, managerial and advisory positions in private enterprise companies'. The state took even more power than this as Article 8 also states: 'as well as any other job in which any kind of confidence is entrusted upon them'. No doubt the authorities would decide which jobs were covered by this provision.

Lastly Freemasons could mitigate the offences against them by betraying their fellow Freemasons to the Franco regime.

Despite the fact that Freemasonry is apolitical that has not stopped it being used by politicians of every hue. In Spain Franco considered it to be allied to the political left whereas in the UK Freemasonry is considered to be part of the establishment and consequently *must* be right wing politically (see Chapter 5).

A reassessment of Spain's past led the government to seek to overturn the penalties Franco's courts imposed on 'Communists and Freemasons'.

Franco's courts to be declared illegitimate, says leftist coalition
'Spain's governing Socialists are to pass a law declaring the political courts that operated under dictator General Francisco Franco to be illegitimate, thus opening the way for thousands of sentences to be declared null, according to Spanish politicians.

Prime Minister José Luis Rodríguez Zapatero's government has cleared the way for death sentences and other decisions of military tribunals and special courts to be challenged, Spain's communist-led United Left coalition group announced.

A new law will declare Franco's court martials, public order tribunals and courts set up specifically to pursue Communists and Freemasons as "contrary to the law" and "illegitimate", said the United Left leader, Gaspar Llamazares. That would allow families of victims to ask the Supreme Court to declare their sentences null and, in turn, seek compensation, said Mr Llamazares. "This is a qualitative leap from impunity towards justice," he said.

Campaigners welcomed the agreement between the Socialists and United Left, who jointly see themselves as representing the republicans who lost the civil war against Franco's rightwing rebels.

Campaigners said the new deal improved on an earlier Socialist proposal which shied away from annulling sentences and prevented the naming of those who administered Franco's political courts until his death in 1975.

The law would concentrate on the victims of Franco's nationalist side during the civil war rather than on the victims of the republic's mainly leftwing defenders, according to Mr Llamazares. Those killed in republican areas included more than 6,000 priests, monks and nuns.

Spain's rightwing opposition People's party accused Mr Zapatero, whose grandfather was shot by Franco's firing squad, of stirring up confrontation and of betraying a tacit agreement in democratic Spain not to rake over the coals of the civil war.

"Parliament has never before been used to look back at that tragic and dramatic moment of history, the civil war," said parliamentary spokesman Eduardo Zaplana.

Mr Llamazares said the draft was not finalised, but that the United Left and the Socialists agreed on the fundamentals.'[287]

The Historical Memory Law was passed by Spain's Congress of Deputies on 31 October 2007.

Great Britain

Freemasons in Britain and Ireland were well aware of laws against Freemasonry such as those enacted in Spain (see above) and is it any wonder that 20 years after the death of Franco, when various branches of the UK government seemed intent on similar persecution, Freemasons shuddered at the thought that such a thing could happen in a liberal democracy?

Thus far we have dealt with examples of what happened to Freemasons in Germany and in the occupied countries. However it should not be forgotten that Nazi Germany had plans to 'deal' with Freemasonry although my fellow British Freemasons never experienced the horrors inflicted upon our Brethren in Europe during the Holocaust. What we ought to be aware of is that those horrors were to be visited upon us had we lost the war. That the Nazis had plans for 'dealing' with Freemasonry within Great Britain is beyond doubt. In 2000 the Nazi invasion plan for Great Britain (*Informationsheft GrossBritannien*) was made public for the first time.[288] The plan assumed the success of Operation Sea Lion (*Unternehmen Seelöwe*) planned for 1940 but abandoned by Hitler in September 1940. The words 'plan for the invasion of Britain' are misleading as it is in effect a handbook for the guidance of those responsible for establishing an occupation regime – including the identification and detention of all opponents. The 'plan' was written by the SS General Walter Schellenberg (1910–1952) and lays out in great detail the duties of the Gestapo and the *Sicherheitsdienst* – the SD – once the Wehrmacht had cleared areas of military opposition.[289] Every aspect of British life is detailed and the scale of the information in the possession of the Germans would have been of grave concern to the British authorities had they been aware of it at the time. Our interest here lies in the fact that separate chapters are devoted to Freemasons and Jews (in that order). The chapter on Freemasonry reveals that there is no doubt that the Nazis had every intention of eliminating British Freemasons, along with all the other 'problem' groups. The plan includes several 'special wanted lists' of people and property. Freemasonry features in both with every Lodge, Provincial Grand Lodge and Grand Lodge in Britain listed 'for a visit' by the *Einsatzgruppen*.[290] [291]

The above is merely an indication of the way Freemasonry and its members were treated during the first half of the 20th century. The focus has very much been on Germany as that became the centre of Masonophobia which spread across the continent, especially the occupied countries. The sheer scale of the Holocaust ensured that it was impossible for some details not to leak into the wider world and the rhetoric against Freemasons ensured that many ceased openly acknowledging their membership of the Order. This was true in Britain which had been on the brink of invasion for some time. Once the war was over and the extent of the Holocaust was revealed the almost unimaginable number of victims served to reinforce the belief that it was not a good idea to publically discuss Freemasonry or admit that one was a Freemason. This attitude became embedded in the membership and without knowing it this would give rise to problems in the not too distant future. The suffering of large groups, especially Jews and Poles, became well known. The Nuremberg Tribunal (1945–1946) revealed a considerable amount of information regarding the Holocaust (and a little about Freemasonry) but the tribunal and its finding were not widely read by the general public. Instead works such as *The Scourge of the Swastika – a short history of Nazi war crimes* (1954) focused on the gruesome aspects, complete with graphic images. It revolted and intrigued at the same time. Everyone came to recognise the suffering of the Jews and, more gradually, other groups, but the silence of Freemasons ensured that their involvement was rarely, if ever, discussed. Masonic activity recommenced in Germany almost immediately after the war with the first known meetings being held in Hamburg just three weeks after the cessation of hostilities but these were small scale and not publicised. It was not long however before 'organised' Freemasonry was re-established in the country.[292]

During the inter-war years churches in the UK were interested in Freemasonry and regularly posed the question is Freemasonry compatible with Christianity? The nature of these enquiries was muted but served to keep the 'pot boiling' on the issue which was to come much more to the fore in the post-war years. Space does not permit details to be provided here but it is important to realise that church interest in Freemasonry has been more or less continuous and can be seen as part of an anti-Masonic process traceable to at least the 17th century.

In the British *Theology* magazine (January 1951) an article entitled 'Should a Christian be a Freemason?' by Walton Hannah (1912–1966) was published.[293] *Theology* is the official magazine for the Society for Promoting Christian Knowledge and was edited at that time by Canon Alec Vidler (1899–1991), who was chaplain to King George VI. The article appears to have been deliberately provocative given that George VI and Geoffrey Fisher (1887–1972), the Archbishop of Canterbury (1945–1961), were Freemasons as were a large number of Anglican clerics.[294] The issue was discussed at the Church of England assembly in June 1951 but no official conclusions were reached.[295] Hannah, obviously disappointed with the attitude of the church, subsequently published *Darkness Visible* in 1952, possibly with the intention of encouraging the church to reconsider its stance.[296] He published another critique of Freemasonry in a book entitled *Christian by Degrees* in 1954.[297] The former deals with the Lodge degrees and the latter with other Orders of Freemasonry such as the Holy Royal Arch, the Ancient and Accepted Rite and the Knights Templar etc.

Hannah converted to Roman Catholicism, and became a priest. Following his conversion, he studied at the Pontifical Collegio Beda, Rome. During his time in Rome he was invited by Archbishop Paul-Émile Léger (1904–1991) to live in Montreal where he served as priest for the Church of the Ascension in Westmount, and St. Willibrord's parish in Verdun, while residing at Loyola College.

Hannah's books have had a lasting effect, being the basis for a BBC television documentary, *The Unlocked Secret*, broadcast in March 1965 and in which parts of Masonic ritual were enacted. The producer, James Dewar, wrote a best-selling book of the programme with the same title published in 1966. Hannah was an advisor to the documentary team. Not only did his books spawn the first television exposure of Masonic ritual (at least in the UK) but also gave inspiration to that most mendacious Masonophobic book *The Brotherhood* (1983) and a sequel *Inside the Brotherhood* (1989). The author of the latter has been cited in the media as an expert on Freemasonry and who suggested that Freemasons were responsible for the Dunblane massacre (see pages 7-9).

Hannah's publications were exposures with the same intended purpose of that of Pritchard and Ludendorff (and all those in between). As one reviewer stated: 'To read *Darkness Visible* is, in a way, to give yourself a vicarious form of Masonic initiation!'[297] The reviewer's comment, together with the writing of Hannah and others, shows that they fail to grasp that Freemasonry is not simply words on a page but a process or a journey and that Freemasonry (as history attests) cannot be destroyed by simply printing Masonic rituals.

Mention of these publications brings me into the post-war period more particularly the 1990's and it is to that decade which I now turn.

CHAPTER 4

FREEMASONRY AND RELIGION[298]

'An atheist is a man who has no invisible means of support.'
John Buchan (1875–1940)

You will recall that earlier in this book it was explained that Freemasons, as Freemasons, may not discuss religion and politics. This age-old, self-imposed rule is followed for a simple and practical purpose. Centuries ago in the early days of stonemasonry (that was to become modern Freemasonry) it was understood that there were two subjects that would always lead to arguments even among friends – religion and politics. For this reason, and the desire to create as harmonious an atmosphere as possible, lodges banned the discussion of these topics. Although this created the desired effect within lodges it later caused a problem in that Freemasons could not (and cannot) easily engage with their detractors in other spheres of human activity. The question might well be asked of me, 'Why, therefore, are you discussing Freemasonry and religion and politics in this book?' The simple answer is that I am not. Instead I am raising, as an historian, questions as to the reasons, causes and effects of the relationship between religion and Freemasonry, not the theological or doctrinal aspects of any particular religion.[299] In the same way I shall not discuss the merits, or otherwise, of any particular political system or its ideology other than the manner in which it interfaces with Freemasonry.[300] Although this distinction is very subtle it is a necessary and valid one to make.

The inability to discuss religion and/or politics as a Freemason therefore imposes on me certain restraints which are not applicable to non-Masons. It is in effect saying to people in those two parts of society who are about to attack me: 'Hang on, wait a minute, I need to have both hands tied behind my back before we go "head to head"' – stupid or what![301] There is no doubt in my mind that Masonophobic individuals understand this self imposed 'no-go-area' and exploit it to the full to attack Freemasons and the Order to which they belong.

On the matter of religion I shall begin with a specific example from which to extrapolate the debate.[302] William L. Brown delivered a lecture entitled Secret Societies in the Light of the Bible, on 1 November 1928 in Illinois.[303] After a preamble Brown asked three questions:

Is Masonry a Religion?
If it is a Religion, is it the Christian Religion?
If it is not the Christian Religion, what kind of religion is it?

The point of the lecture is immediately exposed by the title and the above questions. The author purports to be discussing secret societies but then only goes on to discuss Freemasonry. He does not discuss other societies of a similar nature to Freemasonry and so it is safe to conclude that this is a thinly disguised Masonophobic attack.[304] The question of whether or not Freemasonry is a 'secret' society is something that shall be considered later.

That said, everyone (including Freemasons) must confront a fundamental problem when discussing Freemasonry and religion. Despite the fact that Freemasons all over the world state that 'Freemasonry is not a Religion nor is it a substitute for Religion' many religious groups, particularly Christian, have decided that Freemasonry *is* a religion. That means that many religious groups have imposed *their* religious preconceptions on to a minority group that is not a religion. It is very unlikely that this kind of discrimination would today be tolerated if applied to any other minority group. A subsidiary question must be *who* decides if a particular group is a religion or not? In the case of Freemasonry it seems that this judgment is claimed by religious groups and no one else. This has interesting ramifications which may be discussed together with the previous questions. The notion that certain kinds of groups cannot be 'attacked' as being politically incorrect as opposed to those which are 'fair game' shall be considered later.

However, let us (for the moment) return to the questions posed above. The first question rather gives away the whole point of the argument, as if Freemasonry was not a religion, then the discussion would not exist in the first place. This point is crucial as in order for religions to be able legitimately to discuss Freemasonry, *in their own arenas*, Freemasonry must be able to be considered to be a religion.[305] If not, then churches, etc. would have no obvious legitimate right to comment, theologically, on the activities of another group. This prerequisite determines before any investigation, debate or research takes place that Freemasonry *is* a religion and therefore it does not matter what Freemasons consider Freemasonry to be as that decision has been taken out of their hands. Any attempt by Freemasons to defend the Order is therefore deemed invalid and is often turned around and used against the Craft. This is because Freemasons have fallen into the trap of discussing Freemasonry in a forum provided by the attacker and this is a forum where the issue has already been decided. A recent and detailed example of this relates to an article published in a church magazine and will be discussed shortly. I now return to the first question mentioned above. The author, Brown, thinks to ask Freemasons themselves what is Freemasonry:

> 'If we would ask Masons, as we meet them on the street, if Masonry is a religion some would say, "Yes, and it is good enough for me." Another would answer, "No, it is not a religion. It is only an association of men intended for their mutual benefits and interests." A third would tell us that it is a system of morality, veiled in allegory and illustrated by symbols; while a fourth might hesitate to state his views on the subject, his real motive in uniting perhaps being only for the benefits which he hoped to derive from it.'[306]

However, Brown cannot understand why there are so many different answers from Freemasons. He believes that there must be other, more straightforward, answers that Freemasons are unable or are unwilling to provide.

Like many before and after him, Brown has examined a number of books written by Freemasons about Freemasonry:

> 'How then are we to get a satisfactory answer and make sure whether Masonry is a religion or not? I think all will agree that we should consult the very highest Masonic authority. Since I believe we are united about this and since the writers of these books were all Masons of high degree and their works are regarded as standards in Masonic circles, I can conceive of no other source from which we can get so conclusive an answer.'[307]

Having explained why the opinion of the 'ordinary Mason in the street' has no worth he uses the material written by 'Masons of high degree' to assess whether or not Freemasonry is a religion according to his understanding of the term.[308] One crucial point that he, and others like him, miss is that such writing is not intended for a religious audience. The material is intended for Freemasons and therefore was never intended to be interpreted from a religious viewpoint.

Writing in 1928 Brown used books written by Albert Gallatin Mackey (–1881), A. T. C. Pierson (1817–1889) and Thomas Smith Webb (1771–1819).[309] [310] However, what Brown and others of his ilk simply do not understand is that *no* Freemason can speak *for* Freemasonry and dismiss that suggestion as absurd (see below). This is extremely important because Brown and other Masonophobic writers are simply not prepared to allow that their interpretation may be incorrect.

In making that observation Brown reveals that he is a Masonophobe who is not prepared to allow Freemasons to make any defence. Certainly the likes of Mackey, Pierson and Webb may be considered knowledgeable Freemasons but they are offering their own opinions only. Masonophobes rarely understand (or care) about what Freemasons have to say about Freemasonry except when it feeds their prejudices. Brown quotes the following extract from Mackey (quoting William Hutchinson):

> 'He [the Master Mason] has discovered the knowledge of God and his salvation, and been redeemed from the death of sin and the sepulchre of pollution and unrighteousness.'[311]

This quote, and others, is used by Brown to argue that this proves that Freemasonry is a religion but I disagree with Brown, Mackey and Hutchinson regarding this quote. In fact I violently disagree with the ideas expressed in the statement. However I know that Hutchinson and Mackey are merely expressing their opinions. Thus, whilst I disagree with them, I respect their right to express that opinion in the knowledge that they are not speaking *for me* in respect of Freemasonry. This then is the crux of the argument – Brown and others like him can pick up the ideas and opinions of one, two, three or even 100 Freemasons but they cannot legitimately claim that this proves this, that or the other about Freemasonry.

After the first edition of Brown's lecture was published a copy was purchased by *The Builder,* a Masonic magazine. The editor, Joseph Fort Newton, replied to Brown's polemic, the essence of which was that, although several Masonic writers had been quoted by Brown as being Masonic authorities, none could be taken as speaking on behalf of Freemasonry.[312] The fourth edition of Brown's lecture includes a response to Newton's reply:[313]

> '*The Builder* pities "the religious minded anti-Mason" because he "can never seem to understand that there is no authority in Masonry."
>
> 'Here we are told in substance that whatever has been said, or is to be said, by any Mason about Masonry – even statements from its highest officers – comes without any authority whatever. This is surely a slippery, cunning way for Masons to try to crawl out from all difficulties.

'When quotations from their publications do not please them, and when their real significance is revealed to the "profane" – those who are not members of the Masonic fraternity. If there is no authority in Masonry, why does *The Builder* attempt a reply? Judging it out of its own mouth, it speaks without authority. According to its own testimony, what it says amounts to nothing.

'But we know that Masonry rules with an iron hand and that there is no institution more despotic.'[314]

Brown dismisses Newton's assertion that Masonic authors such as Mackey, Webb and Pierson cannot speak on behalf of Freemasonry. In his mind they are leading Freemasons and so must have authority, particularly authority to speak on behalf of Freemasonry. Like so many others Brown's response is dismissive, even belligerent: 'This is surely a slippery, cunning way for Masons to try to crawl out from all difficulties.'[315] The tone is pejorative. Note the use of the words 'slippery', 'cunning' and 'crawl' in reference to Freemasons.

There is an extremely important point to be made, not only in respect of Brown's lecture, but also about others who have adopted a similar attitude towards Freemasonry. Does Brown (and those before and after him) speak on behalf of Christianity? Does he speak for every Christian whether Roman Catholic, Presbyterian, Baptist or Methodist? No, Brown is merely offering an opinion but at the same time it is not accepted that Freemasons such as Mackey, Pierson and Webb are offering their individual opinions. In other words Masonic writers are taken to represent Freemasonry whereas Christian writers are not taken to represent Christianity. This suggests the application of double standards when it comes to commenting on Freemasonry.

Another quote by Mackey, 'The religion of Masonry is pure Theism', is used by Brown to demonstrate that Freemasonry is a religion.[316] Once again, we find that the meaning of Mackey's words, intended for a Masonic readership, are being re-interpreted from a non-Masonic point of view. Mackey was writing about Freemasonry for Freemasons and his use of the word 'religion' might today appear to Freemasons, especially in light of this discussion, to be an unfortunate choice of word but we ought to try to understand what Mackey was getting at – he was *not* suggesting Freemasonry is a religion in the same way as Buddhism or Taoism but in a more general sense: 'consumerism is the new religion' or 'in this town football is a religion'. By applying *their* understanding of the word religion the religious groups bring it into their realm – somewhere it simply does not belong.

It is understandable why non-Freemasons use the writings of prominent Freemasons to try and explain Freemasonry but they are doing so from their personal point of view and usually from within a particular religion or denomination within a religion. To explain this in another way: because non-Masonic commentators are a member of a church which explains, often in precise detail, what elements of that religion mean and stand for, there is a presumption that Freemasonry can be explained in the same manner. It cannot. For example an image of the crucified Christ, a male human form nailed to a cross, bearing a crown of thorns, with a wound to the right lower abdomen, can, to a Christian, represent only one thing – the Passion of Jesus Christ. It cannot depict anyone other than the Son of God.[317] This means that there is a hard and fast explanation for virtually everything one hears, sees and reads within a Christian setting.[318] Applying that way of understanding Christianity in an attempt to understand Freemasonry is fundamentally flawed. This can perhaps be best explained by way of an example. The letter 'G' features prominently in Masonic symbolism and most non-Masons, and many Freemasons, accept that this is a symbol for God. However, every Muslim Freemason with whom I have discussed this rejects that explanation as it is unacceptable to them for God to be reduced to a mere symbol and one created by one of God's creations at that. Instead their interpretation is that it means 'Geometric' which conforms to the belief that it is not possible for human beings to depict anything created by God.[319] Jewish Freemasons have a similar outlook believing that it is disrespectful to use a letter of the alphabet to represent God.[320] For many of that faith the letter 'G' stands for 'Goodness' – the innate goodness that is inherent in everyone. This is a brief way of explaining that it is not possible to use one, or even a few, individual Freemasons' interpretation of elements of Freemasonry. Just to reinforce the point, I know some Jewish Freemasons who prefer to interpret the letter 'G' as 'Geometric' or 'Geometry' and some Muslim Freemasons who consider it to mean 'Goodness!'

The crux of the matter is that Freemasonry does not have a dogma and does not impose specific interpretations of elements found within Freemasonry upon its members. Aside from the fallacy of attempting to interpret Freemasonry as if it was a religion the absence of a 'Masonic dogma' means that it does not contain one of the most essential elements of a religion.

Perhaps it is as well to remind ourselves here what 'dogma' means – the established doctrine central to a religion. It is authoritative and is not open to question. The given interpretation may not be disputed, doubted or diverged from. Subsidiary to that is 'doctrine' which comprises an extended form of the dogma (it may also include, for example, church law as well as church dogma) which is taught by a particular religion. As we have seen from the above, Freemasonry contains neither a dogma nor a doctrine and as these essential elements of a religion are missing it is impossible for Freemasonry to be classified as a religion.

Despite what Freemasons say, *Freemasonry is not a religion nor is it a substitute for religion;* however, despite the preceding debate many religious groups maintain that Freemasonry is a religion and once that is established, in their minds at least, then it can be compared to other religions and this is usually done in order to decide if Freemasonry is compatible with, for example, Christianity.

The first question is, in my opinion, therefore redundant and consequently the other two questions are rendered irrelevant. However, Masonophobes will have convinced themselves that the question has been answered in the positive: that Freemasonry is a religion. I shall discuss the remaining questions in order not to stand accused of avoiding those very questions. In order to do so I refer again to Brown and his lecture. Under the heading: 'Is it the Christian Religion?' he again turns to Masonic authors to answer the question. He first turns to Mackey:

'The Lodge is then, at the time of the reception of an Entered Apprentice, a symbol of the world, and the initiation is a type of the new life upon which the candidate is about to enter. There he stands [meaning the candidate] without our portals, on the threshold of his new Masonic life, in darkness, helplessness and ignorance. Having been wandering amid the errors, and covered over with the pollutions of the outer and profane world, he comes inquiringly, to our doors, seeking the new birth, and asking a withdrawal of the veil which conceals Divine truth from his uninitiated sight.'[321]

The first comment that I have regarding the above is that this quote is again taken as if it is from a 'Gospel of Freemasonry', of which there is, of course, no such thing. This is one man's interpretation of the admission of a candidate into Freemasonry and as it happens one with which I do not agree. The fact remains that if Brother Mackey wishes to interpret the admission of a candidate into Freemasonry in these terms, using these words, then it is his prerogative to do so. As it happens, as already stated, I do not entirely agree with him because my interpretation is personal, as is his, and so we again come to the point of divergence between non-Masons (particularly Masonophobes) and Freemasons.

Masonophobes interpret Freemasonry from a pre-determined perspective whereas Freemasons, individually and collectively, interpret Freemasonry for themselves, from their own personal life experience without the imposition of any dogma or doctrine.

As Brown is writing as a Christian he therefore uses the New Testament to criticise Freemasonry. Anti-Masonic Christians frequently use two aspects to attack Freemasonry: salvation by good works and the absence of references to Jesus Christ. In particular the Book of Ephesians is cited in support of the first point.[322] Freemasonry makes no pretence at offering any form of religious salvation to its members and so any of the good works that it does cannot be 'used' for that purpose. The second point is discussed more fully below.

It is timely to reiterate that I, as a Freemason, cannot discuss detailed theological aspects of a religion and I must therefore leave it to individuals to follow up on those specific aspects. However, there is a simple and fundamental reason why this argument fails utterly. Masonic Lodge ritual is based entirely on Old Testament stories and therefore it is quite inappropriate for Christians to use the New Testament, and their interpretation thereof, to attack a non-religious organisation.

Having 'proved' that Freemasonry is a religion but that it is not Christian the third question is, inevitably, 'What kind of religion is Freemasonry?' Repeating the same exercise as previously: quoting opinions of individual Freemasons who are increasingly described as being 'leading Masonic authorities' thereby suggests that they are 'leaders' in the same sense as Priest, Pastors and Ministers etc. and thus reinforces the notion that Freemasonry is a religion. It has been stated before but it is essential to bear this in mind – that one individual cannot speak for Freemasonry.[323] Once again setting aside the claim that Freemasonry is a religion and can therefore be judged from (in this example) a Christian point of view but without accepting for a moment that either is true I now wish to examine the conclusion that Brown comes to in answer to his own his question: 'What kind of religion is Masonry?'[324]

After quoting Webb (see below) Brown goes on to discuss the claim that Freemasonry based on the Bible is specifically originating with King Solomon. This he dismisses because in the later part of his reign Solomon fell into bad ways and so if Freemasonry truly is based on Solomon then it is bad because Solomon ultimately became a bad person. 'King Solomon did get into idolatry and many disgraceful things in the latter part of his life.'[325] The fact that Masonic ritual is based on the period when Solomon was 'good' is ignored and is yet another indication that those attacking Freemasonry are not interested in facts. This clearly smacks of the selective use of material in an effort to prove an unsustainable argument. On Brown's behalf I must admit that he could not have known more about the origins of Masonic ritual because the oldest Masonic ritual in the world was not discovered until four years after he delivered his lecture.[326] That said, those that have followed Brown (Walton Hannah mentioned above is an example) have done so religiously (sorry, I could not resist!) by repeating the same argument over and over without taking into account factual historical information let alone how Freemasons themselves understand Freemasonry.

Brown then attempts to answer his rhetorical third question: 'We quote again from Webb's *Masonic Monitor*, page 285: So broad is the religion of Masonry, and so carefully are all sectarian tenets excluded from the system, that the Christian, the Jew and the Mohammedan, in all their numerous sects and divisions, may and do harmoniously combine in its moral and intellectual work with the Buddhist, the Parsee, the Confucian and the worshipers of Deity under every form.'[327] Brown's observation here is that Webb appears to refer to Freemasonry as a religion. The words are 'the religion of Masonry' and here Webb is using the term to describe Freemasonry as being 'moral and intellectual' and not as a religion. One question that Brown does not confront is that if Webb were describing Freemasonry as a religion it would be a religion that combines Christianity, Judaism, Buddhism, Zoroastrianism, Islam, Confucianism and every other religion not mentioned! In other words Brown's question (see above) 'What kind of religion is Freemasonry?' is answered by the statement 'It is all religions.' The accusation is that Freemasonry is syncretic but this is nonsensical, if Brown accepts Webb's statement, as it is impossible to reconcile all religions with each other to create another separate religion.[328] However, this is not the answer that Brown is after and he ignores this obvious conclusion in favour of his own explanation which is that Freemasonry, because it denies Jesus Christ, is a form of devil worship.

Let us turn then to the questions posed at the beginning of this chapter. The first is the matter of Freemasonry allegedly being a secret society. A secret society means that the society is unknown to the general public and so the term ought properly to be applied to the likes of the Mafia, Triads or groups which are secret to the extent that even their names are unknown to us. This lack of precision in describing Freemasonry misleads people into believing Freemasonry is something that it is not and generally serves to reinforce Masonophobic attitudes.

As stated earlier, Freemasonry is not a religion as it is missing some of the essential elements that define the very nature of religion, in particular a dogma. However, the fact that Freemasons openly declare that Freemasonry is not a religion does not stop others from defining it as such. The question must be why? In the first instance I suspect that the original definition of Freemasonry as provided by James Anderson in the *Constitutions* of 1723 – 'oblige them to that Religion in which all Men agree, leaving their particular Opinions to themselves' (see Chapter 1, page 31) – is perceived as a threat by some religions and the use of the word 'religion' as early as 1723 in relation to Freemasonry no doubt confirmed to many that Freemasonry is a religion. However, as explained above this is to take the word, as used by Anderson and Mackey, out of context.

It is noticeable that those writing or speaking against Freemasonry do so in a way that usually excludes Freemasons. Freemasons are not invited to engage in debate, attend the lectures, contribute to Masonophobic publications or as we shall see have a genuine right of reply in the media. One might think that this is a rather silly point to make but I think it is quite important. The reason being that anti-Masonic attacks are not directed at Freemasons! Instead these are given in church, to an invited audience at a seminary, sold in Christian (and other religions') bookshops or posted online on Masonophobic web sites. That tells us one thing – it is not Freemasons who are being told (at least not directly) that Freemasonry is bad and the question again must be why? I suggest that there are several reasons. Some are relatively innocuous, others are decidedly sinister. Most innocuous are the genuine misunderstandings as to the nature of Freemasonry – and there are a range of such misunderstandings. Another function of attacking Freemasonry can be in order to create 'the other', by defining an enemy that a particular group must guard against. This has the purpose, and effect, of bonding the group together in order to protect the group from 'the other'. Creating 'the other' is something which I will explore in more depth later.

What is probably noticeable to all who have read the previous chapters will be that the religions mentioned, in relation to Freemasonry, are almost exclusively Christianity and Judaism. It is equally obvious that attacks on Freemasonry come not from Jews but from Christians of various denominations.[329] In fact, I have been unable to find any Jewish attacks on the Order of Freemasonry.[330] The absence of attacks by other major religions requires to be mentioned. To date I have found no criticism of Freemasonry originating from Buddhists, Shintoists, animists or Pagans.[331] Freemasonry originated in a western Judaeo/Christian milieu, both religions sharing a common origin in so far as sacred texts are concerned. The Hebrew Bible consists of three parts: Torah (Pentateuch), Neviim (Prophets) and Ketuvim (Writings). For Christians this comprises the Old Testament. Both religions therefore share the same origins in respect of their earliest texts. Christianity adds the New Testament consisting of 27 additional books relating, in the main, to events before, during and after the life of Jesus Christ.[332] Christ was a Jew and died a Jew. Christianity arose immediately after his death based on the interpretations by others of his life and activities.[333]

Islam was brought forth by the Prophet Mohammed [Blessed be his Name] approximately 600 years after the death of Christ but unlike Christianity and to a lesser extent Judaism it did not spread to what is now termed the 'western world' and was almost totally absent in much of Europe during the period that Freemasonry originated, became organised, elaborated and developed into what it is today.

Freemasonry does not exclude any religion (or denomination thereof) but some believe, probably because of the historical origins described above, that they are excluded. This is incorrect as Freemasonry has never excluded any religion, although admittedly it may have been unaware of its existence.[334]

Even although the society in which Freemasonry originated has changed beyond recognition the main precepts of Freemasonry have not and it is striking that Masonophobic attacks originate from the same sources as 100, 200 and even 300 years ago. In an ever changing world this seems odd. It is worthwhile to revisit briefly the main objection some religions have against Freemasonry. As we have seen in Chapter 2 the main Protestant accusation against Freemasonry was (and is) based on a tautological argument that because Freemasonry is a religion (even though Freemasonry has never claimed to be one) and, damningly, one that does not acknowledge Jesus Christ, Freemasonry must therefore be anti-Christian.[335] The argument as you will recall eventually comes to the conclusion that Freemasonry is a form of devil worship – the exact opposite to and deadliest enemy of Christianity. However, this argument is based more on the needs of the church(es) concerned and not the facts. To claim that people such as Robert Burns, Winston Churchill, Cardinal Newman, Harry S. Truman and George Washington were devil worshippers is beyond the pale.

In the first place Freemasonry does not acknowledge Jesus Christ because Masonic ritual is based on the Old Testament *not* the New Testament. It would be completely inappropriate for a non-religious body, Freemasonry, whose origins and history have no connection to the main sacred book of the Christian faith (the New Testament).[336] Allow me to put this in another way. Masonic ritual is centred on events described in the Old Testament which occurred thousands of years before the coming of Christ. These events culminate with the building and near completion of King Solomon's Temple and conclude with an allegorical aftermath that does *not* appear in the Old Testament.[337] In these circumstances it is simply not possible, nor would it be proper, to refer to Jesus Christ. For that reason Freemasonry is attacked by (some) Christians who curiously do not attack Jews whose *religious* rituals are entirely based on the Old Testament and who, of course, do not mention Christ. The same argument concerning the absence of Jesus Christ can be applied to other religions. Buddhists do not include Christ in their religion, nor do Sikhs, Taoists, Shintoists, Jainists or Hindus.[338]

It is however of paramount importance to realise that Freemasonry does not make use of any religious text for its religious content but for its historical background. The Old Testament story of King Solomon building the temple in Jerusalem was attractive to stonemasons because it associated their trade of stonemasonry with a building erected at a very early date. It therefore provided the Craft with an air of antiquity and mystique but not religiosity. In light of the theory above the origin and development of Masonic ritual, briefly referred to above, to claim that illiterate stonemasons chose the Old Testament in order to create a religion that worshipped the devil is plainly ridiculous.

Freemasonry is therefore in a bizarre situation, not of its own making, where although not a religion it is attacked for not including the central figure of the Christian religion. Let me put this in another way. There are numerous other groups which declare themselves to be religions and which are recognised as being religions by Christians but they are not abused or vilified for their failure to acknowledge Jesus Christ. Anyone standing back and viewing this dispassionately must find this at least curious. What is even stranger is that the majority of these other religions which have no place for Jesus Christ do not attack Freemasonry for its omission of, for example, the Lord Buddha or Krishna Ahura Mazda or Zoroaster.[339] One must wonder therefore if Freemasonry is being used to attack, by proxy, these non-Christian religions?

The position is therefore this. Religions, of assorted types, respect or at least tolerate each other as being different.[340] However, one group which is not a religion is attacked and vilified because it does not contain a particular central element of a particular religion – Christianity. Logic would dictate that such disputes could only be between religions not a religion attacking a non-religious group.

Explaining this most unusual situation is difficult and I do not pretend to be able to do more than offer a little insight as to the causes. As explained, Freemasonry originated and developed at a time when there were only two religions of any size – Christianity and Judaism. The former (in all its variations) was by far the most numerically dominant. Freemasonry took material from the Old Testament for allegorical and non-religious purposes. It did not impinge at all on the sacred text of Christianity, the New Testament. However, despite the protestations of Freemasonry that it was *not* a religion there seems to have been a fear that whatever the intention a new religion, in competition with Christianity, *might* have been synthesised. Despite the passage of more than 300 years – which has demonstrated that Freemasonry is not a religion, nor a substitute for one – the original attitude adopted all that time ago has remained unchanged and in fact has since been demonstrably reinforced.[341] [342] There was also a suggestion that Freemasonry might lead to a fusion between Christianity and Judaism but as these are two separate religions and Freemasonry is not a religion at all, this suggestion is considered to be mischievous.

However, there is another explanation that Freemasons themselves have never really considered. Down the years the fulminations that have been directed at Freemasonry – Papal Bulls, edicts, proclamations, condemnations and sermons – were not delivered in a Masonic Lodge, or at a meeting of Freemasons. They were directed at members of particular groups who are not Freemasons.[343] In the main therefore Masonophobic 'messages' are not aimed at Freemasons but at people who are *not* Freemasons. I consider this to be a crucial point as it not only applies to the religious but also other sectors of society.

The question must be: If certain religions, and other groups, attack Freemasonry but do not address those attacks directly at Freemasons what is the purpose of doing so? An examination of all the accusations and fulminations against Freemasonry reveals that they do not focus on 'converting' Freemasons to a different point of view, but on reinforcing the belief system of the group being addressed.[344] Many religions actively proselytise but seeking to convert a person from one religion to another is quite different from attempting to persuade a person to renounce membership of a non-religious group and become a member of a religion.[345] Here then I think we come close to an answer to the question, 'Why do so many religious groups claim Freemasonry to be a religion?' The answer, in short, is that if Freemasonry is not a religion then Freemasons cannot be converted to another religion.

It also means that religions would have no automatic right to make theological comments regarding a non-religious group. This too is, I believe, a vitally important point. Let us imagine, but only for the purpose of debating this question, that a religious group (or a denomination of one) decided that Freemasonry was *not* a religion. In that case religious commentators would no longer be automatically nor legitimately entitled to comment on the private activities of Freemasonry and its members without explaining why. By making Freemasonry a religion the need for a religious group to explain and justify why it is commenting on Freemasonry is not required.

This discussion, problematic as it is, becomes even more convoluted once it is understood that many Freemasons *are* members of particular religions. Thus if a Freemason is a Protestant and regularly attends his Masonic Lodge as well as his church how is he to be approached? This conundrum is one possible reason why attacks against Freemasonry are generalised and are not directed against specific individuals.

What religious Masonophobes fail to understand is that Freemasonry is not a religion for one major reason – it has no dogma.[346] This is a sufficiently important point to permit a significant digression. Dogma is a system of belief, a set of principles or doctrines. These are the points of a religion from which believers in that particular belief system cannot deviate as to do so would mean that they no longer believe in what that particular religion teaches. In that case, if they are honest, they cannot remain true members of that religion.[347] Freemasonry is different in that it does not insist on what each member *must* believe in order to remain a member.

A few examples might be of assistance in illustrating this point of difference. Most Christian denominations make use of the Passion Cross (crucifix) in the shape of † and some also depict a figure of a human male nailed to such a cross. This of course is a direct allusion to the crucifixion of Jesus Christ.[348] The image cannot mean anything else. The human figure (the Son of God) is Jesus Christ and the cross is the instrument of his Passion (death). It does not represent anyone else and the Christian church will not allow for any variation in that interpretation. If you, as a member of the church concerned, decide that the figure represents someone other than Jesus Christ then in all conscience you cannot remain a member of that church because you have rejected that church's interpretation (dogma) as to what that symbol represents.[349]

Freemasonry does not function in this manner. As there is no Masonic dogma there are no firm and fixed rules as to what things mean. Allow me to illustrate the point in a manner somewhat similar to the above. The letter 'G' is a fairly well known Masonic symbol and is often seen on its own or in combination with the Square and Compasses. Many

Freemasons, especially those who are Christians, believe that the letter 'G' represents God. However, I am aware of numerous Freemasons who reject that interpretation and do so vehemently and argue that the letter 'G' means 'goodness,' that is the innate goodness that resides within every human being. Others argue that it merely represents geometry or geometric design. This is a view held by members of those faiths who believe that it is simply impossible to 'reduce' God to a mere symbol (a letter of the alphabet) devised by an inferior creature created by God – a human being.[350] In this single example I have provided three interpretations (there are others) of a symbol commonly used by Freemasons. A religion simply would not allow for such a multiplicity of interpretations of its symbolism. When one is aware that this multiplicity of interpretations extends also to Masonic regalia and even the physical position of individuals within a Lodge room, it becomes clear that Freemasonry cannot be considered to be a religion because there is no standard interpretation, explanation or set of instructions as to what things stand for or mean.[351] [352] To make matters even clearer, Grand Lodges do not lay down precise explanations as to the meaning or interpretation of every aspect of Freemasonry under their jurisdiction and even where some attempt to introduce some measure of standardisation within their area of control it tends to be of a bureaucratic nature rather than anything else.[353] Religious commentators who realise that the absence of a Masonic dogma is fatal to the categorisation of Freemasonry as a religion never acknowledge this and fudge the issue by arguing that Freemasonry shares a number of similarities with religion.[354] Even this fudge can be seen to be nothing more than a sleight of hand. Either Freemasonry is a religion or it is not. There can be no half-way house. Even the *Encyclopaedia Britannica* in noting that Freemasonry contains religious elements, does not claim it to be a religion.[355] [356]

In addition to using Masonic symbolism against Freemasonry (often by deliberately distorting or misunderstanding its meaning) another tactic is to use words out of context or arguing that they have a use and meaning that is not based on Masonic usage. Freemasonry uses terms which are also used by religions. For example 'Light', or more precisely 'Masonic Light', which is used in Masonic rituals has been misunderstood, deliberately or otherwise. To use another example by Brown:

'The lodge is, then, at the time of the reception of an Entered
Apprentice, a symbol of the world, and the initiation is a type of the

new life upon which the candidate is about to enter. There he stands [meaning the candidate] without our portals, on the threshold of this new Masonic life, in darkness, helplessness and ignorance. Having been wandering amid the errors and covered over with the pollutions of the outer and profane world, he comes inquiringly to our doors, seeking the new birth, and asking a withdrawal of the veil which conceals Divine truth from his uninitiated sight. In these words Mr. Mackey pictures before us a man who is about to unite with the Masonic order. Morally, he may be one of the best of men. He may be a disciple of the Lord Jesus Christ, whom his Saviour has described as a "light of the world"; but until he crosses the Masonic threshold, he is said to be in "darkness, helplessness and ignorance," not only is he blind, helpless and ignorant, but he is further described as "having been wandering amid errors, and covered over with the pollutions of the outer and profane world." This, according to the highest Masonic authority, is the sad plight in which all of us are who are not Masons. What a magic institution is Masonry, since in so brief a period one can have this darkness and ignorance expelled and so come into possession of "Divine truth" and an effulgence of knowledge which can only be grasped through Masonry!'[357]

Religious commentators such as Brown assume that, in reading a Masonic writer's attempt to define Freemasonry, it must be done from a religious point of view. Thus the Masonic description of a non-Mason being in 'darkness, helpless and ignorance' and initiation meaning being admitted to 'Masonic light' must have a religious explanation. This is simply incorrect. 'Masonic darkness' simply means that a non-Mason does not possess Masonic knowledge. On admission to a Lodge that knowledge is obtained. This way of describing a state of ignorance can be applied to many other fields from the mundane (in terms of car mechanics I am in a state of darkness) to the more profound – gaining previously hidden insights on matters of philosophy or politics for example.

Before leaving the matter of religion and Freemasonry I would like to widen the debate in order to provoke thought and not acrimony. In discussing Freemasonry the following question is repeatedly heard: 'Is Freemasonry compatible with Christianity?' I would like to take the opportunity to turn that question around in the hope of gaining some further insight. My first question is therefore: 'Is Christianity compatible with Freemasonry?' Posing such a question will, I am sure, shock some people but perhaps it serves to illustrate the one-way traffic on this matter. It seems acceptable that a religion, in this instance Christianity, can comment on Freemasonry which is categorised as being a religion yet Freemasonry cannot comment on religions! In posing the question in this way the contradictions inherent in claiming Freemasonry to be a religion are revealed.[358] As Freemasons cannot debate religion I wish to ask and discuss a few short 'what if questions', this being one of them. These are hypothetical and for the purpose of discussion only but I think that they do shed some light on the relationship between Freemasonry and certain religious groups.

Freemasonry as a body has never declared itself to be a religion.[359] My first 'what if question' is what would be the effect if Freemasonry (acting in unity) openly declared that it *was* a religion? Would Christian churches suddenly cease their attacks in the same way that they do not attack Buddhists? Would government provide the same laws and protection that it presently extends to religions? In Britain would Freemasonry be automatically allowed radio and TV 'slots' in the national media, such as BBC Radio 4's *Thought for the Day* and interviews on TV religious programmes? Such a re-classification making Freemasonry a religion would have social, legal and tax implications in many countries. Such wider implications (of which there are very many) are never considered by religions when discussing Freemasonry and further indicate that Freemasonry is discussed for self-serving purposes only and there is no holistic analysis.

Given that it is, in the main, Christians (of various denominations) that insist Freemasonry is a religion would they accept that and welcome Freemasonry into the family of world religions? Would Freemasonry be welcome to participate in the World Communion of Reformed Churches or be placed in the Anglican Communion?[360] The question, a very pointed question, is where exactly would Freemasonry be placed in the world's religions? What would be Freemasonry's relationship with other world religions? Would the present move towards increased ecumenicalism encompass Freemasonry? Again one begins to see contradictions surfacing even in this brief discussion as to 'what if' Freemasonry actually became a religion? I do not expect any responses to these questions but they do, I hope, provide some food for thought.

There is another matter I would like people to consider and Freemasons in particular. Various religions feel free to comment, criticise and condemn the practices of Freemasons and although Freemasons do not comment on religion (or politics) because of our own self-imposed rules there is a hypothetical question I would like to pose:

What would be the response if a Freemason wrote to the leader of a particular Christian denomination and criticised some aspect of its ceremonial (that is, its liturgy)?[361] If a Freemason took exception to 'the blood and body of Christ' as depicting vampirism and cannibalism and demanded that this element be removed from that church's liturgy what would be the likely response? If any answer was forthcoming I suspect that it would along the lines of I had not understood that these aspects of the liturgy were allegorical, acts relating to the Passion and Resurrection of Christ. However, when it is explained that Masonic ceremonies are allegorical they are either dismissed out of hand or more often simply ignored. It is fine for religions to explain that parts of their ceremonies are allegorical but Freemasons cannot possibly be doing the same!

This strongly suggests that there is no desire to try and understand Freemasonry because that might actually reveal it as being deliberately misunderstood. This dismissive attitude of the opinion of Freemasons is again indicative of how Freemasonry is not considered in a wider sense and is merely a self-serving device. Two examples will, I trust, help to illustrate this almost deliberate lack of any attempt to understand Freemasonry in a wider context.

When in early 2003 the Church of Scotland's official magazine, *Life and Work*, suggested an interview in which Freemasons would be allowed to 'state their case' the opportunity was gratefully accepted. In an in-depth interview with the then Grand Secretary and several other Freemasons we explained, in detail, what Freemasonry was 'about' and eagerly anticipated the publication of a favourable article. The article appeared in the March 2003 issue and was entitled 'The Craft and The Kirk' the contents of which came as a shock to those who had participated in the interview. The input of the Grand Lodge of Scotland was then sent, without prior knowledge or consent, to a Professor of Practical Theology at the University of Aberdeen and his extended commentary on Freemasonry was added to the article.[362] Here again is an example of how even today a Christian Church can pick its own field of battle (religion) and judge Freemasonry by its own religious perceptions. Were we naive? Perhaps, but the evidence of the way Scottish Freemasonry was treated by another, younger, Scottish institution is an indication of how some Christian attitudes have changed towards Freemasonry.

Masonophobia, from whatever section of society, manifests itself as generalisations. The focus is entirely on the body and not individuals. This is a classic tactic of depersonalising the 'enemy' by denying him (or her) a face, character and ultimately their humanity.[363] This is done by the detractors of Freemasonry, for the same reason that minorities down the ages have been dehumanised – in order to make them acceptable victims. Individual Freemasons are never mentioned by those who attack the Order. To do so would reveal major rifts in their arguments against Freemasonry. It is far easier to attack Freemasonry in a generalised and abstract manner.

These points bring us neatly to the observation that attacks on Freemasonry are not for the benefit of Freemasonry but serve a purpose designed by its detractors.

To summarise:

Freemasonry is considered to be a religion in order for it to be a legitimate subject for *religious* debate.

Attacks on Freemasonry are intended to provide an 'enemy without the gates' to bind the members of a religious group closer together.

Freemasonry can be used as an example of an impediment to the 'true teachings' of a particular religion (or denomination) without having to attack another, competing, religion (or denomination).

This is a diversionary tactic brought into play when internal matters threaten the cohesion of the group.

A 'what if' question

There is no single organisation that has the ability to decide whether a particular group and its practices constitute a religion. This is probably why some churches, denominations, etc. can claim, without fear of contradiction from other religious groups, that Freemasonry is a religion. They do so for their own purposes, as discussed above, but in doing so they fail to consider the wider implications. This overweening need to classify Freemasonry as religion creates even more contradictions than those mentioned above, which demonstrate that same self-serving purpose. This is an important point for if those who claim Freemasonry is a religion are doing so from a general societal point of view then it would be expected that they would comment on a whole range of ramifications of that classification. In other words, by classifying Freemasonry as a religion are other consequences discussed? Two examples will suffice here to illustrate this point.

In the United Kingdom a number of Christian denominations have in the recent past declared that Freemasonry is a religion and is incompatible with Christianity. Here we see the reason why Freemasonry has to be designated a religion as otherwise compatibility would not be an issue. If it is accepted that the opinion of these churches is valid (and

I do not accept it) then there are other implications that these churches have not considered.

Improvements have been made in the conditions of the citizens of the United Kingdom across a huge range of matters including employment, health care, legal representation and human rights, to name but a few. Included in this process has been the drive to reduce discrimination against minority groups on the grounds of disability, faith and sexual orientation. On the basis of the expert opinion of Christian churches in the UK then Freemasonry ought to be afforded protection against employment discrimination by the state:

Protection from discrimination

There is no specific list that sets out what religion or belief discrimination is. The law defines it as any religion, religious or philosophical belief. This includes all major religions, as well as less widely practised ones.

You are also protected against discrimination if you do not follow any religion or belief, and your employer discriminates against you because of this. Political beliefs are not counted as a religion or belief.[364]

Government legislation in the form of the 'Employment Equality (Religion and Belief) Regulations 2003' would, in theory, protect Freemasons from discrimination in the workplace on the basis of their 'religion' or at least their beliefs. Needless to say, legislation such as this was probably never intended to be applicable to Freemasons. The question must be why not? The detractors of Freemasonry seem to want to ensure that Freemasonry is not considered a legitimate minority group such as the disabled, etc. but maintain the position that Freemasonry is a religion and is one which can be discriminated against!

Detractors of Freemasonry nearly always discuss Freemasonry in an abstract manner as if it were not composed of human beings. This failure to confront the fact that Freemasons are people avoids the need to discuss what individuals think of Freemasonry and to debate their opinion directly or indirectly with them. All organisations are proud to have members who are prominent in some manner but curiously Freemasonry does not record famous members as all are treated equally and so fame, riches, social position are irrrelevant. Those that have been identified have usually been discovered by accident. As discussed above, William L. Brown had a very specific motive for defining Freemasonry as a religion and that was because he believed it to be a form of devil worship. The fact that this conclusion had been decided before he undertook his 'analysis' not only demonstrates the self-serving purpose of the lecture but also that Freemasons were excluded from contributing directly so that Brown could 'cherry pick' from the written musings of individual Freemasons. It is also worth reminding ourselves that theological objections to Freemasonry were developed only after mundane objections had been made against the institution. That tells us two things. Firstly, theological (that is religious) arguments were created in order to provide legitimacy to attacks originating from religious commentators and groups and secondly to create 'the other' or 'the enemy without' for the purpose of binding members of a religious group closer together.

For the last three centuries numerous people have become Freemasons including many religious leaders, politicians and famous individuals. By not discussing individuals who are Freemasons, Masonophobes avoid confronting a very uncomfortable fact – that a huge number of people simply do not agree with their opinion. That many religious leaders have found no conflict between being a Freemason *and* following their faith is not an issue that is discussed. Yet there are a large number of religious leaders who were and are Freemasons. Many church leaders in England and elsewhere have been Freemasons. In Scotland the main church is the Church of Scotland, founded almost 100 years after Scottish Masonic records commence. As has been previously mentioned, the Church initially had no problem with Freemasonry and that tolerance and understanding existed until relatively recently. Many leaders, or moderators of the Church of Scotland were Freemasons.[365] Dr James Lauchlan McLean Watt is but one example. He was minister of the Parish of Alloa, and became a Freemason in the Lodge of Alloa, No. 69, in 1904. In 1930 he became Grand Chaplain of the Grand Lodge of Scotland and officiated at numerous Masonic ceremonies before, during and after his official period of office.

It is timely to remember that Scotland is being used as an example of Masonophobia in a small country in the hope that this introductory study of anti-Masonry might be extrapolated further.

On the rare occasion when it is pointed out that someone prominent is also a Freemason this is excused away by saying that he is a 'good Freemason' or is 'the exception that proves the rule' but that still does not deal with the central point that those who criticise Freemasonry are not speaking on behalf of all members of their particular religion, or religious denomination. That distinction is not applied to Masonic writers. Rather, they are used to bolster a particular, inevitably Christian, view of Freemasonry and is another example of the one-way traffic regarding the subject.

Before leaving the discussion as to why some Christian denominations attack Freemasonry because of its alleged and erroneous denial of Jesus Christ, despite the fact that Freemasonry uses only the Old Testament for its *allegorical* history, another question is pertinent. What do the very same Christian denominations have to say about Buddhist Freemasons? Do they attack them because they are Buddhists or because they are Freemasons? The answer is that they do not make any such distinction. Many Buddhist, Muslim, Jewish and Hindu Freemasons would find this offensive as they are being targeted because they are Freemasons. Those with anti-Masonic views never address this problem. By attacking Freemasonry from their own religious perception (instead of trying to understand it) they are decrying Freemasons who are not Christians. Is there an ulterior motive at work here? Is Freemasonry being used as a guise under which one religion attacks others? Unfortunately, repeated attempts to analyse such possible motives have failed because of the refusal to engage in a meaningful dialogue.[366]

CHAPTER 5

THE MODERN ERA

'All news is lies and all propaganda is disguised as news.'
Willi Münzenberg (1889–1940)

In the previous chapters we have seen how Freemasonry has been the subject of relentless and multi-faceted 'campaigns' of Masonophobia. 'Campaign' is probably not the best word to use in this respect because it implies that there are some kind of orchestrated, organised and repeated attacks on the Order. That is how it may look to a conspiracy theorist but as I do not subscribe to that theory I have a rather different explanation I wish to explore and which will be revealed and fully discussed in the concluding chapter. Here I wish to examine the period where the introduction left off by examining what happened immediately after the article by Fred Bridgland published on 22 March 1996 in *The Scotsman* newspaper. The article was reproduced in full in the introduction and again so here (see below) in order to 'dissect' it as this process reveals some of the tactics adopted in other, later articles regarding Freemasonry. In addition the article, the first of its type, contains some important claims, allegations and observations which were to be repeated in a variety of forms in subsequent years.

In 1989 Martin Short (1943–) published *Inside the Brotherhood: Further Secrets of the Freemasons* which was a sequel to *The Brotherhood: the Secret World of the Freemasons* by Stephen Knight (1951–1985).[367] Both books were avowedly about Freemasonry and contained numerous allegations of a huge variety of wrongdoing on the part of Freemasons. Martin Short quickly became a recognised 'expert' on Freemasonry and was (and is) a frequent commentator on matters relating to Freemasonry in England. This was the first puzzle about the article: 'Secret brotherhood which protects its own' was conducted as an interview by a journalist who was not resident in the UK. The journalist was, and is, a recognised expert on political affairs in the southern part of Africa. Yet here he was interviewing an 'expert' on English Freemasonry. Even more curiously the subject of the interview was a tragic event which had taken place in Scotland only 10 days previously, investigations into which had barely commenced.

The purpose of this book is two-fold: firstly to provide background material about anti-Masonry (or Masonophobia as it is now better known) to show that this is not a new phenomenon but has been around for 300+ years and secondly to examine that phenomenon as contemporary history. The former, as already stated several times, can only be by way of an introduction for the amount of material precludes any attempt at a comprehensive historical account.[368] The latter was intended to be an analysis of Masonophobia of the recent past. It had been hoped that such an analysis would be based on dialogue with numerous individuals involved in the tumultuous affairs of the 1990s and later. As an historian I was, and remain, interested in the process rather than the individuals involved and I anticipated that through dialogue I would come to understand the stages (processes) of Masonophobia, the motives (if any) of those involved and the purpose served by this phenomenon. This was a naive expectation on my part as no such dialogue took place.[369]

When I realised that there was a great deal of information worth observing and collating I began to take notes, record TV programmes etc. One of the latter was *Why Dunblane?*, part of the famous investigative series *World in Action* which was broadcast on 18 March 1996. This was an in-depth exploration of the life of Thomas Hamilton and importantly it made no reference to Freemasonry. It soon became clear that I was in the middle of history in the making. In the absence of any dialogue with those involved in producing the material I was accumulating, and I shall discuss why there was a lack of dialogue in the conclusion, I therefore must turn to the contemporary material itself, and attempt an analysis without the benefit of input from the authors. This form of analysis is not what I would have wished for at the outset as this means that this chapter (in particular) must rely to a much larger degree on descriptive material than originally intended. However, I comfort myself with the fact that I did make the effort to engage in dialogue and continue to do so (without much success). One example will serve for the present to illustrate this point.

Fred Bridgland was known personally to the author who had met him several times in the early days of his career whilst he was still based in Scotland and primarily working for *The Scotsman* newspaper. When I began to accumulate material, jot down notes and keep newspaper clippings from 1996 onward I began to gain an overview that many 'ordinary' Scottish Freemasons probably would not have.[370] In beginning to research and write this book the starting point always returned to Fred Bridgland's piece.[371] This despite the fact that it was clearly necessary to cover a much longer time period in order to put the subject in its historical context. Once this project was decided upon (in the author's mind at least) attempts were made to contact Fred and it was established that he was now based in Johannesburg, South Africa. His e-mail address was obtained and initial contact with him was more than promising until it was mentioned that the article (below) was to be central to the proposed discussion. Suddenly all contact ceased. The e-mail address no longer functioned and messages left at newspapers he contributed to (in South Africa), went unanswered and telephone calls always found him to be unavailable. I now turn to the article and its contents.

– the Secret brotherhood which protects its own
Fred Bridgland

'The Freemasons of Britain are strongly protective of their fellow Masons. They rarely punish brethren who break the criminal law of the land, Martin Short, author of a best-selling investigation into Freemasonry, last night told *The Scotsman*.

'Scotland is a place where one Mason looks after another,' said Mr Short. 'If Thomas Hamilton was one of the brethren it's pretty bad news for the Masons because one is inclined to assume he may well have received favours.' They would not allow one of their own brethren to be exposed to public ridicule and would do everything to avoid his membership being known.

Short, whose book *Inside the Brotherhood: Further Secrets of the Freemasons* was first published in 1989, referred to a local government ombudsman decision in Hamilton's favour in 1983. The ombudsman overturned a decision by Central Regional Council to end his lease of Dunblane High School premises for his boys' club, the Dunblane Rover Group.

'The fact that he managed to bamboozle the ombudsman suggests that the ombudsman was bombarded by letters,' said Mr Short. 'If he managed to convince the ombudsman that he was OK, you can be pretty sure that his lodge would have felt at least equally strongly. The Masons in the lodge would not have wanted to think ill of him and would therefore have tried to protect him from all-comers.'

Social pressures make it difficult for an honest Mason to complain about criminal or immoral conduct by his brothers, said Mr Short. In fact, it would be the complainant, not the wrongdoers, who faced ostracism and probable exclusion from the lodge.

Mr Short said Masonry was an organisation of men only who voluntarily swear mutual aid and to guard each other's secrets: it has its own strict rules, inquiry systems, punishments and courts of appeal. He said that when it became known he was researching his book he lost count of the brethren who cautioned him to 'watch out' or 'take care'.

Mr Short went on: 'One man whose evidence sent a fellow Mason to jail told me of his fears during that trial and the extreme precautions he had taken to stay alive. He advised me to do the same.'

Mr Short's 711-page book lists some of the reasons why he was inclined to take the advice seriously. It also lists some of the bizarre initiation ceremonies of Masonry. Mr Short, for example, describes a Masonic lodge in Lincolnshire where a candidate Mason is lowered into a trap below the temple floor on the Friday before full moon to confront a female skeleton as a symbol of mortality.

Several traditional crafts and professions are bastions of Freemasonry, Mr Short argues.

In his book he points to the example of the Metropolitan Police where, in 1987, he identified one assistant commissioner, two deputy assistant commissioners, 12 commanders, 23 chief superintendents, ten superintendents and seven chief inspectors as members of a single Masonic lodge.

Mr Short argues that Freemasonry extends into local government, the armed services, industry and the intelligence services to an extent which would astonish non-Masons. He says 100,000, or one in 14 of Scotland's working population, are Freemasons.[372][373]

This article is important because it sets the standard of analysis that others would follow in subsequent years. It is therefore worth discussing, albeit briefly.

'*The Freemasons of Britain... rarely punish brethren who break the criminal law...* ', and so the scene is set. Because it is *known*, according to a self-appointed expert (who cites no proof) that Freemasons protect criminals. Having established the 'known truth' the following can be stated with impunity: '*If Thomas Hamilton was one of the brethren...*' and the operative word here is 'if' and this 'if' later turns into fact: ' *...you can be pretty sure that his lodge...*' and so now supposition has turned into fact – that Hamilton was a Freemason. It was not until later that evidence to support this claim was sought and, despite the 'evidence' being false, continues to be used as proof that Hamilton was a Freemason. The rest of the article then provides non-specific support for Short's expertise and anecdotal tales as to what Freemasons do, how and why they protect each other and cites as 'evidence' quotes from his book published almost ten years previously.[374]

The shock, anger and frustration experienced by everyone (especially in Scotland) filled the pages of newspapers, television and the internet. It seems that when there is no quick and clear reason as to why a disaster happened, people begin to guess, even to fantasise, as to the causes. This is a point to which I shall return later. It was not long before the media were supplying answers.

The Scotsman implied that it knew the reasons for the mass murder at Dunblane and made that suggestion within ten days of the event. The reason is as contained in the article above and which I now wish to discuss.[375] A large number of articles appeared in the same newspaper in the succeeding years, a number of which are reproduced below. I have included these articles for two reasons: firstly so that the cumulative effect of the Masonophobic campaign can be gauged and secondly so that they are on record in one place for ease of access.[376]

The above article was published without any reference to any Masonic body and this set a pattern that rarely changed. Articles were written about Freemasonry without any consultation with any Masonic 'authorities'; when Freemasons were quoted this was for a different purpose and I shall highlight those instances as they arise later in the chapter.[377] By adopting this tactic Freemasonry was always 'on the back foot' never knowing what was to come and reacting to events rather than being part of them. Given the duration of the media commentary and that there was never any prior consultation this suggests that a decision had been made early on not to involve Freemasonry in any of the stories in which it featured. The lack of dialogue with the media means that this can be an observation only. Equally the motive(s) for the lack of consultation are also unknown but some tentative suggestions will be made later in the chapter.

Returning to the article it has already been noticed that the expert quoted has only written extensively about Freemasonry in England and that the author of the piece was an expert on southern African affairs and lives there. The article begins by referring to Britain yet this is a story about a single tragic event which took place in Scotland. This, then, suggests that those responsible for the article did not know that Freemasonry in Scotland is separate from that in England. In any event this indicates that the newspaper was implicating all *British* Freemasons in this tragic event.[378]

The first paragraph explains that Freemasons protect each other and rarely take action against Freemasons who are criminals and that Short is a best selling author on the subject of Freemasonry. Although no facts are provided the scene is set. Freemasons protect each other even if they are criminals and this is confirmed by an acknowledged expert.

Switching from Britain the expert declares that Scotland is a place where Masons look after each other and introduces Thomas Hamilton, the man responsible for murdering the children and teacher at Dunblane. However, the article is written in a manner so as not to provide any facts. 'If Thomas Hamilton was one of the brethren...' commences the second paragraph and continues to state that his fellow Freemasons would protect him. Within the space of a couple of sentences the discussion therefore has shifted from whether or not Hamilton was a Freemason to how the Freemasons would protect him thereby suggesting that he was – without saying so!

The use of the word 'if' is common and allows the writers room to manoeuvre if challenged. The sentence 'If he managed to convince the ombudsman that he was OK...' , comes after a sentence that commences, 'The fact that he managed to bamboozle the ombudsman...' The article then proceeds to discuss what Hamilton's fellow Masons would have done in this situation and the question of if he was a Freemason is no longer in any doubt. The assumption, without explicitly saying so, is now that he was a Freemason. The remainder of the article has little to do with the Dunblane Massacre but is a list of the bad things that Freemasons get up to, the fact that a lot of them are policemen and that Short the expert had been put in fear of his life during the writing of his book. The parting shot of the article is the 'fact' that there are 100,000 Freemasons in Scotland representing 10% of the working population. The Grand Lodge of Scotland was not asked for any figures and I can only conclude that this was a scare tactic, implying that there is a veritable army of Thomas Hamiltons out there waiting to prey on innocent citizens.

The newspaper which ran the above article ran another 'story' on the same day, albeit on a different page, which did suggest answers:

Masonic link may explain Hamilton's 'charmed life'

Questions are being asked whether **Thomas Hamilton** abused his position as a **Freemason.**

A Labour MP who has campaigned against secret societies said that Hamilton's membership of the **Freemasons** could explain his apparently 'charmed life'...

A senior Scottish **Freemason** told *The Scotsman* that Hamilton had been a Mason for a number of years.

Thomas Hamilton... would have followed his grandfather into Freemasonry.

Chris Mullin, the Labour MP who has campaigned against secret societies, said he found the alleged Masonic link with Hamilton 'very interesting'.[379] [380]

This is not so much an article as perhaps something intended to 'generate debate'? What was of great concern at the time was that the innuendo and allegations made in Bridgland's piece had already, on the same day, been converted into hard fact.[381] The first point says it all: 'Questions are being asked whether **Thomas Hamilton** abused his position as a **Freemason**.'

What is of major importance here is that on 21 March the British government announced that a Public Inquiry would be held in order to establish the events surrounding the Dunblane shootings. Within 24 hours of that announcement elements of the Scottish Press were suggesting that they knew who was culpable and what is more that they were ordinary Scotsmen who also happened to be Freemasons. It was suggested at the time that the newspaper concerned was deliberately attempting to influence Public Inquiry by 'guiding' them in a certain direction. There was and is no evidence for that suggestion but readers may well be interested in events immediately before, during and after the Public Inquiry.[382]

The world was being told without any doubt that the mass murderer, Thomas Hamilton was a Freemason. The Grand Lodge of Scotland had not been approached to confirm whether or not this was true. This raises a matter which I suggest is of major concern and which comprises two parts. Firstly, is it right and proper for anyone to *appear* to influence a Public Inquiry before it has even begun to gather evidence? The second part relates to Freemasonry and shall be discussed, along with related matters in this chapter.

The preliminary hearing of the Public Inquiry into the Dunblane Shootings was held on 1 May when Lord Cullen issued a call for written submissions to the Inquiry.[383] In addition Lord Cullen had notices placed in the press, on 3 May, making the same appeal.[384] [385]

The Public Inquiry was held at the Albert Halls, Stirling and sat for 26 days commencing on 29 May and closing on Wednesday, 10 July 1996.[386]

Whilst the Public Inquiry was being held the Press ran a number of articles on Freemasonry. As someone commented to me at the time, 'It is almost as if someone is trying to influence the Public Inquiry [into the Dunblane Shootings] against us.' One newspaper in particular published a huge number of column inches over four days during the last week of the Public Inquiry. The series entitled 'Freemasons in Scotland' commenced on Monday, 1 July, and ran also on Tuesday, 2 July,

Wednesday, 3 July and Thursday, 4 July.[387] There were several pages each day and this represents a substantial body of material published in the public domain about Scottish Freemasonry during the course of a Public Inquiry.[388] As it is not so readily available for study today it has been decided to reproduce *all* of that material again for the first time in more than 10 years.[389]

Masons urged to come clean[390]

EXCLUSIVE: Scots councillors face pressure to reveal membership (Stephen Breen and Nic Outterside)

Councillors in Scotland should be forced to declare if they are Freemasons and top local government officers should also be encouraged to reveal their membership when new codes of conduct are drawn up, Scotland's leading councillors believe.

Rosemary McKenna (1941–), who stepped down as president of the Convention of Scottish Local Authorities last month, and her successor, Keith Geddes believe the move is essential to reassure the pubic that there is no favouritism in council decision-making or appointments.

COSLA is revising the code of conduct for council employees and will look at membership of secret societies.[391] The code for council employees in England and Wales recommends that staff should declare membership and says that councils should consider asking job applicants if they are masons.

A separate code of conduct for all councillors in Britain will be revised after Lord Nolan completes his enquiry into local government. The House of Commons home affairs select committee begins taking written evidence this month into the influence of Freemasonry in the police and judiciary in England and Wales.

The Scotsman surveyed leading figures in public life and business in an attempt to discover whether the craft still has influence in Scotland today.

Mrs McKenna said councillors should be compelled to reveal if they are members of secret societies. Mr Geddes, the new president, and the new vice-president, Kate Maclean will support this demand when COSLA is consulted as the new code is drawn up.

Mrs McKenna told *The Scotsman:* 'There should not be an option. Councillors have to make it known. They have to declare business interests so there isn't a conflict of interest in terms of membership of secret societies. Councillors could be sitting on an interview panel when members from the same society are applying for a job and no-one knows that at the time. When there is secrecy there is suspicion, when there is no secrecy there is none.'[392]

The existing code of conduct for UK councillors does not require elected members to register membership of masonic lodges, but they are warned not to create the impression that they put their 'private or personal interests' before the public good. Freemasonry, along with membership of trade unions and voluntary bodies, is listed in the code as a 'private or personal interest'.

The new City of Dundee Council has revised its code of conduct for employees to include a form for senior officers to declare membership of any societies or organisations which might affect their decisions. That would include membership of the masons. Kate Maclean, the council leader, said that when COSLA is consulted over the codes of conduct she would support councillors and senior officials having to declare their membership of secret societies.

She said, 'If you are an officer or a councillor dealing with a range of organisations and taking decisions and possibly awarding grants, it is for your own protection that you have your interests declared on forms. Our declaration (in Dundee) wasn't particularly aimed at the masons or the Knights of St Columba but it would include them.'

COSLA's chief executive, Douglas Sinclair, said: 'We will be looking at existing best practice for staff. There is reference to secret societies in the English code for officers and it is clearly something we will look at.'

A Scottish Office spokesman said councillors were encouraged to name organisations to which they belonged, but making declarations of secret societies mandatory would have to be considered under the new UK code.

The Grand Master Mason of Scotland, Lord Burton of Dochfour, said he saw no need for Masonic councillors to reveal their membership because Freemasonry had no influence in local government.[393]

Freemasonry in Scotland today: Day 1

Two important enquiries begin this year which could have profound implications for the secretive world of Freemasonry. This month the Commons Home Affairs Select Committee begins taking evidence on the influence of the craft in the police and judiciary in England and Wales; and councillors and local government officials will face a new code of conduct demanding more openness. STEPHEN BREEN and NIC OUTTERSIDE begin a four-part investigation into Freemasonry in Scotland today.

Power lodged with the men of secrecy

In April this year two councillors in the new Highland Council were heavily defeated when they attempted to pass an amendment forcing councillors to declare if they were Freemasons. The pair believed it would allay public fears that Freemasons show favours to the brethren when it comes to appointments and council decision-making.[394]

The Scotsman was told by one elected member on a Highland planning committee of an occasion when he became aware of Masons trying to improperly use the Lodge network to secure the passage of a planning application. The night before a site visit he received a telephone call from another councillor, who was a Mason, asking him to support the application.

When he reached the site he found out the application would breach every existing planning regulation. At the site he spoke to another elected member, a Mason, who had also received a call from the Masonic councillor urging him to 'do the right thing' and pass the application because he was in the Lodge.

The non-Masonic Highland councillor told *The Scotsman*: 'That morning the councillor who was in the Masons told me that that was not what the Lodge was for. It's not very often they speak about each other, but I was impressed that he was honest enough to admit to me that this had happened. Another councillor who is in the Lodge didn't show up. It seems that rather than vote against the Lodge he had stayed away.'

The Masonic councillor named to *The Scotsman* as receiving the telephone call denied the incident, but said he was aware that calls were made on the night before the site visit. He said he did not know whether they were connected with Freemasonry.

Cllr Douglas Briggs, an SNP member on the new Highland Council, said he'd been informed about the Cllr being 'leaned on'. 'If these telephone calls happened once, you can be sure they've happened on other occasions. It is tantamount to councillors being intimidated out of their job.

'I have had all sorts of people describing to me discrimination they feel they have suffered in the Highlands because they are not Masons. It has been in local government, the gas and electricity utilities, the fire service and the police.

'People say they were concerned at not getting a job, then a cousin of a brother in the Lodge has told them he had heard their name mentioned at the Lodge in connection with the application and that was why they didn't get it. If there is this belief going around then that is damaging.'

Mr Briggs believes incidents such as these fuel public suspicions of Masonic corruption. To restore public confidence he feels it is essential for elected members to register their membership of secret societies.

However, he was heavily defeated in April when he proposed the amendment requiring elected members to include the Lodge membership on a register of interests.

Rosemary McKenna, who tried as COSLA PRESIDENT for councillors to be compelled by law to declare their membership of secret societies. Councils are attempting to compel councillors to declare that they are members. Her successor, Keith Geddes, and his vice president, Kate MacLean, agree there needs to be transparency in local government. Mr Geddis and Ms MacLean support Mrs McKenna's call for councillors to be compelled by law to declare their membership of secret societies, when a new national code of conduct is drawn up after Lord Nolan examines local government later this year. They would also like a code of conduct which would encourage senior staff to declare membership, bringing Scotland into line with England and Wales.

Freemasonry rarely raises its head in Scottish town halls, but the society has been fiercely debated in more than 100 English local authorities since the 80s, with some councils attempting to compel councillors to declare if they are members.

In an attempt to discover if Freemasonry has influence in local government today, *The Scotsman* wrote to the chief executives of Scotland's 32 new unitary authorities asking them the following questions.

1 Are you a Freemason?

2 To the best of your knowledge, what percentage of your senior officials are Freemasons?

3 Has Freemasonry ever been a divisive or controversial issue during your time in local government?

4 Have members of the public ever raised the issue of Freemasonry in any complaint against any local authority you have worked for?

5 In your opinion has Freemasonry ever been used to influence decisions taken by council officials or councillors – particularly in the areas of planning, grand aid and council contracts?

21 of the 32 chief executives responded and 20 said that they were not Lodge members. Douglas Paterson of Aberdeen Council did not answer but he said *The Scotsman* risked 'creating an issue where one does not necessarily exist'. He said: 'Freemasonry has to my certain knowledge never been mentioned, or even hinted at, in any proceedings of Aberdeen City Council,' adding that all appointments to the authority were based on merit.

Only one of the chief executives who answered said he had come across an instance where he believes Freemasonry could have been misused in local government, the overwhelming majority of chief executives said they had no idea how many senior officers were Lodge members, and of those who gave estimates, most said very few.

Michael Watters, a former district secretary of Dumbarton District Council, who is now chief executive of West Dunbartonshire Council said: 'I was investigating misdemeanours involving employees and a number of people suggested to me that recent Freemasonry might have been an influence.

'I received no evidence to support this apart from when I was going through various papers and came across the minutes of a meeting which had the initials of individuals and some numbers at the top of the page, which could have been a Lodge number.'[395]

In 1994, councils south of the border accepted a code of conduct for employees which recommended staff be given an opportunity to declare membership of secret societies. The code also states that councils should consider addressing the question of secret societies when recruiting staff.

This year, the new Dundee City Council introduced a new declaration form for chief officers, which required them to state membership of any organisation, which would include the Freemasons, which they felt might affect their decisions. I, like Stephen, the council's chief executive, pinpointed a central problem with such a policy: while he would expect his officers to declare their membership, he would soon be surprised if they did. He said: 'If an officer believed his membership of the Masons would affect his decisions we would expect he would put it down on his form. If he didn't put it down and it later emerged that he was a Mason and it didn't influence his decisions, we would take disciplinary action.'[396]

The following chief executives did not respond to *The Scotsman* survey: Sandy Waterson (Angus); James McLellan (Argyll & Bute); Robert Allen (Clackmannanshire); Con Mallon (East Dunbartonshire); John Lindsay (East Lothian); Walter Weir (Falkirk); Andrew Cowe (North Lanarkshire); George Thornley (South Ayrshire); Alistair McNish (South Lanarkshire); Robert Gilbert (Orkney).

The Past
Romance of history carved in stone
Each week men in dark suits congregate in their lodges, reaffirming their loyalty to the craft – or brotherhood . For many years, the 'profane', or non-members, have suspected that Masonic influence is exerted in many

areas, including the corrupt, the acceleration or ruination of individual careers and even the perversion of justice.

Almost 100,000, or one in 14, members of the working male population of Scotland are Freemasons. They come from all walks of life: police officers, solicitors, ministers, bankers, car sales executives, elders, teachers, civil servants, doctors, journalists, and industrialists.

With groups allegedly stretching back 600 years, few Freemasons can sort fact from fantasy, truth from fiction, tradition from travesty.

One tradition of particular English Oration origin is claimed to be descended from the stonemasons of medieval times. Another tradition – and more Scottish in its roots – is that Freemasonry is derived from the Knights Templar, who found sanctuary in the West Coast of Scotland after the Crusades and their excommunication in the 14th century. These knights carved signs and Pictish crosses in stone and became stonemasons in their own right. In succeeding centuries these traditions became hallowed by custom and perverted by a false faith of fanciful rituals, newly coined legends and bloodcurdling oaths. Today's brethren wax poetic about their stonemason ancestors because they built the Gothic cathedrals that rank among Europe's architectural glories. In fact, the Gothic cathedrals were mostly built between 1100 and 1400 A.D., 300 years before the foundation meeting of the Grand Lodge of Scotland in 1736. The construction was also well before the Grand Lodges own record of its 'oldest surviving minute of a Scottish Lodge', in 1598.

However, what is probably true is that medieval stonemasons spent their working lives on a few big sites. Cathedrals, some churches and maybe a secular building such as a castle. On each site some kind of lodge would be erected where Masons could shelter, store tools, organise work and even sleep or 'lodge'.

It could take 100 years to build a cathedral, so the lodges took on a near permanent status. Through them, the stonemasons protected themselves and their jobs and maintained work standards through a controlled rank structure of three degrees: apprentice, fellow craft and Master Mason.

They probably 'worked' rituals in which initiates swore not to reveal the secrets of their craft. To block infiltration, they may also have devised a secret code or passports, handshakes and other signs of recognition.

However, after the Reformation and the destruction of many cathedrals and abbeys, stonemason numbers exceeded demand. By 1600 most fraternities had disappeared along with their records.

A few lodges survived, but only by throwing membership open. By the time of the birth of modern Freemasonry, lodges were claiming to be schools of moral instruction. Each stonemason's tool – the square, composite, level, plumb line, gauge, trowel, chisel – became a symbol of some process in man's moral and spiritual perfection.

The ritual: Sworn to secrecy
In masonry's first degree the initiate, or would be apprentice, swears he will never reveal any of the Craft's secrets or mysteries.

The blindfolded, bare breasted and noosed candidate places his hand on the open Bible and solemnly swears to observe these vows: 'Under no less a penalty than that of having my throat cut across, my tongue torn out by the root, and buried in the sand of the sea at low water mark, or a cable's length from the shore, where the tide regularly ebbs and flows twice in 24 hours.'

Initiation into higher degrees of Freemasonry have carried similar threats to the Initiate's mortality. Martin Short, the author of *Inside the Brotherhood: further secrets of Freemasons*, describes a Masonic Lodge in Lincolnshire, where, on the Friday before full moon, a candidate Mason is lowered into a trap below the temple floor to confront a female skeleton, a symbol of mortality. When the Italian banker and Freemason, Roberto Calvi, was found hanging from London's Blackfriars Bridge in 1982, Masons and non-Masons alike wondered if death 'where the tide ebbs and flows' might still be the punishment inflicted on Masonic traitors.

The Personnel
You might be surprised who is a Freemason.

For example, the prominent Edinburgh solicitor, Walter Sneddon, is a Grand Bard of the Grand Lodge of Scotland, the ruling body of Scotland's 1,100 lodges and its 70,000 accepted Craft degree Masons. Lord Burton of Dochfour is the current Grand Master of the Grand Lodge. The Duke of Argyll – the Queen's representative in Scotland – is a Junior Grand Warden.

The eminent Glasgow Surgeon, Alexander Walker Naddell, is Master of the Scottish Scotia Lodge in Nigeria, while the former Deputy Prime Minister, Viscount Willie Whitelaw, is a senior Scottish Mason and Master of the Scottish St John Lodge in Jamaica.

At the other end of the spectrum the Angus minister, the Rev Joseph Morrow, is one of them. Almost two dozen clergyman hold senior positions within Scottish Freemasonry, while Robert Higgins, the leader of the SNP group on Dumfries and Galloway Council, is an active Mason and past secretary of his Luce Abbey Lodge at Glen Luce.

Scotland's most senior and prestigious Lodge is the Mother Kilwinning Lodge, (Lodge No. 0) which was formed at the foundation in 1736. However, the Scottish Grand Office-bearers each belong to Scotland's most exclusive Lodge, Robert Morey, No. 1641, which meets three times a year at the Lodge room in Hill Street, Edinburgh.

Masters – the third degree of Freemasonry – form the largest proportion of Freemasons, including the Grand Master, and in most cases are unaware of members of a large number of superior degrees 'to which they are never admitted, nor even here mentioned'. These include the Ecossais Scotia and the fourth degree of secret master.

Beyond these degrees are many other secret orders, each with its own arcane jargon and grandiose titles. These include: the Rose Croix, Knights Templar, the Mark, the Red Cross of Constantine, and society master Rosa Christiana in Anglia. Freemasonry's supreme degree is the holy Royal Arch; one Mason in every three or four joins this order.

'People join Freemasonry for the comradeship, the social aspect and the charity aspect,' explains Archibald Orr Ewing, the senior grand warden of the grand Lodge of Scotland.

'It has also got an historical element. The main difference between English and Scottish Freemasonry is that in Scotland we have lodges throughout the country, which are very mixed with all different types from all different backgrounds and professions, whereas in England they have lodges for stockbrokers and lawyers.'

Gerard O'Donnell, an Edinburgh Freemason, defends his craft.

'To become a Freemason certain requirements must be fulfilled,' he wrote in a letter to *The Scotsman*.

'These being: a belief in a supreme being power governing the universe, to be of good character and to have a desire to be of service to all people, regardless of colour or political beliefs. In addition, it is forbidden to seek material gain by becoming a Freemason.

'Freemasonry has been a part of Scottish society for a very long time. It can count people of the standing of Robert Burns, and a Walter Scott amongst its membership.'

The image of the brotherhood, for all its benevolent protestations, is a sinister one for many of the 'profane'. In June 1992 Maria Fyfe, the Labour MP for Glasgow Maryhill, tabled a House of Commons motion challenging MPs to admit their membership of the Freemasons.

'For as long as Freemasonry has existed,' says Maria Fyfe, 'people have suspected that decisions could be made at the highest level where people who are Masons – including royalty, judges, police officers and people who are members of local and national government – congregate.'

Martin Short adds: 'There are rules that say you must not abuse Freemasonry for personal gain, but in most cases in people's eyes it exercises a corrosive influence in local government and business and to some extent in military circles.

'I just think the existence of such a society today, is it is divisive, particularly in times when people are worried about losing their jobs and face uncertainty in life.'

The Grand Lodge of Scotland was not asked to comment on any of the content reproduced above. The numerous inaccuracies (some serious some not) could not therefore be corrected prior to publication. Where necessary I have added a brief end note explaining why there is an error and where it is of major significance in this work I shall expand on the point in the concluding chapter.

Having read day one of 'Freemasons In Scotland' it was with some trepidation that 'Day 2' was awaited – would this be the day that our side to the debate was published? The following was on page 1:

EXCLUSIVE: Freemasonry in Scotland, Day 2
MPs fears over secrecy a threat to democracy.
NIC OUTTERSIDE and STEPHEN BREEN
Six out of ten Scottish male MPs who responded to a *Scotsman* survey say Freemasonry is incompatible with open government or believe that membership should be declared in the register of MPs' interests.

A total of 39 responded.

The Scotsman's investigation revealed unease among MPs about Freemasonry in public life. All 65 of Scotland's male MPs were asked a series of questions:

The brothers in law
Just how influential is the brotherhood, when it comes to where real power lies? In part two of The Scotsman's *four-day examination, Stephen Breen and Nic Outterside report on Masons in Scottish politics.*

In January 1994, the Labour MP Dennis Skinner asked how many Masons held positions within the government and called for the Prime Minister to 'come clean'. He also called on Masons to declare membership in the register of members' interests.

The response of the public services minister, David Davis, was noncommittal: 'I have no notion of whether there are any Freemasons in the Cabinet, although I suspect not.'

Last year, amid fears expressed in the House of Commons by a number of Labour MPs that Masonic influence may be used to build their justice and affect individual careers, it was announced that the Nolan committee might investigate Freemasonry as part of its review of standards in public life.

However, last week, a spokesman for the Nolan committee said it now seems unlikely that the brotherhood would be scrutinised by the committee when it looks at the running of local government, but confirmed that the Masons would be covered by the home affairs select committee when it began enquiries into the police and judiciary this month.

Despite the strong working-class membership of Freemasonry in Scotland, more than three quarters of Labour MPs who responded to a *Scotsman* survey on the subject believe that membership of the brotherhood was either incompatible with open government, or that MPs should be forced to declare whether they are Freemasons.

This is in marked contrast to the response from the Conservative colleagues who either declared that Freemasonry was compatible, or avoided answering the question.

The Scotsman polled Scotland 65 male MPs – female MPs were not included as no Scottish Lodge admits women and their answers may have unfairly skewed the survey. We asked five questions: one, are you a Freemason? Two, to the best of your knowledge, what percentage of MPs are Freemasons? Three, are you aware of any Masonic lodges at Westminster? Four, have you ever experienced or been aware of instances when Masonic influence has been improperly used to gain advantage for Masons? Five, do you think Freemasonry or membership of any secret society is compatible with accountability and open government?

A total of 39 MPs responded to the survey. The 60% response is higher than any other survey of Freemasonry. A total of 24 (53%) of Labour's 45 male MPs returned completed questionnaires.

George Robertson, the shadow Scottish secretary, said: 'I am not a Freemason, have never been a Freemason and do not intend ever to be a Freemason.'

Those that did not respond were: Henry McLeish (Fife Central), Jimmy Hood (Clydesdale), Norman Hogg (Cumbernauld and Kilsyth), John McFall (Dumbarton), Ernie Ross (Dundee West), Gordon Brown (Dunfermline East), Adam Ingram (East Kilbride), Michael Connarty (Falkirk East), John Maxton (Glasgow Cathcart), Ian Davidson (Glasgow Govan), Jimmy Donnachie (Glasgow Pollok), Jimmy Wray (Glasgow Provan), David Marshall (Glasgow Shettleston), Willie McKelvey (Kilmarnock), Dr. Lewis Moonie (Kirkcaldy), Tom Clarke

(Monklands West), Dr. John Reid (Motherwell North). Dr. Jeremy Bray (Motherwell South), Gordon McMaster (Paisley South), Tommy Graham (Renfrew West and Inverclyde), Tommy McAvoy (Glasgow Rutherglen) and Sam Galbraith (Strathfield and Bearsden).

Westminster has at least three lodges, one for MPs and officials – the New Welcome Lodge, which meets five times a year at Freemasons Hall in London. There is another Lodge for journalists and the Lodge of St James's is for members and senior officers of both houses. A fourth Lodge is believed to exist in the House of Lords, although this has never been confirmed.

The Edinburgh South MP, Nigel Griffiths, claimed Freemasonry was 'rife' at Westminster, while his colleague Alistair Darling, the MP for Edinburgh Central, said, 'Rumours abound' in the House of Commons about Masonic lodges. Mr. Darling said he believed membership of any society 'which could influence the judgement or work of an MP ought to be disclosed'.

Dennis Canavan, the Labour MP for Falkirk West, said: 'I daresay there are some good people in Masonic lodges carrying out charitable works, but I would have thought in this day and age for grown men to behave in such a secretive fashion, the rolling up of trouser legs and putting on a blindfold, is a piece of nonsense, full stop.' Mr. Canavan has also called on the Nolan committee to demand that all elected officials publicly register if they are Freemasons.

Brian Donohoe, the Labour MP for Cunningham South, said: 'As a trade union official I saw Freemasonry working at industrial tribunals and at disciplinary appeals. It is particularly prominent in the West of Scotland where people are being dismissed and are in an appeal situation where you can hear and know precisely what they are saying.

'They just signal the fact that they are Masons to whoever is hearing the appeal. It can also be successful, but it can also work in the opposite way when the employer could signal to whom ever is hearing the tribunal and it can go against the poor sod who is being dismissed.'

Brian Wilson, Labour's transport spokesman, believes that Freemasonry *is* compatible with open government, but said membership 'should be declared'.

However, Eric Clarke, the MP for Midlothian, said it should be up to the conscience of MPs to declare if they are Masons. 'I had an old man who took me under his wing, who was an active Mason and never once did he try to influence me,' he said. 'He was a marvellous man, who really practised the brotherhood of man.'

Seven of Scotland's ten Tory MPs replied to *The Scotsman* survey.

Those who did not respond were the Scottish Secretary, Michael Forsyth, and Scottish office ministers, Raymond Robertson and George Kynoch. Five Tory MPs declared they were not Freemasons and Lord James Douglas Hamilton declined to answer the question.

The Ayr MP, Phil Gallie, sent an acerbic letter demanding to know whether *The Scotsman* journalists conducting the survey were trade union members, homosexuals, company shareholders and what salary they received. Mr. Gallie added: 'I trust the questions are not too intrusive, but, given your public role as a journalist, and the influence you have on public perceptions, it is important that I, and others, should be aware of your background, such that we can judge motivation and form a balanced opinion.'

The Scotsman answered Mr. Gallie's questions. Mr. Gallie responded, saying he was a Freemason but had never come across the Lodge at Westminster and believed Freemasonry *is* compatible with democracy.

The Defence Secretary, Malcolm Rifkind, answered the survey directly. But the Galloway MP and President of the Board of Trade, Ian Lang, said as 'a government minister' he 'makes it a rule not to complete any questionnaires'. His secretary answered on his behalf, stating that she 'knew he was not a Freemason' and she was not aware of any Masonic influences in politics.

The Tayside North MP, Bill Walker, was the only Tory MP to show variance from his colleagues, stating: 'In principle, I am against joining secret organisations, but believe that a matter of personal choice.' All eight male Liberal Democrat MPs replied to the survey, each declaring that they were not Freemasons. The Scottish Lib Dem leader, Jim Wallace, along with three of his colleagues, stated that 'membership of any secret society should be declared'. Neither of the SNP's two male MPs, Alex Salmond or Andrew Welsh, responded to the questionnaire.

In 1987, Martin Short, the author of the authoritative *Inside the Brotherhood – Further Secrets of the Freemasons*, conducted his own survey of Freemasonry among all 622 UK male MPs. He received 278 replies.

Mr Short was surprised by the strength of anti-Mason feeling among Labour MPs. A total of 95% of Labour MPs said that MPs should be 'obliged to declare membership of Freemasonry' and 23% of Tory MPs felt the same.

Mr Short established that Nigel Thorne and Sir Gerard Vaughan, the former Conservative Health Minister, were Freemasons from their listing in that year's *Masonic Yearbook*. Seven other MPs told Mr Short that they were Freemasons, including the Ulster Unionist Cecil Walker,

Anthony Nelson (Conservative, Chichester) and Tony Baldry (Conservative, Banbury). Mr. Short identified another four MPs as Freemasons, including the former Tory party chairman, Cecil Parkinson.

'Freemasonry is a mechanism of social control and the Conservative party is one of the main beneficiaries,' asserted Mr Short.

In 1992 the Labour MP Chris Mullin, who has campaigned against Freemasonry in public life, led a House of Commons debate on his Secret Societies (Declaration) Bill, which required holders of other candidates for appointment or election to public office or a post held in public service to declare publicly their membership of any secret society.[397]

Despite tacit support from the Prime Minister, John Major, the bill was 'talked out' but provided the catalyst, later, for the Home Affairs Select Committee enquiry into Freemasonry which begins taking evidence this month and is scheduled to begin hearings in December.

The results of the *Scotsman* survey will be handed to the select committee.[398]

The Class Divide

Freemasonry is a 'fraternity largely made up of mercantile, middle-class England', says Martin Short, the author of *Inside the Brotherhood – further Secrets of the Freemasons.*

In Scotland, the secret brotherhood, which has more than 100,000 members are mainly working-class in the ethos he maintains. However, there is a more complex paradox: Scotland has many more aristocratic Masons than does England. In 1989 Mr Short identified 36 Masons in the house towards whom 27 were senior office holders. Of these Masons, 23 were Conservative, eight independent (which usually means unaffiliated Tories), two Social Democrats, one Labour, one Liberal and one undeclared.

One of the more prominent Masons is John Ganzoni, the 2nd Lord Belstead, and government minister between 1970 and 1974 and 1979 and 1987. In 1988 he became leader of the House of Lords in succession to the Scots-born Viscount Whitelaw, who had been Mrs Thatcher's Deputy Prime Minister.

'To have two leaders of the Lords in succession, who are Freemasons is some achievement for a fraternity whose influence is generally believed to be on the wane,' observed Mr Short.

Lord Whitelaw's Masonic past is well documented, but in 1988 Mr. Short asked him directly whether he had maintained an active role in Freemasonry. Lord Whitelaw responded: 'I am in fact a Freemason and was a member of the Scottish Lodge, many years ago. I have never been an active Freemason since I entered the House of Commons in 1955.'

But according to both the 1990 and 1996 Grand Lodge of Scotland yearbook, the Viscount Whitelaw of Penrith is the Master of the District Lodge No. 623 St John (Jamaica).[399] He is also the Scottish Grand Lodge representative of the Sister Grand Lodge of New South Wales in Australia. To fill both positions Lord Whitelaw would be an active Mason and have maintained a level of activity to attain these leading positions.

One of Lord Whitelaw's close friends is the Duke of Argyll, who as well as being a Junior Grand Warden of the Grand Lodge of Scotland is also Master of her Majesty's Household Scotland.

This follows a long tradition of Royal Patronage of Freemasonry. King George VI was a keen member. The Duke of Edinburgh was initiated in the Navy Lodge No. 2612 in 1952, but claims he has since taken no active part.

However, the Duke of Kent, initiated in 1964, was made a Grand Master of the United Grand Lodge of England in 1967 and since then has been the originator of more openness in Freemasonry.

Among more than 14 Peers with Scottish titles or Scottish lands, identified by *The Scotsman* as Freemasons are: His Royal Highness Prince Michael of Kent; the current Grand Master of the Grand Lodge of Scotland, The Right Honourable Lord Burton of Dochfour; the Earl of Elgin and Kincardine (formerly Lord Bruce), a former Lord High Commissioner to the Gen Assembly of the Church of Scotland and the Past Grand Master; Lord Belhaven and Stenton; the Right Honourable Lord Swansea; the Right Honourable Earl of Balfour; a former East Lothian councillor; the Right Honourable Earl of Eglinton and Winton – whose residence is Perth – a Past Assistant Grand Master of the United Grand Lodge of England.

Freemasons in Scotland: Day 3
Police chiefs stay silent on Lodge openness

As a House of Commons select committee begins taking evidence into whether the police and judiciary south of the border should announce that they are Freemasons, Scotland's chief constables have refused to reveal if they are Lodge members.

The chief constable's decision has been criticised by MPs, who believe that public confidence in the police would increase if officers declared their membership of secret societies.

The Scotsman continues its investigation into Freemasonry in Scotland today with a look at the police, the law and business. [400]

In the grip of the craft[401]

Ten years ago, the right handshake was important for promotion in the Scottish police force. But has the influence of Freemasons declined in the last decade, and does the brotherhood have a mafia-like hold over small businesses in some parts of the country? In the third part of our investigation, Stephen Breen and Nic Outterside examine the reach of the Masons in two of the most sensitive areas.

Scotland's eight chief constables have been criticised by MPs campaigning for openness in the police for failing to disclose that they are Freemasons.

The House of Commons Home Affairs Select Committee begins taking written evidence this month about the influence of Freemasonry in the police and judiciary in England and Wales. It will examine whether police officers, magistrates and judges should be required to declare membership of secret societies.

To find out if the craft holds any sway within the police north of the border, *The Scotsman* wrote to each of Scotland's eight chief constables asking if they were Lodge members, but they declined to answer, referring the matter to the Association of Chief police officers in Scotland. ACPOS said that it was a 'private matter'.

However, Chris Mullin, the Sunderland Labour MP whose efforts secured the Home Affairs Select investigation disagrees. 'It is not a personal matter for chief constables if police officers won't admit they are members of secret societies. It damages public confidence in the police.'

The Labour MP for Edinburgh South, Nigel Griffiths, also expressed concerns: 'It does reinforce my worst suspicions that Freemasonry is something that could be abused, and people don't wish it to be made public. If they declared it would greatly clear the air.' Martin Short, the author of *Inside the Brotherhood*, has estimated that 20% of Britain's officers are Masons. He joined the criticism of Scotland's chief constables saying: 'it is unacceptable that police officers are allowed to be members of secret societies, while at the same time serving the public'.

Mr. Mullen said that police membership of Masonic lodges raised questions about whether they had direct communication with the suspects, influenced the course of investigations, resulting in Masonic criminals being protected from prosecution.

Jim Fraser, chairman of the Scottish Police Federation, said Freemasonry was not an issue among the police in Scotland and he saw no need for officers to declare if they were Lodge members. Twice in the past five years the Police Federation in England and Wales has rejected calls for officers to make it known if they are Masons – by 492 to 391 votes in 1993.

'I don't see any advantage to that,' said Mr. Fraser. The issue is: are police officers discharging their duties to the satisfaction of the public, the procurator fiscal and their superiors? If an officer is doing that, it doesn't matter if he is a Mason, a member of the Knights of St Columba [a Catholic organisation] or a member of a golf club.

'The public have to have confidence that if they have a complaint against a police officer, it will be dealt with properly, and the system is in place already.' The Police Complaints Authority (PCA), which investigates disciplinary cases south of the border told the Home Affairs select committee last December that all police officers should announce if they are Lodge members. This would remove 'lingering suspicions' of Masonic influences in the handling of investigations. There is no equivalent to the PCA in Scotland.

One senior Lothian and Borders officer said, 'the right handshake' was influential in police promotions even up to ten years ago, but equal opportunities legislation has greatly reduced the scope of Masons to elevate their brethren.

The officer said he suspected that in the past Masonic criminals might have been protected by policeman in the Lodge. He had dealt with complaints, which meant he saw some 'curious' decisions by the procurator fiscal not to prosecute. 'I've no concrete evidence, but some of the decisions really made you wonder.'

He had refused on several occasions to join a Lodge and believe his colleagues should be open about membership.

A college lecturer who previously conducted police promotional examinations for Scottish forces said Freemasonry and Protestant sectarianism hampered Catholic officers from rising through the ranks.

'The exams were an educational qualification pre-requisite to promotion, but because officers often had to wait for vacancies to occur, passing the exam did not necessarily mean instant promotion,' he said.

'What I noticed was that in the case of Catholic police officers they often had to wait until they had passed their inspectors' exam before even being considered for a vacancy as a sergeant.

In one division of an East of Scotland force complaints about it being a 'Bastion' of Freemasonry and Protestantism were met with the token promotion of a popular Catholic constable to sergeant, he said.

There have been no Masonic police corruption scandals in Scotland, but in England, hard evidence has emerged that some forces, particularly the Metropolitan police, are riddled with Freemasonry and that Lodge membership has been used.

In 1977, 13 Metropolitan police detectives were jailed for taking bribes whilst working for the pornography squad. Almost all were Masons, claims Martin Short.

In 1985 the then Metropolitan Commissioner, Sir Kenneth Newman, said he believed officers should quit the craft if they wanted to command the respect of their colleagues and the public in a passage in his pamphlet, *The Principles of Policing*, which was written by Newman's assistant commissioner, Albert Laugharne and stated: 'The police officer's special dilemma is a confluence of conflict between his service declaration of impartiality and the sworn obligation to keep the secrets of Freemasonry.

His declaration has its statutory obligation to avoid any activity likely to interfere with the impartiality or to give the impression that it may do so. A Freemason's oath holds inevitably, the implication that loyalty to fellow Freemasons may supersede any other loyalty.

'The discerning officer will probably consider it wise to forego the prospect of pleasure and social advantage in Freemasonry so as to enjoy the unreserved regard of all those around him.'

Lawyers figure prominently amongst the office-bearers listed in the 1996 Grand Lodge of Scotland yearbook, these include: Walter Sneddon; (Grand Committee, Grand Lodge); David A. Brittain (Law Agent to the Grand Lodge); Robert H. Allen, (Wishaw); James S. Grosset (Leven); David M. D. White (Milngavie).

Among numerous Masonic JPs are the following who are Office-bearers of the Grand Lodge: Iain MacLean (Grand Librarian); Rev. Joseph Moreau (Grand Jeweller); Roy Scott (Proxy Senior Warden); Gerald Leven (substitute Grand Master); Sir Ronald Orr Ewing (past Grand Master).

Opinions vary as to whether Freemasonry still has any influence within the law, but *The Scotsman* has found no evidence to suggest that it has any adverse effect within the Scottish legal system.

Glasgow lawyer Martin Smith said he had no personal experience of Freemasonry, but felt it still 'opened doors', although it was probably waning in influence.

'There are sheriffs who are Masons,' he said. 'A number of years ago, a sheriff said to me that on occasions an accused person or a witness made a comment which he was able to interpret as indicating that they wanted the sheriff to know they were Masons. But the sheriff assured me he wouldn't allow it to influence his handling of the case.'

One of Scotland's most senior judges, Lord McCluskey, said he had no reason to believe any High Court judge was a Mason. He had never been conscious of Freemasonry having any influence in the running of the Scottish judiciary.

An advocate who was formerly a Mason said he thought three of Scotland's 26 judges were Masons, but that the influence of masonry had died a death by the 70s.

Business Insiders
Unwritten Laws that Rule Traders

The leader of Scotland's small-business community described one experience of Freemasonry in a small town as like 'dealing with the mafia'.

Bill Anderson said the brotherhood appeared to have an all pervading influence in Argyll, reducing one Lodge member to a state of terror when he became involved in a dispute with one of his brethren.

Leading figures in the Scottish business community told *The Scotsman* that Freemasonry was virtually unheard of at the top of Scottish industry and commerce, but the craft does appear still to have a significant role in some small towns were Lodge membership can be seen as a pre-requisite for success in business.

Mr. Anderson, the Scottish secretary of the Federation of Small Businesses (FSB), said: 'the one time I dealt with the Masons it was like dealing with the mafia. It was over ten years ago in Argyll when a member of the local Masons was running a general shop, but he also started selling flowers. A high-up Mason decided that this was not fair because there was an unwritten law that they must not compete with one another, so he was informed that he should stop selling them. He said no and it was as if the bones were pointed towards him. He was totally ostracised and threatened with being banned from the Lodge. The Lodge was going to tell their members to stop buying produce from him.

'He was very upset and felt real fear, I'd never seen anything quite like it. He appealed to the Grand Master of Scotland, but it was a stonewall he was dealing with.

'My reaction would have been "two fingers" to the Masons, but he was very upset and said I didn't understand how important it was to his family for him to be in the Masons. He said it was just terrible.'

Mr Anderson, a secretary of the FSB, intervened on behalf of the businessman. He said he wrote to the leading Mason in Argyll and to the Grand Master Mason of Scotland, but he again 'met a stonewall'.

'It was made quite clear to me that there was nothing I could do about it. I can't think of any other organisation that could have that kind of hold over people. He was talking as if it was some kind of all-powerful organisation, and that's not healthy, because it inhibits free trade. If the Masons are not allowed to compete with one another in the open market

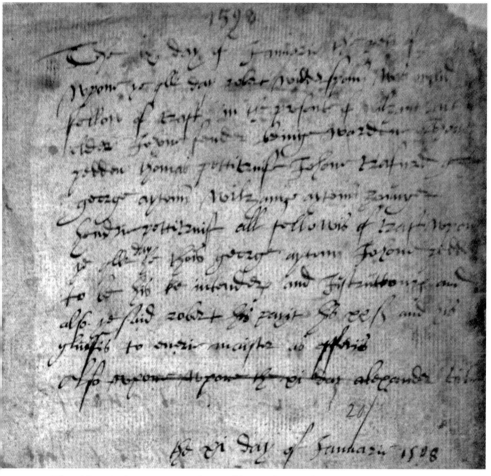

The oldest Lodge Minute in the world – Lodge Aitcheson's Haven Jan. 1599.

Late 17th century depiction of King Solomon's Temple.

Frontispiece of Anderson's *Constitutions* 1723.

Frontispiece from J. Scott's Pocket Companion. London, 1754.

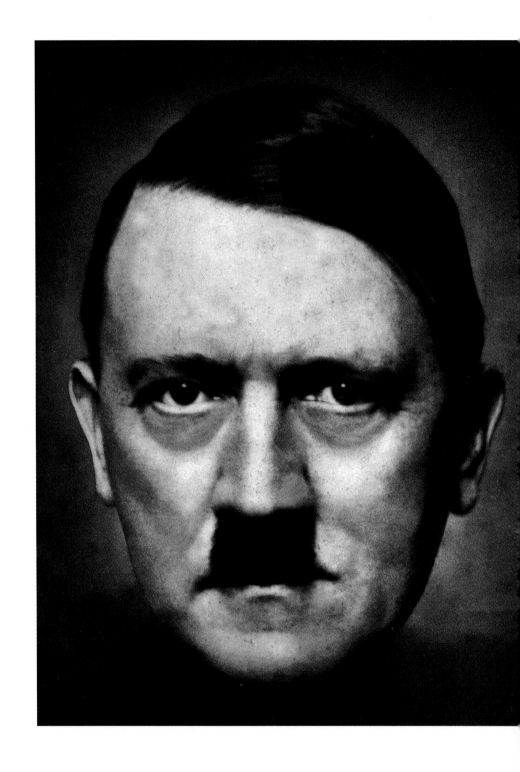

Hitler – persecutor of millions including Freemasons.

Trotsky, a Freemason, a Jew and a Bolshevik. 1921.

Freemasons, Churchill and Roosevelt, being balanced on a see-saw by a Jew. The Jews use Freemasonry to rule the world. Nazi (Serbia) anti-Semitic poster (c.1941)

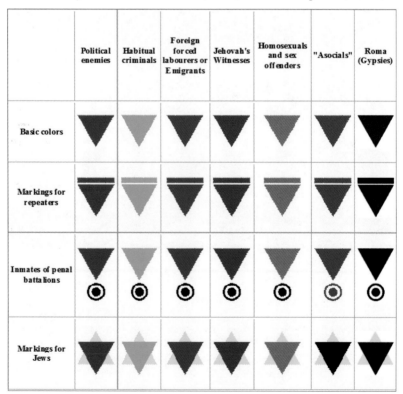

Concentration Camp Badges used to identify the wearer.

Nazi (Serbia) anti-Semitic and Masonophobic postage stamps issued in 1941.

The Duke of York, afterwards King George VI, after his Installation as Grand Master Mason. 1936

Black Freemasons initiated in Scotland in 1904.

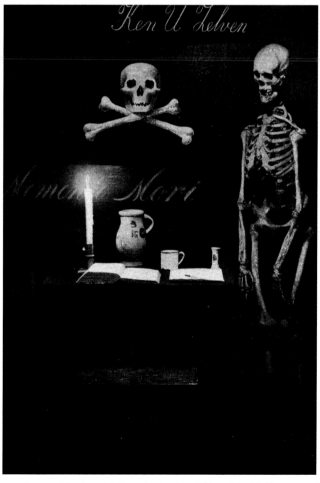
Image from a Nazi anti-Masonic book published in Holland. 1941.

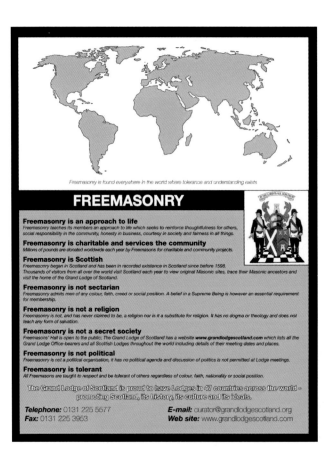

Briefing Notes issued by the Grand Lodge of Scotland
and published in the 'Holyrood Magazine.'

The Grand Lodge of Antient Free and Accepted Masons of Scotland

Caring and Sharing

Care Homes

In 1959 the Grand Lodge of Scotland opened its first care home for older people as part of its Charitable Works. The Organisation now owns facilities in central Scotland which are operated on a non-profit making and open referral basis.

The services comprise residential care, specialist residential care for those suffering from dementia, daycare, respite care and outreach care.

The philosophy of the Grand Lodge is that its services should be run to enable those who use them to have freedom of choice and flexibility, with the care and support being person-centred. The ultimate aim of the Organisation is that the experience of those who use its facilities is positive and meaningful so that their quality of life is enhanced.

Mrs Dawn Oliff,
Homes Superintendent,
Freemasons' Hall,
96 George Street,
Edinburgh,
EH2 3DH.

Telephone: 0131 225 5304
Facsimile: 0131 225 3953
E-mail: glhomes@grandlodgescotland.org
www.grandlodgescotland.com

MPs' fears over secrecy threat to democracy

THE VICTIM'S STORY

'I became a target . . . I was told it would be better if I left town'

THE CHURCHES

Conflict at heart of faith and Freemasonry

HEALTH SERVICE

An 'unhealthy influence' in medical world

Newspaper headlines from the time of the Dunblane Public Enquiry.

DUNBLANE APPEAL

The Grand Master Mason has asked me to indicate to the readers of our Year Book how the "Dunblane Tragedy Fund", organised by our Lodge of Dunblane No. 9, is progressing. The Brethren of The Lodge of Dunblane have given the greatest consideration as to how we, the Freemasons of Scotland, might commemorate the deaths of those involved in the sad tragedy at Dunblane Primary School on 13th March last year in an appropriate manner.

Having consulted with the Grand Master Mason, Grand Almoner and the Chairman of the Masonic Homes Committee, the Brethren of our Lodge of Dunblane have decided that the time is now right to put into action the several projects which they have in mind. In this connection, the commissioning of a piece of music for Dunblane High School has been progressed and this particular project is moving along satisfactorily.

Agreement has, also, been reached with most of the Churches within the Dunblane area for the installation of stained glass windows of commemoration. Due to restrictions imposed on one of the local Churches by its lease, such a window will not be able to be installed and that particular Church is arranging for the erection of a shrine within the Church as a token of remembrance. A donation will be made from the fund to meet all the costs of the stained glass windows and the shrine.

It is anticipated that the eventual costs in regard to these particular projects will not use up all the monies collected by the Lodge and by Grand Lodge by way of kind donation and, therefore, when a final account comes to hand in relation to these ongoing projects, further consideration will be given to an appropriate manner of using the balance of funds.

The Grand Master Mason is sure that all our readers will join with him in expressing their grateful thanks to the Brethren of The Lodge of Dunblane for the amount of work which they have undertaken in order to commemorate the very sad tragedy which took place in their Town and he is sure, also, that the heartfelt sympathy of every member of our Scottish Craft remains with those families who suffered as a result.

Grand Secretary,
February, 1997

Report of the Dunblane Appeal. 1997.

'Filth' A novel by Irvine Welsh. 1998.

A flyer for the play, *'Filth'*. 2001.

February 7, 2002
Conservative leader David McLetchie admits he was once a Mason.

David McLetchie was leader of the Scottish Conservative MSPs from 1999-2005

A 'Masonic angel' in Rosslyn Chapel.

An anti-Semitic postcard (nd.)

Anti-Scottish and anti-Semitic postcard (nd.)

Masonic Monkey. Daily Express. nd.

then that could extend to the awarding of contracts and could go into the council. That's very worrying.'

However, according to leading finance and industry figures, Freemasonry is virtually non-existent at a high level.

Sir Charles Fraser, formerly on the boards of United Biscuits, STV, Stakis and Scottish Widows, said: 'I'm not a Freemason nor have I come across it.'

Another senior Scottish business figure said: 'although I'm not a Mason, I get a few Masonic handshakes. The high seedlings come from distinguished families, but I would guess it's a bit downmarket these days.' Another influential Scottish businessman said: 'I knew business people in Scotland, who became members years before going to America. I don't think it's sinister, but it's prestigious there and you can get an entry into an excellent social circle.'

Fraser Morrison, chairman and managing director of Morrison construction said: 'I have never come across it playing any part at all in Scottish business.

'That may be an indication of how much influence it has. I couldn't quote a single Scottish businessman who is a member.'

Lord Weir, chairman of Weir group, said: 'It's not an issue that's ever come up at all.'

Dr George Mathewson, chief executive of the Royal Bank of Scotland, said: 'I'm not a Mason and I've never found any sinister influence, although like any other social activity, such as membership of golf or rugby clubs, it may oil the wheels of transactions.'

Another senior banking figure said he had heard rumours that Freemasonry was influential in Scottish banking 40 to 50 years ago, but he had no indication that it was important today.

The Victim's Story
'I became a target ... I was told it would be better if I left town.'
I moved to a Scottish town in the 1980s to start a business and quickly became aware that the local Freemasons have had an all pervading influence over the town, but local people said this was the way that things had always been done. I was told on numerous occasions that I would get nowhere in business 'unless I went along to the Lodge'.

Freemasonry came to my attention again when a man I knew joined the cartel of local Freemasons – builders who tendered for council contracts.

I built premises on land close to his premises, and I began to notice building materials were being delivered before the council tenders were open and decided.

In a later incident, a complete renovation was being carried out on the Masonic Lodge and I watched as Masons removed materials from the shed for the council renovations and took them to the Lodge.

The police asked if I knew anything about it and when I told them what I knew, they said they would be back, but that was the last I heard of it.

Until now, although the Lodge had a bar and is very busy with its weekly evening 'harmonies' (policeman, businessmen, council officials, councillors and so on), it did not have a drinks licence because of the overprovision of licences in the area. One non-Masonic club had an application for a drinks licence refused for this reason. When I phoned the police to report illegal drinking at the Masonic Lodge, a drinks licence was granted almost immediately.

I soon became a target of the Masons, I began to have almost weekly problems. I had a dispute with the Masons over the boundary of my present premises when my drains were deliberately blocked, my water pipe cut, and trenches dug to prevent access.

There was an altercation during which he attacked me, the policeman who came round was a Mason and suggested it would be better all round if I left town.

I was charged with breach of the peace and found guilty and the other man pled guilty to the same charge. I later discovered a passerby had seen the incident, but the police did not take the statement and told them to go away. I discovered his version of events was the same as mine, but he was not prepared to make a statement because he had to live in the town.

The procurator fiscal reinvestigated the case and told me he intended to write to the Crown office with a view to prosecuting the policeman who gave evidence at my trial for fabrication of evidence and perjury. Later I received a letter from the Crown office saying no further action would be taken.

I was subject to constant police harassment in one week and was stopped 17 times for a vehicle check when my van was checked over thoroughly, only to be stopped again 50 yards on, and the whole incident repeated.

The police sat outside my house with their blue light flashing and eventually targeted my young son. He was stopped by the police and told him they knew who his father was and that it would be easier for them to prove he did something bad than for him to prove he didn't.

Before reaching his teenage years, he was charged with theft and vandalism, assault and breach of the peace. On each occasion we insisted that the incident be investigated by an outside force and on each occasion the charges were dropped. In his first week of owning a car he was breathalysed three times. He is now in his 20s with no criminal convictions.

Freemasons in Scotland: Day 4
His Master's voice.

To outsiders, it's a secret society; to Lord Burton, 106th Grand Master Mason, it's no different from the golf club. In the final part of our investigation into Freemasonry, Stephen Breen and Nic Outterside talk to Scotland's highest Mason, and examine the craft's influence in churches and the health service.

Sitting in the imposing Grand Master's office at the Grand Lodge of Antient Free and Accepted Masons of Scotland, in Edinburgh, the country's top Freemason asserts that the craft is not a secret society, just a society with secrets.

Lord Burton, of Dochfour, an Eton-educated Inverness-shire landowner, is the 106th Grand Master Mason of Scotland. He follows in the illustrious footsteps of monarchs and some of the nation's most powerful aristocrats; King George VI served as Grand Master for a year until his accession to the throne in 1937 – as did George IV while he was Prince of Wales from 1806-20. The last incumbent who left office in 1993 was a brigadier Sir Gregor MacGregor of MacGregor.

Portraits of previous office-bearers look down on the large wooden table where the inner sanctum of this mysterious organisation, the Grand Lodge committee, holds its meetings.

A prominent member of the Scottish landowners Federation, Lord Buchan was initiated into Lodge Old Inverness Kilwinning St John's in 1952. After being asked by a friend he was attracted by its charitable works and was impressed by the treatment his father-in-law received at Masonic Hospital in England. He is one of 70,000 Masons in Scotland, under the jurisdiction of the grand Lodge, although he admits that membership is in marginal decline.

Flanked by the Grand Secretary, Martin McGibbon, Lord Burton refers *The Scotsman* to an article in a South African newspaper this year, which outlined the principles of Freemasonry. The Grand Master notes that in the picture used he looks like the Pope.

'It is a very old fraternal society,' he told the newspaper. A society of men concerned with the moral and spiritual virtues of members was to learn its precepts by means of ritual dramas, much of which is developed from the ancient Guild of stonemasons. The first condition of admission into membership of this order is belief in the Supreme Being. Membership is open to men of any race or religion, and of good repute.'

Few could argue with those sentiments, but over the years Freemasonry has been dogged by suspicions that some craft members abuse the Lodge to secure promotion, help or favours in business.

So was Lord Burton aware of any cases where membership has been abused? 'No. If you are a member of a Lodge, the same way as if you're a member of a club, and someone in that club is a tradesman, you say: "George, would you like to do a job?" Then you would know someone there who could be relied on, would that be fair?' The question is addressed to Mr McGibbon, who interjects throughout the interview to clarify the Grand Master's views.

Lord Burton cannot think of any occasions when Masons have abused the craft to help themselves or other brethren. 'We frown upon it being used in this way. There is not a great deal we could do about it if it did happen, but I don't know of any particular cases where it is likely to have been done.'

The Grand Lodge is tough with errant members, he says. 'Unfortunately there seems to be an increasing number of Masons we have up before us in our quarterly communications who are debarred from operating, some of them are disowned altogether.'

Mr McGibbon explains that anyone convicted of a criminal offence would be suspended or expelled, though he cannot provide any figures.

If he were faced with three job applicants with equal qualifications, one of whom was a Mason, would Lord Burton employ the Mason?

'It wouldn't influence me at all,' he replies, 'I would expect the Mason to be a man of good character, whereas I might not know about the other two.'

Lord Burton accepts that, in Scotland, Freemasonry is perceived to be an overwhelmingly Protestant craft, but, he points out, there are no religious bars to anyone joining.

He notes that there are Catholic, Jewish, Muslim and Hindu Masons throughout the world. Sadly Freemasonry has fallen foul of the church in recent years, with the free Church of Scotland saying it was incompatible with Christianity and the Church of Scotland asking its members to 'reconsider' their membership of the craft; Lord Burton firmly believes that it and Christianity are 'in no way incompatible'. In light of the *Scotsman* survey showing that the majority of Scottish male MPs believe that Freemasonry is either incompatible with open government or that MPs should declare their membership did the Grand Master believe MPs should do so? 'I would have thought it wasn't necessary, we don't discuss religion or politics.'

If a member of the public asked the Lodge for a membership list, would it provide it? 'The Lodge would not,' he begins, before Mr McGibbon interrupts to say: 'The Lodge would not, because, on the same basis, if you were to call Glasgow golf club and asked if I was a member they would be very unlikely to tell you.'

Lord Buchan does not hide his Freemasonry and would expect his friends to be open if he asked them if they were members of societies. 'I would have thought most Masons, if asked, would say 'Yes, I am' or 'no, I'm not'. You might be told, 'It is no business of yours.'

He did not believe the Lodge policy of not revealing membership lists generated suspicion among the public. Mr McGibbon says: 'I don't see how someone not telling you I was a member of a golf club would engender any suspicion.' To illustrate his claim that Freemasonry is not a secret society, Mr McGibbon points out that a Museum of Masonic Artefacts at the Grand Lodge headquarters in George Street, Edinburgh, is open to members of the public.

Lord Burton rejected a call from presidents past and current of the Confederation of Scottish Local Authorities for councillors to declare their Masonic membership, saying: 'I see absolutely no need for it, having been a Mason for nearly 50 years now and having been in local government, for well over 30 years, in that time. I've never seen any influence of masonry within local government.

'It's a society with some secrets. We have secrets by which we can recognise each other, but that doesn't mean to say we have any subversion.'

Health Service
An 'unhealthy influence' in the medical world
The names of doctors and surgeons are prominent in Masonic year books. Almost all London teaching hospitals have their own lodges, including Barts, Saint Thomas's and Kings College. One doctor listed seven senior surgeons and physicians whom he claimed 'ran' Guy's Hospital.

In Scotland, the influence of Freemasonry in the health service is less obvious there, with no evidence of specific hospital lodges, but Masonic membership is probably more widespread due to a classless ethos within the Scottish brotherhood, which allows everyone from consultant to hospital porter to belong to the same Lodge.

But while less obvious there, there have been occasions when Masonic influence appears to have risen to the surface.

In one instance villagers in Sutherland claimed Masonic influences protected the drunken local GP from being struck off by the General

Medical Council and also explain why more than 100 complaints to the Highland Health Board about his behaviour were ignored. The doctor, who often boasted that the Lodge protected the GP, eventually left the area, after a conviction for drink-driving and faulty prescribing made his position untenable. He is now practising in Australia.

This month, the House of Commons Home Affairs Select Committee will begin taking written evidence about the influence of Freemasonry in the police and judiciary.

Janet Anderson, the Labour MP for Rossendale and Darwen in Lancashire, who was a Select Committee member until last November, had wanted the committee's enquiry to be extended. 'We have a right to know if people in the health service are Masons,' she said at the time, but because the NHS is outside the committee's remit it cannot extend its enquiry.

Ray Rowden, a former director of the Institute of Health Services Management, says Freemasonry should be outlawed in the NHS. 'They parade their good works, but the whole thing is unhealthy,' he said. 'I have been approached twice to join. I also had colleagues told they should join if they want to advance their career – it is almost a veiled threat.'

A former female hospital doctor says Freemasonry is more evident now within management and medicine. She believes the Craft 'explains a great deal of the incomprehensible stuff going on inside the NHS'.

'I used not to be able to understand why some people were in jobs when they were clearly not performing very well,' she said. 'And then I discovered why – there was a whole different system operating; it is more insidious than the old boy network – Freemasonry is all about pulling strings.'

The 1996 Grand Lodge of Scotland Yearbook lists at least ten prominent Masons who are also doctors. These include Dr Iain Thomson, the medical adviser on Marine and Industrial Safety at Herriot-Watt University, and the Edinburgh dental surgeon Robin Jackson.

However, the retired GP, Hector Crawford Campbell, a past Deputy Grand Master of the Grand Lodge of Scotland and founder member of Lodge Loch Lomond, says he has never seen Freemasonry used to influence decisions within the health service.

'It provides a social function, and it's quite separate from what may or may not happen at work. The only benefit I have seen is that in the past, I knew most of my patients personally, as most were in the Lodge,' he said.

The Churches
Conflict at the heart of faith and Freemasonry.
Michael Paterson. *Religious affairs correspondent*

Freemasonry has had a rough ride from Scottish churches over the last decade, although it is estimated that more than half of Scotland's Masons are church members.

While the Roman Catholic Church has long banned its members from being Freemasons, Scottish churches put the craft under the microscope after the Methodists told its own members in 1985 not to become Freemasons.

In 1986, the Free Church of Scotland declared active membership of Freemasonry was 'incompatible with membership or office of the Christian Church'. The free Presbyterians upped the ante by describing the craft as 'anti-Christian and the works of darkness'.

It was in the Church of Scotland that the strongest debate raged. The Kirk – aware that thousands of members had an affiliation to the Church and the craft – undertook a two-year study into Freemasonry.

In 1989, it asked its members to reconsider involvement with Freemasonry. Its doctrine committee defended its decision not to brand faith and the craft incompatible. 'That is not the way we do things in the Church of Scotland, we leave it to people's consciences.'

But there were 'very real theological difficulties' with Freemasonry, the report claimed that the name of Jesus seemed to be suppressed in the Freemason worship.

The Rev. Donald MacDonald, who was later banned from practising as a minister, claimed that four former moderators were Freemasons and the Very Rev. Dr Peter Brodie was one of the Masonic moderators he referred to.

Among 17 other prominent clerics identified as Freemasons are the Reverend Joseph Morrow of Dundee, the Rev. George Gillen of Dunblane and the Rev. Ian Easton of Bearsden.

In 1989 the doctrine committee said: 'any system of morality claiming to be Bible-based, but shunning all mention of Christ is bound to be, for the Christian, seriously deficient.'

In some Masonic worship God is referred to as Jahbulon, a compound of the name of God in three or four languages. This is considered unjustified; other researchers have drawn comparisons between Jahbulon and Baal, a banned deity in the Old Testament.

The request for members to 'reconsider' their involvement did not lead to an appreciable drop in Masonic numbers, according to the Rev. Hugh

Mackay, minister at Duns in Berwickshire, who was a Kirk minister while Deputy Grand Master of the Grand Lodge of Scotland. 'I remember those who said: "The church has asked me to reconsider and I am staying put".

He said that there had been no conflict between his faith and his craft. While Freemasonry focused on God and not Jesus, he said: 'You could also say that about the Old Testament.' There were several specifically Christian Masonic orders in Scotland, he added. The term Jahbulon did not have much place in Freemasonry today, he said, it was a name corrupted by oral transmission.

However, the Rev. Bruce Gardner, formerly a Kirk minister at Carloway on Lewis and now a lecturer at a theological college in Lima, Peru, left the Masons because he was unhappy that it gave Christ 'a lower status of mere equality with other religious leaders'.

Mr. Gardner now says: 'Freemasonry has many worthy aims and motives, but it cannot be said to centre itself sufficiently on the uniqueness of Jesus Christ to be compatible with the historic Christian faith.'

The above represents another 'exposure' of Freemasonry and is essentially the same kind of 'analysis' (some might say an outright attack) of Freemasonry that has been taking place for more than 300 years (see Chapter 1). However, in the modern context this lengthy and sustained 'analysis' was published in a newspaper that had previously suggested that Freemasonry was, at the very least, partly responsible for the Dunblane massacre by protecting the Freemason Thomas Hamilton. What is more, this 'analysis' took place during the final week of the Public Inquiry which was charged with attempting to establish *all* the circumstances regarding the shootings at Dunblane Primary School. Given the length, depth and seriousness of the allegations made in the four-page analysis (above), one might have expected that the findings were passed to the Inquiry and that the writers concerned gave evidence. In fact only two journalists gave evidence, neither of whom had made any allegations of Masonic involvement in the Dunblane tragedy and nor did they offer any at the Inquiry.[402] The timing of this major press 'investigation' is suspicious but could possibly be coincidence. It is perhaps significant that during this extensive examination of the circumstances there is no reference to the alleged involvement of Freemasonry in the Dunblane tragedy, other than to say that Hamilton was not a Freemason. Yet within weeks of the Public Inquiry ending, the same newspaper began making the same allegations that it had made regarding Freemasonry and Dunblane *before but not during* the Public Inquiry.

In light of what Lord Cullen had to say about Freemasonry and Thomas Hamilton, the repetition of the allegations after the public enquiry report was published is worthy of note. Lord Cullen said:

> 'Thomas Hamilton harboured a long-standing grievance against the Scouts and the police. In the large volume of correspondence which he generated, a recurring theme is his assertion that the police were biased in favour of the "brotherhood of masons and that there was a "brotherhood" link between the Scouts and the police. In passing it may be noted that this together with evidence given by Mr Deuchars indicated that Thomas Hamilton had never been a freemason.
>
> 'I am satisfied that he was not a member of the masons.' [403]
> Lord Cullen, Paragraph 5.6.
> Public Inquiry Report.
> October 1996

Before examining the allegations of a Masonic conspiracy regarding Thomas Hamilton and Freemasonry, I would like to discuss the contents of the above newspaper articles. Firstly, I believe that a word analysis would helpfully demonstrate the overall attitude towards Freemasonry.

These terms have all been used in the press in connection with Freemasonry and reveal an overall impression of the perception the press conveys about Freemasonry. That conveyed perception is over-whelmingly negative. This, admittedly brief, word analysis can be divided into three main headings: descriptions of who Freemasons are and what they do; what they are alleged to do (and which is detrimental to groups or individuals); and, lastly, what is required to be done about that situation (which has the effect of turning the assumptions into fact). These three headings are discussed in more detail below.

A Past Master said...
Abused a position
Alleged Masonic link
Allegations fuel public suspicion
Anonymous telephone tip-offs
Applicants to be asked if they are Masons
Bastions of Freemasonry police, military, judiciary etc.
Bizarre ritual
Charmed life Thomas Hamilton

Dozens of Freemasons contacted, all refused to comment
Influence undue
Forced to register membership
Freemasonry might have been an influence
Freemasons show favours to Masons
Local government
Masonic conspiracy
Many members are lawyers
Mutual aid
People in authority
Police and criminals bound together by Freemasonry
Police protecting
Pressure to reveal membership
Protect each other
Put their private interests before the public good
Rumours that he was a Mason
Secret
Secret society
Senior police source said...
Senior police officer said to be a Freemason
Should be compelled to reveal if they are members of secret societies
Should be forced to declare if they are Freemasons
Staff should declare membership of secret societies
Suspicions about favouritism
They feel, because they are not Masons...

Who are the Freemasons?

From the above, we can conclude that Freemasons are claimed to be involved in certain occupations such as the police, the judiciary and politics. The implication is that it is wrong or bad for a Freemason to be in these occupations and professions.[404] Whilst there are undoubtedly some Freemasons who are members of these occupational groups, there is an assumption, which is never challenged, that being a policeman (say) and a Freemason is not desirable. However, that undesirability is rarely, if ever, explained in detail other than to say that *because* Freemasons all take the same obligation that therefore commits them to look after each other to the detriment of everyone else. The fact that the obligation contains the words 'respect for the law etc...' is never mentioned. What we are left with instead is a vague notion, repeated over and over again, that 'Freemasons are in it for themselves' and that they do not care for anyone else. The fact that Freemasons donate millions to charities every year contradicts this, but this is inconvenient to those who hold entrenched views and so usually dismiss charitable giving by Freemasons as a 'smokescreen'.[405] The fact that Freemasons provide care facilities for older people (whether or not the residents are Freemasons) is also rarely mentioned. This absence of positive reports of Freemasonry suggests a desire to present it in a negative light while ignoring any positive contributions made by Freemasons. The focus of the press, as evidenced above, is on people who are in occupations of responsibility, authority, influence and (perhaps) power. The implication of this is that Freemasons in general abuse their position in favour of their friends and relatives, to gain unwarranted income and, ultimately, to create a New World Order.

It is noticeable that almost all press commentary on Freemasonry focuses on public servants, not on people working in the private sector. Here then, I believe that we can see a political agenda at work. Politicians, of whatever 'favour' have control of the public services (judiciary, Customs & Excise, armed forces, local government, for instance). They also have limited influence over non-public bodies, and by that I mean private companies. Government influence over private companies is exercised in a different manner – by legislation, taxation and regulation. However, it cannot demand that private companies ask their employees if they are Freemasons. To do so would be to expose a political rather than an economic agenda. To further emphasise the point: there are no demands that bus drivers, toilet attendants or office cleaners declare if they are Freemasons. You will also notice that I am discussing politics in a general and non-specific manner which is within the self-imposed limitation adopted by all Freemasons.[406]

What Freemasons do

More important is the prior assumption that Freemasons act in a certain way *because* they are Freemasons. This is something that is not (now) applied to any other minority group in society. For example, no one argues that because people are members of a particular fraternity (for example the Knights of St. Columba, the Free Gardeners or the Speculative Society) therefore all their actions in life are predetermined by their membership of these groups.[407] By pre-judging them in this manner they are stigmatised without the ability to defend themselves as would normally be granted to other minority groups. Thus, Freemasons are judged not on the basis of what they actually do, but on the perception of what they do.

Given the gravity of what *The Scotsman* newspaper uncovered (mass murder; corruption; intimidation; bribery; threatening behaviour;

perverting the course of justice and blackmail, etc.), one would expect that the newspaper and/or the journalists concerned would have reported the crimes they had uncovered to the authorities. They did not. Enquiries revealed that none of the allegations made in the above reports (or any others for that matter) were reported. As those individuals, cited in the above reports, who supposedly made the allegations are unnamed, it is not possible to establish if they themselves reported the alleged offence. Enquiries to the Scottish authorities asking if anyone, or any organisation, had made a complaint that alleged offence, crime, discrimination or conspiracy was due to Masonic involvement found that no such complaints had been made. But according to the press (and other parts of the media, of which more later,) the country is permeated by Freemasons who control and manipulate almost every aspect of society. I simply pose the question – is that credible?[408] If so, then almost every event in Scottish life can be laid at the door of Freemasonry, for example:

The cost over-run of the Scottish Parliament building.[409]

The Monklandsgate scandal.

Planning permission for Donald Trump to build his mega golf and hotel complex.

The Dunblane Primary School shootings (see the above newspaper reports).

The decision to install a tram line in Scotland's capital.

Failure of the Mitsubishi plant in Fife to become operational.

The Lockerbie disaster.[410]

'Fitting up' the Birmingham Six.

Similar accusations have been made over the years at a European and International level. For example:

Freemasons assassinated President John F. Kennedy.

Freemasons faked the moon landings.

Freemasons killed Princess Diana.

Freemasonry 'organised' the recent world financial meltdown.

Freemasons were responsible for the French Revolution.

Freemasons were responsible for the Russian Revolution.

Freemasons were responsible for the Spanish Civil War.

Freemasons were responsible for Germany losing WW1.

Freemasons were responsible for the outbreak of Spanish Flu in 1918.

When considered in this context, I would hope that people who are not Freemasons will begin to appreciate how Freemasons feel when they read this kind of material.[411] That aside, this pattern of victimisation at a national level (and Scotland is a small country) may be representative of the kind of treatment Freemasonry receives in other parts of the world.

What's to be done about the Freemasons?

The kind of press reports discussed here provided 'proof' to many people of the true extent of Masonic influence in Scotland. This 'proof' shows that Freemasons control the economy, police forces, local and national government, the military, the NHS, banks and business (large and small). It has been publicly stated that every Prime Minister of Britain has until recently been a Freemason![412] On the basis of this type of 'proof', people and groups from various sectors of Scottish society wrestled with how to 'deal' with the problem. First and foremost, they had to be identified, as without knowing who 'they' are, nothing can be done to deal with them.

A vote on devolution of certain powers to a Scottish Parliament took place in September 1997. The Scotland Act was passed in 1998 and a Scottish Parliament was established following parliamentary elections in 1999.[413] One of the innovative and much applauded initiatives was the creation of a Public Petitions Committee (PPC), which invited citizens to submit petitions on any matter relevant to Scotland and within the powers devolved to the new parliament. These petitions would be processed by the PPC.[414 415] The intention was to allow people to have a direct input to the new Scottish Parliament, the idea was taken up with gusto and petitions were submitted on a huge range of subjects.[416] However, there was an unexpected side effect that impacted on Scottish Freemasonry. Petitions began to be received from people wishing to have legislation enacted to 'expose' Freemasons. The initial occupational focus was on the Scottish Judiciary and a petition submitted to the PPC in November 2000 read:

'Petition calling for the Scottish Parliament to request that all members of the Judiciary declare membership of organisations such as Freemasons and that such a register be made available on request.'[417 418]

The main purpose of an historian in examining past events is to try and attempt to identify patterns, as such patterns can occasionally reveal possible motives. It is most interesting to note that, prior to the above mentioned petition being submitted to the PPC, it was under active discussion in the press and media for more than a month. In other words, the subject of the petition was being debated in the public domain before the petition had even been written. Some might suggest that smacked of attempting to gain, at the very least, publicity prior to the petition being presented or, at the most, attempting to influence those who would consider the petition before they might normally have done so.[419]

One specific example will serve to illustrate this point. The programme: *Newsnight Scotland,* broadcast on BBC2 television on 18 October 2000, interviewed the petitioner at length about his demand to know if the judge who would be hearing his case was a Freemason. The programme explained that this legal challenge was being made under article 14 of the European Convention on Human Rights:

'Prohibition of discrimination.

'The enjoyment of the rights and freedoms set forth in this Convention shall be secured without discrimination on any ground such as sex, race, colour, language, religion, political or other opinion, national or social origin, association with a national minority, property, birth or other status.'[420]

There is no need to provide details of the programme other than to note that it was clear that the challenge to the judge to disclose membership of Freemasonry was merely the first step in creating a public register of all Freemasons in public service.[421] When the representative of the Scottish Centre for Human Rights was asked:

'If this were to go through it would not just stop at judges and sheriffs, would it? It would not just all be down to the police, but it could be all public servants, because anyone could be said to be biased?'
'It will.'[422]

Here then we can see the extent of the debate. Everyone who was employed in serving the public even indirectly would be required, by law, to declare if they were Freemasons or not.[423]

In the years following, there were approximately nine other petitions of a similar nature seeking, in one way or another, to have Freemasons identified. Initially the concern was with members of the judiciary, but this soon escalated to calls for all Freemasons who were in public service to be forced to declare membership of the Order regardless of what position they held. As has been discussed in previous chapters, the first step in creating a scapegoat group is identify a problem (in this instance a potential problem), then establish who is responsible for the (potential) problem and then force them to declare their membership. Freemasons have long memories, and as this suggestion was very reminiscent of the process used by the Nazi regime in Germany, it is no surprise that Scottish Freemasons were bitterly disappointed that this was being actively considered. It is of interest to note that this story was being discussed in the media before the new Scottish Parliament had been petitioned.[424]

The petition was considered on 19 December and the petitioner was invited to appear at the committee meeting to provide details of the reasons behind his petition. Part of the minutes of that meeting of the PPC reads:

> Mr M: 'We need a register of judges who are masons in order to judge whether they are biased.'
>
> Committee Member: 'The basis of your petition is unsubstantiated allegations.'
>
> Mr M: 'Absolutely.'
>
> Committee Member: 'You must have reasons for bringing the petition to the committee. If you have no examples, we are left with allegations.'
>
> Mr M: 'You are quite right. No judge in the country has been convicted of freemasonic bias.'[425]

The petitioner introduced Freemasonry into the Scottish political world early in the life of the new parliament, and subsequent petitions (some of which are discussed below) submitted on a regular basis ensured that Freemasonry was kept in front of politicians over a long period of time.[426]

The petitioner reveals something that I, and many other Freemasons, have suspected for a very long time – Masonophobia is based on an irrational fear (a phobia) of the Order. This irrational fear is based on perception, on not knowing 'something' and a belief that 'unknown forces' were conspiring to do him harm by judging the criminal charges against him in a biased way. That said, he openly admits that, 'The basis of your [his] petition is unsubstantiated allegations.' He also reveals that he wants a register of Freemasons who are judges in order that they might be judged as to whether or not they are biased, and here we come close to one of the fundamental problems – does anyone have the right to 'judge' the activities of anyone's private life? Politicians of all shades have repeatedly claimed that what they do in their private life cannot be used to judge their political decisions, and in the main that has been accepted other than in cases where their private activities go beyond the pale (such as soliciting a prostitute or committing perjury). The latter examples are 'beyond the pale' because there is an element of criminality involved. However, we can see that Freemasons who are judges (in this particular example) are not being allowed that same self defence.[427] But this committee debate confirms another fundamental problem for Freemasons – proof of guilt is not considered to be a requirement in demanding that they be 'exposed' by means of a public register. As far as I am aware, the only group in British society considered in this way is Freemasons. Let me make the point even more forcibly.

Paedophiles have been found guilty of one of the most heinous crimes in modern society. The abuse of children is seen as striking at the very heart of our civilisation, and consequently they are considered to be the ultimate pariahs. They have been detected, arrested, processed through the legal system and punished quite often by a prison sentence. Their names and addresses are placed on a sex offenders' register and they are monitored for the rest of their lives. However, the register is confidential and no member of the public has access to it. In other words, despite being the most despicable of criminals, the state protects their privacy. This is in complete contrast to what we have here: an attempt to have Freemasons, who have been found guilty of no crime, in fact have not even been accused of any crime, named in a public register![428] In other words, everyone except Freemasons is judged on the basis of facts, but Freemasons are to be judged on the basis of perception only. Of utmost importance is that this means that Freemasons are deprived of all rights to defend themselves, for it is not possible to fight proposed legislation which is based on perception. It denies the Freemason the right to have his day in court, a right enjoyed by every other individual in this country. [429] This method of 'dealing' with minority groups has been used in the past and led directly to the gas chamber.

The petition mentioned above was referred to another committee known as the Justice 2 Committee for their observations, and they in turn sought advice from the then Minister for Justice – Mr Jim Wallace.[430] They did so because new procedures for judicial appointments were under consideration by the Minister for Justice and this issue might be considered for inclusion in that new procedure. The minute of the Justice 2 Committee of 29 January 2003 states:

'The Committee considered PE306 [the petition number] by Mr M. on Freemasonry and the judiciary. The Committee agreed to take no further action on this petition. However, if the petitioner was able to provide evidence of further specific cases where difficulties have arisen over the question of Sheriff/Judicial membership of the Freemasons the Committee would consider revisiting the matter.'

The next meeting of the PPC received the advice (above) from the Justice 2 Committee, 11 February 2003, and decided to write to the petitioner asking if he had any 'evidence of further specific cases where difficulties have arisen over the question of Sheriff/Judicial membership of the Freemasons...' The petitioner provided additional material which was considered by the PPC at its next meeting.

In reply to a written question on the same issue, the Minister of Justice replied that the Judicial Oath taken by judges was sufficient to ensure the inpartiality, and proposed no further action.[431]

All of the above might be considered to be a bit of a yawn, but I do not apologise for reproducing it here as it sets the scene for subsequent events. I believe that this serves two important functions.[432] Firstly, to provide some brief material that indicates some of the political perceptions of Freemasonry and places them into their time context. Secondly, to suggest individual motives and perceptions which give rise to Masonophobia. I can only provide a few examples here of the attitudes of some politicians regarding Freemasonry, but they are indicative of a general attitude. (These ought, I believe, to be available for future reference.[433]) For example, the Convener of the PPC expressed 'sympathy' with the petition but the Committee had decided otherwise. This expression of 'sympathy' was stated despite the previously recorded fact that the petition was based on 'unsubstantiated allegations', something that the petitioner himself had acknowledged.

In between the petition being submitted and a final conclusion being reached in 2003, the press reported at length on the issue and I was increasingly aware that, despite the view of the parties and committees involved in this issue, no further action was required to be taken on this petition. The press continued to take an opposite view.[434]

In the same year that the petition discussed above was dismissed by the PPC, another was submitted to the same committee:

'Petition calling for the Scottish Parliament to introduce legislation requiring that anyone involved in legal proceedings must declare membership of secret societies such as the Freemasons.'[435]

The scope of this petition, albeit from a different individual, adds more Freemasons who are to be 'required' to reveal their membership of the Order. Instead of targeting Freemasons who might be members of the judiciary, this petition calls on the Scottish Parliament to demand, by means of legislation, that 'anyone involved in legal proceedings must declare membership of secret societies such as the Freemasons'. The number of people tempted by proposed legislation would now range from the 'bobby on the beat', to all judges, solicitors in private practice and a huge number of civil servants engaged, directly or indirectly, in the legal process. For example it would include:

Scottish Government Legal Directorate
Scottish Prison Service
Government Legal Service for Scotland
Lord Advocate and Solicitor General for Scotland[436]
Directorate for Criminal Justice
Directorate for Constitution, Law and Courts
Court staff
Prosecution and defence witnesses

The PPC decided to send the petition to the Justice 2 Committee 'for information' but, despite this apparent dismissal by the PPC of the petition by sending it on to another committee of the parliament, it served to keep the issue alive within the machinery of government. Shortly afterwards, the committee decided to take no further action regarding this petition.

These decisions did not stop more petitions being submitted and, as they covered a period in excess of five years, they served to keep the 'pot boiling' and, despite the best efforts of the Grand Lodge of Scotland nearly all attempts to correct the worst errors and false allegations were unsuccessful. It cannot fail to be noticed that those submitting petitions seeking in different ways to curtail, identify or otherwise 'expose' Freemasons and their activities were always permitted to present their case in full, often in person before the PPC. The Grand Lodge of Scotland was never able to present the view on behalf of the Freemasons of Scotland.[437] That a minority group (Freemasons) were the subject of such intense investigation and public discussion without being afforded the right to represent their views as citizens is of concern enough, but there is also a 'democratic deficit' to consider. Some of those submitting petitions to the PPC were not resident in Scotland.[438] In other words people who did not reside in Scotland were allowed to submit petitions, which could lead to action being taken against citizens resident in Scotland, while at the same time those very same citizens were denied the right to present their side of the argument. I confess that, given that this 'democratic deficit' so glaringly disenfranchised Freemasons living in Scotland, I assumed, naively, that when it was brought to the attention of those responsible for administering our new form of devolved democracy, they would instantly recognise the serious nature of this problem. Having communicated with the clerk of the PPC, the author was taken aback at the reply to the effect that no one in the Scottish Parliament considered this to be in any way a problem! One might be forgiven in thinking that this is yet another example of Masonophobia, and it is difficult to think of another minority group in modern society which is treated in this dismissive manner.[439] There is one other consequence that is not appreciated by many, including Freemasons themselves, and that is that their opinions are nowhere to be found within official records. If one examines the Scottish Parliament website and searches for 'Freemasonry' or similar terminology (Masons, Masonic, Freemasons etc), then all that is found is information provided by Masonophobes. The voices and opinions of 'ordinary' Freemasons are nowhere recorded. Here is revealed the inherent weakness of Freemasonry in modern society: a minority group is deprived of normal protection within a so-called liberal western democracy. Sadly, the aspirations of the Scottish Parliament appear to have failed – at least so far as an apolitical minority group, Freemasonry, is concerned.

The Queen opened the new Scottish Parliament on 1 July 1999 after which, Donald Dewar (1937–2000) made comments which included the following:[440]

'The past is part of us. But today there is a new voice in the land, the voice of a democratic Parliament. A voice to shape Scotland, a voice for the future.

'Walter Scott wrote that only a man with soul so dead could have no sense, no feel of his native land. For me, for any Scot, today is a proud moment; a new stage on a journey begun long ago and which has no end. This is a proud day for all of us.

'A Scottish Parliament. Not an end: a means to greater ends. And those too are part of our mace. Woven into its symbolic thistles are these four words:

'**Wisdom. Justice. Compassion. Integrity.**

'Burns would have understood that. We have just heard – beautifully sung – one of his most enduring works. At the heart of that song is a very Scottish conviction: that honesty and simple dignity are priceless virtues, not imparted by rank or birth or privilege but part of the soul.

'Burns believed that sense and worth ultimately prevail. He believed that was the core of politics; that without it, ours would be an impoverished profession.

'Wisdom. Justice. Compassion. Integrity.' Timeless values. Honourable aspirations for this new forum of democracy, born on the cusp of a new century.' [441] [Emphasis added]

With these words, the man whom many believe to have been the main architect of Scottish devolution, Donald Dewar, opened the new parliament. It is ironic that he quoted two Freemasons: Robert Burns (1759–1796) and Sir Walter Scott (1771–1832). No Freemasons, not even the Grand Lodge of Scotland, as one of the oldest institutions of the country, were invited to the opening ceremony. Freemasonry has been part and parcel of Scottish history and culture since at least 1598. [442] I have heard it said that some political parties (and some religious groups) are intent on a form of 'ethnic cleansing', meaning the destruction of parts of Britain's history, culture and social activity, because it does not suit those in power who hold a prejudicial view of certain groups. [443] If this seems to be provocative then the aim has been achieved – why should a particular group in the UK today be treated in this manner? As Freemasonry is an apolitical, non-religious body but it is attacked from these very same bases, it appears that these attacks are made for political and/or religious purposes. This is a theme to which I shall return in the conclusion.

In order to demonstrate the 'system' at work again, we turn to a petition lodged with the Scottish Parliament. The last petition submitted to the PPC of the Scottish Parliament which related to Freemasonry was on 14 January 2006. [444]

However, there were two other issues under discussion during this period which were to have an effect on Freemasonry. The first was local and the second European.

The first of these concerns the standards expected of MSPs in the conduct of their affairs. These had been drafted prior to the Scottish Parliament being officially opened in 1999, but in light of the early experiences of that new body it was recognised that the rules governing the conduct of MSPs required some revision. Proposals for new legislation governing the declaration of members' interests were published by the Scottish Parliament's Standards Committee on 19 February 2002. The Standards Committee invited comments from all interested parties and a large number were submitted. I do not intend to go into these to the same extent as I have with the Masonophobic petitions discussed above. However, there are a few pertinent comments to make that will provide some understanding of why this is equally important and how the European aspect later became part of the consultation process. Briefly, many of the comments submitted demanded that all MSPs must be made to declare whether they were Freemasons.[445] Frequently, the submissions included demands that details of all those who were Freemasons must be made available in a public register, or that other restrictions must be placed upon them and their activities, and some went so far as to demand that Freemasons could not be MSPs at all.

As has been repeatedly said in this book, Freemasons cannot become involved in politics *as* Freemasons. It is therefore not possible to *instigate* any activity which might be construed as political. However, if Freemasonry is approached and asked to comment (this is a function of Grand Lodge), then the example of providing an interview for the magazine *Life and Work*, mentioned above, is an indication of what is acceptable. What is not acceptable, for example, is commenting on a particular system of government or its policies.

During the course of the PPC's deliberations on the dozen or so petitions which in some way involved Freemasonry, the Grand Lodge of Scotland was not once asked to present evidence. This seemed to be most odd, as third parties involved in petitions were often invited to give evidence either in writing or in person to the committee. The importance of this will be explained shortly.

The Holyrood Magazine is an independent magazine specialising in news, views and interviews about the Scottish political scene. In the knowledge that the Standards Committee were to ask for public input into revising the Code of Conduct for MSPs, the magazine commented that Freemasonry was thought to be incompatible with democracy. Grand Lodge was asked to comment and its response was published in the issue of 26 February 2002 reproduced in full below:

'Freemasonry and Democracy' by the Grand Secretary of the Grand Lodge of Antient Free and Accepted Masons of Scotland

Whilst Freemasonry as an institution is, and always has been, strictly non-political and non-religious, we always have had amongst our membership individuals who were active in political life and in the various religions of the world.

I would emphasise that our membership includes individuals from all the World's faiths, including Christians of all denominations and we always have had, over the years, members of the various political parties active at the time.

I am delighted when members of our Order, including those in prominent public positions, such as MSP's, voluntarily choose to acknowledge their membership of our Order. Freemasons are encouraged in terms of our own 'Rules and Regulations' to acknowledge their membership on all proper occasions but I do have difficulty with any form of compulsion being placed upon individuals to 'force' them to register or declare their Masonic Membership.

Democracy and Freemasonry are found together wherever governments believe in tolerance and the right of citizens to a private life, including Freedom of Association.

The first President of the United States, George Washington, was a Freemason. Indeed, it was Freemasons from Edinburgh, who were also stonemasons, who built The White House; a Scotsman, who was Grand Master of the Freemasons of New York, laid the foundation stone of the Statue of Liberty and many Scottish Freemasons have made a lasting contribution in other democracies, for example in Canada, New Zealand and India.

Many famous Scots were proud to have been Freemasons, for example, Robert Burns, Sir Walter Scott, Adam Smith and very many more.

However, it should be borne in mind that for every famous individual who was, or is, a Freemason there were, and are, many, many more 'ordinary' members drawn from all walks of life.

Many old Scottish Lodges, such as George Washington's, are still in existence and are cherished by the Freemasons in those countries.

Scottish Lodges exist in countries as diverse as: Malaysia, New Zealand, Australia, South Africa, Botswana, Jamaica, Chile and India – to name but a few. However, there is not a single continent where Scottish Freemasonry does not exist. Scottish attitudes and culture are therefore disseminated across the democratic world and Freemasons in these countries are proud to be Scottish Freemasons.

Freemasons (whether Scottish or otherwise) throughout the world look to Scotland as being the home of Freemasonry. Each year many thousands visit this country to attend meetings of the Grand Lodge of Scotland and the Masonic Lodges here 'at home', making a useful contribution to our national tourist industry.

That said, in living memory, regimes which have suppressed Freemasonry have included Hitler's Germany, Franco's Spain, Mussolini's Italy and Stalin's Soviet Union.

The suppression of Freemasonry in those countries began with a seemingly innocuous request from the 'authorities' for a list of Freemasons in public service – the police, judiciary, civil service, etc, and I hope that your readers, therefore, can understand why Freemasons are gravely concerned that they may be, in this liberal democracy of ours, compelled to disclose their membership.

The German Gestapo had a special section to 'deal' with Freemasons just as it had sections to 'deal' with other groups and whilst, in comparison to some of those other groups, Freemasonry was numerically small, very many Freemasons were tortured and executed but, unlike other persecuted groups, the Freemasons are seldom mentioned.

All Freemasons are taught that their responsibilities to the organisation come a long way behind their duties to their family, their civic responsibilities, their faith, and their occupation. Thus a question posed to a Judge as to his impartiality because he is a Freemason is spurious, for it is clear that the duties and responsibilities of a Judge would, at all times, take precedence.

Freemasons' Hall (including our Museum and Library) at 96 George Street, Edinburgh, EH2 3DH (telephone 0131 225 5304) is very much open to the public.

The Grand Lodge of Scotland website is:
www.grandlodgescotland.com

These are hardly the trappings of a "secret" society.

The existence of Freemasonry is sometimes likened to a 'litmus test' of democracy, a test of 'democratic health' if you like, and I am sure that for Scotland to be placed in a position where it could be compared with countries with intolerant regimes, countries that have a poor human rights record and have persecuted or have suppressed Freemasonry, would be distasteful to the large majority of Scots. Across the world, Scottish Freemasons would be appalled and people throughout world would, in my view, consider Scotland to have failed, abysmally, this 'test' of democracy.

Freemasonry has been part of Scottish society and culture for well over 400 years. Indeed, the oldest Masonic record in existence is held within our building here in Edinburgh, and is dated 1598. It is an ongoing record, so to speak, and proves the existence of Freemasonry here, in Scotland, well before that date.[446]

During all this time Freemasons have attended Masonic meetings, raised money for charity and encouraged one another to be better citizens.

All this has been done quietly and without fuss.

It is surely ironic that the tradition of quiet good works, liberty and Freedom of Association so valued by Scottish Freemasons is now being used to argue for the removal of that Freedom by some of those who ultimately are charged with protecting the rights of all citizens.

Voluntary acknowledgement of membership – no problem!
Compulsory lists – no thank you!

As might be imagined, this caused quite a stir. After years of Freemasons being unable to get their message across here was a magazine that allowed them to do so![447] The Freemasons were no longer remaining silent! No one realised that until then Freemasons had been denied a public voice – but then why would they?

Not only did this alert the media that Freemasons were prepared to defend themselves and had found an avenue to do so, but it also showed that the media 'blockage' could be bypassed. Every issue of *The Holyrood Magazine* carries 'Briefing Notes' by a host of diverse organisations such as charities, trade unions, international businesses, pressure groups etc. In March 2004 *The Holyrood Magazine* was to publish an issue with the theme 'Arts and Culture' (in Scotland) and as these subjects do not fall into the realm of religion or politics, Grand Lodge thought that it would be worthwhile providing some information about the contribution that Freemasonry had made to the cultural life of the nation over time. (See picture section)

The reaction of the press was something of a shock, as the very next day Freemasonry was accused in a front page headline of trying to recruit MSPs! See below:

Masons out to woo MSPs
The Freemasons, one of Scotland's most secretive organisations, is enticing new members by advertising in a magazine aimed at politicians.

The Grand Lodge of Antient Free and Accepted Masons of Scotland has put a notice in the latest edition of *Holyrood*, the Scottish Parliament magazine.

A spokesman for the Freemasons insisted the notice was not designed to promote recruitment and was merely done to promote the work of the organisation.

However, by setting out what the Freemasons do, naming famous former Freemasons and including a contact number and address, the notice does appear to be the next best thing to a recruitment advertisement.

Two years ago Tricia Marwick, the SNP MSP, called for all MSPs to register their membership of the organisation, to prevent a conflict of interest during their public duties.

Bob Cooper, curator of the library at Freemasons' Hall, Edinburgh, said: 'We don't recruit.

'We are pointing out that we have a history we are very proud of and we would welcome people to contact us to find out more about what we do.'

He added: 'The magazine has a very strong focus on arts and culture. We are pointing out that Freemasons are part and parcel of Scottish history.'

Freemasons have about 660 lodges in Scotland.[448]

The *Edinburgh Evening News*, part of the same newspaper group, also reported the day following the 'Briefing Notes' and it too focused on the supposed attempt of Freemasons to recruit MSPs.[449]

Freemasons deny MSP recruiting bid

Scotland's Freemasons today denied hoping to recruit members by advertising in a magazine read by Holyrood politicians.

The latest edition of *Holyrood Magazine* includes an advertisement placed by the Grand Lodge of Antient Free and Accepted Masons of Scotland, the organisation's official name, listing famous masons.

But Bob Cooper, curator of the library at Freemason's Hall in Edinburgh, said the aim was to show the part played by masons in Scotland's cultural life. 'Each issue has a particular theme, and the theme of this issue is the arts and culture,' he said. We are simply letting people know that people such as Sir Walter Scott and Arthur Conan Doyle were Freemasons. We are pleased to be part of the cultural scene – it's as simple as that.'

Mr Cooper said the masons had previously advertised in the same magazine when it focused on issues like health and the elderly.

This extreme reaction suggested that a raw nerve had been touched. My understanding is that some members of the press were incensed that Freemasons had found a way of bypassing them, the mainstream print media. They were now in the position of having to react to the views of Freemasons which were appearing in print first.[450] It seems also that attempting to be open undermined the position of those accusing Freemasonry of being secretive and this was something they did not like.

This and subsequent 'Briefing Notes' (See Plate 14) also had the effect that people and institutions began to realise that Freemasons would speak about Freemasonry but only under circumstances which, to a non-Mason, appear bizarre, by not engaging in political and religious matters and not instigating debate. However, the appearance of these briefing notes did bring the attention of certain institutions to our (limited) ability to comment and one institution in particular, the Scottish Parliament, took notice.

On 19 February 2002 the Standards Committee had submitted a report to parliament entitled 'Report on Replacing the Members' Interests Order: Interim Proposals for Consultation'. Under the section entitled 'Non Pecuniary Interests' the following is included:

30. The Committee is particularly keen to seek the views of interested parties on whether the replacement legislation should contain a provision requiring the mandatory registration of non-pecuniary interests. The Committee notes the argument that such interests could potentially wield the same influence over a Member's participation in Parliamentary proceedings as a pecuniary interest. The Committee has also noted concerns in relation to membership of organisations such as the *Freemasons* which, rightly or wrongly, may be perceived by some observers as 'secret societies'. The National Assembly for Wales currently requires Members to register membership of the *Freemasons*. However, the legality of the provision has been challenged in two cases which have been considered by the European Court of Human Rights. The Assembly's Standards of Conduct Committee is currently considering the implications of these judgements.'[451] [Emphasis added]

The amount of material which had been received by the Standards Committee commenting on Freemasonry was so extensive that in light of the 'Briefing Notes' the committee decided to contact Grand Lodge seeking opinion on the material received and in particular the proposal that MSPs must be compelled to reveal their membership of the Order. A long submission was made on 12 April 2002, vigorously defending the Craft and offering to give verbal evidence to the committee.[452] The material that was submitted was so extensive that it is not possible to reproduce it here, but there was one point that I think was very telling.

'The European Court of Human Rights (ECHR) had ruled in 2000 that "prejudice" and "perception" were neither "an identified object" nor were "proportionate" in setting aside the rights of privacy or the right not to be discriminated against.'[453]

Like the petition referred to above (PE306), the submissions to the Standards Committee were almost entirely based on perception, unsubstantiated allegation, prejudice and supposition. It was therefore argued that to demand that members of one minority group, and one minority group only, be forced in a Code of Conduct to identify themselves was discriminatory and disproportionate.

You might well be asking by now why this degree of detail is required here, but it is what subsequently took place within that committee that is most revealing.

'When the issue last came up in the Standards Committee, the press ran wild with suggestions that we just want freemasonry to be registered. In fact, we were talking about the registration of all non-pecuniary interests. In the National Assembly for Wales, there was a requirement to register freemasonry in isolation. I want to test Professor Miller on human rights and the European Convention on Human Rights. I understand that if we singled out one organisation for registration, that would be an infringement, but if we required members to register all non-pecuniary interests, that would not be in contravention of the ECHR.'[454] [455]

This is disingenuous to say the least. The report delivered to parliament on 19 February (see above) specifically mentions membership of only one minority group – Freemasonry.[456] The press reported that, albeit with considerable additional commentary. The Grand Lodge submission alerted the committee to the possible human rights implications of singling out Freemasons to declare their membership under the proposed new Code of Conduct. From the above extract from the committee minutes, it is clear that the target remained Freemasonry, but in order to get round the judgment of the ECHR the committee would require membership of all groups to be declared. In the committee's own words the human rights of Freemasons counted for nothing in its desire to force people to declare their membership of the Craft.

The question must be asked, what disciplinary action would be taken against an MSP who failed to declare membership of, say, a trade union compared to one who failed to declare being a Freemason? In addition, the committee decided that breaching the Code of Conduct would not result in criminal proceedings but any breaches of Parliament's Code of Conduct would be dealt with via internal disciplinary procedures. This had the effect, yet again, of denying Freemasons access to a public forum in which to defend themselves, in this case the courts, but would leave them at the mercy of internal parliamentary procedures.

That this was mere posturing can be demonstrated by two things. Firstly, there was and is no mechanism for the Standards Committee to find out who is a Freemason and who is not. If someone alleged that an MSP was a Freemason and that this had not been declared in the Register of Members' Interests, how was that to be dealt with? The committee made no provision for this eventuality. The second point relates to a particular individual.

In the weeks before the Standards Committee published its proposals for a new Code of Conduct, there was considerable speculation as to whether any MSPs were Freemasons. Several at that time were 'outed', including one who openly admitted that he was a Freemason but was no longer active.[457] He declined to register this fact in the Register of Members' Interests but no disciplinary action was taken. It seems that this witch-hunt against Freemasons was not intended to identify MSPs who were Freemasons and discipline those who failed to reveal their membership. Instead, it appears that this was more about sending a message to one and all that being a Freemason was not a good thing. If it was not desirable for an MSP to be a Freemason who *could* be a Freemason? This is likely to be the political end result and is discussed in the conclusion.

On 1 May 2002, in another report submitted by the committee to Parliament, the wording had changed to:

52. The Committee has also indicated that it wishes to consult interested parties on whether Members should be required to register non-pecuniary interests such as the membership of professional bodies, trade unions or other organisations such as the Freemasons.

On 3 July:

43. The Committee has decided to recommend that the replacement legislation adopts the approach used in the Ethical Standards legislation: Members should be required to register interests which the public might reasonably think could influence an MSP's actions. This will be supplemented by extensive guidance in the Code of Conduct which will provide illustrative examples. These are likely to include positions held in or membership of professional bodies, trade unions, pressure groups, the Freemasons, and cultural and sporting organisations.

Thereafter references to Freemasonry cease and are replaced by wording such as:

'MSPs should be required to register non-financial interests which the public might reasonably think could influence an MSP's actions.'

Grand Lodge was again invited to submit evidence to the committee and on 1 November 2004 it duly did so. By this time the ECHR had handed down judgments on two cases previously laid before it in 1997 regarding Freemasonry and the Italian government. The judgment was not received by the Grand Lodge of Scotland for some considerable time and even then the full implications had to be assessed by legal experts.[458]

In 1997 a regional government in Italy introduced rules which required applicants for public posts to declare whether or not they were Freemasons. A Freemason applied for a post on a public body which was overseen by the regional authority which was also responsible for staff recruitment. The Freemason concerned was successful but objected to the fact that, during the application process, he was required to declare his membership of a Masonic Lodge. At approximately the same time in another part of Italy, disciplinary proceedings were instituted against a judge who was a Freemason although he was not active. Both these cases were eventually heard before the European Court of Human Rights (ECHR), which sits at Strasbourg, and the judgments (N.F. v. Italy [Application No. 37119/97] and Maestri v. Italy [Application No. 39748/98]) were delivered in 2001 and 2004 respectively. The full text of both judgments can be found in the Member Services area of the Grand Lodge of Scotland website.[459]

The two individuals concerned were members of lodges under the Grande Oriente of Italy and that body objected to the fact that, because their members were being discriminated against, so too, as a consequence, was the Grande Oriente *as a body*. It was granted permission to bring cases before the ECHR against the Italian government on the grounds that it was a victim of discrimination in light of the two aforementioned cases. This was an extremely important decision by the court because the Grande Oriente of Italy, like the Grand Lodge of Scotland, is an unincorporated body and therefore it is not a legal entity. The reason why the court decided to hear the representations of the Grande Oriente of Italy are complex, but essentially revolve around fundamental tenets of the *Convention for the Protection of Human Rights and Fundamental Freedoms* – that everyone is entitled to freedom of association and the right to a private life. The court recognised that in this case discriminating against a group (The Grande Oriente of Italy) would consequently affect the fundamental rights of the individual.

Judgments in these two cases were delivered in 2001 and in 2007 (Grande Oriente D'Italia di Palazzo Giustiniani v. Italy [Application No. 35972/97] and Grande Oriente D'Italia di Palazzo Giustiniani v. Italy No. 2 [application No. 26740/02]). The text of both can be downloaded from the Member Services area of the Grand Lodge website. It is the latter judgment which brings to a conclusion the issue of discrimination against Freemasons (as individuals) and Freemasonry (as an institution).

In essence the court has ruled that Freemasons cannot be discriminated against, and specifically cannot be discriminated against when seeking public office – whether appointed or elected. By implication, therefore, Freemasons cannot be discriminated against in any walk of life, for that would strike a mortal blow to the fundamental human rights of the individual.

However, the significance of the fact that the Grande Oriente of Italy was permitted to bring two cases against the Italian government is enormous. From the court's deliberations and final judgments, the following points can be made:

Freemasonry is a legal, legitimate institution.
Freemasonry is not a criminal organisation.
Freemasonry is not a secret society.
Freemasons have a right to freedom of association.
Freemasons have a right to a private life.
Freemasons cannot be discriminated against on the grounds that they are Freemasons.
Government cannot victimise the institution of Freemasonry (or its members) because it believes there is an adverse public perception of Freemasonry.
Restrictions on Freemasons are not necessary in a democratic society.
Section 11 of the Human Rights Convention (freedom of association) applies to Freemasonry as an organisation in the same way as to a trade union or a political party (specifically cited by the court).

The court held that there had been a violation of Article 11 of the Convention in respect of the reputation and image of the Grande Oriente of Italy, thereby creating and perpetuating the very perception it claimed to be the reason for the discrimination! In finding that such a violation had taken place constituted *in itself* 'just satisfaction' for the damage sustained by the applicant association, and it was awarded damages against the Italian government accordingly.

It will be interesting to see what action, if any, the new Scottish government takes to revoke the discriminatory rules introduced (by the previous Scottish Executive) regarding Freemasonry and MSPs. The above cases and subsequent judgments would seem to provide more than sufficient grounds to submit to the ECHR that Freemasons in Scotland are the subject of institutionalised discrimination orchestrated at the highest levels of government. What an embarrassment for the Scottish Parliament should this fledgling devolved democracy stand convicted by the ECHR of discrimination against its own citizens.

Freemasons in Scotland have an advantage in that the deliberations of the Standards Committee (which laid down the rules governing the conduct of MSPs) and those of the Public Petitions Committee are a matter of public record, and so the actual *process* of discrimination can clearly be demonstrated.

However, the judgments will take some time to be digested by all concerned and it will no doubt take more time for these rules which are 'not necessary in a democratic society' to be rescinded.[460]

The European Court of Human Rights considered that freedom of association is of such importance that it cannot be restricted in any way, even in respect of a candidate for public office, so long as the person concerned does not himself commit any reprehensible act by reason of his membership of the association.

The submission by Grand Lodge seemed to have a real impact and the wording again changed. What is more, the terms of disclosure of membership also changed yet again:

14 January 2005
49. [extract] The Committee therefore proposes that Members should be required to register non-financial interests which the public might reasonably think could influence an MSP's actions, using the objective influence test discussed at paragraphs 13 to 16 above.

50. The Committee also recommends that contravention of any provision requiring the registration and declaration of non-financial interests should not be a criminal offence.

The machinations of the Scottish Parliament and its committees, not to mention the press, are tedious but I cannot apologise for that. Please remember that one of the purposes of this book is to record the *progress* of Masonophobia in a small democratic country known as Scotland (hopefully thereby allowing others to make comparisons with their own countries), and although I agree that this is not of the calibre of popular novels such as *The Da Vinci Code* this is an account of how Freemasonry has been, and therefore can be, used and abused. If only Dan Brown had been called to give evidence to the various committees of the parliament north and south of the border, this account of events might have been a more pleasant read.

Even while the Standards Committee was considering Freemasonry and an amended Code of Conduct for MSPs, Freemasonry was being kept to the forefront of political debate. The Movement for a Register of Freemasons submitted a petition (PE739) on 6 May 2004 requesting that solicitors be forced to declare whether or not they were Freemasons. The arguments are a repetition of previous (and later) petitions and need not delay us here, but there are two aspects that ought to be mentioned. First, the press once again picked up on the fact that the petition had been submitted and yet another wave of Masonophobia spread throughout the media.[461] However, the submission of this petition raised a question not only in relation to Freemasons but also for Scots in general. I make this point as a matter of observation only, not as a commentary on the political process. This petition was submitted by an individual who was not resident in Scotland but whose petition sought to change laws applicable only in Scotland. The concern is that a Scottish minority group could have been the subject of discriminatory legislation as a consequence of an external (that is non-Scottish) initiative.[462]

After the report by the Standards Committee (see above) was delivered matters seemed to settle down and Freemasons began to feel that they were no longer the target of politicians, religious groups and the media.[463] They were wrong. A petition submitted on 14 December 2006 was described in the following terms:

'Petition by Mr G. calling for the Scottish Parliament to urge the Scottish Executive to commission research into membership of the freemasons within the police and judiciary.'

This petition was considered by the committee on 8 February and what transpired is very interesting. The meeting was opened with the comment by the convener (chairman) to the effect that, as the subject had previously been investigated several times (as a result of similar petitions) by the Justice 2 Committee:

The Convener
We have received a number of petitions on this subject. Some time ago, we passed them on to the Justice 2 Committee, which conducted a full

inquiry. I do not think that PE912 adds anything to the conclusions of that inquiry. We can note the petition, but there would be no value in considering it further because the relevant committee has already made its judgment on the issue.

Helen Eadie: I suggest that we note the petition and close our consideration of it.

Rosie Kane: I hear what the convener says, but there are a few points that I want to raise. We have heard in this morning's news that a raft of new measures on Scottish judges is coming in, which will deal with such matters as whether they are competent. In future, they will be accountable and could, in certain circumstances, lose their position. In my view, that is a missed opportunity. MSPs are required to disclose their membership of and support for other organisations, as well as their allegiances and interests. It is right that that is the case because we can be influenced by such factors. I am certainly influenced by the bodies to which I am affiliated, such as the environmental movement – that is why I am affiliated to them.

It is important that we disclose such information and it beggars belief that membership of the Freemasons does not have to be disclosed. I do not understand why that is the case – perhaps it is a secret. It is regrettable that the Parliament has not taken up the issue. For a number of reasons, the petitioner has worked incredibly hard on his case and continues to do so at great cost to himself. If members of the police and the judiciary were to disclose their membership of the Freemasons, it would take away the suspicion that hangs around, which gives rise to the accusations that are made. One would think that it would be in the best interests of justice, democracy, openness and accountability for membership of the Freemasons to be disclosed. I want to put that on the record.

I wish that we did not have to close our consideration of the petition. If I could think of a viable way of keeping it open, I would suggest it, but I cannot – perhaps another member can help me. I do not think that we have even asked the first set of questions that need to be asked, the answers to which would give rise to a further set of questions.

The Convener: I have a great deal of sympathy with what you have said. We have received petitions on the subject in the past. They were passed on to the Justice 2 Committee, which conducted an inquiry. That is why there is nothing more that we can do. The issue has been addressed by the Parliament.

Although I sympathise with the sentiments of your comments, the issue is what we can do to progress the petition. Given that a full parliamentary inquiry on the matter has already been held, I do not think that there would be any value in our considering the petition further.

Campbell Martin: I agree with what Rosie Kane has said, but I think that there is a problem with the petition in that it seems to call on the Executive simply to commission research into membership of the Freemasons by members of the police and the judiciary. That would just establish that there are masons in the police and the judiciary. Although it might give an idea of the extent of such membership, it would probably not give an accurate reflection of the situation. That would not take us much further forward; it would simply establish that there were masons in the police and the judiciary. Although I agree with Rosie Kane, I do not think that there is much that we can do with the petition.

Rosie Kane: It sounds as if a new petition is required.

Helen Eadie: I agree with what has been said, but there is another issue. The petition focuses on Freemasonry, but we all know that there are secret organisations throughout the world. We would be tackling just one part of the problem.

The convener is right. The relevant committee has undertaken an in-depth inquiry, so I do not see how we can make progress. All the evidence that was taken will be in the Official Report and every document that the Parliament has on the issue will be accessible to any member of the public, so they will be able to find out whether all the questions that all of us would be concerned about have been asked. I agree with the convener. I do not think that we can make progress on the petition. I suggest that we simply note the petition and take no further action on it.

The Convener: Do members agree to that proposal?

Members *indicated agreement* [*Interruption*]'[464]

I make no apology for once again inflicting upon you a long chunk of text from a committee minute. This provides us with a clear insight to the attitude of some of the members of this committee towards Freemasonry. I urge you to read it in full. Despite an almost immediate acknowledgement by the Convener and other members of the committee that there was nothing that could be done to progress the petition, some members of the committee expressed frustration and disappointment that it seemed that there was nothing they could do to further it. The Convener expressed his sympathy with that attitude. One member suggested that another petition was needed – almost an invitation for someone to do so. All of this indicates a Masonophobic attitude on the part of some members of the committee. Because of the self-imposed constraints by which Freemasons conduct their lives, an expression of an opinion as to the political ideology that might be the basis for this attitude, as expressed above, cannot be given here but readers may wish to come to their own judgement in that respect.[465]

In May 2007, the Scottish National Party narrowly won the Scottish General Election and formed a minority government. What has that got to do with Scottish Freemasonry? you might well ask. Because Freemasonry is a fraternal organisation and does not get involved in religion or politics, it might be construed that I am straying from our own self-imposed rules. However, I do so in order to make a general observation which concerns politics, rather than one that makes a political comment. I know the wording is tortuous but it is necessary! Immediately before the Scottish Parliament was established, there was a great deal of Masonophobia in the media (the Dunblane massacre etc.) and during the first few years of the Parliament petitions were received demanding a public register of Freemasons be created and rules governing the conduct of MSPs, including references to Freemasonry in negative terms. From the point of view of the ordinary Scottish Freemason, this was very confusing. The vast majority of Scottish Freemasons are ordinary working people and tend to vote accordingly. Yet, here they found themselves in a situation, year upon year, being told that being a Freemason was a bad thing. The problem was that, as members, they knew this was not true. They had never met a mass-murderer in their lodge, they did not get promotion because they were Freemasons (indeed many of them became unemployed) and they knew that anyone who committed a crime was expelled from the Craft. Squaring the circle was impossible for many and the effect was disillusionment. Did they give up their innocent pastime? Most do not appear to have done so but there is anecdotal evidence that their voting habits changed or that they simply stopped voting. There is no evidence, other than the occasional remarks I heard across the country, that the sustained period of Masonophobia had an effect on the election of May 2007, but it is an intriguing thought nevertheless.

To return to the matter of Thomas Hamilton and the Dunblane massacre. As early as ten days after the mass murders, the press suggested that Freemasonry was responsible (directly or indirectly) for the killings. The argument, with some slight variations, went along these lines: Thomas Hamilton was known to be mentally unstable but, despite this fact, he was allowed to keep handguns and ammunition at home. He could only be allowed to do so with the permission of the police. They did so despite knowing that he was unstable.[466] This meant that, regardless of the fact that he had mental health problems of which the police were aware, they allowed him to keep the guns and ammunition.

He was therefore protected by the police. 'Everyone knows' that all policemen are Freemasons, so it was obvious that Hamilton was himself a Freemason and was being protected by his Masonic policeman friends. That being the case, Freemasonry was ultimately responsible for the Dunblane massacre.

This 'story' was repeated many times after 1996, and became so embedded in the public consciousness that regardless of the truth, many people refuse to accept anything other than this explanation. This is an excellent example of how the repetition of something untrue becomes accepted as being true even in the face of hard facts. Hitler knew the value of propaganda and how it could be used to influence, even to control, how people thought. Indicating how deeply ingrained this story has become, people began to accuse Lord Cullen and the Public Inquiry he conducted of being a whitewash devised to hide the truth of Freemasonry's involvement in the Dunblane shootings. The private evidence taken at the Public Inquiry was subject to a 100-year rule in order to protect those who had given evidence as well as the survivors of the mass murders. This is normal practice and not considered to be in any way unusual. However, almost immediately the media reported claims that this was a conspiracy designed to maintain the whitewash. The press demanded to know who was really being protected by the evidence being kept unavailable to the public for 100 years. Petitions were submitted to the PPC demanding that the 100-year rule be removed so that the Masonic conspiracy could be revealed. This was subsequently done and many people went to the public archive to review the previously 'secret' evidence. It revealed no Masonic conspiracy whatsoever, and in fact, the opposite was true. Hamilton had complained that Freemasons were part of a conspiracy against him running his boys' clubs. The previously closed material confirmed the statement made by the Public Inquiry:

'In the large volume of correspondence which he generated, a recurring theme is his assertion that the police were biased in favour of the "brotherhood of masons" and against Hamilton and his boys' clubs.'[467]

Interestingly, he also claimed that there was another 'brotherhood' at work against him – a link between the Scouts and the police.[468] Despite all this, the press continued to suggest that Hamilton was a Freemason and that Freemasonry was therefore responsible in part for the mass murder at Dunblane Primary School in 1996.

First and foremost, there is a need to consider the widely held and fundamental belief that Freemasons act in a particular way *because* they are Freemasons. This is grounded in the fact that all Freemasons go through a similar process in becoming a Freemason. People such as Martin Short conclude that that process means that Freemasons are bound to assist each other to the extent that they will protect someone who cold bloodedly killed 16 children and one adult and wounded 17 others. This is a fantastic claim and is founded not on fact but on prejudice.[469] As has been seen above, the avoidance of hard fact can permit anyone to blame Freemasons for anything. That Freemasonry is made up of an incredibly diverse membership (all creeds, colours, faiths, ethnic, social, political or economic backgrounds) spread across the world with no single central body or 'Head Office' means that it is impossible for it to act in such a concerted manner – but here we are, almost falling into the trap of believing what is being argued against!

Freemasonry fell into such a trap when Hamilton was claimed to be a Freemason and the race was on to prove that he was not. Rather than confront the general slur on Freemasonry that its members all act in a certain manner because they *are* Freemasons the press claimed that they had proof that Hamilton was a member of Lodge Garrowhill, No. 1413 (Ballieston, Glasgow).[470] The 'evidence' was an alleged conversation with a 'senior Freemason'. That Lodge's records were examined in exhaustive detail and there was no trace of Hamilton becoming a member of that lodge but it was discovered that his grandfather, James, had been a member of that Lodge from his initiation on 2 December 1957 until his death in 2000. James Hamilton adopted his grandson, Thomas, in 1956 and in 1963 they both moved to Stirling. James then became a frequent visitor to Lodge Stirling Royal Arch, No. 76. On 21 November 2003, Lodge Stirling Royal Arch, No. 76 issued the following statement:

'Thomas Hamilton's grandfather was a regular attender at this Lodge. Thomas Hamilton was not a member. His grandfather said on several occasions that he would never consider proposing Thomas for membership.'

All these details were provided to the press, in which they were reported in the following manner:

'And last week, in a historic and unprecedented move, six volumes were thrown open to *Scotland on Sunday* as part of Freemasonry's attempts to dispel its secretive image and counter a damaging association with Dunblane killer Thomas Hamilton. It is the first time that an outside organisation has had such open access to masonic files.

'The registration books, and the equally-voluminous attendance books for two individual lodges, cover the period during which

Hamilton could have been a member or a visitor. Exhaustive searches by senior staff of the Grand Lodge of Scotland – effectively head office – has failed to find any record of Hamilton ever being a mason or even stepping over the threshold of the masonic lodges in Glasgow and Stirling to which he has been most closely linked.'

And

'We are going to ask for members' permission from two lodges that Thomas Hamilton has been linked with to print the membership book on the internet to put an end to speculation over whether he was a Freemason or not. We know he wasn't but we want everyone else to be sure as well. It's not just an academic exercise. The Hamilton connection has haunted the Freemasons since he shot dead 16 children, one of their teachers and himself in the school gym of Dunblane Primary in 1996. Last month, a petition was submitted by a local resident to the Scottish parliament asking for the Cullen Inquiry into the murders to be reopened to re-examine alleged masonic links.

'Cooper is more familiar than most with how the theory goes. It sprang, he says, from the clearly-recorded membership of Hamilton's grandfather, James, a welder who joined the Garrowhill Lodge in the working class district of Baillieston in December 1957 and, after moving home, was a regular attendee at the Royal Arch Lodge in Stirling until his death in 2000.

'As the grandfather was a member, then so was the grandson, so the theory progresses. As a mason, Thomas Hamilton would mix socially with other masons, many of them local police officers, the theory dictates. "Thomas Hamilton was unstable but was allowed to keep guns in his house by the police because they were all masons together," Cooper said. "None of this is true."

'Membership records were scrutinised for the years in which Hamilton, who was born in 1952, could have been a member. They were from 1973, after he was 21 (you can only join at 18 if your father has been a member), to 1996 when he died. Another two Thomas Hamiltons were unearthed in Scotland but they were both the wrong ages.'[471]

As well as reporting as above, the press were also allowed full access to all the relevant books and other records and were even invited to take them away to have them independently assessed for evidence of any tampering, but they declined the invitation.[472] The manner in which the media released details about Freemasonry and Hamilton is interesting, and the sequence of their revelation of Hamilton's Masonic career, is most revealing.

Hamilton stated to be a Freemason. (No proof provided.)

The area where he was an active Freemason is revealed. (This was merely where he had previously lived with his grandfather.)

His lodge is eventually named. (He was not a member or a visitor.)

A Freemason 'who does not wish to be named' confirms his membership. (No proof provided.)

Hamilton's grandfather (who raised him as a child) is revealed to have been a Freemason. (The grandfather was by then deceased.)

Hamilton's name cannot be found be in any record locally or centrally. This was reported, in writing, to the press.

The fact that Hamilton was not a Freemason is not reported by the press.

The findings of the Public Inquiry reveal that Hamilton had a grudge against Freemasonry (see above).

The Public Inquiry is condemned as a 'whitewash' designed to bury a Masonic conspiracy of monumental proportions involving people at the highest level.

The press reports demand that the information gathered by the Public Inquiry be released in order to confirm that Hamilton was a Freemason.[473]

Another exhaustive examination of the membership records shows (again) that Hamilton was not a Freemason. Although reported to the media, this was again ignored by the press.

The material gathered by the Public Inquiry is made available to the public. Hamilton is revealed not to be a Freemason.[474] In fact, Hamilton accused Freemasons of conspiring against him.[475] This is not reported by the press.

The Public Inquiry into the Shootings at Dunblane Primary School on 13 March 1996 by The Hon. Lord Cullen was held between Wednesday, 29 May and Wednesday, 10 July 1996. On 1, 2, 3 and 4 July 1996, *The Scotsman* ran a four-day, multi-page exposé of Freemasonry. (See Plate 15)

Some have noted that these press reports were published during the last full week before the end of the Public Inquiry and some cynics have suggested that this was a deliberate attempt to influence the Public Inquiry against Freemasonry. Anyone wishing to do so had a much more direct means. On 1 May 1996 at a preliminary hearing Lord Cullen made a public call for written evidence. This call was repeated, on 3 May 1996, in press notices inserted in *all* the national newspapers, including those of Scotland. Those submitting evidence are detailed in an appendix (No. 4) of the Public Inquiry report. None of the newspapers or journalists reporting on Freemasonry made any submissions in response to the call issued by Lord Cullen. That the press, in particular, published claims that Hamilton was a Freemason and that there was a Masonic conspiracy at work to protect Hamilton, but did not provide the Public Inquiry with the information is curious. There is one further interesting detail. The press reports published during the course of the Public Inquiry are entirely negative regarding Freemasonry, but none mention the Dunblane murders nor do they repeat the earlier claims that Hamilton was a Freemason and was receiving their protection.

Despite attempts to provide the media with accurate information regarding Freemasonry and any possible involvement with the Dunblane massacre, these were ignored. There are two aspects which were alluded to in the introduction and, despite being explained to the media, have never been published by the press. The Grand Lodge of Scotland had a home for older people at Dunblane and one of the children murdered by Thomas Hamilton was the grandson of one of the employees at the home.[476] Freemasons in Scotland were shocked and greatly saddened but the press made no mention of this throughout their reporting of the Dunblane massacre. Not only did that have the effect of denying the facts it omitted that Freemasons were as upset as anyone else. In other words, the omission refused them a human face. Freemasons across the world were shocked; many felt the need to respond in some way. Thousands did so by sending money to the Dunblane Tragedy Appeal Fund. (See Plate 16) This fund was used to contribute to the installation of commemorative stained glass windows in Dunblane churches. As might have been expected, the generosity of Freemasons from all over the world was not reported by the press.

The existence of widespread Masonophobia as reproduced in the press has been more than demonstrated above. Although lengthy, no apology is made for including so much material, because it is essential to demonstrate the variety and scope produced during this period. It is also important to reproduce a representative sample of that material in one place.[477]

Home Affairs Select Committee

At the same time the Scottish Press were 'investigating' Freemasonry, another investigation was underway in England.

On 21 November 1974, two bombs exploded in two public houses in Birmingham.[478] A total of 21 people were killed and 162 injured. The bombings were claimed to be the work of the Provisional IRA. Six people were arrested, charged and convicted of carrying out the bombings.[479] All six were sentenced to life imprisonment on 15 August 1975. Christopher J. Mullin (1947–), an investigative journalist working for Granada Television, took up the case and a *World in Action* programme broadcast in 1985 cast serious doubt on the convictions. His subsequent book, *Error of Judgment – The Truth about the Birmingham Pub Bombings*, published in 1986, further reinforced that view. What is significant is that neither this *World in Action* programme, nor Mullin's book makes any mention of Freemasonry. A Case of Appeal in 1988 upheld the convictions. Christopher Mullin was elected a Member of Parliament in 1987 and subsequently Member of the Home Affairs Select Committee from 1992–1997 and was chairman of that Committee 1997–1999.[480]

In 1992 the following was proposed:

'That leave be given to bring in a Bill to require that an occupant of, or candidate for appointment or election to, a public office or a post in a public service shall make a public declaration as to his membership or otherwise of any secret society; and for connected purposes. My Bill seeks to ensure that candidates either for appointment or election to public office should declare their membership or otherwise of any secret society. It will require also that the record of any such declarations is made available to the public.'

It is to be noticed that this quote refers to 'secret societies' and shares that phrase in common with all other Masonophobic rhetoric, including that used by the Press and the Scottish and Welsh Assemblies. This is something that will be discussed more fully in the conclusion.

'Although no particular organisation is mentioned and the scope of my Bill is not limited to any particular organisations, you, Madam Speaker may not be surprised to learn that Freemasons will be among those who fall within its scope.'[481]

It is perhaps revealing to note that the person making this proposal identified only one so-called 'secret society' – Freemasonry. This is a common tactic employed by Masonophobes. The suggestion is that all 'secret societies' are being targeted, but only one is actually ever identified!

In 1994, during a debate on the Queen's Speech, the following statement was made:

'There is also a problem, which we should acknowledge, of police forces being riddled with freemasonry, especially in the detective squads. Those who have been down some of the alleyways that I went down during the Birmingham and Guildford investigations know that *almost everyone* involved in those cases, up to the level of chief constable in some cases, is a mason.'[482] [483] [Emphasis added]

The latter comment was made in response to the announcement in the Queen's Speech that a criminal cases review authority was to be created to investigate miscarriages of justice. On 1 January 1997 the Criminal Cases Review Commission came into being.[484]

On 1 May 1997 a general election brought another party to government.[485] Soon after, the Home Affairs Select Committee began an investigation into the possible influence of Freemasonry in the Police and judiciary.

It was during Chris Mullin's tenure as chairman that allegations were made that Freemasonry was involved in a conspiracy to pervert the course of justice by ensuring innocent people were convicted of the bombings and, by implication, was protecting the real culprits.

Effect of Masonophobic Attacks
Although it is not possible to know with any certainty what effect this constant Masonophobic reporting had on any particular part of society, it seems some change in voting patterns has taken place. There is anecdotal evidence that Masonophobic attacks have had an effect on voting. Scotland is generally accepted by many to be a place where left-of-centre parties do well even when other parts of the United Kingdom have voted in an different manner. During the 1990's and early 2000's, while the media and various branches of government were 'investigating' Freemasonry and taking action against it (see below), many Scottish Freemasons were placed in a quandary. Scottish Freemasonry is historically rooted in the working class and today the largest percentage of the membership is not within the 'A' and 'B' categories.[486] The very party that they voted for now attacked the organisation of which they were proud to be a member. In 2007 another left-of-centre party won the majority of seats in the Scottish Parliament.[487]

Many other sectors of society followed the lead of the government and Freemasonry became the whipping boy for many. Local authorities quickly added a question about Freemasonry to their recruitment application forms, inserting a requirement to declare Masonic membership to their codes of practice and encouraging those whom they dealt with in the private sector to do the same. The implication was that private firms which had dealings with local government would not be considered favourably. Exactly how this was to be policed was not explained. *That* suggested that there was an element of not-too-subtle coercion involved, for how else would a private company know what a local authority knew about Freemasons in the local community?

Some local authorities, no doubt taking their lead from the party in power nationally, decided not only to require applicants for employment to declare their membership but also existing members of staff to reveal if they were Freemasons. For example, at the time of writing Fife Regional Council's code of conduct includes the following under the heading 'Conflicts of Interest':

'If you are a member of an organisation or a club, and membership might result in a conflict of interest or could reasonably be perceived by a member of the public as creating a possible conflict of interest in relation to any aspect of your work with the Council, then you must declare this membership to your line manager. This applies equally to membership of organisations or clubs which are not open to the public, e.g. Freemasonry.'[488]

The Masonophobic bias of those who drew up this regulation, applicable to all employees of the local authority, is revealed by the use of the terms:

not open to the public
perceived by a member of the public
might result in a conflict of interest
Freemasonry

The requirement that all employees of the council disclose their membership of organisations or clubs (specifically Freemasonry) remains in force today. The only 'club' or 'organisation' that is cited as an example is Freemasonry. Many might think that this is a clear example of Masonophoia embedded in Scotland's system of democratic local government.[489] Some might well consider that institutionalised Masonophobia is more widespread than previously thought.

The extent of the witch-hunt became clear when even trade unions required prospective members to declare whether or not they were Freemasons. UNISON is the largest public sector union in the UK. In

Scotland it is the largest trade union by a considerable margin. UNISON is also one of the largest financial contributors to a particular political party. Like any organisation it has rules and regulations by which members must abide. In 1997, it was proposed that the following addition to rule 5.1 be made:

> 'Any person who is, or has been, in membership of the Freemasons must declare this, in writing, at the time of completing the application form for UNISON membership.'[490]

This proposal to change the rules was made by the National Executive Council – not the 'grass roots' of the union – and was submitted to the annual conference. The motion was carried at the 1997 annual conference and was incorporated into its rulebook.

The application form was reworded to read:
'I wish to join UNISON and accept its rules and constitution.
'I authorise deduction of the following Political Fund payment as part of my subscription.
'Tick one box only
'*Affiliated Political Fund*
'*General Political Fund*
'I authorise deduction of UNISON subscriptions from my salary/wages at the rate determined by UNISON to be paid over to them on my behalf and I authorise my employer to provide to UNISON information to keep my records up to date.
'If you are, or have been, a member of the Freemasons you must declare this in writing when completing the form.
'I wish to pay by direct debit/cheque.
'(please tick if appropriate)
'Now please sign and date below and return this form'

Rule 6.1 states, 'Every member shall observe all the Rules of the Union.' The nature of sanctions to be applied against those who failed to declare 'membership of the Freemasons' (past or present) at the time of joining UNISON is not provided.[491]

What is to be made of this? Here we have a legal voluntary group (a trade union) demanding a declaration be made if an applicant is, or ever has been, a member of another legal voluntary group (Freemasonry).[492] What is more, it is explicit that anyone who fails to reveal their existing or previous membership of that legal voluntary organisation known as Freemasonry is liable to disciplinary action![493]

Here we come to a crucial point that applies not only to the matter of membership of a trade union or other body, but the assumptions being made about being a Freemason. In the first place how would a trade union find out if an applicant was, or ever had been a Freemason? There are two further points. If the applicant answered 'yes' to that question, how would that information be used and what potential action could be taken against him or her? If the answer was 'no', then would the trade union write to Grand Lodge, asking if the applicant was or ever had been a Freemason? Clearly this is ridiculous. If nothing else, it would create a bureaucratic nightmare for the organisation instigating the request – assuming that a reply was forthcoming from any of the Grand Lodges concerned.

It is believed that there is another motive involved here, and not just in relation to this example. The question is not intended to actually find out if the person is, or was, a Freemason but is a deliberate attempt to blackmail or intimidate the individual into believing that being a Freemason is incompatible with being a trade unionist.[494]

Although Masonophobia is no longer prevalent in the press, the effects of the relentless denigration of the Craft during the 1990's and early 2000's remain with us today as evidenced by the trade union and council examples discussed above.

Human Rights
The Scottish government decided that a Scottish Human Rights Commission (SHRC) was necessary and in order to inform interested parties and obtain feedback, a conference (Establishing Our Rights) was held in February 2003. In light of the court cases before the European Court of Human Rights involving Freemasonry as discussed above, it was decided that an observer be sent to that conference.[495] The conference was most interesting, but it remained unclear why Scotland alone in the UK thought that it ought to have its own commission on human rights which would in any event be subservient to the ECHR. The commission was set up by an act of the Scottish Parliament in 2006 and is now a department of the Scottish government.[496] [497]

Subsequent to the conference, Establishing Our Rights, the Scottish government solicited the participants for their views. Below is the formal response to that invitation sent by the Grand Lodge of Scotland to the Scottish government, on behalf of all Freemasons resident in Scotland.

Scottish Freemasonry and Human Rights
Since 1997 the political and social landscape of Scotland has changed and

that has impacted on many areas of life and culture. Freemasons may not engage, as Freemasons, in matters of politics although of course in other walks of life they are free to do so. This means that Freemasonry is not in any way politically active. However, the GLoS can, and does, take note of matters which might have an effect on Freemasonry as an institution and on individual Freemasons.

One example of this lies in the field of Human Rights. The GLoS notes the intention of the Scottish Executive to establish a Scottish Human Rights Commission (SHRC) and indeed a representative was present at the conference, Establishing Our Rights on 17 February 2003 when the (then) Deputy First Minister and Minister for Justice, Jim Wallace, QC, MSP, 'set the scene' for the creation of a SHRC.

Minority groups in Scotland have a right to expect and receive fair and even handed treatment. They further have the right to have their beliefs and practices respected by those who do not hold the same beliefs and opinions. Mutual respect of all who live in Scotland is a laudable aim to be promoted wherever and whenever possible. When the beliefs and practices of minorities are abused it is quite right and proper that the abusers are called to account. The GLoS notes the efforts of the Scottish Executive to reduce tensions as indicated by moves to eliminate sectarianism and through the 'One Country – Many Cultures' campaign to promote tolerance and understanding between diverse sections of Scottish society.

When a minority is accused of: paedophilia, organised fraud, murder, political manipulation, assassination, perverting the course of justice and religious persecution then the members of that minority must be brought to justice. To accuse any minority of such heinous crimes and not bring them to justice is an abuse of their Human Rights (as well as everyone, such as their families, 'contaminated' by such false allegations). Such repeated claims being made against a minority, without evidence and without any criminal charges ever having been brought, would lead to a public outcry, with demands that the rights of the minority concerned be protected and the accusers and abusers be brought to book – except, that is, when the minority concerned are Freemasons.

In the introduction to the Scottish Executive's consultation paper: 'The Scottish Human Rights Commission' (2003) it states:

Human rights are those rights which could be described as the most basic and fundamental values on which our society has been built... This includes things like:

The right to life.

The right to freely express your views.

The right to respect for your private and family life.

With these sentiments the GLoS concurs. Freemasonry in Scotland is a private activity, undertaken by private individuals exercising their inalienable right of free association.

The Grand Secretary
The Grand Lodge of Antient Free and Accepted Masons of Scotland[498]
Freemasons' Hall
96 George Street
Edinburgh
EH2 3DH

A letter was received acknowledging this contribution, but nothing further was heard on the subject.[499]

Popular Culture

When a subject becomes part of popular culture it is usually a good indication that it has been talked about so much, so often and by so many people that it is a good bet for further exploitation. This was the case in respect of Freemasonry in Scotland and there are numerous examples. In order to make the point I need only refer to two.

In 1998, in the immediate aftermath of the tirade of accusations of all types against Freemasonry, a novel entitled *Filth* was published by Irvine Welsh (1958). (See Plate 17) This novel is based on his home town of Edinburgh and the plot's central character is a police detective. In the novel Detective Sergeant Bruce Robertson is assigned a case of racially motivated murder. The victim is a black journalist and the novel charts Robertson's investigation of the case.[500] Welsh commented that he had been influenced by the 1992 film, *Bad Lieutenant* by Abel Ferrara (1951):

' ... when I wrote *Filth* I had this idea that I would do the same thing only with environmental health officers working for the council – but like really dirty bastards working for the council... so instead of Bad Lieutenant, Bad Environmental Health Officers. But I thought I can't fucking do that, you've got to have some fucking corrupt cop – I mean, if an environmental health officer has fucked up you get food poisoning, but if a cop has fucked up you can go down for years, you know. So I wanted to get to the fucking soul of corruption there, that's what I was trying to do.'[501]

The plot is complex, based on Welsh's political views and I will not attempt to provide a comprehensive synopsis here.[502] It is sufficient for our purposes, particularly in light of his comment, 'I wanted to get to the fucking soul of corruption' to note that Welsh depicts Detective Sergeant Robertson as an alcoholic, a drug addict, a sexual predator, a rapist, a racist and a sociopath. He is also a senior Freemason.[503] Needless to say, this linkage of corruption, police and Freemasonry accords very well with the Masonophobic press that was in wide circulation during the period when Welsh was writing his book. What influence this had on his novel is hard to say, but it was certainly a remarkable coincidence.

Filth was rewritten as a play which was performed during the Edinburgh International Fringe Festival in 2001. It was performed over the course of a week and the city was plastered with flyers advertising the play.[504] (see Plate 18)

The design of the flyer is deliberately provocative (as some advertising is intended to be) but this particular image turns history on its head. We have seen in previous chapters that Freemasons were persecuted by the Nazi regime both in Germany and occupied Europe. The combination of the Nazi swastika and the Masonic Square and Compasses is a gross distortion. However, I have no doubt that it accords with the idea of those involved that British police officers are both Nazis and Freemasons. This is an example of how perception is created regardless of the facts and in this case, because the novel and play were hugely popular, this gross misrepresentation entered popular culture where it remains, perpetuating a false perception of the Craft.

As shall be explored in the conclusion, there are certain elements that can be identified as part of the process of creating scapegoats. One we have already briefly discussed above is that of gross misrepresentation of the facts; the other is ridicule.

Ridicule is often underestimated as a means of stigmatising minority groups. It can take different forms from jokes to caricatures. These highlight the obvious differences of a minority by over-emphasising some aspect common to the group. At one time, jokes about Irish people, disabled people and black people were common. Often this was due to ignorance and a lack of knowledge about the group concerned. It is no longer politically correct to denigrate groups in this manner, but it remains acceptable to do so regarding Freemasons. I shall return to this theme in the conclusion. Here, as we have discussed the misrepresentation of Freemasonry in the book and play *Filth*, it is appropriate to mention other misrepresentations of Freemasonry in popular culture.

An episode of the very popular 'courtroom soap', *Judge John Deed* [played by Martin Shaw], entitled 'Abuse of Power' was first broadcast on 28 November 2002.[505] [506]As is usual with popular television series like *Judge John Deed*, this episode had two main stories or plots:[507] [508]

'After a young woman is battered to death, the mentally retarded Gary Patterson confesses and the police consider the case solved. However, Gary later withdraws his confession, leaving Judge Deed's court struggling with limited evidence.

'Meanwhile, Deed is also busy looking into a case about a multi-million pound mortgage fraud and comes up against a masonic conspiracy. The fraud case is due to go before a brother judge who himself proves to be implicated, and who commits suicide.

'In Deed's own court, the jury finds Gary Patterson not guilty, Deed asks who the killer was, and Gary says he witnessed the killing and knows the answer.'[509]

The voiceover introducing the episode states, 'Now though, battling a Masonic conspiracy, it's *Judge John Deed*.' This prejudicial introduction makes it clear which of the two plots will be the dominant theme in this episode. More than that, before this fictional courtroom drama is even viewed the public are informed that there *is* a 'Masonic conspiracy' and although the programme is fiction the emphatic statement serves to confirm the suggestion. The repetition of an alleged conspiracy in a programme viewed by millions perpetuates the perception that Freemasons are therefore corrupt. But there is also a subtle linkage between the two plots. One concerns the inadequacy of a police investigation into the circumstances surrounding a vulnerable individual, and at the same time the major plot is about Masonic corruption in the highest levels of the English judicial system. Some of the programme's dialogue as it relates to Freemasonry is illuminating:

'Doesn't the old school tie system tend to discourage corrupt judges in this country?'(Deed)

'The police suspect a network of corrupt lawyers – all Masons. There has to be a judge or two among them.' (A senior police officer)

'Is that what you know or what you want to believe?' (Deed)

'It is the only way it [the conspiracy] could work consistently.' (A senior police officer)

Later, after Judge John Deed's daughter, Charlie Deed, [played by Louisa Clein] has begun investigating the legal figures thought to be involved:

'This could cause a huge scandal... Your starter for ten is to guess the other connection.' (Charlie Deed)

'Wearing aprons and rolling up their trouser legs?' (John Deed)

(Snigger) 'Haven't got the time to check if they are Masons yet.' (Charlie Deed)

And in discussion with a policeman:

'You are a Mason aren't you? (John Deed to a senior police officer)

'Is that the connection? [you are trying to make] it's a pretty weak connection.' (A senior police officer)

'John, the Masons aren't proscribed.' (A senior police officer)

'I am simply looking for a thread.' (John Deed)

'There is no indication of criminal intent.' (A senior police officer)

'Charlie is working on it.' (John Deed)

Deed's daughter, Charlie, undertakes some research on behalf of her father and compiles damning evidence against a group of judges, solicitors and others in the judicial system which strongly indicates a Masonic conspiracy. It is at Companies House that Charlie obtains much of this evidence (including share ownership and directorships held by the Masonic conspirators) with the assistance of very helpful staff. On her way home she is mugged and her research is stolen. After explaining what happened to her father:

'We should stop this right now.' (John Deed to Charlie Deed)

'You can't be serious, they're all Masons.' (Charlie Deed to John Deed)

Charlie then agrees to reconstruct her research by returning to Companies House, this time accompanied by her father's personal police bodyguard. (Constable Stephen Ashurst, played by Dave Norman). On arriving at Companies House, Charlie finds that the staff are no longer helpful but are downright obstructive. On the way home the bodyguard offers to help analyse the reconstituted data, and he takes the file with him on his return to duty with Judge John Deed. Before reaching the judge's chambers he is intercepted by the internal investigations branch of the police, who confiscate the material given to him by Charlie and threaten him with disciplinary action. What they are unaware of is the fact that the confiscated material consists only of copies – Charlie has the originals.

A last ditch attempt by the Masonic conspirators is to have a senior judge, Sir Joseph Canning (played by Donald Sinden) confront Judge John Deed:[510]

'You must stop [Deed's investigation] if not for your sake then for the sake of your daughter [Charlie], for those who you cherish, your sister, Mrs Mills [played by Jenny Seagrove] and her family, and your new girlfriend. [Carol Hayman, played by Simone Lahbib]'

Deed rejects this advice and points his right hand at Canning as if firing a pistol. Soon after, Mrs Jo Mills is informed that her son, Tom, has been injured in a car 'accident' and has been hospitalised.

'A car, which did not stop, forced him off the road' (Jo Mills)

In a subsequent scene Deed goes with his new girlfriend, Carol Hayman, to her home to have sex, but their arrival disturbs an intruder who flees out of a window. Deed immediately phones the police, asking that they come immediately. As soon he puts down the phone there is a loud knocking on the front door; in response he comments, 'That was quick.' The Drug Squad have arrived with a warrant following a tip-off. A search taking less than a minute finds a bag of white powder which is suspected of being heroin. Deed and Hayman are arrested and taken to a police station where they are accused of being drug dealers. Once Deed's identity is established, the planted drugs are traced to a store of drugs in police custody which are to be used as evidence in another criminal case.

The judge presiding over the trial of the lawyers accused of mortgage fraud amounting to several hundred millions of pounds, Judge Robert Home (played by Sheridan Morley) on realising that the 'game is up', commits suicide rather than reveal that he is protecting fellow Freemasons.

This hugely popular television series was watched by millions of people in the UK. It was also sold to numerous other countries which broadcast it in English or dubbed it into the native language. This episode, along with all the others, continues to be repeated on television more than eight years after the original broadcast. As in the instance of the book *Filth* (see pp208-9), the negative perception of Freemasonry is reinforced by this form of Masonophobia embedded in popular culture. Needless to say, Freemasons have no 'right of reply' to such fictional parodies of the truth. This is hardly surprising, given the fact that Freemasons apparently have been denied a 'right of reply' to disinformation reported in the mainstream press and media.

Anti-Masonic attitudes, or at least the perpetuation of inaccurate depictions of what Freemasonry is, crop up in all sorts of places. *From Hell* is a 'graphic novel' (that is it is illustrated with sequential line drawings) about Jack the Ripper based on a variety of disparate sources including Stephen Knight's (1951–1985) *Jack the Ripper: The Final Solution*. *From Hell* presents a distorted mishmash of images of Freemasonry, its rituals and regalia, together with a repetition of the unsubstantiated claim that Freemasons were deeply involved in the Ripper murders and actively protected the guilty party. This form of accusation without evidence was to be repeated by Knight in a later book devoted entirely to Freemasonry: *The Brotherhood*.[511] *From Hell* was made into a film of the same title starring Johnny Depp in the lead role, which was released in the UK in 2002.

These UK examples are indicative of how widespread and ingrained is this perception of Freemasonry. Like *From Hell*, the extremely popular US television series *Star Trek: Deep Space Nine* includes an example of how this perception in popular culture has become international. In one episode the character Quark (Armin Shimerman, 1949–) seeking a way out of a desperate situation, appeals to Commander Sisko:

> 'Oh, come on now, you people [humans] have rituals for everything, except waste extraction, you must have a ceremony or secret handshake or something ...'

Quark's plea contains the words *'ritual'*, *'ceremony'* and *'handshake'* of which he knows nothing other than that they exist. Quark is therefore not a Freemason, but has some idea of what they claimed to be able to achieve – use of secret knowledge, secret ritual and secret communication to alter the natural course of events. These references, originating in the UK and the USA and broadcast around the world, were produced without reference to Freemasons or any of the Masonic organisations which represent 'ordinary' Freemasons.[512]

It is worth examining the content of the episode of the extremely popular UK TV series, *Judge John Deed*, in order to discuss common perceptions of Freemasonry and how they serve to keep these misconceptions in the public mind.[513] A brief résumé of the main points will have to suffice.

The scriptwriter, Gordon F. Newman, obviously picked up on government and media perception that Freemasonry was a corrupting influence within the judiciary. The TV programme begins with the presumption that there is a Masonic conspiracy within the judiciary and then proceeds to investigate that conspiracy. It is noticeable that this is the same approach adopted by media and government – Freemasonry is presumed guilty, it is simply a matter of uncovering the facts. Obviously this programme is designed to entertain and it is fiction, but it serves to reinforce the perception created elsewhere. In order to entertain, the programme goes further than other commentators on Freemasonry. The conspiracy initially only concerns mortgage fraud, but in order to avoid further investigation the Freemasons involved resort to increasingly desperate tactics: corruption; obstructing the course of justice; attempted murder; burglary and blackmail. Freemasons therefore are capable of virtually any crime. On several occasions it is said that, 'Freemasonry is not proscribed,' and the implication is, given the context in which the comments are made, that Freemasonry should be outlawed. The programme did not miss the opportunity to ridicule Masonic practices such as rolling up trouser legs, etc. and was broadcast at the height of the debate in the Scottish Parliament on rules of conduct for MSPs (see below), but whether one informed the other is unknown.

During 2001/02 there was a great deal of debate regarding (a 'Code of Conduct') for Members of the Scottish Parliament (MSPs) – (see pp187, 192) above. The press made a great deal of the need for 'transparency' and petitions were submitted to the Public Petitions Committee of the Scottish Parliament, demanding that MSPs be forced to declare whether or not they were Freemasons. This allowed the issue to be continuously discussed before the committee responsible for drawing up recommendations governing the conduct expected of MSPs.[514] We have already seen how some politicians, having been made aware of the ruling of the European Court of Human Rights that no one could be discriminated against because they were a Freemason, sought to circumvent that ECHR ruling (see pp187–9 above). It was during that period that the then leader of the Conservative Party, David McLetchie (1952–), thought it wise to disclose that he 'was once a Mason.' (See Plate 19)

Newspaper cartoons, such as this, are intended to make a humorous commentary on a topical issue and the author confesses to smiling when he saw this in the local evening newspaper.[515] Frank Boyle is a superb political cartoonist and a keen observer of the Scottish political scene. Following David McLetchie's admission that he was 'once a Freemason' it was almost inevitable that Boyle would use his talents to comment on that fact.[516]

In general, the cartoon pokes fun at Mr McLetchie and the Conservative Party. However, it contains elements that are exactly the kind of thing that creates misperception and reinforces prejudice. If we look at the two ladies at the far right, one is holding a Masonic apron, 'a nice wee pinny', as she calls it.[517] She obviously does not understand what it actually is, despite the Masonic symbolism it bears. The other woman, with a question mark above her head, is holding a pair of trousers, the left leg of which is partially rolled up. This is, yet again, poking fun at Freemasonry's symbolic practices. While this is apparently gentle humour, and there can be no doubt that this is what it was intended to be, of more concern is what it represents and what it perpetuates. Freemasons are an object of fun because they wear 'wee pinnies' and have a trouser leg rolled up, but there is no attempt at understanding or explanation.[518] This cartoon serves to perpetuate a stereotypical image of Freemasons, what they wear and what they do and it is therefore alright to make them the objects of ridicule. Furthermore the overall thrust of the cartoon is that Freemasonry is closely associated with the Conservative and Unionist party (note the banner on the rear wall). A fearsome-looking bust of Margaret Thatcher (1925–) is shown at the bottom right bearing the words 'SMASH THE MINERS'. Taken together it implies that Freemasonry has a particular place in society and a party political agenda.[519] [520]

The use of cartoons to ridicule a minority group is a powerful visual medium. There are other ways to do the same without any images, whether cartoons, photographs or engravings. Below is a 'send-up' of Freemasonry published in the 'Politics and Focus' section of a Scottish national newspaper.[521] The suggestion that Freemasonry has a political bias is inescapable.

Masonic Notes
Holyrood Lodge number 3245, meeting 22/01/02.
Present: The Sixty Brothers on the Mound.
All trousers were raised.
Visier Blue Lion (Mr Gallie) handled the blade and Exposed the novices.
Apologies
Mr David McLetchie: Grand Master of the Trouser Press
Promoted Third Degree
Mr Jamie McGrigor: Apron in waiting.
Mr Brian Montieth: High Bigot of Hibernian.
Mr Annabel Goldie: Apprentice to the Goat, Second Degree.
Brothers were reminded by the Worshipful Grand Master that Membership of clandestine organizations, like the Conservative Party, must be registered with the Ruling Council of the Radiant Star.

All repeat the Oath

'Hand to hand I greet you as a brother; foot to foot I will support
you in all your undertakings; knee to knee, the posture of my daily
supplications shall remind me of your wants; breast to breast,
your lawful secrets when entrusted to me as such I will keep as
my own; and hand over back, I will support your character in
your absence as in your presence.

'Aye. And may our hearts be plucked beating from our breasts
and fed to the ravens at high tide.'

1) Relations with Profanes: Brothers in the Edinburgh Legal lodges
on the importance of observing their promise to form 'a column of
mutual defence' advancing the interests of Brothers of the Divine
Order in all walks of professional life.

2) Admission of Catholics. Upon submission to the absolute power
of the Grand Architect of the Universe. Or when Hell freezes over,
whichever is the sooner.

3) Women's Lodge. Brothers to be reminded of the inability of
women to enter the Light. Until further notice.

4) New Masonry. New Labour Brothers to advise on promotion of
better image of order by advertising slogans: 'Masons:
building for the future'; 'Only a handshake away';
'Embrace a Mason'; 'Masons Do It in an Apron.'

Time for reflection
Upon Masons-in-denial. Any such wilful and perjured individual
Shall be cast from the Brother of the Light into the Great
Darkness. Unless he repenteth to the Grand Architect of the
Universe.

Once a Mason, always a Mason
The text makes it clear what that political bias is – Freemasonry is
allied with the Conservative Party. In the process of attempting to
politicise Freemasonry, the unknown (secret) author reveals a multitude
of erroneous prejudices attributed to Freemasonry which are used to
attack the political party. Freemasonry is therefore being used by the
press as a proxy for party political purposes.

Although ridicule is often produced in visual forms, such as cartoons,
it can also take written and verbal form. The above is such an example,
and the fact that it appeared on the front page of a broadsheet newspaper
demonstrates the depth of Masonophobia. The piece, which is in the
form of a Lodge Summons, also highlights the main grievances that the
authors have against Freemasonry, as well as ridiculing Masonic

practices. It names a number of prominent members of the Conservative Party, suggesting that the writers believe Freemasons are natural supporters of that party. One of these politicians is a woman (Annabel Goldie who is described as 'Mr') but the contradiction between this and the 'fact' that women cannot become Freemasons is another small indication that Masonophobes are not interested in the facts but merely wish to peddle their prejudices to anyone who will listen. It is appropriate to provide here some information regarding women and Freemasonry. There were no women in stonemasons' lodges and the modern form of Freemasonry is merely a continuation of that historical fact. However, that is rarely a satisfactory answer to those who hold prejudiced views of Freemasonry. They are either unaware of, or choose to ignore, the fact that a woman can become a Freemason if she so wishes. There exists a body which admits men and women and another which refuses to admit men. Therefore there are three Masonic groups: one for women only, one for women and men, and one for men only. All possible permutations of the sexes are provided for and it is hard to see what point the Masonophobes are trying to make regarding the non-admission of women, unless it is merely a weapon with which to attack Freemasonry. However this is a digression. The skit above refers to 'Edinburgh Legal lodges' and that the members of such Lodge are to protect one another to the detriment of non-members. Particularly obnoxious is the statement:

'Admission of Catholics. Upon submission to the absolute power of the Grand Architect of the Universe. Or when Hell freezes over, whichever is the sooner.'

Here we see the same old prejudicial error being rolled out once more. Freemasonry does not exclude anyone because of their faith. What can happen is that some people exclude themselves and some churches recommend to their members not to become members. That is quite different from stating that Freemasonry excludes those of a particular faith.

Before ending this chapter, another more subtle problem ought to be discussed regarding Freemasonry and the media. Two examples will suffice to make the point. On 8 March 2004 a group of men who were all Freemasons met in a Masonic building in Suffolk, New York State. They were not there for a Masonic meeting but attending a casual unofficial meeting of a social group. A new member was to be admitted and part of that included 'hazing' with an unloaded pistol. Unfortunately, the gentleman with the unloaded pistol also had with him his own, legally held weapon and he confused which weapon was which. To cut a sad story short, the new member was accidentally shot dead. The full details were investigated by the police, the district attorney and the owners of the building. All agreed that the death was as a result of a stupid, unnecessary stunt that should never have happened. It was reported in the Scottish Press under the headline that Freemasons were now killing each other! That story appeared in the same newspaper every day for a week with slight variations to each account. Two weeks later a Freemason in New York City was brutally murdered in a back alley. The motive was the theft of his gold Masonic ring. Before he was killed his finger bearing the ring was hacked off. All the details were established and the culprit apprehended and charged with murder. That story was also reported in a small paragraph in the same newspaper – for one day only.[522]

This chapter and those preceding it are an attempt to provide some information about the Masonophobia which appeared almost as soon as Freemasonry came to the attention of the public. It must be stressed that this book ought to be treated as merely an introduction to the subject at best, as a detailed investigation into this enduring phenomenon would surely take up several volumes.

CONCLUSION

'The term Masonophobia accurately conveys the level
of nastiness used in attacks on Freemasonry.'
Robert L. D. Cooper.

Why Masonophobia? There is no doubt that Masonophobia is a curious word. Certainly it is not to be found in any current dictionary. Until now the term 'anti-Masonry' and 'anti-Masons' have been used by Freemasons to describe those who attack the Order and its members. However, 'anti-Masonry' is wishy-washy and is in the same league as 'anti-car', 'anti-smoking' etc. As accurate as these terms are in respect of their subjects they convey nothing of the nastiness, spite and sheer malevolence directed at Freemasonry. Something that conveyed the viciousness of the attacks on Freemasonry had to be found, and 'Masonophobia' fulfils that purpose.

From the content of the preceding chapters, it will be seen that a large amount of material and the discussion of it relates to Scotland. While one is aware that England also experienced a sustained period of Masonophobia, the reason is simply, time and space. The amount of English material is so great that it would have taken too long to examine it all and most of it could not have been used here. As Scotland is smaller, so too is the amount of Masonophobic material available. This made it much easier to handle and, of course, I am much more familiar with the events in Scotland than those elsewhere.

Apart from those who hold a genuine belief that Freemasons pose a danger in some form or another there are other groups that use and abuse Freemasonry who have other motives. It is those groups and motives that will now be examined. However, it is timely to recall that it was hoped that this would primarily be an analytical work. Sadly, that was not possible, due in the main to the avoidance of all discussion with the author. This occurred many, many times and suggests a fundamental need for non-Masons to do nothing that would lead to their perceptions and prejudices being challenged. This attitude seems to be held by all Masonophobes often without them realising it, and this is one of the reasons why all prejudice can be so insidious – people do not always appreciate that they are prejudiced. Where society has challenged prejudice, attitudes have been altered for the better. But how can prejudice be challenged and corrected when there are forces determined not to allow that process to take place? Before discussing that, I wish to turn to those who are unconsciously Masonophobic.

Freemasonry has attracted a lot of attention in recent years, particularly in the popular press and media. A flurry of books since 1982 have made numerous suggestions as to the origins of Freemasonry, its history and more especially its alleged involvement in hidden or unknown history. The scale of Freemasonry's involvement in a huge number of different areas means that it is impossible to detail with them all here, but a few will suffice to indicate that diversity. The most commonly debated and popular is the suggested connection between Freemasonry and the medieval Order of the Knights Templar. A veritable industry has grown up around that speculation with books, movies, documentaries, newspaper and magazine articles, websites and even tourist attractions being created. Most of this is quite innocuous and is merely a product of inquisitive minds linked with an entrepreneurial spirit. There was, therefore, no malice intended in these activities but yet, as we shall see, there have been unintended consequences.

The first thing to note is the inherent contradiction embedded in these claims. Essentially Freemasonry is claimed to be a secret society which operates in secret to promote itself as a body and its individual members. Yet these claims are made in public and discuss all aspects of Freemasonry as if it was *not* a secret. This contradiction exists because, although Freemasonry is discussed in public, usually discussed is Freemasonry in relation to the past. Modern Freemasonry is in the curious situation of being perceived as secret because modern writers continue to perpetuate the notion that Freemasonry is a secret society! This is despite the obvious fact that it is not a secret society, something confirmed by the European Court of Human Rights.[523] *Bona fide* researchers can and do make use of Masonic membership records and many websites exist that are run and paid for by Freemasons to explain what they are 'all about'. Part of the confusion lies in the meaning and misunderstanding of the word 'secret'. Secret means clandestine, unknown, hidden, undetectable yet this word is used to describe Freemasonry when it is obviously inaccurate. A real secret society operates with no public profile whatsoever. The Mafia, Triads, terrorist organisations are a few examples, but of course they are nothing like Freemasonry. Such organisations are illegal and are subject to society's censure. Freemasonry is not illegal, is not the subject of legal scrutiny and is not on any government watch list. The inaccurate and repetitive description of Freemasonry as being 'secret' creates the perception that it has dubious characteristics. When Freemasonry and politics are discussed below I shall offer an explanation of why this perception continues to be perpetuated despite Freemasonry being vindicated at the highest levels.

It it is also appropriate to discuss possible motives people have in claiming that Freemasonry poses some kind of a danger.

Political ideology

As has been discussed previously, some political parties at different periods of time have labelled Freemasonry as a danger, usually to the state or some part of it such as the judiciary. The recent past has shown that in the UK, Freemasonry, despite being a legal and legitimate organisation, has been the subject of a sustained witch-hunt originating in the political sphere. Although this form of Masonophobia has always been around, its most recent and intense form can been identified as originating in the early 1990's when it was alleged that Freemasonry was involved in a conspiracy involving the Birmingham Six. The conspiracy gathered pace when it was claimed that the mass-murderer, Thomas Hamilton, was a Freemason. The number and type of allegations against Freemasonry continued to mount, culminating in England with an investigation by the powerful Home Affairs Select Committee into Freemasonry and the Judiciary. In Scotland there was no equivalent investigation, but the Scottish Parliament, Local Authorities and other public bodies introduced rules requiring Freemasons to declare their membership. Various methods of enforcing disclosure were introduced but curiously there was no mechanism to identify whether anyone in the public sector was a Freemason. The outcome of the Home Affairs Select Committee was that the then Home Secretary, Jack Straw (1946–), issued a ministerial instruction requiring that all applicants for positions within the English judicial system declare whether or not they were Freemasons.

It would, however, be a mistake to suggest that Masonophobia is the sole preserve of one part of the political spectrum. Both right-wing and left-wing groupings have attacked Freemasonry in the past. Although some political beliefs seem to have a particular view of Freemasonry this is not consistent across Europe, with different political ideologies adopting different stances. These attitudes also appear to change over time. Although a particular political ideology identifies Freemasonry as an 'enemy', this does not mean that opposing ideologies view Freemasonry as a 'friend'. On the contrary, recent history has shown that the opposing ideology does not defend Freemasonry even when it might be assumed that, in the rough and tumble world of politics, this would be the usual reaction. The first thing that is striking is that Freemasonry suffers doubly – attacked on one hand but not defended on the other. What then is to be made of all this? It seems that Freemasonry does not have a fixed point on the political compass therefore allowing opportunistic attacks. However, there may be other motives or combinations of motives at work, some of which originate outside the political sphere. Examples of this are religious attacks channelled through the political arena.

Religious orthodoxy

Masonophobia emanating from the religious sphere is obviously different from that in the political world, but there may be some commonality which will be discussed shortly. As has been seen previously, attacks on Freemasonry by religious leaders or groups generally have a narrow focus and do not consider wider implications. A couple of examples have served to demonstrate the need to define Freemasonry as a religion before religious attacks can be made. The focus of religious attacks is therefore almost entirely given over to proving that Freemasonry *is* a religion, and only once that has been achieved can an analysis on that basis commence. This extremely narrow treatment of Freemasonry reveals numerous ambiguities, the first of which is that the consequences of categorising Freemasonry as a religion are neither understood – nor discussed – whether deliberately or not. This shows that those making such a claim have only one intention and that is to bring Freemasonry into their field of expertise, nothing more. By exploring what they do not discuss in relation to their view of Freemasonry, it can be seen that this definition is for their ends only. In Chapter 4, an example of this was briefly explored in a 'what if' scenario. If religions, particularly the Christian religion in its various denominations, are the accepted authority that determines what is a religion and what is not, then one would expect that others who are not authorities on the subject would defer to their judgment. This is quite normal and part of everyday practice. Government takes advice on economic matters from economic experts and the same applies to a whole host of other disciplines, ranging from health to education.

The 'what if' example in Chapter 4 connected the claim that Freemasonry was a religion with the consequences of what might occur if that claim was adopted and generally accepted. Freemasonry would have to be accorded protection by the state as being a religion, its members afforded 'Protection from discrimination... on the basis of... religion or belief'. The crucial point here is that the claim of the experts, in this example Christians, that Freemasonry is a religion has not been accepted by the state, or anyone else for that matter. This is another indication that this description of Freemasonry is exclusive to a particular group.

This lack of transference of definition from one power group to another (the religious sphere to the political sphere) is very important, as it indicates a lack of a commonly defined understanding of *what is* Freemasonry.

It seems that this very lack of definition means that Freemasonry is 'available' to every group, every political party, every religion, everyone with a complaint or grievance, to use as a whipping boy. This lack of definition, and how to resolve it, will be discussed below.

Although Masonophobia originates, in the main, from the religious and political realms, there are other bodies that make use of Freemasonry for their own purposes. Rather than attack Freemasonry they use it in a more benign manner, but because the people concerned are not Freemasons they distort Freemasonry for their own ends. Such distortions are a disservice to Freemasonry but that is rarely a consideration. I therefore turn to these users and abusers of Freemasonry and their possible motives.

Freemasonry and politics

As with the section above, on Freemasonry and religion, it must again be made very clear that Freemasons, as Freemasons, cannot discuss politics.[524] What I shall do, is discuss the interface between Freemasonry and politics. The word 'interface' is used tentatively, because there has been very little direct communication between the world of politics and Freemasonry (as a body) and any politicians. The 'interface' is therefore the media through which politicians have made their opinions known, commented on, made allegations about or proposed legislation to deal with Freemasonry. This section might equally have been entitled 'Freemasonry and the media'. However, although a considerable amount of the material reproduced in previous chapters may have originated with the media and not with politicians, I have no way of confirming this despite attempts to do so. I must therefore rely on the general observation that much of the media comment appears to have originated in the world of politics and to a lesser extent that of religion.[525]

Government in the UK is controlled and operated by a specific political party elected by the citizens of the country for that purpose. The leading political party therefore drives much of what the country does as a nation. In the UK it governs what is loosely known as the public sector, which contains such bodies as the National Health Service, local authorities, government departments (defence, finance, international relations, and so on). The other large sector of activity is commonly known as the private sector which is principally concerned with running industry and commerce. The public sector is controlled directly by government and the private sector only indirectly, but it may be influenced in numerous ways.[526] Freemasonry by comparison lies outside the control of government. In the past, as we have previously seen, some governments would not tolerate a body remaining beyond their control and Freemasonry suffered accordingly.

When politicians claim that their private lives have nothing to do with their public duty, I am sure that Freemasons will express exasperation in that they have been threatened with legislation to force them to reveal details of their private lives because they are of interest to politicians! This goes right to the heart of an important point. Does the state have the right to know private details of the lives of a few selected citizens solely on the basis of perception? The question becomes even more important when one understands that this erroneous perception has, in part, been created and perpetuated by, among others, politicians.

Following the investigation by the Home Affairs Select Committee in 1996/97, the committee concluded:

'We recommend that police officers, magistrates, judges, and crown prosecutors should be required to register membership of any secret society and that the record should be available publicly. However, it is our firm belief that the better solution lies in the hands of freemasonry itself. By openness and disclosure, all suspicion would be removed and we would welcome the taking of such steps by the United Grand Lodge.'[527]

A general election in May 1997 returned a different political party to government. The members of the Home Affairs Committee membership changed and the new chairman was Chris Mullin.[528] Under this committee the investigation went much further. The investigation was entitled 'Freemasonry in Public Life'. A preliminary observation built on the previous committee's recommendation (see above) was:

'All new appointments to the judiciary (including part-time offices such as Recorders, Deputy High Court Judges etc.), to the magistracy, to the police, to the legally qualified staff of the CPS, to the Probation Service and Prison Service shall have as a condition of appointment a requirement to declare membership of the freemasons (and any later admission to them). We will consult the relevant bodies on the extent to which new appointments may include those currently in service but who are appointed to a wholly new position or transfer in service or who are promoted.'

The then Home Secretary, Jack Straw, consequently introduced a requirement in England and Wales that all applicants for work as judges, magistrates, police and prison officers had to disclose whether or not they were Freemasons.[529] Less well known is that this requirement also applied to all who were transferred or promoted within the judicial system. The effect of this would mean that, in time, the need to disclose Masonic membership would apply to everyone employed within the judicial system.[530]

As well as demanding that individuals declare their membership, the committee also anticipated that the UGLE might be unwilling or unable to provide the information that the committee thought was needed for a public register of Freemasons in public life:

> 'If the United Grand Lodge is unwilling or unable to comply with this request, or to comply only partially (for example because it does not itself have the data in the required form), the Government will initially make arrangements for registers to be opened for all the specified professions and occupations. All would be invited to register. Although at this stage a failure to return information would not of itself be a breach of conditions of employment, any nil returns would be shown as such on the register.'[531]

As far as is known, none of the three home Grand Lodges (England, Ireland and Scotland) had ever been asked if any applicant was a Freemason. As the government insisted on asking this question, logic dictates that a mechanism would have been put in place to check whether or not an applicant was being truthful as to whether or not he was a Freemason. The home Grand Lodges have never been asked to co-operate in creating such a mechanism. In that light it must be asked, what was the real purpose in asking that question in the first place if it was not to identify Freemasons? Was this perhaps a way of telling public servants that, so far as certain politicians were concerned, being a Freemason was undesirable? If the government was announcing that it was not a good thing for a judge to be a Freemason, what did that convey to a policeman, a civil service clerk or indeed anyone employed directly or indirectly by the state?[532]

This committee extended its enquiries to include an investigation of:

The West Midlands Serious Crime Squad
Conclusion
On the basis of the information supplied, we conclude that

freemasonry was not a primary cause of the difficulties within the Serious Crime Squad although we cannot entirely exclude the possibility that it may have been a contributory factor.

The Birmingham pub bombings investigation
Conclusion
Overall, we conclude that freemasonry was not a significant factor in the Birmingham pub bombings case.

The Stalker-Sampson Inquiry
Conclusion
On the basis of the information supplied, we cannot conclude that freemasonry played a significant part in the Stalker affair. We cannot, however, entirely exclude the possibility that it did.

From this some might uncharitably suggest that the committee was on a second 'fishing expedition' and, even though it found no evidence of undue Masonic influence in any of these three major incidents, could not quite believe Freemasons to be innocent.

As has been previously detailed, the Home Affairs Select Committee report 'Freemasonry in the Police and the Judiciary' (the first inquiry by the committee) found that there was nothing inherently wrong with Freemasonry:

> 'When the oaths are taken in context there is nothing in them that would appear sinister and nothing in the evidence we have heard that would show a conflict between the oath taken by a judge or policeman and that taken by a Freemason.
>
> 'We do not believe that there is anything sinister about freemasonry and are confident that freemasonry does not encourage malpractice.'[533]

In making its recommendations, the Home Affairs Committee(s), a part of the machinery of government, was motivated by perception and not facts. To clarify this further, the matter of perception needs to be very briefly discussed. The committee decided to enquire into Freemasonry *before* it had received or heard any evidence. It therefore acted on some of the committee members' own preconceived perceptions of Freemasonry. This is an important point in that, by instituting the inquiry, they were acting on their own opinions and not evidence. Subsequent submissions to the committee consisted of a large amount of unsubstantiated allegation and innuendo that further perpetuated the perception that Freemasonry was in some way dubious. The (first) committee (1996/97) recognised this and stated that a great deal of the material submitted to it could not be considered as evidence.

'We have given careful consideration to each of the submissions received and note that many of them are devoid of real evidence, or are anecdotal in nature, or where there is evidence it has been largely circumstantial.'[534]

Despite this, the committee concluded on the basis of perception and not evidence that:

'It is obvious that there is a great deal of unjustified paranoia about freemasonry and we have no wish to add to it. We believe that there would be practical difficulties in requiring a register of freemasons in all areas of the Criminal Justice system, but it would certainly be possible to establish one. We also note that the Prime Minister himself has said that he was in favour of a requirement for public officials to declare whether they are freemasons or not, and that the Shadow Home Secretary believes that membership of the freemasons should be a declarable and registrable interest. We believe however that nothing so much undermines public confidence in public institutions as the knowledge that some public servants are members of a secret society, one of whose aims is mutual self-advancement – or a column of mutual support, to use the masonic phrase. We note the claim by United Grand Lodge that freemasons are not a secret society but a society with secrets. We believe, however, that this distinction is lost on most non-masons. The solution is not bans or proscriptions or any form of intolerance. We acknowledge that a lot of honest people derive innocent social pleasure from membership of freemasonry and we have no wish to deprive them of such pleasure. The solution is disclosure. We recommend that police officers, magistrates, judges, and crown prosecutors should be required to register membership of any secret society and that the record should be available publicly. However, it is our firm belief that the better solution lies in the hands of freemasonry itself. By openness and disclosure, all suspicion would be removed and we would welcome the taking of such steps by the United Grand Lodge.'

It is worthy of note that in discussing the evidence presented to the committee it agreed that it was *all* either not real evidence, anecdotal or circumstantial. It did not cite any actual evidence whatsoever.

The Committee admitted that there exists 'a great deal of unjustified paranoia about freemasonry' and states that 'we have no wish to add to it'. Offering that single crumb of comfort, the committee quickly moves on. Despite the committee's acknowledgement that Freemasonry is the victim of 'unjustified paranoia', and that, 'The solution is not bans or proscriptions or any form of intolerance', the committee's answer is not to tackle that paranoia that it accepts is the root cause of the problem. Instead their solution is that:

'police officers, magistrates, judges, and crown prosecutors should be required to register membership of any secret society and that the record should be available publicly.'

It is to be noted that the committee recognises that creating such a register would be difficult but not impossible, and suggests, 'By openness and disclosure, all suspicion would be removed', therefore Freemasonry would serve its own best interests, but significantly would provide the solution desired by the committee without the need for government action and subsequent bureaucracy. As mentioned elsewhere (see below), there is no discussion whatsoever as to *how* Freemasons are to be made to disclose their membership.

At the same time the Home Affairs Select Committee was meeting, a case against the Italian government had been lodged with the European Court of Human Rights (ECHR) and another followed in 1998 (see Chapter 5) – about the same time that the ministerial instruction had been issued by Jack Straw.

In the first case, a Freemason applied for a post on a public body which was overseen by a local authority and which was also responsible for staff recruitment. The Freemason concerned was successful, but objected to the fact that during the application process he was required to declare his membership of a Masonic lodge. In the second case, in another part of Italy, disciplinary proceedings were instituted against a judge who was a Freemason, although he was not active.

The two individuals were members of lodges under the Grande Oriente of Italy and it objected to the fact that, because its members were being discriminated against, consequently so too was the Grande Oriente as a body. It was granted permission to bring cases before the ECHR against the Italian government on the grounds that it was a victim of discrimination in light of the two aforementioned cases. This was an extremely important decision by the court because the Grande Oriente of Italy, like the Grand Lodges of England and Scotland, is an incorporated body and therefore not a legal entity. The reason why the court decided to hear the representations of the Grande Oriente of Italy are complex, but essentially revolve around fundamental tenets of the Convention for the Protection of Human Rights and Fundamental Freedoms – that everyone is entitled to freedom of association and the right to a private life. The court recognised that in this case discriminating against a group (the Grande Oriente of Italy) would affect these fundamental rights of the individual *and* of the group. They did so because Freemasonry is an 'unincorporated body' or, in their terms:

> 'In Italian law the applicant association has the status of an unrecognised private-law association under Article 36 of the Civil Code. It therefore does not have legal personality.'[535]

This point is also immensely significant. Freemasonry in the United Kingdom, and Italy, has no 'legal personality'; that is, Freemasonry is not a legal entity and therefore has no recourse to law on its own behalf. The ECHR therefore understood that Freemasonry (in this instance in the form of the Grande Oriente of Italy) could not therefore defend itself as could a political party or a trade union. In recognition of this, it allowed Freemasonry to be legally represented by way of the fact that individuals were members of the Order. Not being a lawyer, nor a theologian nor a politician for that matter (!), I can only but wonder at the ramifications of this as it seems that, for once, Freemasonry has been provided with a legal precedent that at the very least recognises it as a body on a par with a trade union or political party.

In essence, the court has ruled that Freemasons cannot be discriminated against, and specifically cannot be discriminated against when seeking public office – whether appointed or elected. By implication therefore, Freemasons cannot be discriminated against in any walk of life for that would strike a mortal blow at the fundamental human rights of the individual.

However, the significance of the fact that the Grande Oriente of Italy was permitted to bring two cases against the Italian government is enormous. From the court's deliberations and final judgments the following points can be made:

Freemasonry is a legal, legitimate institution.

Freemasonry is not a criminal organisation.

Freemasonry is not a secret society.

Freemasons have a right to freedom of association.

Freemasons have a right to a private life.

Freemasons cannot be discriminated against on the grounds that they are Freemasons.

Government cannot victimise the institution of Freemasonry (or its members) because it believes there is an adverse public perception of Freemasonry.

Restrictions on Freemasons are not necessary in a democratic society.

Section 11 of the Human Rights Convention (freedom of association) applies to Freemasonry as an organisation in the same way as to a trade union or a political party. (This comparison was specifically cited by the court.)

The court held that there had been a violation of Article 11 of the convention in respect of the reputation and image of the Grande Oriente of Italy. The Italian government had therefore perpetuated the very perception it claimed to be the reason for the discrimination against Freemasons in the first place! In finding that such a violation had taken place, the ECHR ruled that this constituted *in itself* 'just satisfaction' for the damage sustained and the applicant association (the Grande Oriente of Italy) was awarded damages against the Italian government accordingly.

The importance of this judgment, handed down by the highest authority in Europe on matters of human rights, cannot be underestimated. It firstly reaffirmed the status of Freemasonry as being a legal and legitimate organisation. It further confirmed that it is not a criminal organisation and, significantly, also confirmed that it is not a secret society. At last a body that is superior to any single national government had affirmed the status of Freemasonry across Europe. The ECHR took the very unusual step of allowing an organisation to bring a case against a government, unusual because the court is concerned with matters of individual human rights. It recognised that Freemasonry as a body was being discriminated against because individual members were being attacked. This is of the utmost importance, because for the first time Freemasonry, as an institution, has had its rights clearly defined. In doing so the court placed Freemasonry on a par (by way of example) with political parties and trade unions. The judgment therefore applies not only to individuals but also the institution to which they belong.

Here then is an important point for consideration by all Freemasons in Europe. As the ECHR has declared that Freemasonry is not a secret society, any Freemason confronted with the question 'Are you a member of a secret society? (whether written, verbal or by any other means), can now answer, 'No I am not,' with confidence born of a legal judgment.

The court went further in making clear that Freemasons, like members of a political party, a trade union or any other legal, legitimate organisation, have the right to freedom of association and a right to a private life. While this might seem to be self-evident, the court felt the need to repeat those basic human rights and went on to reinforce those rights by stating that Freemasons cannot be discriminated against on the grounds that they are Freemasons. The court also found that Freemasonry is not a secret society:

> 'Accordingly, there was a difference of treatment between the members of the applicant association [the Grande Oriente of Italy] and the members of any other non-secret association.'[536]

As previously mentioned, the detractors of Freemasonry usually launch their attacks from the political or religious spheres. These are categorised as being 'aggressive' attacks. Others which emanate from, for example, the tourist or financial fields are usually 'opportunistic' and are generally designed to make money, generate publicity or arouse curiosity. Others are considered 'passive' and these are more difficult to assess, as they do not obviously attack nor use Freemasonry for their own ends. These are usually more insidious, hidden and deep rooted than the other categories, but are no less obnoxious. These can be described as 'gratuitous', and examples range from the use of the terms, 'Masonic Mafia', 'CIA Freemasons' and 'Catholic Freemasonry'. This gratuitous way of associating Freemasonry with shadowy or even sinister groups is as worrying as the overt attacks, because they are embedded in the committee report, newspaper article, book or edict, etc., quite normal and natural.

One of the dichotomies that has become apparent in this study is the fact that there is no 'transference' between the religious and political sphere. This is made manifest by the judgments of the ECHR. Freemasonry is not a secret society and it is not a criminal organisation. The ECHR made no judgment as to whether or not Freemasonry was a religion, but the absence of comment by the ECHR suggests that it did not view it in that light. The lack of any mention that Freemasonry is a religion by a secular court must have major implications. This court defined Freemasonry as an association similar to a trade union or a political party. Both of these are clearly not religions. However, both 'look after and promote their own' – an accusation that is frequently thrown at Freemasonry. That trade unions and political parties have a central function of looking after particular groups (especially the former) and that function is considered to be legitimate is accepted by most people. That the ECHR chose to compare Freemasonry to those two particular groups is therefore as revealing as it is important. Now that there is a legal ruling that Freemasonry is a legal, legitimate organisation which is not a secret society and, by implication, is not a religion, it must be wondered what effect that will have on those who claim that Freemasonry is a religion. Freemasonry has always rejected the label of a secret society and now it is supported by one of the highest authorities in Europe. The allegation that Freemasonry is a secret society has been used since the early 18th century to bring it under the umbrella of 'religion', and this was done not to welcome Freemasonry into the 'family of religions' but in order to allow it to be criticised on religious grounds. Now that Freemasonry has been legally judged not to be a secret society, and by implication is a secular society, will religious commentators now cease to judge it as if it were a religion? The ECHR also compared Freemasonry to a political party and to a trade union and *not* to any religion, suggesting that it was perceived as a voluntary association. That a supreme secular court has come to that judgment would seem to finally remove Freemasonry from the claimed authority of any church or religion.

This court's judgment comes as near as is possible to a legal definition of Freemasonry. The highest secular court of human rights in Europe has therefore vindicated Freemasonry and the speed, or lack of, the adoption of that judgment by European governments will first and foremost demonstrate their attitude towards Freemasonry and secondly their commitment to human rights.

Freemasonry has few, if any, people in positions of power within the UK willing to come to its defence, and one can but wonder why a legal, legitimate institution that has existed within our liberal democracies for hundreds of years has had to chance to luck that the European Court of Human Rights heard a case that provided vindication.

Now that the ECHR has removed the suggestion that being a Freemason and a public servant is incompatible, one would have assumed that, given the media's obsessive coverage of anything at all to do with Freemasonry, the vindication of Freemasonry would certainly have been newsworthy. Not so. The decision by the Justice Secretary, Jack Straw, to withdraw his own ministerial instruction which he had issued in 1998 (while Home Secretary 1997–2001), was said to be due to the fact that, in the ten years it had been in force, nothing had been found to suggest impropriety within the judiciary as a consequence of being a

Freemason![537] The fact that Freemasonry had been vindicated by the ECHR, something recognised by Jack Straw, did not stop some politicians from attacking it.[538] More important surely is the fact that the United Grand Lodge of England (UGLE) had communicated their intention to seek a judicial review of his ministerial instruction. The full text of the Justice Minister's decision, as reported in the *Guardian* newspaper, is as follows:

'The United Grand Lodge of England made representations in May. They drew attention to the decision of the European Court of Human Rights in Grande Oriente D'Italia di Palazzo Giustiniani v Italy (No 1) and Grande Oriente D'Italia di Palazzo Giustiniani v Italy (No 2) and indicated that they might seek judicially to review the application of the policy to the judiciary. In the light of my consideration of those representations I decided to review the policy.

'As a result of this review we have decided to end the current policy of requiring applicants for judicial office to declare membership of the freemasons. The review of the policy operating since 1998 has shown no evidence of impropriety or malpractice within the judiciary as a result of a judge being a freemason and in my judgment, therefore, it would be disproportionate to continue the collection or retention of this information.'[539]

The fact that Her Majesty's government had to be made aware that a judicial review was being considered before accepting, and adopting, a judgment issued by the European Court of Human Rights several years previously must be something of an embarrassment, to say the least. The ECHR's observation that Freemasonry was not a secret society challenged the very basis of the Home Affairs Select Committees recommendation 'that police officers, magistrates, judges, and crown prosecutors should be required to register membership of any secret society and that the record should be available publicly' and Jack Straw issued his ministerial instruction based on that recommendation. Once the ECHR had made it clear that Freemasonry was not a secret society, the Home Affairs Select Committee's recommendation and Jack Straw's subsequent ministerial instruction was therefore without foundation.

This vindication of Freemasonry was reported not with any fanfare but by a low key, without-comment, entry in the least prominent pages of our national newspapers. This is a far cry from the front-page proclamation that Freemasons were attempting to recruit Members of the Scottish Parliament. There was no discussion of the past or of the pain and anguish experienced by ordinary Freemasons. Simply put, Freemasons are human beings, they have feelings, they have families and they are voters. It is fortunate that, in this 'free and democratic' country, this minority group was able to rely on an authority higher than that of the UK government. However, the damage has been done. As has been seen previously, history shows that projecting a negative image over and over again of a minority group, especially when the allegations, 'evidence' and opinion are presented in a plausible manner which invokes the need to protect the 'majority', is very potent. This form of alienation can be a precursor to persecution. It must be hoped that the ECHR judgment will end the treatment of Freemasons on the basis of perception and paranoia.

Effect of Masonophobic Attacks

Although it is not possible to know with any certainty what effect this constant Masonophobic reporting had on any particular part of society, it seems some change in voting patterns may have taken place. There is anecdotal evidence that attitudes of some voters have been changed by Masonophobic material. It may be that some Freemasons who traditionally tend to vote for a particular political party have been caught in a dilemma when that party has been in the vanguard of attacks on Freemasonry.[540]

Anti-discrimination legislation has been enacted in the UK, all of which is intended to move towards a fairer, more equal society. The latest piece of legislation is the Equality Act 2010 and forms the basis of anti-discrimination legislation in the UK at the present time. It requires: 'equal treatment in access to employment as well as private and public services, regardless of gender, race, disability, sexual orientation, belief and age'.[541] The act contains the following definitions:

Religion means any religion and a reference to religion includes a reference to a lack of religion.

Belief means any religious or philosophical belief and a reference to belief includes a reference to a lack of belief.

If, as some churches claim, Freemasonry is a religion, would anti-discrimination legislation not apply to Freemasons? The problem here lies in the fact that Freemasonry is described as a religion for the internal purposes of any particular church. Churches that claim Freemasonry is a religion are not doing so with an eye on anti-discrimination legislation. This discussion also highlights the fact that there is no body with the right to decide what organisations can be defined as a religion and those that cannot – despite the fact that some churches have assumed that right!

It is intriguing to note that the legislation also defines 'belief' as being 'any religious or philosophical belief' and so provides protection to those who have a philosophical belief. This is something much wider than a religious belief.

We have seen, particularly in the previous chapter, that a huge number of allegations were made in the recent past against Freemasonry and some of these have been of a serious nature including corruption, murder, blackmail and paedophilia. In a society as organised as ours, such grave crimes committed by an identified organisation over a period of decades could not have failed to attract the attention of the authorities.

One way of categorising attacks on Freemasonry is to define any particular attack as passive or aggressive, which can be helpful in determining the seriousness of such attacks. The former can, for example, be based on ignorance or repetition of error. The latter tends to be based on clear understanding of what Freemasonry is believed to be, and this is almost always negative. It usually is based on perception and an element of malice can occasionally be identified. A brief discussion of this form of categorisation follows.

Holocaust Memorial Day (Passive)
It has previously been demonstrated in Chapter 3 that Freemasonry was a very specific victim group brought to the pinnacle of persecution during the Nazi and Fascist regimes of the mid-20th century – although that certainly does not mean Freemasons today wish to be considered as victims. That the Gestapo had a section to deal solely with Freemasonry shows that it was considered in much the same light as Judaism, Communism, trade unionism, Sinti, Jehovah's Witnesses, homosexuals, blacks, Slavs and Poles. It was only a twist of fate that one of the primary functionaries of the Final Solution, Adolf Eichmann, was transferred from dealing with Freemasons to dealing with the Jews. The list of groups persecuted by the Nazis is based on those targeted by the Gestapo and other branches of the regime. Most of these, including Freemasonry, were specifically mentioned at the Nuremberg Trials and have been repeated by subsequent researchers and historians.

On Thursday, 27 January 2000, representatives of 44 countries attended a meeting in Stockholm, Sweden, of the Stockholm Forum on Holocaust Education, Remembrance and Research. This inter-governmental conference was convened by the Swedish government to give support for education and research in an attempt to better equip governments to combat racism, anti-Semitism and intolerance as they manifest themselves in modern-day society. At the conclusion of the conference, the heads of delegations unanimously agreed to sign the Declaration of the Stockholm Forum.[542] As part of Britain's Holocaust Memorial Day, the principles of the declaration were adopted and adapted into the Statement of Commitment, as a benchmark for understanding the aims and objectives of Holocaust Memorial Day. In 2000 the United Kingdom government decided that a special day ought to be set aside to commemorate those who suffered and died during the Holocaust of World War 2 (1939–1945). In so doing, the government was acknowledging that particular groups of people were subject to 'special treatment' – a euphemism for systematic arrest, torture, starvation and death by a variety of means. While it is common knowledge that during WW2 particular groups were selected for 'special treatment' by the Nazi regime, it is almost unknown that Freemasons also came into that category. Few people are aware that Freemasons suffered at the hands of the Nazis following Hitler's rise to power in 1933. This is most likely due to the fact that Freemasons were numerically a much smaller group than most others.

As early as 1924 in his book, *Mein Kampf*, Hitler had made it clear that as far as he was concerned Freemasons and Jews were responsible for the condition of post-war Germany. Essentially, Hitler's argument was that Freemasons and Jews had colluded in taking over large parts of German society and had brought the country to its knees – politically, culturally and economically.

Few people are aware of the persecution of Freemasons by the Nazi regime and fewer still know that many Freemasons were hunted down and executed by Franco (Spain), Stalin (USSR) and Mussolini (Italy). In addition, we have seen that the apparatus of persecution was exported to countries occupied by German forces and that Freemasons were also executed, and their property stolen by Nazis, in Norway, Denmark, Holland, Belgium, France, Luxembourg, Poland, Czechoslovakia, Hungary, Greece, Austria, Romania, etc. As no accurate figures are known, the exact total death toll of Freemasons must be partly guess work. However, using those figures which are available, such as those for Czechoslovakia, it is possible to tentatively extrapolate. One such estimate suggests that the number of Freemasons who died because they *were* Freemasons would be approximately 80,000.

It is curious therefore that the Holocaust Memorial Day Trust does not recognise Freemasonry as a single identifiable group selected for 'special treatment' by the Nazi regime.[543] [544] Despite repeated attempts, I have been unable to obtain an explanation as to why this should be.[545] The statement above – 'Freemasons who died because they were Freemasons' might provide a clue and also is indicative of the institutionalised Masonophobia that exists in the United Kingdom at the present time. What feedback I have obtained from those involved in Holocaust studies suggests one simple reason.[546] If Freemasonry was accepted to have been a group targeted for 'special treatment' then they would become a 'victim group', a minority that was deserving of sympathy and support. This would fly in the face of the present perception of Freemasonry, that it is elitist and part of the establishment. For that reason Masonophobes will fight tooth and nail to ensure that Freemasonry is never allowed to be seen in a sympathetic manner, as to do otherwise would be to deprive them of their prejudice. Here again, the judgement of a minority group can been seen to be made on the basis of perception and not facts. The fact that Adolf Eichmann spent months compiling a card index of German Freemasons before moving on to do the same for German Jews is an inconvenient fact and one that cannot be allowed to disturb long-cherished prejudice.

A less emotive explanation has been offered for not accepting that Freemasonry was a group targeted for 'special treatment' and that is because it is not possible to show that Freemasons were victimised solely for being Freemasons. The argument is that Freemasons are often referred to in the same breath: 'Jews and Freemasons' or 'Freemasons and Jews'. This is a disingenuous argument, as mentioning two distinct and separate groups in the same breath does not make them into one group and does not mean that one, or the other, does not exist. Curiously this argument is only applied to Freemasonry. No one, for example, claims that neither Communism nor trade unionism do not exist even though both are often discussed 'in the same breath'. Both are, of course, included in the list of persecuted minorities. The argument has been further refined by explaining that, as the Jews were numerically far larger and their sufferings much more comprehensively documented, there was no need to refer separately to Freemasons!

The fact remains that the names of many Freemasons who were tortured, confined to concentration camps or executed because they *were* Freemasons are known. Denying recognition of their suffering is a denial of their humanity.

Dunblane Massacre (Aggressive)

The mass murder of 16 children and one adult in March 1996 was claimed to be the result of a Masonic conspiracy to protect the murderer Thomas Hamilton. In racing to rebut the claim that Hamilton was a Freemason a very important point was missed, and that was the assumption that being a Freemason was in some way bad. A deeper assumption, even more disturbing, is that Freemasons act in certain ways because they *are* Freemasons. Disproving that Hamilton was a Freemason did nothing to dismiss that assumption and, in any event, the proof that he was not a Freemason was not widely reported and so too this limited objective was not achieved. Let us, however, return to the main point. The presumption that Freemasons act in a particular way because they are Freemasons is bound up with the idea that because all take the same oath, they are bound to always protect each other regardless of the circumstances, Freemasonry, it seems, is the only institution that is seen in this way and it appears to be, yet again, a matter of perception not fact. The argument that Hamilton was a Freemason went something like this: Hamilton was mentally unstable; a mentally unstable man would not be allowed to own guns; the police issue firearms certificates and they did so to Hamilton; all police officers are Freemasons, so they would only issue a firearms certificate to a mentally unstable person if he too was a Freemason. Putting the argument in this way highlights its ridiculous nature. In any event, what one person does cannot be expanded to include every member of all organisations of which the individual is a member – except in the case of Freemasonry! A priest must take an oath, or vow, on entering the priesthood. These are essentially vows of chastity, poverty, and obedience to the Church.[547] When a priest sexually molests a child, the automatic reaction is horror then sympathy for the child and family, closely followed by sympathy for the Church concerned. This reaction is the result of the reality that the Church is not responsible for the aberrant actions of a single individual. Sadly, in the recent past there has been more than the occasional and isolated case of child abuse, and yet the church of which the priest or minister was a member has not been held directly responsible.[548] There have been a number of court cases which have revealed the sordid details, and the resultant anguish of other members of the church is understandable. However, so far as Freemasonry is concerned, normal human understanding is suspended and the organisation as a whole is held to be culpable for the actions of one individual. How many cases have been brought to court on the basis that a person committed a criminal act because he was a member of the Church of Scotland? None. How many cases have been brought to court because the individual was a Freemason? None. Crimes are prosecuted because of what was alleged to have been done, not on the basis of belonging to a voluntary association such as Freemasonry.

Masonophobic Websites (Aggressive)

Masonophobia is big business! Google Freemasonry and the results might shock you. What appears is not a list of *Masonic* sites but, in the main, a list of Masonophobic websites. They appear to be very adroit at using internet search engines or paying to have their sites promoted by the likes of Google.[549] Their content and nature vary enormously, much like Masonic sites it must be admitted, but all do not have the interests of Freemasonry at heart. These sites can be divided into three main types:

Conspiracy theorist sites which may or may not focus entirely on Freemasonry as the cause of all the world's ills.

Religious sites which claim that Freemasonry is anti-Christian (at the very least) or is a devil-worshipping cult.

News sites which report all the bad news about Freemasonry and none of the good news.

Some sites contain elements of all three, but there is one common thread – money. Some sites are quite open about this in offering material (e.g. books and DVDs of religious tracts) which support their Masonophobic views. The other way such sites make money is by advertising. Advertisers will pay to have links from heavily visited sites and therefore the purpose of these sites becomes one of making money rather than their original purpose. Some Masonophobic website owners even pay search engines to guarantee that their website is prominently displayed when people search for information about Freemasonry.

Tourist Attractions (Passive)

Rosslyn Chapel is the prime example of how Freemasonry was used, and arguably abused, in the course of promoting a tourist attraction. I would not use the term Masonophobia in this instance. This subject has been touched upon elsewhere and therefore only a brief discussion is necessary.[550] When Freemasonry has been accused of criminal activity in the press, examples of which have been provided previously, Freemasonry itself (specifically a head office – a Grand Lodge) has rarely been invited to comment in advance of the publication. In the same way other organisations have 'hijacked' Freemasonry for their own use and have done so without consulting Freemasons. There are numerous examples that could be cited, but probably the best known one is Rosslyn Chapel. In the early 1980s books began to appear which made a variety of claims about Freemasonry and the chapel. The number of books claiming some kind of hidden history which usually linked modern Freemasonry to the medieval Order of Knights Templar, the Holy Grail, lost treasure, etc, began to accelerate throughout the 1990's. Each new book elaborated the claims made in earlier books. As each claim became more sensational, more and more people began to visit the chapel in order to see what all the fuss was about.

The claims about Freemasonry, its history and alleged links with various shadowy organisations came to be incorporated into the official account of the chapel. In 1989 a new guide book was produced which included many of the sensational notions of some writers. Freemasonry was not consulted prior to the publication and this led to a number of problems for Freemasonry – not the chapel. This is a case of what I call 'passive anti-Masonry'; that is, there was no conscious malicious attempt to abuse Freemasonry, but rather there was an unthinking use of dubious material. One example will suffice to illustrate the point. In the chapel there are three pillars at the east end, one of which (that at the southeast side) is known as the Apprentice Pillar. There is a story associated with this pillar which is briefly recounted as follows. The owner of the chapel wanted a copy made of an ornate pillar, the original being in Rome. The master mason was provided with a drawing of the original pillar, but was not confident enough to create the copy without first examining the original. He was permitted to travel to Italy to see the pillar. In his absence, an apprentice stonemason completed the pillar. The master mason on his return to the chapel was outraged to see the pillar so brilliantly finished by the apprentice. In a fit of jealous rage, he struck the apprentice a fatal blow to the forehead.

This tale was claimed by some to be related directly to the allegorical tale incorporated in the third or Master Mason's degree of Freemasonry.[551] On this erroneous basis the other two pillars became associated with the second or Fellow of Craft degree and the third with the Master Mason's degree. This was done despite the obvious contradiction that the story of the apprentice pillar was said to relate to the third or Master Mason's degree! From that point on, other carvings near to these three pillars were considered Masonic. In particular, there are three carvings of angels which have adopted a variety of postures. These angels were described as being in positions of significance to Freemasons (see Plate 20). It was a small step for these carvings to then be described as being 'Masonic Angels'![552] At the same time Freemasonry was claiming not to be a religion. Rosslyn Chapel staff were telling people from all over the world that there was such a thing as Masonic angels. Try telling the church that it was not Freemasons who were claiming that Masonic angels existed! Had Grand Lodge been consulted, this problem might have been resolved earlier.[553] This hardly indicates that Freemasonry is an all-powerful organisation that rules the world!

This example is not about 'bashing the Masons'; the aim was not to assist Freemasonry but to use it for the chapel's own purposes. Rosslyn Chapel is 550 years old and in need of repair. One way of raising the necessary funds is to charge visitors a fee. Obviously, the more visitors, the faster the much needed money will be collected. This serves to show non-Masons are quite happy to use Freemasonry to achieve quite different goals.

Jews and Freemasonry

It is now difficult to separate Freemasonry from Judaism, as the two have been constantly linked by non-Masons since the early 19th century. Initially, Freemasons and Jews were *not* connected and were attacked separately, and for different reasons, until such a connection was made by those who followed Barruel. Thereafter, Freemasonry and Judaism are often mentioned in the same breath. The pattern that developed illustrates some important points as to how some groups can be made into society's scapegoats.

The first condition, and one that is required to kick-start the process of creating a scapegoat, must be an unexplained or unexplainable event such as the French Revolution or the defeat of Germany in 1918. In order to explain the unexplainable a likely culprit is sought. This culprit must be an 'acceptable' group rather than an individual, and this usually means that the group is easily identifiable and not part of mainstream society. Freemasons and Jews fit this profile as they are in a minority, and those who are not members do not know what takes place in their meeting places (Lodges and synagogues). This casting about for a suitable culprit, who is almost always innocent, is part of the process of creating an 'enemy within'. Such groups are part of society but are also obviously separate because of their different history, culture and practices. If there is already a body of evidence, no matter how spurious, the need to justify the presumption of guilt is much reduced. Thus, after the defeat of the German army in 1918, the existence of the *Protocols of the Elders of Zion* provided so-called evidence of a Judaeo/Masonic conspiracy that had stabbed Germany in the back. Once identified as an 'enemy within', the process is reinforced in a number of ways which today are deemed politically incorrect. These consist of polemics against the group, emphasising differences (often physical characteristics, see Plate 21), ridiculing unusual practices often by means of caricature. The culmination of the process saw members of the minority group being identified and then officially designated by the state as non-citizens, leading to segregation, systematic harassment, torture and genocide.

Many will be at least vaguely aware that this process reached its ultimate conclusion in Nazi Germany and occupied countries. However, the initial parts of this process also took place in the victorious liberal democracies. (See Plate 21).

Once the full extent of the Holocaust became generally known, anti-Semitism declined sharply. Curiously, and despite the repeated and emphatic allegations of a link between Freemasonry and Judaism, Masonophobia did not decline in comparison with anti-Semitism. If anything, attacks on Freemasonry increased and escalated during the period after the war, reaching, as we have seen, a high water mark in the 1990's as manifest by the Home Affairs Select Committee investigation into Freemasonry, the Dunblane Masonic conspiracy allegations, the demands that Freemasons in public service be identified and the various codes of conduct introduced by national and local government and trade unions, requiring that individuals declare whether or not they were Freemasons. Part of the process, briefly explained above, in relation to post-WW1 Germany which led to the deaths of thousands of Freemasons during the Nazi period was recommenced in the UK after WW2, as demonstrated by publication of exposures such as that of Walton Hannah, calls for the compulsory identification of Freemasons in public service and the ridicule of Masonic practices (see Plate 23). Fortunately, the post-war wave of Masonophobia did not come close to the conclusion experienced during the war, but for many the repetition of the first stages of persecution was deeply worrying. The fact that a similar pattern of persecution had again commenced suggested that if any conspiracy existed, it was a conspiracy against Freemasonry. Once a minority becomes the focus of prejudice and spite, it is not possible to predict the eventual outcome of the process – as the Nazi experience proved.

A working hypothesis as to why Masonophobia exists

Given the unwarranted reputation of Freemasonry since the 18th century, it has been used and abused by almost everyone with an axe to grind. From the taking of an oath, causing the Spanish Civil War, to the assassination of John F. Kennedy (1917–1963), Freemasonry is the alleged culprit. When the magnitude and longevity of the accusations against Freemasonry are considered one cannot but wonder why such an allegedly vile, corrupt, revolutionary and criminal organisation remains in existence and has done so for at least 500 years.[554] The mere fact that Freemasonry continues to exist means that no government seriously believes that Freemasonry is a threat. Had governments, and people in power, really believed that Freemasonry could be capable of such base attitudes and acts, then Freemasonry would have been proscribed. The European Court of Human Rights does not agree with that view of Freemasonry, declaring it not to be a 'secret society'. What therefore is the motive for the use of Freemasonry in explaining a huge number of events both momentous and minor?

The first clue is the fact that some of the events laid at the door of Freemasonry have no obvious cause. That perhaps ought to be refined: some of the events laid at the door of Freemasonry had no obvious cause *at the time*.

Human beings seem to have an innate desire to understand events and to see a pattern in everything that takes place. Many people experience frustration over events which have no apparent cause and the need to explain the unexplainable becomes overwhelming. Speculation as to possible causes can lead to the development of conspiracy theories. These theories have the benefit of fulfilling the need for an explanation; any explanation. There are a multitude of such unexplained events and associated conspiracy theories. Some of these have been mentioned earlier and range from the assassination of John F. Kennedy (JFK) to the death of Princess Diana and the Dunblane massacre. One of the common characteristics in such events is that most, if not all, of the (possible) perpetrators have died or have disappeared. This means that there is no one available to reveal who was involved and what were the motives. Where momentous events such as revolutions have no obvious cause, or at least there is no obvious cause at the time, the need for an explanation is also strong. The theories which develop to explain such events rarely suggest that they were caused by a single individual, for that would not constitute a conspiracy. It is much more common to believe that the event was the result of a group of people. Thus the assassination of JFK by Lee H. Oswald (1939–1963) is not acceptable to conspiracy theorists, especially as Oswald was murdered before he could explain his motives.[555] Various groups have been claimed to be responsible, including the CIA, Mafia, KGB, Cuban exiles and, of course, Freemasonry.[556]

Freemasonry also fits the needs of others, of non-Masons. As society, quite correctly, seeks to reduce discrimination against minorities, the number of 'available' politically correct groups has been reduced. Many will recall that it was common to hear jokes about the disabled, Irish people, homosexuals, black people and Jews. Various forms of discrimination against these groups was commonplace in the UK as well as elsewhere. Measures have been taken, including education and legislation, to try to end such discrimination. This is very laudable, but means there are fewer and fewer available groups to blame. Regrettably, it remains acceptable to attack Freemasonry despite the Order being legal and legitimate. As with conspiracy theorists who seek to identify groups responsible for major traumatic events, so too do some individuals seek to allocate blame for their misfortunes onto someone other than themselves.

In this way, Freemasonry is used to explain away calamitous national and international events such as the collapse of the German military at the end of World War 1, as well as personal misfortunes of all types. For more than 200 years Freemasonry has served as society's 'whipping boy', available to assuage the psychological needs of people in every part of the world. The perception of Freemasonry as being responsible for a host of undesirable and/or unfortunate events both general and personal is reinforced each time it is accused.

Concluding the conclusion

The question has been asked, 'Why rake it all up again?' There are several answers. First and foremost, just because Masonophobic hysteria has reduced in the recent past does not mean that it has gone away, quite the contrary. As has been shown in these pages, attacks on Freemasonry are many and varied and have continued for more than 300 years. A pattern of sorts can be discerned relating to major inexplicable events (assassinations, revolutions, wars, economic crises among others) which are inevitably followed by an upsurge in anti-Masonic sentiment. However, Masonophobia presents itself according to the motives of those attacking Freemasonry. An example is when an individual, or a group of people wishes to divert attention from something that is embarrassing, or to disguise information or events that are unfavourable to the group concerned. Such tactics are by no means restricted to attacks on Freemasonry, but it does seem that Freemasonry is 'handy', as has previously been discussed.[557] Although no 'events pattern' can be identified when attacks are based on other motives, it is important to appreciate the causes and this will, hopefully, identify them more easily and quicker than hitherto.

Attacks on Freemasonry also serve another important function in binding members of a particular group together. In this situation, Freemasonry is not attacked in order to change or 'convert' Freemasons to another point of view, but to provide a particular group with an enemy which the group is required to defend itself against. This has the additional effect of preventing members of the group from straying beyond specific bounds and minimises the risk of defection. An element of fear is therefore involved. When Freemasonry is chosen as the enemy, Masonophobic attacks inevitably follow as the group seeks to defend itself. It matters not that the 'enemy' in fact poses no threat whatsoever to the group. It might be argued that the lack of any real threat is actually beneficial, for there is no actual risk involved in designating Freemasonry as an enemy.[558]

A more subtle and often overlooked motive is that Freemasonry is an indirect attack on another group. This motivation has existed as long as Masonophobia as indicated by the Burgess Oath controversy of the 18th century. (See Chapter 2, pp36-9.) Rather than attack the establishment over oath taking, the General Associate Synod attacked Freemasonry as substitute for their belief that the taking of oaths was anti-Christian. As Freemasonry was not in a position of power this attack could be made with impunity, but served the purpose of highlighting the religious belief that all oath taking was anti-Christian. The General Associate Synod therefore made its point in public and without adverse reaction, yet Freemasonry is still attacked on this basis even although the original religious motives have long since been relegated to a historical backwater.

As a Freemason I also believe that it is important to bear witness to more recent events for the benefit of future generations. Press material, a very small proportion of which is reproduced in this volume, might assist others who are unaware of the scale and nature of attacks on Freemasonry. The reproduction of this material, much from the period when Masonophobia was at its most intense, is, I believe, a representative sample of the type of press reports that had huge circulation at the time. For those who have not the time to locate examples such as these, it ought to provide an indication of not only the intensity but also the form of 'evidence' used to make the case against Freemasonry.

The most recent significant advance for Freemasonry must be the judgment handed down by the ECHR and discussed above (see pp229-35). In the analytical and dispassionate courtroom, emotion is removed from the examination of facts and evidence. Prejudice, perception, ungrounded belief and pure spite play no part in the search for truth and justice. When examined in that fair and unbiased manner Freemasonry is exonerated at the highest level. One is led to believe that, in this knowledge, those whose faces are set against Freemasonry have done all in their power to avoid allowing Freemasonry the opportunity to publicly defend itself. The saddest aspect of the recent wave of Masonophobia is that not one individual in a position of power and authority came forward to defend a legal, legitimate minority group. As in Nazi

Germany, no powerful voices were raised against the demands that the state should force private individuals to register with the state that they were Freemasons.[559] To what use such a register would be put has never been explained. This raises suspicions that the information would be used not for the benefit of Freemasons, but for other, darker purposes.

Freemasons are entitled to have Masonophobic actions and attitudes placed on record, in the hope that the political and religious tolerance and understanding already extended to other minority groups will soon encompass Freemasonry.

Finally, a large part of the problem seems to centre on repeated attempts to define, explain or otherwise understand Freemasonry as an institution. By its very nature, Freemasonry cannot be compared to any existing group or body. This is very difficult for many people to accept, because we all have a good idea of what groups in society 'are about', what they do, what they stand for and what their aims and objectives are. Freemasonry is the exception to this because individual Freemasons do not have a dogma to guide their actions. One way to consider Freemasonry is as a framework through which individuals can move as they wish, in any direction they wish, interpreting and understanding what they see and hear. They might well be offered opinions and interpretations by other Freemasons also navigating the same framework, but these opinions can be accepted, rejected or modified. There is no central authority that dictates where the framework begins or ends or what various symbols, words and objects mean. Thus Freemasonry means different things to different people at different times. As a self-interpreting system it therefore defies classification.

Once it is understood that Freemasonry cannot be classified, labelled and filed away, then perhaps comparisons will no longer be made. Freemasonry will be accepted for what it is: a peculiar system of morality, veiled in allegory and illustrated with symbols.

APPENDICES

ONE

Statutum penes regimen magistrii latimi ecclesie collegiate Beati Egidij burgi

(Statute anent [about] the government of the master masons of the College Kirk of St. Giles of the Burgh of Edinburgh.)

The quhilk day, the prouest dene of gild haillies and counsale of the burgh of Edinburgh thinkis expedient and als ordanis that thair maister masoun and the laif of his colleges and seruandis of thair kirk wark that now ar and sall happin to be for the tyme sail diligentlie fulfill and keip thair seruice at all tymes and houiris as after followes : That is to say, The said maister and his seruandis sail begyn to thair werk ilk day in somer at the straik of v houris in the morning, and to continew besylie into thair lawbour quhill viij houris thairafter, and than to pas to thair disione and to remane thairat half ane hour, and till enter agane to thair lawbouris at half hour to ix houris before none, and swa towirk thairat quhill that xj houris be strikken, and afternone to forgather agane to their wark at the hour of ane, and than to remayne quhill iiij houris afternone, and than to gett a recreatioun in the commoun luge be the space of half ane hour, and fra thine furth to abyde at thair lawbour continually quhill the hour of vii be strikkin: And in winter to begyn with day Licht in the morning kepand the houris abouewritten, and to haif bot their none shanks allanerly afternone, and to remayne quhill day licht be gane. And gif the said maister quhatsumeuir or his collegis and seruandis faillis in ony poyntis abouewritten, or remainis fra his said seruice ony tyme, he to be correctit and pvnist in his wages at the plesour of the dene of gild that sell happin to be for the tyme, as the said dene will ansuer to God and the guid towne theirvpon.

TWO

The Protocols of the Learned Elders of Zion

PROTOCOL 1

What I am about to set forth, then, is our system from the two points of view, that of ourselves and that of the goyim, i.e. non-Jews...[560]

Our power in the present tottering conditions of all forms of power will be more invincible than any other, because it will remain invisible until the moment when it has gained such strength that no cunning can any longer undermine it...

Let us, however, in our plans, direct our attention not so much to what is good and moral as to what is necessary and useful...

We must not stop at bribery, deceit and treachery when they should serve toward the attainment of our end...

Far back in ancient times we were the first to cry among the masses of the people the words "Liberty, Equality, Fraternity"... [These words] brought to our ranks, thanks to our blind agents, whole legions who bore our banners with enthusiasm. And all the time these words were cankerworms at work boring into the well-being of the goyim, and putting an end everywhere to peace, quiet, solidarity, and destroying all the foundations of the goya states. As you will see later, this helped us to our triumph; it gave us the possibility among other things of getting into our hands the master card – the destruction of the privileges, or in other words of the very existence of the aristocracy of the goyim, that class which was the only defence peoples and countries had against us. On the ruins of the natural and genealogical aristocracy of the goyim we have set up the aristocracy of our educated class headed by the aristocracy of money. The qualifications for this aristocracy we have established in wealth, which is dependent upon us, and in knowledge, for which our learned elders provide the motive force.

PROTOCOL 2

It is indispensable, for our purpose, that wars, so far as possible, should not result in territorial gains; war will thus be brought onto the economic ground, where the nations will not fail to perceive in the assistance we give the strength of our predominance and this state of things will put both sides at the mercy of our international agentur; which possesses millions of eyes ever on the watch and unhampered by any limitations whatsoever. Our international rights will then wipe out national rights, in the proper sense of right, and will rule the nations precisely as the civil law of States rule the relations of their subjects among themselves.

The intellectuals of the goyim will puff themselves up with their knowledge and without any logical verification of them will put into effect all the information available from science, which our agentur specialists have cunningly pieced together for the purpose of educating their minds in the direction we want. Do not suppose for a moment that these statements are empty words: think carefully of the successes we arranged for Darwinism, Marxism, Nietzscheism. To us Jews, at any rate, it should be plain to see what a disintegrating importance these directives have had upon the minds of the *goyim*...

It is in the Press that the triumph of freedom of speech finds its incarnation. But the goyim States have not known how to make use of this force; and it has fallen into our hands. Through the Press we have gained the power to influence while remaining ourselves in the shade; thanks to the Press we have got the gold in our hands, notwithstanding that we have had to gather it out of oceans of blood and tears.

PROTOCOL 3

Today I may tell you that our goal is now only a few steps off. There remains a small space to cross and the whole long path we have trodden is ready now to close its cycle of the Symbolic Snake by which we symbolize our people. When this ring closes, all the States of Europe will be locked in its coil as in a powerful vice...

In order to incite seekers after power to a misuse of power we have set all forces in opposition one to another... The people under our guidance have annihilated the aristocracy who were their one and only defence and foster-mother for the sake of their own advantage which is inseparably bound up with the well-being of the people. Nowadays, with the destruction of the aristocracy, the people have fallen into the grips of merciless money-grinding scoundrels who have laid a pitiless and cruel yoke upon the necks of the workers. We appear on the scene as alleged saviours of the worker from this oppression when we propose to him to enter the ranks of our fighting forces – Socialists, Anarchists, Communists – to whom we always give support in accordance with an alleged brotherly rule (of the solidarity of all humanity) of our social masonry. The aristocracy, which enjoyed by law the labour of the workers, was interested in seeing that the workers were well fed, healthy and strong. We are interested in just the opposite, in the diminution, *the killing out of the goyim*...

This hatred will be still further magnified by the effects of an *economic crisis*, which will stop dealings on the exchanges and bring industry to a standstill. We shall create by all the secret subterranean methods open to us and with the aid of gold, which is all in our hands, *a universal economic crisis whereby we shall throw upon the streets whole mobs of workers simultaneously in all the countries of Europe...*

Remember the French Revolution, to which it was we who gave the name of *Great*: the secrets of its preparation are well known to us for it was wholly the work of our hands. Ever since that time we have been leading the peoples from one dis-enchantment to another, so that in the end they should turn also from us in favour of that *King Despot of the blood of Zion, whom we are preparing for the world.*

PROTOCOL 4

Gentile masonry blindly serves as a screen for us and our objects, but the plan of action of our force, even its very abiding place, remains for the whole people an unknown mystery...

But even freedom might be harmless and have its place in the State economy without injury to the well-being of the peoples if it rested upon the foundation of faith in God, upon the brotherhood of humanity, unconnected with the conception of equality, which is negative by the very laws of creation, for they have established subordination. With such a faith as this a people might be governed by a wardship of parishes and would walk contentedly and humbly under the guiding hand of its spiritual pastor submitting to the dispositions of God on earth. This is the reason: why it is *indispensable for us to undermine all faith, to tear out of the minds of the* GOYIM *the very principle of the Godhead, and the spirit, and to put in its place arithmetical calculations and material needs.* In order to give the goyim no time to think and take note, their minds must be diverted towards industry and trade. Thus, all the nations will be swallowed up in the pursuit of gain and in the race for it will not take note of their common foe.

PROTOCOL 5

In the times when peoples looked upon kings on their thrones as on a pure manifestation of the will of God, they submitted without a murmur to the despotic power of kings; but from the day when we insinuated into their minds the conception of their own rights they began to regard the occupants of the thrones as mere ordinary mortals. The holy unction of the Lord's Anointed has fallen from the heads of kings in the eye of the people, and when we also robbed them of their faith in God the might of power was flung upon the streets into the place of public proprietorship and was seized by us...

Reared on analysis, observation, on delicacies of fine calculation, in this species of skill we have no rivals, any more than we have either in the drawing up of plans of political actions and solidarity. In this respect the Jesuits alone might have compared with us, but we have contrived to discredit them in the eyes of the unthinking mob as an overt organization, while we ourselves all the while have kept our secret organization in the shade. However, it is probably all the same to the world who is its sovereign lord, whether the head of Catholicism or our despot of the blood of Zion! But to us, the Chosen People, it is very far from being a matter of indifference...

The nations cannot come to even an inconsiderable private agreement without our secretly having a hand in it... All the wheels of the machinery of all States go by the force of the engine, which is in our hands, and that engine of the machinery of States is – Gold. The science of political economy invented by our learned elders has for long past been giving royal prestige to capital...

The principal object of our directorate consists in this: to debilitate the public mind by criticism... In order to put the public opinion into our hands we must bring it into a state of bewilderment by giving expression from all sides to so many contradictory opinions and for such length of time as will suffice to make the GOYIM lose their heads and come to see that the best thing is to have no opinion of any kind in matters political, which is not given to the public to understand, because they are understood only by him who guides the public. This is the first secret. The second secret requisite for the success of our government is comprised in the following: to multiply to such an extent national failings, habits, passions, conditions of civil life, that it will be impossible for anyone to know where he is in the resulting chaos, so that the people in consequence will fail to understand one another. This measure will also serve us in another way, namely, to sow discord in all parties, to dislocate all collective forces, which are still unwilling to submit to us, and to discourage any kind of personal initiative which might in any degree hinder our affair. *There is nothing more dangerous than personal initiative*; if it has genius behind it, such initiative can do more than can be done by millions of people among whom we have sown discord...

By all these means we shall so wear down the GOYIM they will be compelled to offer us international power of a nature that by its position will enable us without any violence gradually to absorb all the State forces of the world and to form a Super-Government. In place of the rulers of today we shall set up a bogey which will be called the Super-Government administration. Its hands will reach out in all directions like nippers and its organization will be of such colossal dimensions that it cannot fail to subdue all the nations of the world.

PROTOCOL 6

1) We shall soon begin to establish huge monopolies, reservoirs of colossal riches upon which even large fortunes of the *goyim* will depend to such an extent that they will go to the bottom together with the credit of the states on the day after the political smash...

2) The aristocracy of the goyim as a political force is dead – we need not take it into account; but as landed proprietors they can still be harmful to us from the fact that they are self-sufficing in the resources upon which they live. It is essential therefore for us at whatever cost to deprive them of their land. This object will be best attained by increasing the burdens upon landed property in loading lands with debts... What we want is that industry should drain off from the land both labour and capital and by means of speculation transfer into our hands all the money of the world, and thereby throw all the goyim into the ranks of the proletariat. Then the goyim will bow down before us, if for no other reason but to get the right to exist.

3) *We shall further undermine artfully and deeply sources of production by accustoming the workers to anarchy and to drunkenness and side by side therewith taking all measure to extirpate from the face of the earth all the educated forces of the* GOYIM.

PROTOCOL 7

1) Throughout all Europe, and by means of relations with Europe, in other continents also, we must create ferments, discords, and hostility... By our intrigues we shall tangle up all the threads which we have stretched into the cabinets of all states by means of the political, by economic treaties, or loan obligations...

2) The principal factor of success in the political is the secrecy of its undertakings... We must compel the governments of the *goyim* to take action in the direction favoured by our widely conceived plan, already approaching the desired consummation, by what we shall represent as public opinion, secretly prompted by us through the means of that so-called 'Great Power' – *the Press, which, with a few exceptions that may be disregarded, is already entirely in our hands.*

PROTOCOL 8

Our directorate must surround itself with all these forces of civilization among which it will have to work. It will surround itself with publicists, practical jurists, administrators, diplomats and, finally, with persons prepared by a special super-educational training *in our special schools...*

Around us again will be a whole constellation of bankers, industrialists, capitalists and – *the main thing – millionaires – because in substance everything will be settled by the question of figures.* For a time, until there will no longer be any risk in entrusting responsible posts in our states to our brother-Jews, we shall put them in the hands of persons whose past and reputation are such that between them and the people lies an abyss, persons who in case of disobedience to our instructions, must face criminal charges or disappear – this in order to make them defend our interests to their last gasp.

PROTOCOL 9

De facto we have already wiped out every kind of rule except our own... Nowadays, if any States raise a protest against us, it is only pro forma at our discretion and by our direction, *for their anti-Semitism is indispensable to us for the management of our lesser brethren.*

And the weapons in our hands are limitless ambitions, burning greediness, merciless vengeance, hatreds and malice. It is from us that the all-engulfing terror proceeds. We have in our service persons of all opinions, of all doctrines, monarchists, demagogues, socialists, communists, and utopian dreamers of every kind. We have harnessed them all to the task: each one of them on his own account is boring away at the last remnants of authority, is striving to overthrow all established forms of order. By these acts, all states are in torture: they exhort to tranquillity, are ready to sacrifice everything for peace: but we will not give them peace until they openly acknowledge our international Super-Government, and with submissiveness.

Division into fractional parties has given them into our hands, for in order to carry on a contested struggle one must have money, and the money is all in our hands.

We have got our hands into the administration of the law, into the conduct of elections, into the press, into the liberty of the person, but principally into education and training as being the cornerstones of a free existence. We have fooled, bemused and corrupted the youth of the goyim by rearing them in principles and theories which are known to us to be false although it is by us that they have been inculcated.

PROTOCOL 10

... We must have everybody vote without distinction of classes and qualifications, in order to establish an absolute majority, which cannot

be got from the educated propertied classes... When we introduced into the State organism the poison of Liberalism, its whole political complexion underwent a change. States have been seized with a mortal illness – blood poisoning. All that remains is to await the end of their death agony. Liberalism produced Constitutional States, which took the place of what was the only safeguard of the *goyim*, namely, Despotism; and *a constitution, as you well know, is nothing else but a school of discords*, misunderstandings, quarrels, disagreements, fruitless party agitations, party whims – in a word, a school of everything that serves to destroy the personality of State activity.

... We shall arrange elections in favour of such presidents as have in their past some dark, undiscovered stain, some 'Panama' or other – then they will be trustworthy agents for the accomplishment of our plans out of fear of revelations and from the natural desire of everyone who has attained power, namely, the retention of the privileges, advantages, and honour connected with the office of president. The chamber of deputies will provide cover for, will protect, will elect, presidents, but we shall take from it the right to propose new, or make changes in existing laws, for this right will be given by us to the responsible president, a puppet in our hands.

But you yourselves perfectly well know that *to produce the possibility of the expression of such wishes by all the nations it is indispensable to trouble in all countries the people's relations with their governments so as to utterly exhaust humanity with dissension, hatred, struggle, envy and even by the use of torture, by starvation, BY THE INOCULATION OF DISEASES, by want, so that the GOYIM see no other issue than to take refuge in our complete sovereignty in money and in all else. But if we give the nations of the world a breathing space the moment we long for is hardly likely ever to arrive.*

PROTOCOL 11

1) Having established approximately the *modus agendi* we will occupy ourselves with details of those combinations by which we have still to complete the revolution in the course of the machinery of State in the direction already indicated. By these combinations I mean the freedom of the Press, the right of association, freedom of conscience, the voting principle, and many another that must disappear forever from the memory of man...

2) The *goyim* are a flock of sheep, and we are their wolves. And you know what happens when the wolves get hold of the flock?... for what purpose then have we invented this whole policy and insinuated it into the minds

of the goys without giving them any chance to examine its underlying meaning? For what indeed if not in order to obtain in a roundabout way what is for our scattered tribe unattainable by the direct road? It is this which has served as the basis for our organization of SECRET MASONRY WHICH IS NOT KNOWN TO, AND AIMS WHICH ARE NOT EVEN SO MUCH AS SUSPECTED BY, THESE GOY CATTLE, ATTRACTED BY US INTO THE 'SHOW' ARMY OF MASONIC LODGES IN ORDER TO THROW DUST IN THE EYES OF THEIR FELLOWS.

3) God has granted to us, His Chosen People, the gift of the dispersion, and in this which appears in all eyes to be our weakness, has come forth all our strength, which has now brought us to the threshold of sovereignty over all the world.

PROTOCOL 12

What is the part played by the press today? It serves to excite and inflame those passions which are needed for our purpose or else it serves selfish ends of parties. It is often vapid, unjust, mendacious, and the majority of the public have not the slightest idea what ends the press really serves. We shall saddle and bridle it with a tight curb; we shall do the same also with all productions of the printing press, for where would be the sense of getting rid of the attacks of the press if we remain targets for pamphlets and books?

... *I beg you to note that among those making attacks upon US will also be organs established by us, but they will attack exclusively points that we have predetermined to alter. Not a single announcement will reach the public without our control.*

Is there any one of us who does not know that these phantom blessings are the direct roads to foolish imaginings which give birth to anarchical relations of men among themselves and towards authority, because progress, or rather the idea of progress, has introduced the conception of every kind of emancipation, but has failed to establish its limits... All the so-called liberals are anarchists, if not in fact, at any rate in thought. Every one of them is hunting after phantoms of freedom, and falling exclusively into license, that is into the anarchy of protest for the sake of protest...

All our newspapers will be of all possible complexions – aristocratic, republican, revolutionary, even anarchical... Like the Indian idol Vishnu they will have a hundred hands, and every one of them will have a finger on any one of the public opinions as required. When a pulse quickens, these hands will lead opinion in the direction of our aims, for an excited patient loses all power of judgment and easily yields to suggestions. Those fools who will think they are repeating the opinion of a newspaper of their own camp will be repeating our opinion or any opinion that seems desirable for us. In the vain belief that they are following the orders of their party they will in fact follow the flag which we hang out for them.

PROTOCOL 13

The need for daily bread forces the goyim to keep silence and be our humble servants...

In order that they themselves may not guess what we are about we further distract them with amusements, games, pastimes, passions, people's palaces... these interests will finally distract their minds from questions in which we should find ourselves compelled to oppose them.

... Have we not with complete success turned the brainless heads of the goyim with progress, till there is not among the goyim one mind able to perceive that under this word lies a departure from truth in all cases where it is not a question of material inventions, for truth is one and in it there is no place for progress. Progress, like a fallacious idea, serves to obscure truth so that none may know it except us, the Chosen of God, its guardians.

When we come into our kingdom, our orators will expound great problems which have turned humanity upside down in order to bring it at the end under our beneficent rule. Who will ever suspect then that ALL THESE PEOPLES WERE STAGE-MANAGED BY US ACCORDING TO A POLITICAL PLAN WHICH NO ONE HAS SO MUCH AS GUESSED AT IN THE COURSE OF MANY CENTURIES.

PROTOCOL 14

When we come into our kingdom, it will be undesirable for us that there should exist any other religion than ours of the One God with whom our destiny is bound up by our position as the Chosen People and through whom our same destiny is united with the destinies of the world. We must therefore sweep away all other forms of belief...

Our philosophers will discuss all the shortcomings of the various beliefs of the goyim. BUT NO ONE WILL EVER BRING US UNDER DISCUSSION OUR FAITH FROM ITS TRUE POINT OF VIEW SINCE THIS WILL BE FULLY LEARNED BY NONE SAVE OURS, WHO WILL NEVER DARE TO BETRAY ITS SECRETS.

PROTOCOL 15

The principal guarantee of stability of rule is to confirm the aureole of power, and this aureole is attained only by such a majestic inflexibility of might as shall carry on its face the emblems of inviolability from mystical causes – from the choice of God. *Such was, until recent times, the Russian autocracy, the one and only serious foe we had in the world, without counting the Papacy.*

... We shall create and multiply free Masonic lodges in all the countries of the world, absorb into them all who may become or who are prominent in public activity, for in these lodges we shall find our principal intelligence office and means of influence. All these lodges we shall bring under one central administration, known to us alone and to all others absolutely unknown, which will be composed of our learned elders. The lodges will have their representatives who will serve to screen the above-mentioned administration of *masonry* and from whom will issue the watchword and programme. In these lodges we shall tie together the knot which binds together all revolutionary and liberal elements...

... Death is the inevitable end for all. It is better to bring that end nearer to those who hinder our affairs than to ourselves, to the founders of this affair. *We execute masons in such wise that none save the brotherhood can ever have a suspicion of it, not even the victims themselves of our death sentence, they all die when required as if from a normal kind of illness...* Knowing this, even the brotherhood in its turn dare not protest. By such methods we have plucked out of the midst of masonry the very root of protest against our disposition. While preaching liberalism to the *goyim* we at the same time keep our own people and our agents in a state of unquestioning submission...

... When the King of Israel sets upon his sacred head the crown offered him by Europe he will become patriarch of the world. The indispensable victims offered by him in consequence of their suitability will never reach the number of victims offered in the course of centuries by the mania of magnificence, the emulation between the *goy* governments.

PROTOCOL 16
In order to effect the destruction of all collective forces except ours we shall emasculate the first stage of collectivism – *the universities* by re-educating them in a new direction. *Their officials and professors will be prepared for their business by detailed secret programmes of action from which they will not with immunity diverge, not by one iota. They will be appointed with especial precaution and will be so placed as to be wholly dependent upon the Government.*

We must introduce into [gentile] education all those principles which have so brilliantly broken up their order. But when we are in power we shall remove every kind of disturbing subject from the course of education and shall make out of the youth obedient children of authority, loving him who rules as the support and hope of peace and quiet.

... The occasional genius has always managed and always will manage to slip through into other states of life, but it is the most perfect folly for the sake of this rare occasional genius to let through into ranks foreign to them the untalented who thus rob of their places those who belong to those ranks by birth or employment. You know yourselves in what all this has ended for the goyim who allowed this crying absurdity.

PROTOCOL 17

... We have long past taken care to discredit the priesthood of the goyim and thereby to ruin their mission on earth which in these days might still be a great hindrance to us. Day by day its influence on the peoples of the world is falling lower. *Freedom of conscience* has been declared everywhere, *so that now only years divide us from the moment of the complete wrecking of that Christian religion.* As to other religions we shall have still less difficulty in dealing with them, but it would be premature to speak of this now. We shall set clericalism and clericals into such narrow frames as to make their influence move in retrogressive proportion to its former progress.

Just as nowadays our brethren are obliged at their own risk to denounce to the kabal apostates of their own family or members who have been noticed doing anything in opposition to the *kabal so in our kingdom over all the world it will be obligatory for all our subjects to observe the duty of service to the State in this direction.*

PROTOCOL 18

... It must be remembered that the prestige of authority is lessened if it frequently discovers conspiracies against itself: this implies a presumption of consciousness of weakness, or what is still worse, of injustice. You are aware that we have broken the prestige of the *goy* kings by frequent attempts upon their lives through our agents, blind sheep of our flock, who are easily moved by a few liberal phrases to crimes provided only they be painted in political colours. *We have compelled the rulers to acknowledge their weakness in advertising overt measures of secret defence and thereby we shall bring the promise of authority or destruction.*

PROTOCOL 19

We have done our best, and I hope we have succeeded to obtain that the *goyim* should not arrive at this means of contending with sedition. It was for this reason that through the Press and in speeches, indirectly – in cleverly compiled schoolbooks on history, we have advertised the martyrdom alleged to have been accepted by sedition-mongers for the idea of the commonweal. This advertisement has increased the contingent of liberals and has brought thousands of *goyim* into the ranks of our livestock cattle.

PROTOCOL 20

Today we shall touch upon the financial programme, which I put off to the end of my report as being the most difficult, the crowning and the decisive point of our plans... Taxation will best be covered by a progressive tax on property... State needs must be paid by those who will not feel the burden and have enough to take from... Purchase, receipt of money or inheritance will be subject to payment of a stamp progressive tax...

From these sums will be organized public works. The initiative in works of this kind, proceeding from State sources, will bind the working class firmly to the interests of the State and to those who reign.

Economic crises have been produced by us for the goyim by no other means than the withdrawal of money from circulation. Huge capitals have stagnated, withdrawing money from States, which were constantly obliged to apply to those same stagnant capitals for loans. These loans burdened the finances of the State with the payment of interest and made them the bond slaves of these capitals... The concentration of industry in the hands of capitalists out of the hands of small masters has drained away all the juices of the peoples and with them also of the States.

You are aware that the gold standard has been the ruin of the States which adopted it, for it has not been able to satisfy the demands for money, the more so that we have removed gold from circulation as far as possible.

With us the standard that must be introduced is the cost of working-man power, whether it be reckoned in paper or in wood. We shall make the issue of money in accordance with the normal requirement of each subject, adding to the quantity with every birth and subtracting with every death.

PROTOCOL 21

We shall replace the money markets by grandiose government credit institutions, the object of which will be to fix the price of industrial values in accordance with government views. These institutions will be in a position to fling upon the market five hundred millions of industrial paper in one day, or to buy up for the same amount. In this way all industrial undertakings will come into dependence upon us.

PROTOCOL 22

In our hands is the greatest power of our day – gold: in two days we can procure from our storehouses any quantity we may please. Surely there is no need to seek further proof that our rule is predestined by God? Surely we shall not fail with such wealth to prove that all that evil which for so many centuries we have had to commit has served at the end of ends the cause of true well being – the bringing of everything into order?

PROTOCOL 23

The supreme lord who will replace all now existing rulers, dragging on their existence among societies demoralized by us, societies that have denied even the authority of God, from whose midst breaks out on all sides the fire of anarchy, must first of all proceed to quench this all-devouring name. Therefore he will be obliged to kill off those existing societies, though he should drench them with his own blood, that he may resurrect them again in the form of regularly organized troops fighting consciously with every kind of infection that may cover the body of the State with sores. This chosen One of God is chosen from above to demolish the senseless forces moved by instinct and not reason, by brutishness and not humanness. These forces now triumph in manifestations of robbery and every kind of violence under the mask of principles of freedom and rights. They have overthrown all forms of social order to erect on the ruins the throne of the King of the Jews; but their part will be played out the moment he enters into his kingdom. Then it will be necessary to sweep them away from his path, on which must be left no knot, no splinter.

PROTOCOL 24

I pass now to the method of confirming the dynastic roots of King David to the last strata of the earth... Certain members of the seed of David will prepare the kings and their heirs, selecting not by right of heritage but by eminent capacities, inducting them into the most secret mysteries of the political, into schemes of government, but providing always that none may come to knowledge of the secrets. The object of this mode of action is that all may know that government cannot be entrusted to those who have not been inducted into the secret places of its art. To those persons only will be taught the practical application of the aforenamed plans...

all the observations on the politico-economic moves and social sciences – in a word, all the spirit of laws which have been unshakably established by nature herself for the regulation of the relations of humanity.

THREE

Organisation of Security Office 1933-1934
Chief of Sicherheitsamt (SHA)
Adjudant
Department Z (Zentral) (Registry and correspondence of CdSHA)

Department I. Organisation
Personnel
Personnel file
Civil service reinforcements for state organisations
General organisational matters; activity reports
Training officer

Department II. Administration (pay, finances, supplies)

Department III. Information (Domestic, political)
NS, *völkisch*, monarchical opposition, etc.
Religion and ideology, including separatism
Marxists
Scientists
Constitution and law
Strengthening of ideological awareness of the public

Department IV. Counterespionage and Foreign Enquiry
Foreign intelligence
Jews; pacifists; hate propaganda; emigrants
GPU; espionage; immigrants
Counterespionage, military and economic
Armament
Economy and corruption

Department V. Freemasonry
Freemasonry card file (domestic – foreign)
Evaluation

Lodge file
Archive
Museum

Department VI. Independent Desk. Press
Monitoring and evaluating
Information service

Department VII. Independent. Technical Support and Radio
Enemy organisations file
Photography; laboratory; drafting
Statistics
Library
Radio (wireless communications)

This was the structure of the SICHERHEITSDIENST (SD) during the time Eichmann worked in Department V – Freemasonry.

(Reproduced from: *Hitler's Enforcers. The Gestapo and the SS Security Service in the Nazi Revolution.* By George C. Browder, pp.252-253).

FOUR

TRANSLATION OF DOCUMENT I76-PS

Nazi Conspiracy and Aggression.Volume III.

Source: USGPO, Washington, 1946/pp.203-209
Report on Einsatzstab Rosenberg
Working Group in the Occupied Western Territories and the
Netherlands

REPORT
On the activities of the Einsatzstab of the Bureau of the Reichsleiter Rosenberg in the occupied Western Territories and the Netherlands. Working Group Netherland.

The Working Group Netherland of the Einsatzstab Reichsleiter Rosenberg began its work in agreement with the competent representative of the Reichskommissar during the first days of September, 1940. The execution of the past, conforming with the Führer's orders, coordinated itself with the liquidation, that is confiscation, according to civil law, of the various subversive institutions – as set forth in the circulars of the OKW (A2 Nr. 2850/40g Adj. Chief OKW), dated 5 July 1940, and of the Chief of the OKW to the Commander in Chief of the Wehrmacht in France (2 f 28.14WZ Nr. 3812/40g) dated 17 September 1940, as well as to the Commander in Chief of the OKW in the Netherlands, (AZ 2 f 28 J [IA] Nr. 1338/40g) dated 30 October 1940. The screening of the material of the various Masonic lodges was taken care of primarily, and the library and the archives of the following lodges were sifted and all useful material was packed.

[There follows a list of lodges that has been omitted for reasons of space, pp. 203-206.]

All together 470 cases combining material from the here mentioned lodges and from organisations of a similar status were packed and transported to Germany. Furthermore, everything the temple of the lodge in Nijmegen and the temple of the I.O.O.F. in Haarlem contained was sent to Germany. Also, steel shelves for about 30,000 books were taken from the building belonging to the Grooten Oosten in Den Haag where they have so far been used for the Bibliotheka Klossiana, containing parts of one library of the Grooten Oosten, and the library of the Vrijmetselar-Stichting, Amsterdam, are of great value. And so are the archives of the Grooten Oosten in Den Haag, containing all the historical documents of the lodges affiliated with the Grooten Oosten.

To estimate the value of the Bibliotheka Klossiana, containing many rare pieces, it is to be remembered that in 1930 the Grooten Oosten der Nederlande was offered $5,000,000 for the Bibliotheka Klossiana by Freemasons in the U.S.

A particularly valuable discovery was made by the working group searching the altars in the building of the Grooten Oosten in Den Haag. The Master-Hammer of the Grooten Oosten, made of pure gold, which some of its members had presented to the Grooten Oosten on its 60th Anniversary, fell into our hands. It is a piece of high quality whose money-value alone is estimated to be 3,000 Reichsmark.

The Working Group took over the International Institute for Social History in Amsterdam with its library and archives, boxes of extraordinary value. It seems that this institute was founded in 1934 with the intention of creating a centre of intellectual resistance against

National Socialism. Its employees were mainly Jewish refugees from Germany. The contents of its library and its archives with many very valuable items were brought together from all over the world. In the library, there are about 160,000 volumes, though most of them will have to be catalogued. Of particular interest is the German, French and Russian Department. According to the decision made by Reichsleiter Rosenberg, the Institute was taken over in its entirety. A member of the Dienststelle was nominated as director of the Institute – he, together with his collaborators, will arrange the books, catalogue the scientific material and get the Institute ready for the work of the Party. What may be said already above the scientific value of the library and the archives is that they contain a complete collection of material on the social and socialist movements in certain countries.

The libraries of the Societas Spinozana in Den Haag and of the Spinoza-House in Rijnsburg also were packed. Packed in 18 cases, they, too, contain extremely valuable early works of great importance for the exploration of the Spinoza problem. Not without reason did the Director of the Societas Spinozana try, under false pretences which we uncovered, to withhold the library from us.

Then the library of the Alliance Francaise, Den Haag, was packed (six cases) as well as the German publication of the refugee-publishers Aller de Lange, Querido, Fischer-Beerman, Forum-Zeek, of the Kultura Bookshop and the publications of the Pegasus-Verlag, all in Amsterdam, a total of 17 cases. After that, the Working Group concentrated on packing the newspaper and magazine stocks of the International Institute for Social History. The very exclusive racks which had been brought together from all over the world were kept at the Institute in complete disorder and left to self-destruction; they were properly packed into 776 cases and stored, for the time being, in the Working Group's storehouses. It is very strongly suggested that these newspapers and magazines be bound and the volumes be put up in proper libraries as fast as possible; otherwise, an irreparable loss will be the result since these newspapers and magazines are from all over the world.

A large unknown amount of material classified as 'Enemy Goods' and coming from the so-called 'Overseas-Gifts', that is; household goods of Jewish refugees, is falling into our hands daily. These gifts are being kept at the so-called 'House in Holland', and so far 43 cases were packed there, including the private library of the former Minister of the Eisner-Government, Neurath.

In agreement with the Commander-in-Chief of the Wehrmacht in the Netherlands, all libraries in houses of Jewish refugees and confiscated by the Wehrmacht, are being turned over to the Working Group. So far, the library of the Jew De Cat in Haarlem was packed into four cases.

An extremely valuable library, containing inestimable works in Sanskrit, was confiscated when the Theosophic Society in Amsterdam was dissolved, and packed into 96 cases.

A number of smaller libraries belonging to the Bellamy Movement, the Spiritists, Esperanto Movement, the International Biblical Research and various other minor international organisations were packed into seven cases; texts belonging to various minor Jewish organisations were packed into four cases, and a library of the Anthroposophic Society in Amsterdam into three.

It is safe to say that the racks of books confiscated, packed and so far sent to Germany by the Working Group are of extraordinary scientific value and shall contribute an integral part of the library of the 'Hohe Schule'. The money-value of these libraries, as shown in the case of the 'Klossiana', can only be estimated, but surely amount to 30-40,000,000 Reichsmarks.

For the coming months, action is planned on the following, enumerated here in chronological order:

1. The libraries of the Theosophic Society and similar organisations in Den Haag, Rotterdam and several other places.

2. Continuous sifting of objects confiscated in the 'House in Holland' and other buildings.

3. Screening of several archives with press-photos, consisting altogether of 2.6 million pictures which shall be turned over to us by the Reichskommissariat.

4. The Jewish private libraries in Amsterdam, particularly:

A. The Israelite Library Beth-Hamidrasch Etz Chaim, Amsterdam, Rapenburgerstraat 109. This library, founded in 1740, contains about 4,000 volumes, particularly Jewish theology.

B. Library of the Netherland Israelite Seminar, Amsterdam, Rapenburgerstraat 177. It contains 4,300 volumes of Hebraica and 2,000 volumes of Joudaica. At the time, it took over the library of the Jewish Society for Literature, Thoelet (X330-1837) and valuable Jewish private collections. Amongst other things, it contains precious old prints from the years 1480 to 1560 and some manuscripts.

C. The Portuguese-Israelite Seminar, Amsterdam, Jonas Daniel Meyerplein 5. There are 25,000 volumes, 450 manuscripts, 600 prints [Inkunablen] and numerous Exlibris, coins and the like and the famous material on Talmud literature.

D. The so-called Rosenthaliana, primarily a foundation by the Jew

Rosenthal from Hannover. From there, it was at the time transferred and affiliated with the local university library. In the meantime, it has on account of donations, grown considerably. Technically, it belongs to the Municipality of Amsterdam, but in the Catalogue of Libraries in the Netherlands of 1931, it is designated as 'Private'. According to the catalogue, it contains 25,000 volumes and 300 manuscripts. However, the amount of volumes reaches 100,000 indeed.

The libraries mentioned under 4. ought to be of particular interest for the history of Western Europe. It is very likely that hitherto unknown facts may be brought into the open, on the era of Cromwell and that of the glorious Revolution of 1688 and the resulting personal union between England and the Netherlands. In particular, light may be thrown on Cromwell's attitude towards the Jews, possibly even on the Jewish influence on the development of the Secret Service.

The temple and the museum of the Grooten Oosten der Nederlande. At present, both are needed for exhibitions on behalf of the Dienststelle of the Reichskommissar. With the end of the exhibition temple, furnishings and museum shall be turned over to us.

A very conservative estimate of the value of the objects enumerated in 1. to 5. may be about three times as much as that of the libraries already packed. Therefore, it is safe to say that the library of the Hohe Schule shall, with very little effort, receive an extraordinary amount of treasures which shall give it a unique position in the realm of questions regarding Judaism and Free-Masonism.

The Working Group, in executing the aforementioned tasks, is bound strictly to the pace set by the Reichskommissar for the handling of the Jewish questions and that of the international organisations. This pace again is determined by the political evolution which is taking shape according to decisions made on a higher level, and which must not be hampered by individual acts. Work that has been authorised to be done by the Working Group, but has not yet been accomplished should now, with twice as much personnel as before, be finished within two to three months. It may be mentioned that the Working Group has been working overtime for weeks now, and also is working, as is done on the battlefield, on Sundays.

The leader of the Working Group Netherland.
Schimmer
Oberbereichsleiter.

BIBLIOGRAPHY

The Red Triangle

I wish to record my sincere thanks to the publisher, Lewis Masonic, for indulging me yet again in printing such an extensive bibliography. I thought that the bibliography included with the book *The Rosslyn Hoax?* was fairly large, but appropriate for that particular publication. However, when it came to research for *The Red Triangle* I was almost overwhelmed by the source material necessary to consult in the production of this work. I now realise that this was entirely due to my attempt to combine two subjects, both of which have a huge amount of material published on each. Please be assured that this lengthy bibliography is in no way comprehensive and has been reduced to what I believe the publisher will tolerate.

Allan, David. *Virtue, Learning and the Scottish Enlightenment.* Edinburgh University Press Ltd. Edinburgh. 1993.

Allen, John L. Jr. *Pope Benedict XVI – A Biography of Joseph Ratzinger.* Continuum International Publishing Group Ltd. London. 2005.

Aly, Götz and Heim, Susanne. *Architects of Annihilation – Auschwitz and the Logic of Destruction.* (Trans. Blunden, A. G.) Weidenfeld & Nicolson. London, 2002.

Ankerberg, John and Weldon, John. *The Facts on the Masonic Lodge.* Eugene, Oregon. 1989.

Ankerberg, John and Weldon, John. *Encyclopedia of Cults and New Religions.* Eugene, Oregon. 1999. (p.214)

Ankerberg, John and Weldon, John. *Fast Facts on the Masonic Lodge.* Eugene, Oregon. 2004.

Armitage, Frederick. *The Old Guilds of England.* London. 1918.

Ars Quatuor Coronatorum. Transactions of the Quatuor Coronati Lodge, No. 2076. London. (1892-) Various volumes.

Ashlar Magazine. Various Vols. – 1997 to date. Circle Publications Ltd. Helensburgh.

Bach, H. I. *The German Jew... A Synthesis of Judaism and Western Civilization 1730-1930.* Published for the Littman Library by Oxford University Press. Oxford. 1984.

Baigent, Michael and Leigh, Richard. *The Inquisition.* London. 1999.

Baker, Alan. *Invisible Eagle – The History of Nazi Occultism.* Virgin Publishing Ltd. London. 2000.

Barbour, John. *The Bruce. c.*1375. Reprinted by Canongate Classics. 1997.

Barrett, David V. *Sects, 'Cults' and Alternative Religions: A World Survey and Source Book.* London. 1996.

Baum, Steven K. *The Psychology of Genocide: Perpetrators, Bystanders and Rescuers.* Cambridge University Press. Cambridge. 2008.

Baynes, Norman H. (Ed.) *The Speeches of Adolf Hitler, April 1922-August 1939 – an English translation of representative passages arranged under subjects*. Royal Institute of International Affairs. London. 1942.

Berenbaum, Michael. (ed.) *A Mosaic of Victims – Non-Jews Persecuted and Murdered by the Nazis*. New York University Press. 1990.

Berry, Harold J. *Masons – What they Believe*. Omaha, Nebraska. 1990.

Berry, Harold J. *Rosicrucians – What they Believe*. Omaha, Nebraska. 1987.

Bessel, Richard. *Nazism and War*. Weidenfeld & Nicolson. London. 2004.

Boyle, Frank. *Hooray for Holyrood – Political Cartoons by Frank Boyle*. Glendaruel. 2002.

Breitman, Richard. *The Architect of Genocide: Himmler and the Final Solution*. Alfred A. Knopf Inc. New York. 1991.

Brendon, Piers. *The Dark Valley – a Panorama of the 1930's*. New York. 2000.

Britannica Encyclopedia of World Religions. Chicago. 2006.

Bronner, Stephen E. *A Rumor About the Jews: Reflections on Antisemitism and the Protocols of the Learned Elders of Zion*. St. Martin's Press. New York. 2002.

Broszat, Martin. *Hitler and the Collapse of Weimar Germany*. Berg Publishers Ltd. Leamington Spa. 1987. (First published as: *Die Machtergreifung. Der Aufstieg der NSDAP und die Zerstörung der Weimarer Republik*. Taschenbuch Verlag. Munich. 1984.)

Browder, George C. *Foundations of the Nazi Police State – The Formation of SIPO and SD*. University Press of Kentucky. 2004. (First published 1990.)

Brown, William A., Rt., Ex. *Facts, Fables and Fantasies of Freemasonry*. New York. 1968.

Brown, William L. *Secret Societies in the Light of the Bible*. Wheaton, Illinois. 1928.

Burleigh, Michael. *The Third Reich – A New History*. Macmillan. London. 2000.

Burrin, Philippe. *Nazi Anti-Semitism: From Prejudice to the Holocaust*. The New Press. New York. 2005.

Cameron, Nigel M. de S., (Organising Editor). *Dictionary of Scottish Church History and Theology*. Edinburgh. 1993.

Campbell, Joseph. *The Hero with a Thousand Faces*. Fontana Press. 1993. (First published by Princeton University Press. 1949.)

Cartwright, Dr E. H. *Masonic Ritual – A Commentary on the Freemasonic Ritual*. (Third edition) Shepperton. 1985.

Castells, F. de. *The Genuine Secrets of Freemasonry*. London. 1978.

Cawthorne, Nigel. *Witch Hunt – History of a Persecution*. London. 2003.

Cecil, Robert. *The Myth of the Master Race – Alfred Rosenberg and Nazi Ideology*. Dodd Mead & Company. New York. 1972.

Cerza, Alphonse. *The Courts and Freemasonry – Case histories that have or could affect Freemasonry*. Research Lodge, No. 2 (Iowa). Anchor Communications. Highland Springs, Virginia. 1986.

Cohn, Norman. *Warrant for Genocide: The Myth of the Jewish World-Conspiracy and the Protocols of the Elders of Zion*. Eyre & Spottiswoode. London. 1976.

Connery, Sean and Grigor, Murray. *Being a Scot*. London. 2008.

Cooper, Robert L. D. 'The Revenge of the Operatives?' in: *Marking Well: Essays on the Occasion of the 150th Anniversary of the Grand Lodge of Mark Master*

Masons of England and Wales and its Districts and Lodges Overseas. Ed. Andrew Prescott. Hersham. 2006.

Cooper, Robert L. D. *The Rosslyn Hoax?* London. 2006.

Cooper, Robert L. D. *Cracking the Freemasons' Code.* London. 2006.

Cornwell, Rupert. *God's Banker: An Account of the Life and Death of Roberto Calvi.* London. 1983.

Cowan Ian B., and Easson, David E. *Medieval Religious Houses – Scotland.* Longman. 1957 and 1976.

Cowan, William. *A Bibliography of the Book of Common Order and Psalm Book of the Church of Scotland – 1556-1644.* Edinburgh. 1913.

Craig, John. *A Shorte Summe of the Whole Catechisme.* Edinburgh. 1581.

Cullen, W. Douglas, The Rt. Hon. Lord *The Public Inquiry on the Shootings at Dunblane Primary School 13th March 1996.* HMSO. 1996. The full text of the document is available online at:
www.archive.official-documents.co.uk/document/scottish/dunblane/dunblane.htm

Curtin, Nancy J. *The United Irishmen: Popular Politics in Ulster and Dublin, 1791-1798.* Oxford. 1994.

Facsimile reprint by Law, Thomas Graves. Edinburgh. 1883.

Daraul, Arkon. *Secret Societies – A History.* New York. 1989. (First published 1961.)

Davies, Peter and Lynch, Derek. *The Routledge Companion to Fascism and the Far Right.* London. 2002.

De Hoyos, Arturo and Morris, Brent S. *Is It True What They Say About Freemasonry?* Masonic Information Centre. Silver Spring, Maryland. 1997.

De Hoyos, Arturo and Morris, Brent S. (Eds.) *Freemasonry in Context – History, Ritual and Controversy.* Lanham, Maryland. 2004.

Delzell, Charles F. *Mediterranean Fascism, 1919-1945.* Walker Publishing Co., Inc. New York. 1971.

Denslow, Ray A. *Freemasonry in the Eastern Hemisphere.* Trenton, Montana. 1954.

Dewar, James. *The Unlocked Secrets – Freemasonry Examined.* London. 1966.

Dickie, John. *Cosa Nostra – A History of the Sicilian Mafia.* Hodder & Stoughton. London. 2004.

Draffen, George of Newington. *The Mason Word – Another early reference.* AQC. Vo.65 1952.

Edwards, John. *Inquisition.* Stroud. 2003.

Elliott, Paul. *Brotherhoods of Fear – History of Violent Organisations.* London. 1998.

Elon, Amos. *The Pity of It All – A Portrait of Jews in Germany 1743-1933.* London. 2003.

Evans, Richard J. *The Third Reich in Power.* London. 2005.

Faulks, Pip and Cooper, Robert L. D. *The Masonic Magician.* Watkins Publishing. London. 2008.

Finlay, Anthony. *Demons – The Devil, Possession and Exorcism.* Vega. London. 2002.

Finney, Charles G. *The Character and Claims of Freemasonry.* Stoke-on-Trent. 1996.

Fischer, Klaus P. *The History of an Obsession – German Judeophobia and the Holocaust*. New York and London. 1998.

Forbes, Camille F. *Introducing Bert Williams – Burnt Cork, Broadway, and the Story of America's First Black Star*. New York. 2008.

Friedländer, Saul. *Nazi Germany and the Jews – The Years of Persecution 1933-39*. London. 1997.

Fry, L. *Waters Flowing Eastward*. Second edition. Paris. 1933.

Fuchs, Eduard. *Die Juden in der Karikatur: ein Beitrage zur Kulturgeschichte*. Albert Langen Verlag. München. 1921.

Gellately, Robert. *The Gestapo and German Society – Enforcing Racial Policy 1933-1945*. Oxford University Press. Paperback edition 1991. (First published 1990.)

Gellately, Robert. *Backing Hitler: Consent and Coercion in Nazi Germany*. Oxford University Press Inc. New York. 2001.

Gellately, Robert and Kiernan, Ben. (Eds.) *The Spectre of Genocide – Mass Murder in Historical Perspective*. Cambridge University Press. 2001.

Gellately, Robert and Stoltzfus, Nathan. (Eds) *Social Outsiders in Nazi Germany*. Princeton University Press. New Jersey. 2001.

Gilbert, Martin. *The Holocaust – The Jewish Tragedy*. London. 1987.

Gill, Anthony. *The Political Origins of Religious Liberty*. Cambridge University Press. Cambridge. 2008.

Gordon, Sarah. *Hitler, Germans, and the Jewish 'Question'*. Princeton University Press. New Jersey. 1984.

Gould, Robert F. *Military Lodges 1732-1899*. London. 1899.

Grand Lodge of Scotland. *Year Book (1952-to date)*. Various volumes. Edinburgh.

Grand Lodge of Scotland. *The Laws and Constitutions of the Grand Lodge of Ancient and Honourable Fraternity of Free and Accepted Masons of Scotland*. Edinburgh. 1836 and 1848.

Hamill, John. *The History of English Freemasonry*. Addlestone. 1994.

Hanfstaengl, Ernst. *Hitler in der Karikatur der Welt – Tat gegen Tinte*. Duderstadt, (Hannover). 1933.

Hannah, Walton. *Darkness Visible – A Revelation and Interpretation of Freemasonry*. Augustine Press. London. 1952.

Harding, Nick. *Secret Societies*. Pocket Essentials. Harpenden. 2005.

Harris, Jack, *Freemasonry – the Invisible Cult*. Whitaker House. New Kensington, PA. 1983

Harvey, John. *The Master Builders: Architecture in the Middle Ages*. Book Club Associates. 1973. (First published by Thames and Hudson Ltd. 1971.)

Hausner, Gideon. *Justice in Jerusalem – The Trial of Adolf Eichmann*. Camden, New Jersey. London. 1967.

Headings, Mildred, J. *French Freemasonry under the Third Republic*. Baltimore. 1949.

Heiden, Konrad. *The Führer*. New York. 1999. (First published 1944.)

Hellig, Jocelyn. *The Holocaust and Antisemitism – A Short History*. Oneworld Publications. Oxford. 2003.

Henderson, Kent. 'The Craft in Islamic Countries: An Analytical Review.' In: *Transactions*. Vol.13 2006. Walter F. Meier Lodge of Research, No. 281. Seattle, Washington. 2008.

Herf, Jeffrey. *The Jewish Enemy: Nazi Propaganda During World War II and the Holocaust.* Harvard University Press. 2008.

Hobsbawm, Eric and Ranger, Terence (Eds). *The Invention of Tradition.* Cambridge University Press. 2004. (First published 1983.)

Hobsbawm, Eric. *The Age of Revolution – 1789-1848.* Abacus. London. 2002.

Holden, Andrew. *Jehovah's Witnesses – Portrait of a Contemporary Religious Movement.* London. 2002.

Howard, Michael. *The Occult Conspiracy – The Power of Secret Societies in World History.* New York. 1989.

Howe, Ellic. *The Collapse of Freemasonry in Nazi Germany 1933-5. AQC.* Vol. 95 (1982) pp.21-36.

Huyghebaert, Jacques. *A Short History of Freemasonry in the Czech Republic.* Prague. 2005. The Grand Lodge of the Czech Republic was 're-awakened' in 1990.

International Military Tribunal. *Trial of the major war criminals before the International Military Tribunal, Nuremberg, 14 November 1945-1 October 1946.* Nuremberg. 1947-1949.

Jackson, A. C. F. *English Masonic Exposures 1760-1769.* Lewis Masonic Publishing. Shepperton. 1986.

Jones, Bernard E. *Freemasons' Book of the Royal Arch.* George G. Harrap & Co. Ltd. London. 1957.

Junior, Allan. (pseud. John Allan) *The Aberdeen Jew.* Valentine & Sons Ltd. Illustrated by Gregor McGregor. Third Edition. Dundee. 1927.

Kahler, Lisa Dr. *Freemasonry in Edinburgh 1721-1746: Institutions and Context.* Unpublished Thesis. University of St Andrews. 1998.

Kallis, Aristotle A. (Ed.) *The Fascism Reader.* London. 2003.

Katz, Jacob. *Jews and Freemasons in Europe, 1723-1939.* (Trans. Oschry, Leonard.) Harvard University Press. 1970.

Kelly, Aaron. *Irvine Welsh.* Manchester. 2005.

Kieckhefer, Richard. *Magic in the Middle Ages.* Canto. Cambridge. 2000. (First published by Cambridge University Press, 1989.)

Knight, Stephen. *The Brotherhood – The Secret World of the Freemasons.* London. 1984.

Knoop, Douglas; Jones, G. P., and Hamer, Douglas. Carr, Harry (Ed.) *The Early Masonic Catechisms.* Manchester. 1943.

Koch, H. W. (Ed.) *Aspects of the Third Reich.* Macmillan. London. 1985.

Krieg, Robert A. *Catholic Theologians in Nazi Germany.* New York. 2004.

Landau, Ronnie S. *The Nazi Holocaust: Its History and Meaning.* I. B. Tauris & Co. Ltd. London. 2006.

Langer, Walter C. *The Mind of Adolf Hitler – The Secret Wartime Report.* Pan Books Ltd. London. 1974. (First published as: *The Mind of Adolf Hitler – The Secret Wartime Report,* by Martin Secker & Warburg Ltd. 1973.)

Lawler, Justus G. *Popes and Politics. Reform, Resentment and the Holocaust.* New York. 2002.

Lawrence, John. *Freemasonry – a religion?* Kingsway Publications. Eastbourne. 1987.

Lawrence, John. *Freemasonry – A Christian Perspective.* Gazelle Books. London. 1999.

Letson, Douglas and Higgins, Michael. *The Jesuit Mystique.* Fount Paperbacks.

London. 1995.

Lewis, David. *The Man Who Invented Hitler – The Making of the Führer*. London. 2003.

Lewy, Guenter. *The Catholic Church and Nazi Germany*. New York, USA. 2000.

Lewy, Guenter. *The Nazi Persecution of the Gypsies*. Oxford. 2000.

Lindsay, Robert Strathern. *The Royal Order of Scotland*. Edinburgh. 1972.

Lindsay, Robert Strathern. *The Scottish Rite for Scotland*. Edinburgh. 1958.

Linklater, Magnus; Hilton, Isabel and Ascherson, Neal. *The Nazi Legacy – Klaus Barbie and the International Fascist Connection*. New York. 1985.

Litvinoff, Barnet. *The Burning Bush – Anti-Semitism and World History*. London. 1988.

Longerich, Peter. *The Unwritten Order – Hitler's Role in the Final Solution*. Tempus. Stroud. 2003.

McArthur, Joseph Ewart. *The Lodge of Edinburgh (Mary's Chapel), No. 1 – Quatercentenary of Minutes 1599-1999*. Published by the Lodge. 1999.

McCalman, Iain. *The Last Alchemist: Count Cagliostro, Master of Magic in the Age of Reason*. New York. 2003.

McCann, John. *Essays on the Lodge of Stirling, Ancient and Modern – A Quadricentennial Review of the Lodge, 'Antient' Stirling*. Privately printed. 1998.

McCann, John. *Essays on the Lodge of Stirling, Ancient and Modern*. Privately printed. 1998.

McCormick, William James McKendrick. *Christ, the Christian and Freemasonry*. Belfast. 1977.

McFarland, Elaine. *Protestant First – Orangeism in 19th Century Scotland*. Edinburgh University Press. Edinburgh. 1990.

McKale, Donald M. *The Nazi Party Courts: Hitler's Management of Conflict in His Movement, 1921-1945*. The University Press of Kansas. Lawrence. 1974.

Madden, Charles. *Freemasonry – Mankind's Hidden Enemy*. Rockford, Illinois. 1995.

Malcolm, Janet. *Two Lives: Gertrude and Alice*. Yale University Press. New Haven and London. 2007.

Marshall, William S. *The Billy Boys: A Concise History of Orangeism in Scotland*. Mercat Press. Edinburgh. 1996.

Mather, George A. and Nichols, Larry A. *Masonic Lodge*. Grand Rapids, Michigan. 1995.

Melzer, Ralf. 'In the Eye of the Hurricane: German Freemasonry in the Weimar Republic and the Third Reich'. Contained within: *Totalitarian Movements and Political Religions*. Vol. 4, No.2 (Autumn 2003) pp.113-132. London. 2004.

Mohr, Lt. Col. Gordon 'Jack', AUS Ret. *The Hidden Power behind Freemasonry*. GSG Associates Publishers. CA. 1990.

Moore, Alan and Campbell, Eddie. *From Hell: being a melodrama in sixteen parts*. London. 2001. (The book was made into a film of the same title, starring Johnny Depp in the lead role. Released in the UK in 2002.)

Moore, R. I. *The Formation of a Persecuting Society*. Blackwell Publishing. Oxford. 2005.

Morley, John. *Oliver Cromwell*. London. 1900.

Mosley, Leonard. *The Reich Marshal: A Biography of Hermann Goering*. Doubleday & Co. New York. 1974.

Mullin, Christopher J. *Error of Judgment – The Truth About the Birmingham Pub Bombings*, Chatto & Windus. London. 1986.

National [English] Archives, The. *Germany 1944 – The British Soldier's Pocketbook*. London. 2006.

Newton, Toyne. *The Dark Worship – The Occult's Quest for World Domination*. Vega. London. 2002.

Oldridge, Darren. *The Devil in Early Modern England*. Stroud. 2000.

Owen, James. *Nuremberg – Evil on Trial*. Headline Review. London. 2006.

Piatigorsky, Alexander. *Who's Afraid of Freemasons? – The Phenomenon of Freemasonry*. London. 1997.

Poliakov, Leon. Kochan, Miriam (Trans.) *History of Anti-Semitism: From Voltaire to Wagner*. Vol. Three. London. 1975.

P. R. M. (Translator. No author given.) *Fascism and Freemasonry*. (No date.) The Polygraphic Society. London.

Rice, John R. *Lodges Examined by the Bible – Is It a Sin for a Christian to Have Membership in Secret Orders?* Murfreesboro, Tennessee. 1971.

Ridley, Jasper. *The Freemasons*. London. 1999.

Roberts, Allen E. *The Mystic Tie*. Macoy Publishing. Masonic Supply Co., Inc. Richmond, Virginia. 1991.

Roberts, Stephen H. *The House that Hitler Built*. Ninth Edition with Supplementary Chapter. London. 1938.

Robison, John (Professor of Natural Philosophy and Secretary to the Royal Society of Edinburgh). *Proofs of a Conspiracy against all the Religions and Governments of Europe Carried on in the Secret Meetings of the Free Masons, Illumminati and Reading Societies*. Edinburgh. 1797.

Roland, Paul. *The Nazis and the Occult – The Dark Forces Unleashed by the Third Reich*. London. 2007.

Rubenstein, Richard L. and Roth, John K. *Approaches to Auschwitz: The Holocaust and its Legacy*. Atlanta, Georgia. 1987.

Samson, Peter and Crow, Alan. *Dunblane – Our Year of Tears*. Edinburgh. 1997.

Schellenberg, Walter, SS General. (Introduction by Erickson, John.) *Invasion 1940. The Nazi Invasion Plan for Britain by SS General Walter Schellenberg*. St. Ermin's Press Book. London. 2001.

Schnoebelen, William. *Masonry – Beyond the Light*. Chino, California. 1991.

Scottish Burgh Records Society. *Extracts from the Records of the Burgh of Edinburgh. A.D. 1403-1528*. Edinburgh. 1869.

Shankey, Catherine. *Islamophobia in Scotland – a Conference*. Edinburgh. 2004. (The conference was held in Glasgow on 24 June 2004)

Short, Martin. *Inside the Brotherhood – Further Secrets of the Freemasons*. London. 1989.

Smout, T. C. *A History of the Scottish People 1560-1830*. Fontana Press. London. 1985.

Snyder, Louis L. *Encyclopedia of the Third Reich*. Wordsworth Editions Ltd. Ware, Hertfordshire. 1998.

Stevenson, David. *The First Freemasons – Scotland's Early Lodges and their Members*. Second Edition. The Grand Lodge of Scotland. 2001. (First published by the Aberdeen University Press. 1988.)

Stevenson, David. *The Origins of Freemasonry – Scotland's Century 1590-1710*.

Cambridge University Press. 1988.

Stewart, A. Trevor (Ed.) *Freemasonry and Religion – Many Faiths, One Brotherhood.* The Canonbury Papers, Vol.Three. Canonbury Masonic Research Centre, London. 2006.

Taylor, James and Shaw, Warren. *Dictionary of the Third Reich.* Penguin Books. 1997. (First published as *A Dictionary of the Third Reich.* Grafton Books. 1987.)

Tennent, James B. *Records of the Incorporation of Barbers, Glasgow.* Glasgow. 1930.

Thomas, Hugh. *The Spanish Civil War.* (Revised Edition.) The Modern Library. New York. 2001. (First published in 1961.)

Thomas, Keith. *Religion and the Decline of Magic.* Fourth Edition. London. 1991.

Turner, Henry Ashby Jnr. *German Big Business and the Rise of Hitler.* Oxford University Press. 1985.

Turner, John M. *Conflict and Reconciliation: Studies in Methodism and Ecumenism in England 1740-1982.* London. 1985.

Vernon, W. Fred. *History of Freemasonry in the Province of Roxburgh, Peebles and Selkirkshires from 1674 to the Present Time.* George Kenning. 1893.

Walker, Corey D. B. *A Noble Fight – African American Freemasonry and the Struggle for Democracy in America.* University of Illinois Press. 2008.

Warden, Alex. J. *Burgh Laws of Dundee, with the History, Statutes, and Proceedings of the Guild of Merchants and Fraternities of Craftsmen.* London. 1872.

Wartski, Lionel. *Freemasonry and the Early Secret Societies Acts.* Privately printed. Natal, South Africa. 1983.

Webster, Paul. *Pétain's Crime: The Full Story of French Collaboration in the Holocaust.* Pan Books. London. 2001.

Weir, John, DSO, OBE, JP, MA, FEIS. (Ed.) *Robert Burns – the Freemason.* Addlestone. 1996.

Welsh, Irvine. *Filth.* Jonathan Cape. London. 1998.

Wichtl, Friedrich. *Weltfreimaurerei – Weltrevolution – Weltrepublik: Ein Untersuchung über Ursprung und Endziele des Weltkrieges.* Munich. 1919.

Williams, Charles. *Pétain – How the Hero of France Became a Convicted Traitor and Changed the Course of History.* New York. 2005.

Withers, W. J. and Wood, Paul (Eds.) *Science and Medicine in the Scottish Enlightenment.* East Linton. 2002.

Wolf, Lucien. *The Jewish Bogey and the Forged Protocols of the Learned Elders of Zion.* London. 1920.

World Committee for the Victims of German Fascism. *The Brown Book of the Hitler Terror and the Burning of the Reichstag.* London. 1933.

Year Books of the Grand Lodge of Scotland. Numerous. 1952 – to date.

Young, Richard Martin. *Oaths, Oath Taking and Mental Reservation.* ND.

Other sources

There are numerous other sources that have been examined for relevant information. As with the above bibliography the range of material is daunting but only works actually consulted by me are cited here. I have no doubt that there is a great deal of other information available that I have not had the opportunity to consult. It is to be hoped that this will stimulate others to investigate these other sources.

ENDNOTES

1 *The Public Inquiry into the Shootings at Dunblane Primary School on 13 March 1996.* Lord Cullen. HMSO/1996.
2 *The Scotsman* newspaper was founded on 25th January 1817, and its 'mission statement' was and is:
   'The Conductors pledge themselves to impartiality, firmness and independence... their first desire is to be honest, the second is to be useful... the great requisites for the task are only good sense, courage and industry...'
3 The reclusive Barclay brothers had purchased the newspaper on 3rd November 1995 for £87 million. *The Independent.* 4th November 1995. It was reported that 'they did not interfere with editorial policy'. I admit to knowing nothing about them.
4 *The Scotsman* 22nd March 1996.
5 This article appeared the day after it was announced in the House of Commons that there would be a public inquiry into the shootings.
6 Freemasonry was allegedly involved in the assassination of JFK and no doubt someone 'out there' will also accuse us of being involved in the 9/11 attacks, if they have not already done so.
7 The library is open to the public although an appointment is recommended.
8 The then Grand Secretary was Brother C. Martin McGibbon.
9 Freemasons tolerated this because it *was* fun and took no offence. How times have changed.
10 There is ample material available for a study to be made of this earlier type of Masonophobia.
11 I use the word 'campaign' in its loosest possible sense, as I am not suggesting that there was any co-ordinated or orchestrated attempt to denigrate the Order.
12 England is approximately 10 times the size of Scotland certainly in terms of population.
13 A secondary answer might be that, as a Scot I don't like being kicked!
14 Masonophobia is more than simply an irrational fear of Freemasonry but also indicates a malign and malicious attitude towards the order and its members.
15 Explain what Masonophobia actually is.
16 This in a country that had only recently re-acquired a measure of self-determination in the form of a devolved parliament, and was proclaiming itself to be tolerant and welcoming to all, regardless of faith, creed or colour. It was, 'the best small country in the world'.
17 When I say here, I am the 'historian' of Scottish Freemasonry, I must make it clear I am but one of many who can also rightly make that claim. But I tended to be the one consulted because of my position in the Grand Lodge of Scotland.
18 There are occasions when there is a general consensus on certain matters, but even then such consensus cannot be imposed by anyone on the body known as Freemasonry.
19 For a straightforward but more detailed reason why, see *Cracking the Freemasons' Code*, p. xiii-xvi.

20 Modern Freemasonry is generally considered to have begun when Head Offices (known as Grand Lodges) were created to oversee the affairs of Lodges. The first of these Grand Lodges was the Grand Lodge of England, founded in London in 1717. However, recent scholarly debate now sees Grand Lodges merely as a 'stepping stone' in the development of Freemasonry, as Lodge records exist in Scotland dating from 1599.

21 These precious documents are the property of the Grand Lodge of Scotland.

22 This is one of the claims used to attack Freemasonry and will be further discussed in this book.

23 This is tantamount to suggesting that: 'Yes, I was baptised, but I am not baptised any longer!'

24 Briefing notes are essentially 'advertisements', providing a statement of purpose for the organisation concerned.

25 Of all the oldest institutions in Scotland, Freemasonry was the only organisation not invited to the official opening of the newly devolved Scottish Parliament.

26 The occurrence of Masonophobia is in itself very interesting and, although I will comment on this in general, I am quite sure that a study of when Masonophobia erupts, compared to events also occurring at or about the same time, might produce some interesting results.

27 Many of these events have been discussed elsewhere in detail, although perhaps not from the perspective adopted in this book.

28 As shall be seen it is not possible for any one Freemason, or even a group of Freemasons, to speak 'for' Freemasonry.

29 In my view, his work is essential reading for anyone interested in the origins and development of modern Freemasonry. See Bibliography for more details.

30 A burgh was a town with a defensive wall and was not part of the rural feudal system of government.

31 All other trades had their own patron saint and more often than not were responsible for the upkeep of aisles (in various towns) dedicated to those saints. For example, the Wobsters' (Weavers') Patron Saint was St. Michael (Archangel).

32 The procedure was known as the granting of a 'Seal of Cause' – a charter granted by a town council erecting a trade or group of related trades into an incorporation.

33 The exact nature of these ceremonies is now unknown, but they were likely to be relatively simple and probably with religious connotations.

34 There are, of course, substantial differences when compared to modern trade unions, the latter being born as a consequence of the Industrial Revolution. Incorporations were decidedly medieval in character.

35 This was when the town was occupied by General Monck's forces. See *Burgh Laws of Dundee* etc. p.493.

36 Additional trades were part of the Incorporation from time to time, and would probably change according to economic necessity. Coopers (barrel makers), for example, were for a time part of the Incorporation of Wrights [carpenters] and Masons.

37 *Extracts from the records of the burgh of Edinburgh 1403-1528*, Pp.61-62.

38 The English Reformation was due more to the dynastic and political aspirations of Henry VIII (1509–1547; b.1491) rather than doctrinal considerations.

39 They are all now, without exception, charitable and social institutions.

40 It would be rash to jump to the conclusion that this is why lodges and the masons' esoteric knowledge survived when other trade 'secrets' disappeared but we do know that reference to 'secrets' in the other trades ceased to be mentioned in their records.

41 The earliest reference is contained within the Edinburgh city records, which minute the granting of permission to the masons (stonemasons) of the city to use the lodge for 'recreational purposes', indicating that the lodge was a place larger than a tool store and capable of holding a number of people. Unfortunately, the nature of the 'recreation' is not specified.

42 Apart from this single reference, nothing else is known of this lodge. It is thought that lodges such as these were 'occasional' lodges, in which case they are unlike the lodges in Scotland which had a long recorded existence and some of which exist to this day.

43 Cited in *Coil's Masonic Encyclopedia*. 1995. p.73.

44 I dislike the term 'Speculative Freemason' in this particular debate as it obscures the argument. Either the individuals concerned were stonemasons or they were not.

45 A hamlet and staging post near the village of Stow, Selkirkshire.

46 The frequency of attendance prior to 1599 and more particularly prior to the Reformation (1559/60) is not known.

47 Now known as the Lodge of Edinburgh (Mary's Chapel), No.1. The Lodge continues to meet in Edinburgh.

48 Members of the lodge were then besieging Newcastle on Tyne and held a special meeting for this purpose.

49 Whether this can be considered a permanent lodge of the Scottish type is unlikely as we hear nothing more of it after Ashmole's admission.

50 What he understood the accusation to mean is not known, nor what weight, if any, was given to the accusation.

51 Threnodie: a form of the Scots word 'thrain' or 'thren' meaning a sad refrain or lamentation.

52 Cited in *The Origins of Freemasonry – Scotland's Century 1590-1710*. pp.125-126. Readers may well wish to read Stevenson's fascinating discussion as to the possible interpretation of this passage.

53 Ibid.

54 Ibid.pp.127-129. This complex situation and the various possible implications are expertly discussed by Stevenson.

55 *The Mason Word – Another early reference*. AQC. Vol.65 (1952). p.54.

56 Stillingfleet described it as 'Rabbinical Mystery'.

57 *Miracles no violations of the Laws of Nature*. London. 1683.

58 *Science and Religion in Seventeenth-Century England*. 1958. p.99.

59 *Oliver Cromwell*. 1900. p.433.

60 See for example: *Orbis Miraculum or the Temple of Solomon Portrayed by Scripture Light*. London. 1659.

61 See: *Cracking the Freemasons' Code*. 2006. Appendix 1. pp.214-217.

62 The ERH MS and other very similar MSS all reveal that the second Fellow Craft ceremony was also known as the Master Mason's ceremony and that the terms were interchangeable.

63 *Accounts of the Masters of Works for building and repairing Royal Palaces and Castles.* Vol. One. p.17.

64 *Accounts of the Treasurer of Scotland.* Vol. 13. p.140.

65 There are two additional and near-identical manuscripts which make up the body of evidence known as the 'Scottish School'. These are the Airlie MS (1705) and the Chetwode Crawley MS (*c*.1710).

66 This last stonemasons' lodge was Lodge St. John, No.1² (Melrose).

67 I admit that this is pure speculation on my part and that there is no supporting evidence whatsoever.

68 See note 30 above.

69 For details of pre-1717 English evidence, see *The History of English Freemasonry*. 1994.

70 I use the term 'speculative' here despite my dislike of its usage in a Scottish context. Although it was a 'speculative' lodge it rather surprisingly never joined the 'speculative' Grand Lodge of Scotland when that body was founded in 1736. The Lodge at Haughfoot preferred to maintain an independent existence until it finally ceased to exist in 1762.

71 The four known lodges were: The Goose and Gridiron, St Paul's Churchyard, established 1691; Crown Ale House Lodge, Lincoln Inn Fields, established 1712; The Rummer and Grapes, Channel Row, Westminster, (later known as Horn Lodge) and The Apple Tree Tavern, Covent Garden (now known as the Lodge of Fortitude and Old Cumberland No.12). According to Anderson (*New Constitutions*, 1738) this was a revival, not the creation of a new body.

72 This was quite different from lodges in Scotland, which acknowledged St. John the Evangelist as their patron. His feast day is 27 December, and that Scottish lodges met annually on that day is confirmed by records from the late 16th century and throughout the 17th century to the present day.

73 *The History of English Freemasonry*. 1994. p.87.

74 The definition of 'cowan' is not precise and seems to have several meanings. It may refer to those who have the skill and ability of a stonemason but who have not been admitted into a lodge.

75 In Scotland this was a slow process; the last independent stonemasons' lodge joined the Grand Lodge of Scotland only in 1891.

76 Grand Lodge MS No. 2. This document does not refer to the situation in Scotland.

77 The first of these mock-Masonic processions was reported in the *London Daily Post* of 20 March 1741.

78 It is perhaps significant that this lodge, known to have been in existence in 1670, had less than 20% members who were stonemasons.

79 And one, I believe, that was first discussed in this particular manner in: *The Masonic Magician.* p.137.

80 Freemasonry was also intended to appeal to members of other religious groups but they made up a minuscule element of the population.

81 *Jews and Freemasons in Europe 1723-1939.* 1970.

82 There are numerous branches of Freemasonry, all with their own ceremonies and oaths, but for the purposes of this book the reader should assume that I am referring to the first three degrees of Freemasonry: the Entered Apprentice, Fellow of Craft and Master Mason.

⁸³ *Oaths, Oath Taking and Mental Reservation.* ND.

⁸⁴ Some would argue that laws etc, are not easily enforced today but the point here is in comparison to previous centuries. We have improved somewhat!

⁸⁵ This was particularly important for small business transactions (often by barter) where formal contracts simply could not apply.

⁸⁶ It could well be argued that this reveals the dramatic reduction of the weight given to one's word in the past, compared with today.

⁸⁷ For more information see:
http://www.mercers.co.uk/netbuildpro/process/146/History.php

⁸⁸ Such Guilds are recorded as being in existence in England during the 14th century and there are suggestions of an even earlier existence. See, for example, *The Old Guilds of England*, p.101.

⁸⁹ 'Ecclesiastical property' seemed to have been loosely applied to take in all guild property.

⁹⁰ For example: obits for the dead, lamps for chantry services.

⁹¹ Although inevitably politics and dynastic considerations did intrude, the religious dimension was dominant.

⁹² Caution must be exercised in using the Scottish experience to compare events in other countries.

⁹³ Being a Burgess, and the associated privileges, were important to merchants and tradesmen, as it was not possible to engage in business unless one was a member of the merchant guild, and a tradesman could not practise his trade unless he belonged to the burgh's incorporation.

⁹⁴ *Records of the Incorporation of Barbers, Glasgow.* pp. 105-106.

⁹⁵ This particular version of the Burgess Oath was introduced in 1744.

⁹⁶ It could be, and was, argued that the religion of the realm was Protestantism and not simply the type practised by the Church of Scotland. The dominant view was, however, that the oath, strictly interpreted, would exclude people who were not members of the Church of Scotland.

⁹⁷ People who had a trade that had no incorporation, such as a water carrier or carter, were unaffected, but unincorporated trades paid less and were generally lower down the social scale.

⁹⁸ These references to Ebenezer and Ralph Erskine provide a little insight to their extraordinary lives.

⁹⁹ Examples: 'The Tree of Life' and 'The Plant of Renown'. See *An Introduction to the Origins and History of the Order of Free Gardeners,* p.30.

¹⁰⁰ The Illuminati are the most common exception, but even they are usually referred to in the same breath as Freemasons.

¹⁰¹ Erskine wrote extensively and many of his sermons and pamphlets were translated into several European languages. Of his six pamphlets on the Burgess Oath, his first and probably (then) best known was: 'Fancy no faith: or, a seasonable admonition and information to seceders, against the sinful constitution of some brethren into a pretended judicatory: and against a pamphlet lately published by them, intitled, Acts and proceedings of the Associate Synod at Edinburgh, April 1747, &c. Together with some remarks upon ... The warrantableness of the Associate Synod's sentence.'

¹⁰² I specifically use the term 'pseudo-religious' as Freemasonry is not a religion.

¹⁰³ The Burgess Oath was abolished in 1819, but it was by then too late for

Freemasonry. The nature of oath-taking had been well and truly debated for more than 60 years. The focus had moved from the Burgess Oath, which was after all sanctioned and administered by the establishment, to the non-established Freemasonry.

104 Burns' Burgess Ticket (certificate) from Jedburgh records: 'Robert Burns Esquire was entered and received into the Libertys of this Burgh, Create and make a free Burges and Guild Brother of the same, who gave his Oath with all Ceremonies used and wont. Whereupon he required Acts of Court and protested for an Extract of the same under the Common Seal of this Burgh.' (11 May 1787) *Burns Chronicle*, 1942.

105 See the seminal works of Prof. David Stevenson: *The First Freemasons – Scotland's Early Lodges and their Members* and *The Origins of Freemasonry – Scotland's Century 1690-1710.*

106 Scots were instrumental in that process also, for details of which again see the works of Stevenson, as detailed above.

107 The army was in France during the war of the Spanish Succession (1701-1714).

108 Fénelon was a Quietist, which is an approach that attempts to make the mind inactive and passive in order that God can act through it without any encumbrances. It was this idea of the mind becoming a 'blank sheet' on which God could write that attracted Ramsay.

109 He was made a cardinal in 1726.

110 For the text of the *Oration* and a detailed discussion of the two extant versions see *Heredom*, Vol.One.

111 Although some authors have claimed that when Ramsay mentioned Crusaders in his oration, he was actually referring to the Knights Templar. This is incorrect as he never mentioned that Order.

112 Now part of Italy, it was then governed by the Austrians (1713–96).

113 As far as I can tell, there is no evidence of Quietism within Freemasonry.

114 The rituals of Freemasonry were first revealed in 1730, when they were published by Samuel Pritchard in London under the title *Masonry Dissected*. He claimed to be a Freemason and revealed the rituals (they are known as 'exposures' within the Craft) in order to enlighten the unwary. French editions were published soon after and so it seems odd that the church focuses entirely on the private nature of lodge meetings rather than the ritual content.

115 Although not the first to attack formally Freemasonry it was, I believe, the first religious institution to do so.

116 *The Free Masons Pocket Companion*. Ruddiman and Auld. Edinburgh, 1761, and Joseph Galbriath, Glasgow, 1765.

117 *An Apology for the Free and Accepted Masons, Occasioned by their Persecution in the Canton of Berne with the present state of Masonry in Germany, Italy, France, Flanders and Holland.* Contained within *The Pocket Companion*, printed for J. Scott,. London. 1754. pp. 237-281.

118 It is not thought necessary here to reproduce the 'Providas Romanorum'.

119 For a definition of religious indifferentism, see: http://en.wikipedia.org/wiki/Religious_indifferentism

120 Theology is the underlying philosophy of a church.

121 In 1991 Pope John Paul II (1978–2005; b. 1920) said, 'This does not lessen the sincere respect that the Church has for the various religious traditions,

recognising in them elements of truth and goodness.' If Freemasonry is considered to be a religion, one must judge for one's self if the 'sincere respect' accorded other religions is also granted to Freemasonry.

[122] I admit that this is an extreme simplification of this period of Italian history.

[123] See, for example, *The Masonic Magician*.

[124] *The Life of Joseph Balsamo commonly called Count Cagliostro*, p.vii.

[125] Lenten sermon at Aix-la-Chapelle (now Aachen) in 1779.

[126] The priests were members of a minor order of friars known as Capuchins.

[127] *The Masonic Magician*, pp.156-160.

[128] He was one of the first, if not *the* first, to claim that modern Freemasonry was merely a continuation of the medieval Order of Knights Templar and was bent on revenge against the Church and all who supported her.

[129] Prof. Andrew Prescott suggests that Robison supported a Newtonian view of Freemasonry, and that consequently the more speculative and mystical continential form was aberrant. This opinion accords well with Robison's rationalist scientific methodology.

[130] Barruel's work is error-prone when promoting his ecclesiastical prejudices.

[131] *The United Irishmen: Popular Politics in Ulster and Dublin, 1791-1798*, p.246.

[132] This is often used to accuse Freemasons of dubious practices, whereas instead the nature of the organisation making use of such methods is a far better gauge.

[133] The aims of Freemasonry remain quite different from organisations with a political and/or religious agenda, but differentiating between the numerous groups was not an easy task.

[134] *The United Irishmen: Popular Politics in Ulster and Dublin, 1791-1798*, p.247.

[135] Mutiny was included because of the two naval mutinies which took place at Nore and Spithead in 1797.

[136] Freemasons held processions, laid foundation stones and had many of their activities reported in the press.

[137] The Grand Lodges at this time had many senior political figures as members. For example: the Prince of Wales (later George IV, 1820–1830; b.1762) and Francis Rawdon (later Second Earl of Moira and First Marquess of Hastings (1754–1826). Mother Kilwinning was at a disadvantage but was up to the task and approached the Ayrshire MP, Col. William Fullerton, who was able to obtain the same concessions as for the Grand Lodges.

[138] The concessions required Grand Lodges to create another layer of bureaucracy to satisfy the authorities that its Lodges were legal, legitimate and not seditious.

[139] Although these figures are quoted in *Coil's Masonic Encyclopedia*, p.264, I prefer to accept them as approximate.

[140] *Coil's Masonic Encyclopedia*, p.274.

[141] *Warrant for Genocide*, p.31.

[142] Reported in October 1794 and reproduced in *Chronicle of the French Revolution*, p.452.

[143] In the third century AD, the Persian Mani established a religion known as Manicheism in direct competition with Christianity. The Assassins were a Muslim sect. Neither of these had been founded by Jews, although during the Crusades Europeans came into contact with the latter and possibly the former.

[144] For example, he wanted an end to the practice of money lending still prevalent in some Jewish parts of France.

[145] *History of Anti-Semitism: From Voltaire to Wagner*, p.282.

[146] Ibid., p.283.

[147] For a discussion of this in relation to the more recent myths relating to Freemasonry, see *The Rosslyn Hoax?*, pp.14-24.

[148] The plural of *carbonaro*, Italian for charcoal burner, a trade whose activities were used as a model for its rituals.

[149] Members of the Carbonari included Marquis de La Fayette (or Lafayette) (1757–1834), George Gordon, Sixth Baron Byron, (commonly known as 'Lord Byron') (1788–1824) and Louis-Napoléon Bonaparte, later Emperor Napoleon III (1851–1873; b. 1808).

[150] At this time the Papal States were a large geographic as well as religious entity.

[151] An encyclical is essentially a circular letter sent to bishops.

[152] This Pope is famous for the convocation of Vatican Council I (1869–1870), as well as being the longest serving Pope in Church history.

[153] This is not a comprehensive list of revolutions.

[154] The potato famines of 1846 and 1867 affected not only Ireland but also Scotland, Silesia, the Low Countries, northern France and parts of Germany.

[155] As refugees from Silesia etc., crammed into Vienna, they brought with them typhus which spread like wildfire in the overcrowded city.

[156] Once more I have to admit to reducing these enormous subjects and the period covered to the bare minimum.

[157] I can do no better than recommend the reader to *The Age of Revolution 1789-1848* by Eric Hobsbawm for an excellent overview of the period.

[158] In 1849 the people of Dresden, capital of the Kingdom of Saxony, rose to demand that King Frederick Augustus II of Saxony (1797–1854) enact liberal electoral reforms and address social injustice. Richard Wagner (1813–1883), the composer, was actively engaged in the revolution. He was not a Freemason. It is ironic that Adolf Hitler (1889–1945) would adopt Wagner as an example of the need to purify the German Volk. Neither Wagner nor Hitler knew that the revolution that freed Saxony Germans was engineered by Freemasonry!

[159] The book was translated into French in 1854 by Abbot Gyr of Liege.

[160] *Historisch-politische Blätter*. Vol. 49. pp.185-193. There were two volumes published annually in Munich, Bavaria. This article was included in the first volume for that year.

[161] This may have been written by the poet, philosopher and Catholic convert Georg Friedrich Daumer (1800–1875), but absolute proof is lacking.

[162] This periodical was first published in 1838 and continued until 1923.

[163] Palmerston was not a Freemason. See *The Rosslyn Hoax?*, pp.18-19.

[164] Goedsche's chapter on the meeting in a Jewish cemetery was translated into a Russian pamphlet in 1872.

[165] *The Freemasons*, p.214.

[166] It is admitted that this is a very brief and therefore deficient account of an extremely complex period of history.

[167] By Chapman and Hall, Piccadilly, London, 264 pages in total.

[168] Even the first writer to 'expose' Freemasonry in print during 1730, Samuel Pritchard, was never identified.

[169] Although acquitted on the second day of his trial, the guilty party was almost certainly Major Ferdinand W. Esterhazy (1847–1923).

[170] In 1898 the Grand Orient promised its support to obtain justice and legality and denounced those who opposed those aims. In other words it tacitly expressed pro-Dreyfus ideals and decried those who maintained Dreyfus's guilt (regardless of personal cost).

[171] In 1899 a meeting of the Grand Orient called to discuss the Dreyfus Affair was attended by so many Freemasons that a second meeting had to be held.

[172] The notion of regular and irregular Freemasonry must be as difficult to grasp by non-Masons as it is for many Freemasons. Essentially, there are certain 'rules' that Grand Lodges must abide by in order to be considered a 'regular' (that is, genuine) Grand Lodge. The Grand Lodges of England had ceased to recognise the Grand Orient of France in 1870 when it ceased to apply some of those rules.

[173] *Antisemitism: a historical encyclopedia of prejudice and persecution. Volume 1.* p.289.

[174] In 1887 Böckel published a pamphlet, *Die Juden – die Könige unserer Zeit*, which attacked Jews because of their perceived dominance over German life and culture. He led the *Antisemitische Volkspartei* (Antisemitic People's Party) which won four Parliamentary seats in 1890, but his personal dislike of Fritsch ensured his political demise in 1903.

[175] This is reminiscent of Napoleon's summoning an assembly of the Great Sanhedrin in 1806.

[176] It may also be a direct reference to the First Congress of Reform Judaism held in 1869 in Leipzig.

[177] *Warrant for Genocide*, p.43.

[178] The Italians had signed a secret agreement with France in 1902 nullifying the Triple Alliance as Italy wanted Austrian territory, particularly in Dalmatia and Trentino.

[179] No evidence has ever been produced to support this contention. Some sources give the date of the speech as August 1918. Ellic Howe's date seems more likely. See *The Collapse of Freemasonry in Nazi Germany, 1933 – 5*. AQC. Vol.95. p.22.

[180] The first of these was *Masonry Dissected* by Samuel Pritchard. London. 1730.

[181] An interesting article from *The Builder* (1929) entitled 'Freemasonry, Judaism and Gen. Erich Ludendorff' is to be found on line at: http//www.graidlodgesotad.com/index.php?option=com_content &task=view&id=95&Itemid=29

[182] The *Protocols* continue to be published, uncritically, in some countries and are often cited as 'proof' of the existence of a Judaeo/Masonic New World Order conspiracy.

[183] Vol.One was published in 1925 and Vol.Two in 1926.

[184] The adaptation and elaboration of their ideology is somewhat tortuous, given the number of people and ideas being contributed but some insight can be gained from the explanation and discussion contained in Chapter 2 regarding the origins and history of anti-Semitism and Masonophobia.

[185] The German assault in early August 1914 through neutral Belgium, according to the Schlieffen Plan for invading France, gained him national recognition. He was responsible for the eastern front victory at the battle of Tannenberg in 1914 and, after Hindenburg was appointed Chief General, Ludendorff became Quartermaster-General in 1916. In this position he became politically influential

and together with Hindenburg more or less conducted the war from that date. Following the early successes, he went with Hindenburg to the Western Front where they jointly planned and carried out the Verdun attack of 1916. His military and administrative skills were used to re-organise the army while at the same time creating a strategy of advancing on the Eastern Front and holding the French and British in check in the west until forces could be released from the Eastern Front. On the collapse of Russia, he was able to mount a spring offensive in 1918. However, British forces breached the Hindenburg Line during September which, together with the collapse of Bulgaria soon after, caused a crisis of confidence. Believing the war to be lost, Ludendorff called for peace negotiations to commence. Once talks began he changed his mind and refused to co-operate. He was consequently dismissed in October 1918 and took a leading part in the unsuccessful Nazi *Putsch* in Munich in 1923. He was elected to the Reichstag (Parliament) as a right-wing Nationalist in 1924 as a representative of the NSFB (a coalition of the German Völkisch Freedom Party and members of the Nazi Party).

[186] That does not minimise the part it played in the anti-Semitism which led to the Holocaust.

[187] Principally George Shanks, Nesta H. Webster and the editor of *The Morning Post*, Howell Arthur Gwynne. The latter is generally accepted as being the main compiler of both works.

[188] *The Protocols of Zion* – An Exposure. *The Times*, Tuesday, 16 August 1921. Jewish Peril Exposed. Historic Fake. Details of the Forgery. *The Times*, Wednesday, 17 August 1921. The Protocols Forgery. Use in Russian Politics. Methods of the Secret Police. *The Times*, Thursday, 18 August 1921. As Graves was not cited as the author (the writer was stated to be *The Times'* Constantinople correspondent), this probably diminished their authority.

[189] These were:

The Old Prussian Grand Lodges:
Grosseloge von Preussen, genannt (Royal York) Zur Freundschaft
Grosse Nationalmutterloge zu den drei Weltkugeln
Grosse Landesloge der Freimaurer von Deutschland

The Humanitarian Grand Lodges:
Grosse Landesloge von Sachsen
Eklektischer Bund
Grosseloge von Hamburg
Grosseloge zur Sonne
Grosseloge von Darmstadt
Grosseloge Deutsche Bruderkette

The above do not include those other so-called Masonic organisations which existed in Germany and were deemed 'irregular' by most other regular Grand Lodges, etc.

[190] An attempt had been made to create an umbrella organisation for all German Grand Lodges, known as *Deutscher Grosslogenbund*, founded in 1872. This was only partly effective, especially after the Old Prussian Grand Lodges withdrew in 1922.

191 These can only be generalisations as there has never been, so far as I am aware, a detailed comprehensive analysis of the economic/social background of German Freemasons of this period.

192 *The Collapse of Freemasonry in Nazi Germany, 1933-5. AQC.* Vol.95. p.21.

193 *Vernichtung der Freimaurerei durch Enthüllung ihrer Geheimnisse.* Munich. 1927.

194 The so-called Masonic 'secrets' were first published in print form available to the public in London in 1730 by Samuel Pritchard. These 'exposures', as Freemasons call them, continue to be published all over the world and reveal that their publishers and, presumably, the readers simply do not understand the nature of Freemasonry.

195 Although Ludendorff had taken part in Hitler's failed 1923 Beer Hall *Putsch* in the following year he was a founder of the National Socialist Freedom Movement (NSFM) and ran, and lost heavily, for President of the Weimar Republic. In 1925, after Hitler's release, the NSFM was absorbed into the Nazi Party. These facts are important, as Ludendorff was by now treated with suspicion. 'By 1927 Hitler was openly attacking his former ally – and accusing him of Freemasonry [sic]' *Hitler 1889-1936: Hubris.* p.269.

196 As previously noted, the use of an assumed name seemed to be a characteristic common to those mounting anti-Semitic and Masonophobic attacks in print.

197 The use of the term 'victors' and 'defeated' of WW1 are used advisedly here.

198 Hitler was appointed German Chancellor on 30 January 1933. Another general election was held on 5 March, after which, with the support of the Nationalists, he was able to pass the so-called Enabling Act (24 March 1933) which granted him dictatorial powers.

199 In the anti-Semitic journal *La Vieille France*, April 1921.

200 The article was widely circulated and reprinted in Russian and German.

201 He also had to pay for the substantial costs of the court case and publish a retraction of his allegations.

202 Edward Hampshire, Modern Records Specialist, The National [English] Archives, London. In: *Germany 1944 – The British Soldier's Pocketbook.* p.x.

203 Cited in, *The Holocaust – The Jewish Tragedy.* 1987. p.30.

204 Cited in, *In the Eye of the Hurricane: German Freemasonry in Weimar Republic and the Third Reich.* 2003. p.130. (fn)

205 Engelbert Dollfuss (1892–1934)

206 'The young [Himmler] nationalist idealist, already imagining dire conspiracies involving "the Red International", Jews, Jesuits and Freemasons ranged against Germany, had joined the NSDAP in the summer of 1923.' *Hitler 1889-1936: Hubris.* p.301.

207 Canaris was the leader of the July Plot to kill Hitler. He was executed in April 1945.

208 The Nuremberg Tribunal spent a considerable amount of time and effort in detailing the structure and functions of the Gestapo, SD and SS. They identified the departments and sections which had responsibility for 'dealing' with Freemasonry. See *Nuremberg Trial Proceedings.* Vol.Four. 20 December 1945. pp.235-236. *Supporting documents Nazi Conspiracy and Aggression Volume IV:* Nos.1551-PS, No.1815-PS and 192-A-PS also refer to Freemasonry and the arrangements to 'deal' with the problem.

[209] The fragmented nature of Freemasonry in Germany required that not only was an index of individuals created, but also of the various Masonic bodies to which they belonged. See note 206 above.

[210] *Hitler 1889-1936: Hubris.* p.541.

[211] In 1922 he published a book, *Freemasonry and the Russian Revolution.* His reputation as an expert on Freemasonry was enhanced with the publication of his book *The Freemasons* in 1928.

[212] This appears to be an inflated figure perhaps due to duplication, but in any event the card index remained the main SD tool for 'dealing' with German Freemasons. Another suggestion is that the card index also included Freemasons in other countries.

[213] Proving that Masonic Lodges had been looted.

[214] The omission as to whether this referred to St. John the Evangelist or St. John the Baptist suggests a lack of in-depth knowledge of Freemasonry.

[215] See *Eichmann – His Life and Crimes.* 2004.

[216] Freemasonry in Germany is still therefore relatively small as a consequence.

[217] The snake as a symbol of evil was considered very suitable for depicting the Judaeo-Masonic conspiracy.

[218] *The Jewish Community in Hamburg 1860-1943.* See: www.1.uni-hamburg.de/rz3a035/jew_history4.html

[219] *Nuremberg Trial Proceedings.* Vol.12. 30 April 1946. p.418.

[220] Ibid. Vol.13. 3 May 1946. p.63.

[221] Robert H. Jackson was himself a Freemason. I am grateful to Brother Mark Tabbert of the George Washington National Masonic Memorial, Virginia, for this information.

[222] He was one of only three defendants to be acquitted at Nuremberg.

[223] I am grateful to Brother Alain Bernheim, who provided me with this information before I knew I would use it! Bro. Bernheim has a number of useful and interesting papers, on this subject and others, on the Pietre-Stones Review of Freemasonry website at: http://www.freemasons-freemasonry.com/bernheim12.html

[224] As we have seen elsewhere in this chapter, this was in a vain attempt to avert the wrath of the regime.

[225] The German authorities were actively encouraging emigration to Palestine at this time.

[226] See *In the Eye of the Hurricane: German Freemasonry in the Weimar Republic and the Third Reich,* 2003, for a detailed discussion of various tactics used by German Grand Lodges to survive.

[227] This decree removed most civil liberties and was used to imprison anyone not considered to support the state.

[228] Eichmann transferred to the Jewish section of the SD in summer 1935, his work on Freemasonry unfinished.

[229] Care must be taken here, as details of prominent Freemasons were more likely to be noticed and recorded whereas the fate of 'ordinary' Freemasons was not.

[230] In addition to the veiled threat that the state would prohibit Freemasonry unless it voluntarily dissolved itself, there was the fact that Freemasons were already being refused certain jobs and admission to professional organisations. *The Collapse of Freemasonry in Nazi Germany, 1933-5, AQC.* Vo.95. p.30.

[231] *Encyclopedia of the Third Reich.* p.101.

[232] These were quite numerous: National Socialist Association of University Lecturers, Hitler Youth (and its several sub-divisions) the *Nationalsozialistischer Reichsbund für Leibesübungen* (NSRL) the umbrella organisation for sport in the Third Reich.

[233] The German name can loosely be translated as the [National] Committee for Investigation and Settlement.

[234] *The Nazi Party Courts*, p.111.

[235] Ibid, p.112.

[236] In December 1933, the Reich-Uschla was reorganised and renamed Oberstes Parteigericht (Supreme Party Court or OPG) with district and local courts.

[237] *The Nazi Party Courts.* p.133.

[238] *Hitler 1938-1945: Nemesis.* p.24.

[239] George VI, when Duke of York, was installed on 30 November 1936. (See Plate 10)

[240] Complaints regarding this disruption were made. See *The Nazi Party Courts*, p.132.

[241] Further confusion was caused when it was decreed in 1938 that Freemasons who were never 'higher' than a third-degree Mason, and who had never held office or been in a leadership position within a lodge should not be disadvantaged because of their lodge membership. But this relaxation of the rules *only* applied to Freemasons who had left their lodges and joined the Nazi Party before 30 January 1933.

[242] Translating 'Volk' into English is not straightforward. Initially it could be translated as 'folk', as in 'the people', but under nationalistic jingoism it began to have other aspects attached such as occultism, romanticism and folklore. It could therefore be used to identify those who were *not* of the 'Volk' – Jews etc.

[243] *German Primer – Words to Comrades.* 1940.

[244] A co-ordinated, comprehensive, survey of material relating to Freemasonry and the Holocaust would be a way forward. The same could be said for all material relating to Masonophobia, but the former proposal would be sufficiently daunting.

[245] This is particularly true in respect of the English language. I am aware of *Freimaurerei and Nationalsozialsmus. Die Verfolgung der deutschen Freimaurerei durch völkische Bewegung und Nationalsozialismus 1918-1945*, by Helmut Neuberger (two volumes Hamburg, 1980), but my lack of understanding of the German language means that I can but hope that one day this important work will be translated into English.

[246] It is not possible in a work of this size to provide details for every country occupied by Axis forces.

[247] I hesitate to describe Freemasonry as an 'organisation', as there are many elements which are commonly accepted as defining an organisation which are absent from Freemasonry.

[248] Becoming a member of the SD automatically meant becoming a member of the SS. His membership number was 272284.

[249] The SD (and associated organisations) went through numerous phases of reorganisation and renumbering, but it is not the purpose of this book to go into such detail here.

[250] It is estimated that 45,000 Dutch Jews perished in the former and 65,000 in the latter, but these are approximate figures only.

[251] Barbie evaded capture at the end of the war and eventually reached South America. He was deported from Bolivia to France in 1983, put on trial for crimes against humanity and found guilty in 1987. He was sentenced to life imprisonment and died in Lyon prison in 1991 of leukaemia.

[252] I have written seven times to the Holocaust Memorial Day Trust and they have yet to reply.

[253] As stated elsewhere, this book can be considered merely an introduction.

[254] *Freemasonry in the Eastern Hemisphere.* p.146.

[255] I have no knowledge of where Tas was arrested as a result of his resistance activities, or if he had been identified as a Freemason.

[256] *Nazi Attacks against Freemasonry in the Netherlands.* Elliot, Allen; Lodge, Richard W. and Sandstrom, Mark. 1994. UK Masonic Online Forum.

[257] *Vrijmetselarij Een Volksvijandige Organisatie.* 1941.

[258] *Nuremberg Trial Proceedings.* Vol.16. 14 June 1946. p.203.

[259] For example, leather Masonic aprons were used in shoemaking, and paperwork was shredded and reused to make new paper.

[260] *Nuremberg Trial Proceedings,* Vol.7. 7 February 1946. p.15.

[261] Ibid. p.79-80.

[262] Named after where the government was based.

[263] *Freemasonry in the Eastern Hemisphere.* p.177.

[264] I make no judgements whatsoever here of motives, merely noting the almost impossible position of 'target' groups.

[265] Much research could be done, but many will no doubt argue that, 'Masons might not come out looking good, so why bother?' I understand that reluctance. Freemasons are, after all human beings, and will act much the same as others when under threat.

[266] How wise it was to make such a provocative statement might well be indicated by subsequent events.

[267] Off the north coast of Sicily.

[268] *Coil's Masonic Encyclopedia.* p.59.

[269] *Proceedings of the Grand Lodge 'Lessing zu den drei Ringen'.* Prague, Czechoslovakia. 1936-1937. p 1.

[270] *A Short History of Freemasonry in the Czech Republic.* 2005. p.7.

[271] See, for example: http://mill-valley.freemasonry.biz/persecution.htm

[272] This was in Upper Austria, about 12 miles east of Linz.

[273] Correspondence in *The Northern Light* magazine. March 1990.

[274] There is a great deal of anecdotal material where although there is no reason to doubt the essential accuracy of such reports, lack of corroboration often means that it is discounted. For example, the editor of *The Northern Light* magazine stated (February 1990) that a French Freemason, Brother M. Jattefaux who had been incarcerated in Buchenwald concentration camp, had reported that there were approximately 100 Freemasons in that camp. Unfortunately, no other details are (presently) available.

[275] There is a large material which, although accessible, is not usable due to my linguistic deficiencies. Examples are (at random): RG-43.026M – French Freemasons Registrations Cards. Included is biographical and

employment information that was used by French police and other agencies to remove Freemasons from jobs and enforce other restrictions on their lives). In French. 1940–1944. RG-43.044 – Selected Records of Archives Département du Nord. (This collection contains materials pertaining to the persecution of Jews and Freemasons in the Département du Nord in French and German. 1941-1944). RG-65.010 – Selected Records Related to Anti-Masonic Measures in Belgium. (This collection contains materials about the repression of Freemasons. It also contains documentation on the persecution of other organisations such as a Buddhist association. At the end of the collection are alphabetical lists of Freemasons. In German, Flemish and French. 1940-1943). RG-11.001M.21 – *Einsatzstab Reichsleiter Rosenberg* (Most of this material pertains to Yugoslavia and ERR efforts to collect and remove to Germany cultural material, and to conduct propaganda against Jews and Freemasons. Included are lists of confiscated Jewish property, and protocols of interrogations of Jews and Freemasons regarding their property). In German. 1939–1943. The above is a small sample of material housed in the United States Holocaust Memorial Museum, Washington D.C. I have no doubt that there is other similar material in archives in America and Europe.

276 *Warrant for Genocide*, at page 242, citing H. Rollin, *L'Apocalypse de notre temps*. p.514. There were odd Masonic Lodges in China but they were almost exclusively made up of European expatriates.

277 Although there were relatively few Freemasons in the Far East after the outbreak of war, those in the Allied armed forces were sought out by the Japanese *Kempeitai*, often called the 'Japanese Gestapo', and executed. It is impossible to estimate the number involved. See, for example, River Valley Road POW Camp, The. *Grand Lodge of Scotland Year Book 1996*.

278 There may be some confusion with the book, *Coming War*. 1931.

279 *Freemasonry in the Eastern Hemisphere*. 1954. p.223.

280 This period and the events which took place are highly complex and I make no pretence of providing anything other than the sparest of details.

281 This is also a very simplistic rendition of the facts.

282 *Freemasonry in the Eastern Hemisphere*. 1954. p.224.

283 Hundreds of thousands died during the occupation of Yugoslavia. They belonged to diverse groups and very many were civilians. Many were killed as reprisals for partisan attacks. Even the Gestapo noted the brutality of the Serbs in dealing with the 'enemy', which included men, women and children indiscriminately.

284 Yugoslavia was invaded simultaneously by Hungarian and Italian armies as well as that of Germany.

285 These posters and postage stamps (together with captions) have been posted online by the University of Minnesota at: http://www.chgs.umn.edu/Histories/otherness/otherness2.html

286 The longevity of the regime has probably hindered research into this aspect of Spain's history.

287 *The Guardian*. Giles Tremlett in Madrid. Saturday April 21, 2007.

288 The 'plan' was published in an abbreviated form in 2000. There is only one known original and that is in the care of the Imperial War Museum, London.

289 Schellenberg was a member of the SD and therefore also the Gestapo.

290 Special mobile formations charged with carrying out liquidations in occupied countries. Individual detachments were known as *Einsatzstabkommando*, the operations staff *Einsatzstab* and the smallest unit as the *Einsatztrupp*.

291 Their Scottish headquarters were to be in Edinburgh Castle.

292 The subsequent history of Freemasonry in Germany, although interesting, is not of direct relevance here.

293 Full name: William Walton Thomson Hannah.

294 George VI was installed as Grand Master Mason of the Grand Lodge of Scotland on 30 November 1930.

295 For a detailed discussion of the circumstances see, 'The Churches' concern with Freemasonry' by the Rev. Neville B. Cryer in *AQC* Vol. 95 (1981).

296 The book is still in print and is published by the Augustinian Press.

297 The Augustine Publishing Company (run by Timothy Tindal-Robertson 1976–1995.

298 It is important that I define what I mean by religion in order that there is no confusion. I am not delving into the minutiae of religious theology (which is a matter for the religions and denominations concerned). Therefore, although I cannot as a Freemason discuss religion in a specific manner, I can do so in generalities – the abstract mass of thought that might have some religious connotation in the widest possible sense. The former is therefore 'Religion' with a capital 'R' whereas my terms of intent is to discuss religion with a lower case 'r'. See also note 439 and 524 below in relation to politics. If I stray from these definitions, as I understand them to be applicable, then I apologise and ask forgiveness.

299 Inevitably these might be hinted at but it must be borne in mind that even if a specific reference is made that is an inadvertent mistake.

300 Therefore I shall not discuss the merits (or otherwise) of Communism as compared to those of Socialism!

301 Please remember that I am a Scot, and may be considered to have a different attitude of mind to many others.

302 Brown's publication is used here as a representative example (albeit from the USA) of the arguments made by some Christians against Freemasonry. This is because it is a cogent and well-argued case of its type.

303 *Secret Societies in the Light of the Bible.* 1928. Fourth Edition.

304 He makes no mention, for example, of the Free Gardeners, the Knights of St. Columba, the Knights Templar (non-Masonic version), etc, but claims that all 'secret societies' originate from Freemasonry and are therefore contaminated by reason of birth.

305 By 'religions', I include all those groups and individuals who comment on Freemasonry and claim to do so from a religious perspective.

306 *Secret Societies in the Light of the Bible.* 1928. p.6.

307 Ibid.

308 Again, we can see that the assessment takes place on his terms, not ours.

309 As *Secret Societies in the Light of the Bible* is now out of copyright it is reproduced online at: www.grandlodgescotland.com

310 Specifically, *A Lexicon of Freemasonry*, 1845, by the former and *The Freemasons' Monitor*, 1797, by the latter.

311 *Secret Societies in the Light of the Bible.* 1928. p.6.

312 *The Builder* magazine was published from 1915 to 1930 by the National Masonic Research Society. See: http://www.phoenixmasonry.org/the_builder_1915-1930_toc.htm for online copies of the magazine.

313 I have not located copies of the first, second or third editions but it is clear that a reply was sent by Newton between the publication of the first and fourth editions.

314 *Secret Societies in the Light of the Bible.* 1928. p.29.

315 Ibid.

316 Theism is a belief that a Supreme Being created and governs the world of humankind. Many Freemasons therefore accept this as a neutral, non-religious statement, and that Freemasonry has no comment to offer as to the nature of a Supreme Being. At this point Freemasonry accepts that it is the function of any particular religion to provide a religious definition.

317 This is a simplification and there are numerous sub-meanings and symbolic interpretations, but I think this is sufficient to make the point without going into further detail.

318 There are, of course, different interpretations depending on denomination, etc.

319 This is why Muslim sacred architecture emphasises abstract patterns and geometric designs, rather than attempting to paint, draw etc, anything from nature.

320 This is why members of that faith avoid spelling out 'God' in full and nearly always write G_D instead.

321 *Secret Societies in the Light of the Bible.* 1928, pp.6-7.

322 In particular, Chapter 2 Verses 8-9.

323 This is true regardless of the fact that the individual might be a prominent and/or senior Freemason. Not even a group of prominent and/or senior Freemasons can do so either.

324 It must be borne in mind that I am citing Brown as only one example, because his lecture contains all the elements that are still being repeated today to attack Freemasonry.

325 *Secret Societies in the Light of the Bible.* 1928. p.9.

326 The discovery of such historical documents is of little interest to those holding anti-Masonic views.

327 *The Freemasons' Monitor.* p.285.

328 Syncretism is the successful combination of different systems of religious belief or practice and for that reason has been used to classify Freemasonry as being anti-Christian. As Freemasonry is not a religion this attempt to classify Freemasonry by this means also fails.

329 These are numerous even if not mentioned in the text, Roman Catholics, Protestants of various types (such as anti-Burghers, the Church of Scotland and Baptists) including Methodists, Anglicans, Congregationalists etc.

330 I am sure that some could be found if I took a lot of time and trouble to dig them out, but the fact remains that there are none that could be picked up as easily as those by Christians to be cited in this book.

331 Note 330 above is equally applicable here.

332 For the sake of simplicity I am not going to discuss the various arguments as to what should or should not be included in the Bible, for example the Apocrypha,

and other texts more recently discovered.

333 In particular the Gospels of four of his disciples: Matthew, Mark, Luke and John.

334 When I say 'Freemasonry has never...' it is important to bear in mind that Freemasonry across the world does not act as a single unified entity. This means that there have, unfortunately, been localised examples of exclusion contrary to Masonic precepts.

335 Here I am referring only to the original three Craft degrees conferred on Masonic Lodges.

336 Freemasonry is in a no-win situation here; erroneous religious interpretations are being applied to a group which is not a religion. Even if (and I can *never* imagine this happening) Freemasonry decided to acknowledge Christ in some shape or form in its lodges, it would probably be castigated even more than it is at present.

337 Or anywhere else in the Bible for that matter. But the point here is to appreciate, and I know that I am repeating myself, that portions of the Old Testament used in Freemasonry are for *allegorical* purposes.

338 There are numerous others. The major religion that is missing from this short list is Islam. It is not included here because Jesus Christ is recognised by Muslims as being one of the Prophets.

339 Buddhism, Hinduism and Zoroastrianism respectively.

340 I am conscious that this is an idealised situation, but I trust my reasoning here will be understood.

341 Successive Papal Bulls following the first in 1738 are one example.

342 There is also the problem of inertia. Once a decision has been made, at the highest level, religions are notoriously slow to reassess the situation.

343 Some in such audiences, congregations, etc, may well be Freemasons, but that is by accident not design.

344 Convincing Freemasons to change their point of view would be considered by many to be an additional benefit but it is not the primary intention.

345 Proselytising is religiously specific in that members of one religion actively attempt to convince members of another to convert to theirs. Thus most Christian denominations have missions which actively seek to convert Jews from Judaism to their version of Christianity. There are many other possible combinations.

346 The existence of a dogma is an essential part of any religion. People who come together for a common purpose which does not have a dogma cannot be considered a religion. For example, no one claims that the Boy Scouts, Boys' Brigade or Rotary International are religions.

347 This is the reason why there have been so many schisms within religions which are almost as old as religion itself as a system of thought.

348 The Passion Cross without a human figure still represents the crucifixion.

349 You could simply not tell anyone of your alternative (heretical) beliefs and remain a member of the church concerned, but that still means that as an individual you no longer accept the dogma of the church.

350 As previously stated, I know many Muslim Freemasons who adopt this view.

351 This does not mean that a group of Freemasons cannot agree on how they interpret a Masonic symbol, but it remains *their* interpretation and is not one

that can be imposed upon all other Freemasons.

352 Respected works on Religion make no mention of Freemasonry whatsoever. See *Living Religions – An Encyclopaedia of the World's Faiths.*

353 To further qualify this, unlike a church that sets a dogma for all its members, whatever Grand Lodges might decide applies only to a particular geographic area and not to Freemasonry as a whole.

354 *Dictionary of Scottish Church History and Theology.* p.340.

355 *Britannica Encyclopedia of World Religions.* p.359.

356 In a volume of 1181 tightly packed pages, Freemasonry warrants a mere 209 words.

357 *Secret Societies in the Light of the Bible.* pp.6-7.

358 Christianity or more particularly denominations thereof, is the main religion that attempts to classify Freemasonry as a religion. As far as I can tell neither Islam nor Judaism (or sub-divisions thereof) attempt to describe Freemasonry in this manner.

359 No doubt there will have been a few misguided Freemasons who have said exactly that but they cannot speak for Freemasonry as a whole.

360 See: http://www.reformedchurches.org/ and http://www.anglicancommunion.org/

361 Liturgy: a form and arrangement of worship as laid down by a church or religion.

362 Dr. John Drane.

363 As has been stated elsewhere, there *are* female Freemasons although Masonophobic attacks inevitably assume that there are only male.

364 This is available online at: http:www.direct.gov.uk/en/employment/resolvingworkplacedisputes/ discriminationatwork/index.htm

365 Some Christian denominations seem bent on re-writing their own history by denying that any of their prominent members were Freemasons. A full list of moderators of the Church of Scotland can be found at: Moderators_of_the_General_Assembly_of_the_Church_of_Scotland. It would be a very interesting exercise to trawl through the membership to find all those who were Freemasons.

366 Several attempts have been made over a number of years to engage in dialogue with several major churches in Scotland, but all have failed.

367 Martin Short has authored, or co-authored, a number of books on 'true crime' although his book on Freemasonry is thought to have been his most successful.

368 Even then I have had to limit this 'introduction' to Europe and have been forced to ignore other interesting episodes, such as the P2 Lodge (Italy) affair. But I have done so because the subjects have been discussed in detail elsewhere.

369 This is not quite true, as there was some very limited but indirect communication and this will be mentioned where appropriate.

370 Relatively few people read every daily newspaper and take notes and cuttings from them! Such was one of my duties.

371 This is probably because it was, for me, this article that led me to observe subsequent events.

372 *The Scotsman.* 22 March 1996.

373 The 'Mission Statement' of *The Scotsman* from the Prospectus published on 30

November 1816 read: The Conductors pledge themselves for impartiality, firmness and independence... their first desire is to be honest, the second is to be useful... the great requisites for the task are only good sense, courage and industry.

374 The full title, number of pages and date of publication are provided.

375 These are the questions I had wished to ask Fred Bridgland regarding the article:

Dunblane Questions

What prompted the suspicion that Thomas Hamilton was a Freemason?

Who was the source that made that suggestion? (I am after the types of source, e.g. politicians, other newspapers, etc, not the name of any individual.)

What prompted the 'interview' with Martin Short as an 'expert' on Freemasonry?

How was the interview with Martin Short conducted?

Prior to interviewing Short, had his book been read?

Why was it thought appropriate to use an English author writing about an English subject for information on a Scottish matter?

Was the validity of the claims made by Short checked against any other sources?

Was comment sought from the Grand Lodge of Scotland regarding Short's claims? If not why not?

Is it normal practice for a newspaper (in this case *The Scotsman*) to use a foreign affairs expert to write about a Scottish domestic matter?

376 It was not possible to reproduce all the articles during the 1990's that impugned Freemasonry and therefore those reproduced are a selection.

377 When I say 'articles written about...' etc, I also include this to mean news articles in other parts of the media (TV, radio, etc).

378 Whether this was a deliberate decision is not known.

379 *The Scotsman* 22 March 1996.

380 No author provided.

381 It goes without saying that the Grand Lodge of Scotland was not consulted prior to either article being published.

382 The full text of the Public Inquiry into the shootings at Dunblane Primary School on 13 March 1996 is available online at: http://www.archive.official-documents.co.uk/document/scottish/dunblane/dunblane.htm

383 The exact terms were: At the preliminary hearing I also invited written submissions in regard to three particular topics and *any other topic which was relevant*, (My emphasis). *The Public Inquiry on the Shootings at Dunblane Primary School 13th March 1996*. Chapter 2 (2:8 [i]).

384 This invitation was repeated in a press notice on 3 May 1996. Ibid.

385 The three particular topics were: control of the possession and use of firearms and ammunition; school security; vetting and supervision of adults working with children. *The Public Inquiry on the Shootings at Dunblane Primary School 13th March 1996*. Chapter 2 (2:8 (i)).

386 The preliminary Inquiry (1 May) was also held at the Albert Halls, Stirling.

387 Ironically, the date Brother Robert Burns was initiated into Freemasonry.

388 In *The Scotsman* newspaper. The principal authors of the four features were Stephen Breen and Nic Outterside.

389 I express many thanks to the publisher for permitting me this indulgence but they, like myself, appreciate the historical value in having all this material

together in the one place for immediate as well as future reference.

[390] In other words they were 'dirty'.

[391] Freemasonry is not a secret society as confirmed by the European Court of Human Rights. See the concluding chapter for more details.

[392] Given that Freemasonry is not a secret society then this cannot apply.

[393] This article was published on the front page.

[394] This becomes a self-serving claim. If I say there is public concern there must be public concern. The statement is wrong in that no evidence other than opinion is used to support the claim.

[395] If there was a 'suspicion', what was done to investigate it and why were the results not reported?

[396] How would they know? Where would they go to obtain details of membership?

[397] The full text is available, at the time of writing, on the *They Work for You* website at:
http://www.theyworkforyou.com/debates/?id=1992-07-01a.853.0&s=secret+societies+%28declaration%29#g853.1

[398] Neither *The Scotsman* newspaper nor either of the journalists submitted their 'findings' to the committee. They were not called as witnesses. See: *List of Witnesses* (that is, who appeared before the committee), p.xxiv; *List of Appendices to the Minutes of Evidence* (names of those individuals and organisations making written submissions which were published by the committee) p.xxv; and *List of Unprinted Memoranda* (material received by the committee but not printed. This material is located in the Record Office of the House of Lords). *Freemasonry in the Police and the Judiciary*. Vol.One. London. 1997.

[399] He was named as Proxy Master but it is assumed that the authors were unaware of the significant difference.

[400] This brief introductory article was published on the front page on 4th July.

[401] Page 8 *et seq* of the same issue.

[402] They were Margaret Butterwick and Susan Ovenstone, both of whom worked for local newspapers.

[403] See: http://www.archive.official-documents.co.uk/document/scottish/dunblane/dun05a.htm

[404] The list of occupations is by no means exhaustive and those cited here are by way of example only.

[405] If it really is a smokescreen and everybody knows it is a smokescreen, including the Masons, why do they continue to put so much time and effort into supporting charities?

[406] I am sure that there has been the odd exception, but that does not negate the fact that Freemasons, *as Freemasons*, ought to avoid discussing religion and politics.

[407] This form of scapegoating of a particular group is not restricted to fraternities. As we have seen elsewhere in this book it also can be, and has been, applied to religions such as Islam, Judaism and Christianity.

[408] The question must again be asked: why would they do so and where is the evidence?

[409] From the initial estimated cost of £40 million to a 'final' figure of £450 million.

[410] Colonel Gaddafi and his foreign minister were Freemasons and were stated to

be involved in an international Masonic conspiracy, according to a witness at the Lockerbie trial. *The Herald* and *The Daily Express.* 28 September 2000.

[411] Freemasons are people just like you and me!

[412] See: *The Rosslyn Hoax?* pp.18-19.

[413] To read the Scotland Act, see:
http://www.opsi.gov.uk/acts/acts1998/ukpga_19980046_en_1

[414] The committee's function is stated to be: to carry out the initial consideration of each admissible petition before making a recommendation as to the progress of a petition. The initial consideration generally includes hearing from petitioners where the petition raises a new issue, conducting background research and *seeking comments from various organisations with an interest in the issues raised* by each petition. Having conducted its own consideration of the issues the committee may decide that a more detailed investigation is required and refer the petition to the relevant subject committee. Alternatively, the committee may refer a petition to the Scottish Executive or other statutory bodies where work is ongoing in relation to the matters raised by a petition.' Emphasis added. Scottish Freemasonry was never invited to comment, despite the stated remit of the PPC.

[415] For more information about the work of the committee. see:
http://www.scottish.parliament.uk/s3/committees/petitions/index.htm

[416] In excess of 1,200 had been received at the time of writing.

[417] The petitioner had fears that as an accused person he might not be dealt with fairly if the judge hearing the case was a Freemason.

[418] The petition was dated 21st November and received by the committee on 27th November 2000.

[419] It has been suggested that this was an organised 'campaign' against Freemasonry, but that must remain mere speculation.

[420] It seems that quoting this article might have been a mistake as article six 'The Right to a fair trial', might have been more appropriate.

[421] The programme was presented by Anne MacKenzie.

[422] John Scott.

[423] On this basis, people employed in government agencies, quangos and council 'arms length' businesses, etc, would be included.

[424] See the reports at:
http://news.bbc.co.uk/1/hi/scotland/969317.stm and
http://news.bbc.co.uk/1/hi/scotland/979055.stm
both one month before the petition was submitted.

[425] The full minute is too lengthy to be reproduced here, but it is reproduced in full at: http//www.scottish.parliament.uk/business/committees/historic/petitions/or-00/pu00-1902.htm

[426] Some might be tempted to suggest that there was a Masonophobic campaign taking place, but there is no evidence to support this. A conspiracy against Freemasons? Heaven forbid!

[427] Although this appears to be a clear case of double standards, we ought to bear in mind that the argument is rarely considered in this manner.

[428] One has to wonder if the intention was to 'name and shame' those on such a register.

[429] If legislation were to be enacted on the basis of perception alone, then that

would set a precedent which would take us into realms I shudder to think about.

430 Scottish Parliament, Justice 2 Committee – Official Report. Meeting No. 38, 2002, Columns. 1998–1991.

431 Scottish Parliament, Justice 2 Committee, Tuesday 4 March 2003. Judicial Appointments, columns 2582-2595.

432 All petitions, whether closed or open, can be viewed by links from the Scottish parliament PPC web page at:
http://www.scottish.parliament.uk/s3/committees/petitions/index.htm

433 As an historian I am concerned that, with the increasing use of electronic recording methods and the internet, it may become increasingly difficult to obtain information such as that which is discussed in this book.

434 There are numerous press reports about Freemasonry and the judiciary during this period and as most of the content is repetitive they need not be detailed here, but examples are: 'Come out with your trouser-leg up', *The Sunday Herald*, 3 February 2002, and, 'Judges should say if they are Freemasons.' *The [Glasgow] Herald. 5 March 2003.

435 Petition No. PE693, submitted in December 2003 on behalf of the Movement for a Register of Freemasons (MFRFM).

436 These are the principal ministerial advisors to the government on legal matters. At the time of writing it utilises 122 lawyers, plus a range of support staff.

437 The Grand Lodge of Scotland is the highest body representing all the Craft Lodges in the country. There are other head offices which represent other branches of Freemasonry, for example, the Supreme Grand Royal Arch Chapter of Scotland (SGRAC).

438 Petition No. PE693 was submitted by the MFRFM which is based in England, and the individual signing the petition on behalf of MFRFM is resident in England.

439 This is a commentary on Freemasonry and politics (with a small 'p'), but I would like to think that someone, somewhere, might like to take up this discrimination against a minority at a Political level – note the capital 'P'.

440 Queen Elizabeth II (I in Scotland) is the daughter of a Grand Master Mason of the Grand Lodge of Scotland. He was installed on 30th November 1936. See Plate 10.

441 For a full text of the opening speeches see:
http://www.scottish.parliament.uk/vli/history/firstDays/1999opening4.htm

442 There is evidence to suggest that Freemasonry first began in Scotland in the 15th century, if not earlier.

443 Ignoring a minority is bad enough, but actively denying it any voice must be a major worry to all who believe in a democratic society.

444 The petitions together with the dates of receipt by the PPC were as follows:

PE306	27 November 2000
PE652	26 June 2003
PE685	10 November 2003
PE693	4 December 2003
PE731	15 April 2004
PE739	6 May 2004
PE761	17 August 2004

PE803	20 December 2004
PE848	26 April 2005
PE912	14 December 2005
PE927	14 January 2006

[445] A typical example of the kind of submission can be viewed (and downloaded) online at: Scottish.parliament.uk/business/committees/historic/justice1/inquiries-02/j102-rlpc-pdfs/j102-rlpc-37.pdf

[446] This means that Freemasonry is almost 100 years older than the Church of Scotland, founded in 1696.

[447] Grand Lodge had tried innumerable times to be allowed to answer allegations in the press against Freemasonry, but was rarely permitted to do so. The reasons why are not known with any certainty, but it is not unreasonable to offer some suggestions as to why and this will be done in the conclusion.

[448] *The Scotsman*, Thursday, 25th March 2004, by Hamish MacDonell.

[449] *Edinburgh Evening News*, 25th March 2004. The headline belies the content of the article.

[450] I have no evidence that this is true, but it was certainly communicated to me by a journalist who was expressing her opinion of the situation.

[451] See note, 456.

[452] As before and after, these offers were never taken up.

[453] Lustig-Prean and Beckett v. The United Kingdom and Smith and Grady v. the United Kingdom (2000), EHRR548.

[454] Tricia Marwick, MSP.

[455] Professor Alan Miller is Director of Human Rights and a visiting Professor of Law at the University of Strathclyde, where he specialised in Human Rights. In 2007 he was appointed Chairman of the new Scottish Human Rights Commission.

[456] As far as is known, Freemasonry was the only minority group contacted for comment again, indicating that there was only one minority group being considered for inclusion in this Code of Conduct.

[457] Phil Gallie was a Scottish Conservative MSP for South Ayrshire 1999–2007.

[458] One of the reasons for the delay was due to the fact that the case involved the Grande Oriente of Italy, which is an unrecognised Masonic organisation and so there are no official 'lines of communication'.

[459] GRANDE ORIENTE D'ITALIA DI PALAZZO GIUSTINIANI v. ITALY (Application No. 35972/97) and N.F. v. ITALY (Application No. 37119/97).

[460] At the time of writing, no moves have been made to remove the discriminatory elements of the Code of Conduct.

[461] See for example: Bid to make judges admit secret membership – Lawyers' Masonic link to be exposed. *Scottish Sunday Express*, 9th May 2004.

[462] This petition was dismissed on 26th May. The effect of submissions by people not resident in Scotland, seeking to amend in some way the laws of Scotland, appears to be an anomaly not discussed by Parliament.

[463] Even when not being discussed in the political or religious spheres of society other uses were being found for Freemasonry: Sword attacker feared Masons

A psychiatric patient attacked police with a samurai sword because he feared that they were Masons and planned to kill him, a court heard yesterday.

One officer was badly wounded as he used his baton to block Roy Kumar Gajree's blows.

Police went to his Edinburgh flat on August 5 after a neighbour complained about hearing shouting and swearing.

But when Gajree opened the door, he attacked them. PC Craig McCall later required a five-hour operation to his left hand.

Consultant psychiatrist Dr. John Crichton told the High Court in Edinburgh that Gajree, 40, believed the officers who came to his door were Masons and had the intention of killing him.

Dr. Crichton added: 'I think, with the benefit of hindsight, the dosage of his medication was low.'

Psychiatric outpatient Gajree was initially charged with attempting to murder PC McCall and his colleagues Andrew Kendall, John Starling and Brian Manchester.

But he was tried on a reduced charge of assaulting the officer, striking PC McCall with the sword to his severe injury and injuring PC Starling.

After a 20 minute hearing, the jury returned a verdict of not guilty on the grounds that Gajree was insane at the time.

Lord Reed ordered that he should be detained in a mental hospital.

Daily Mail, 25 November 2004.

[464] There is no indication of what caused the interruption, but given the tenor of the previous discussion it would not be unreasonable that some individual(s) expressed their disagreement rather loudly.

[465] The members of the committee who were present were:
Michael McMahon (Convener) [Scottish Labour]
Jackie Baillie [Scottish Labour]
Helen Eadie [Scottish Labour]
Rosie Kane [Scottish Socialist Party]
Campbell Martin [Independent]
John Scott (Deputy Convener) [Scottish Conservative and Unionist Party]
Ms Sandra White [Scottish National Party]
Also in attendance were:
Andrew Arbuckle [Scottish Liberal Democrat]
Rob Gibson [Scottish National Party]
Dr Sylvia Jackson [Scottish Labour]
Those absent were:
Charlie Gordon [Scottish Labour]
John Farquhar Munro [Scottish Liberal Democrat]

[466] Hamilton's mental instability was reported later in the press. See 'Hamilton branded mentally unstable in 1974, report reveals'. *The Scotsman*. 4 October 2005.

[467] *The Public Inquiry into the Shootings at Dunblane Primary School on 13 March 1996*. The Hon. Lord Cullen. Chapter Five, paragraph six. The full text of the Public Inquiry is available online at: http://www.archive.official-documents.co.uk/document/scottish/dunblane/dunblane.htm

[468] See note 94 above.

[469] Some might go so far as to suggest that it is based on extreme paranoia and/or prejudice.

[470] Hamilton was also alleged to have regularly attended Lodge Stirling Royal Arch, No.76, but a detailed examination found no trace of him.

[471] 'Masons to reveal secret list of names', *The Scotsman*. 23 November 2003.

[472] The independent examination would not have been paid for by the press.

[473] This was picked up from the submission of petition to the PPC of the Scottish Parliament entitled:
'Petition calling for the Scottish Parliament to consider a range of issues including the initiation of a new inquiry into the events surrounding the Dunblane massacre, the 100-year closure order on certain files related to the previous Cullen Inquiry and membership of the Freemasons, the Speculative Society and other similar organisations by the Scottish judiciary.'
See: http://www.scottish.parliament.uk/business/petitions/docs/PE652.htm

[474] 'Secret files on Dunblane massacre to be unveiled', *The Scotsman*. 29 September 2005.

[475] I personally went to the National Archive to examine the material produced by the Public Inquiry. This took several days and found confirmation that Hamilton was not a Freemason, and that in fact he believed Freemasons were conspiring against him.

[476] Kevin A. Hasell.

[477] Much, much more could have been included.

[478] The Mulberry Bush and the Tavern in the Town.

[479] Hugh Callaghan, Patrick Hill, Gerard Hunter, Richard McIlkenny, William Power and John Walker.

[480] His constituency is Sunderland South. For details of the career of this MP, see: http://www.theyworkforyou.com/mp/chris_mullin/sunderland_south. In May 2008 he announced his decision not to stand for re-election in the 2010 general election.

[481] Secret Societies (Declaration). House of Commons. Christopher Mullin. 1st July 1992. At the time of writing a full transcript was available online at: http://www.theyworkforyou.com/debates/?id=1992-07-01a.853.0&s=freemasonry+speaker%3A10451#g853.1

[482] Home Affairs and Environment (Debate on the Queen's Speech). 18th November 1994. At the time of writing a full transcript of the debate was available online at: http://www.theyworkforyou.com/debates/?id=1994-11-18a.238.5&s=freemasonry+speaker%3A10451#g278.0

[483] There are several other parliamentary comments and questions on this matter, a number of which were made by other MPs. These quotes by Christopher Mullin are, therefore, merely illustrations of the general attitudes prevailing at that time and place.

[484] A brochure outlining the functions of the commission is available for download at: http://www.ccrc.gov.uk/CCRC_Uploads/report1998_1999.pdf

[485] The Labour Party, with a majority of 179.

[486] I am aware that these categories are deficient in many ways, but I think that they serve to make clear the point being made.

[487] In May 2007 the SNP won one seat more than the next largest party and so formed a minority administration.

[488] The code of conduct of Fife Regional Council is, at the time of writing, available online at: http://www.fifedirect.org.uk/publications/index.cfm?fuseaction=publication.

pop&pubid=978DCF3C-788E-444C-B3BDF5DF549F922D.

It is stated that the code of conduct was: *Approved by Standards and Audit Committee 6th September 2005*. Agreed by Joint Negotiation and Consultation Forum 28th November 2005. A copy of this and other associated material has been preserved in the Grand Lodge of Scotland Library.

[489] Until the requirement that MSPs declare that they are Freemasons, thinly disguised as requiring that they declare their membership of 'other organisations' most Scottish Freemasons are unlikely to fully commit to the democratic process.

[490] *UNISON Rules*. pp.6-7. London. 2000 Edition.

[491] Ibid. p.7.

[492] A protracted correspondence, between one individual and the trade union to which I have been granted access, failed to obtain an explanation as to why being a Freemason required declaration on the application form.

[493] The question relating to Freemasonry was not found in the union's application form obtained in October 2004.

[494] Yet again this demonstrates a lack of understanding regarding the structure, let alone the nature and purpose, of Freemasonry. For example, would the trade union concerned write to the Grand Lodges of England, Scotland and Ireland to ask whether any applicant was, or had been, a Freemason?

[495] I was that observer, sent with strict instructions not to engage in any kind of debate or discussion (with anyone) if the subject could remotely be considered to be in any way political.

[496] Scottish Commission for Human Rights Act 2006.
See: http://www.opsi.gov.uk/legislation/scotland/acts2006/asp_20060016_en_1

[497] See: http://www.scottishhumanrights.com/

[498] Yes, the word 'Antient' is spelt correctly! It is the medieval Scottish spelling of the word 'ancient' and the Grand Lodge of Scotland prefers to continue to use that spelling which first appeared in a Masonic document dated 1599.

[499] To be fair, the consultation exercise had been concluded and the legislation then enacted. Shortly thereafter an election changed the party in government. The lack of a detailed response was, however, disappointing to say the least.

[500] This plot might be considered by some Freemasons to be ironic, in that this book suggests that some journalists seem determined to 'assassinate' Freemasonry!

[501] *Irvine Welsh*, pp.152-153.

[502] The book is readily available.

[503] This aspect of Robertson's life is not mentioned by his creator.

[504] The one reproduced here was affixed to a lamppost outside Freemasons' Hall, Edinburgh.

[505] The main actors were: Martin Shaw as Judge John Deed; T. R. Bowen as Sir Michael Niven; Jenny Seagrove as Jo Mills and Simon Chandler as Sir Ian Rochester.

[506] The initial episode was watched by 6.2 million viewers. It has been repeated many times by both the BBC and other cable providers such as BSkyB and Virgin Media.

[507] Series 2, episode 2.

[508] The script was written by Gordon F. Newman.

[509]This description of the plots is taken from:

http://www.tv.com/judge-john-deed/abuse-of-power/episode/214676/summary.html
    On viewing the programme this latter statement is incorrect. The judge attempts suicide but fails.

[510] For extra drama, Canning is Deed's ex-father-in-law!

[511] The success of this book was followed by another in a similar vein by Martin Short, *Inside the Brotherhood*.

[512] If Freemasons were actually responsible for controlling a 'World Government' or in the process of creating a 'New World Order' would this be in any way possible?

[513] As has already been discussed, the repetition of a particular view of a minority group (in this case Freemasonry) in the popular media (such as TV, theatre and books) serves to reinforce that perception. The use (actually abuse) of popular mediums to project a particular ideology is well known, as in the case of Nazi Germany, but its appearance in western liberal democracies is much more insidious.

[514] The present code of conduct (at the time of writing) can be viewed online at: http://www.scottish.parliament.uk/msp/conduct/index.htm

[515] *Edinburgh Evening News*. February 2002.

[516] Frank Boyle graciously granted permission to reproduce this image. It remains his copyright.

[517] 'Pinny' is a Scots word meaning an apron, although usually intended to mean a much larger version, hence the addition of the word 'wee' [small].

[518] It could be argued that it is not the function of the cartoonist to educate in this way, but that is exactly my point.

[519] Some might claim that Freemasonry's place in society is as part of the establishment and that it is therefore conservative (with a small 'c'). This is, yet again, based on perception and not fact. Freemasonry does not adopt a political or religious stance despite persistent attempts to pigeon-hole the Order in this way.

[520] As has been discussed elsewhere in this book, attempts to define Freemasonry according to a particular ideology are inherently biased as Freemasonry can be defined as being in opposition to any given political ideology. Thus, right-wing and left-wing regimes have declared Freemasonry to be their 'enemies' and Freemasons have suffered accordingly.

[521] *The Sunday Herald*. Glasgow. 10th February 2002. p.17

[522] It will be recalled that early in this chapter there were attempts made to have a dialogue with those in the media writing about Freemasonry – not to name the writers concerned but to try and grasp the processes and motives involved. Two newspaper editors stated that under no circumstances were any journalists to be approached without permission. When asked for such permission it was refused! Although numerous newspaper cuttings had been accumulated, some needed to be replaced (including cartoons), copies of those were also denied when requested.

[523] There are all sorts of other indicators of this, such as the fact that most Grand Lodges have websites and many of their buildings are open to the public.

[524] It is necessary that I define what I mean by politics. The politics that I cannot discuss as a Freemason refers to the political decision-making, debate and party

politics which are part and parcel of everyday life. Instead, I define politics here as the amorphous mass of non-specific interaction in the widest possible sense. The former is, if you will, Politics with a capital 'P' whereas the latter is politics with a lower-case 'p'.

525 This also is a consequence of the refusal of the media to allow me, as an historian, to discuss with individual members of the press, TV, etc, the *process* of how Masonophobia developed and continues to be perpetuated.

526 I am conscious that I am using huge generalisations here, but this simple division of present-day society is sufficient for the point at discussion.

527 Home Affairs Select Committee. Third Report. *Freemasonry in the Police and the Judiciary.* Session 1996-97. Vol. 1. p.xxi.

528 The new members of the committee were:
Mr Richard Allan (discharged 8.6.98)
Mr Robin Corbett
Mr Ross Cranston (discharged 9.11.98)
Mrs Janet Dean (added 1.2.99)
Mr Nick Hawkins (added 2.3.98)
Mr Douglas Hogg (discharged 2.3.98)
Mr Gerald Howarth
Ms Beverley Hughes (discharged 9.11.98)
Miss Melanie Johnson (added 9.11.98) (discharged 1.2.99)
Mr Martin Linton
Mr Humfrey Malins
Mr Bob Russell (added 8.6.98)
Mrs Marsha Singh
Mr Paul Stinchcombe (added 9.11.98)
Mr David Winnick

529 By means of a 'ministerial instruction' – essentially an administrative instruction to the relevant government department.

530 Assuming of course that the requirement to disclose membership remained in force.

531 The full text of the committee's deliberations is available online at: http://www.publications.parliament.uk/pa/cm199899/cmselect/cmhaff/467/46701.htm

532 There is a distinction between politicians and the government that ought to be borne in mind. However, in the case of Freemasonry some politicians have managed to convince the government that their opinion should become policy as evidenced by Home Secretary Jack Straw's ministerial instruction of 1998 concerning Freemasonry and the Judiciary.

533 Home Affairs Select Committee. Third Report. *Freemasonry in the Police and the Judiciary.* Session 1996-97. Vol. One. p.xiv.

534 Ibid. p.vi.

535 Grande Oriente D'Italia di Palazzo Giustiniani v. Italy (Application no. 35972/97). Page six.

536 Grande Oriente D'Italia di Palazzo Giustiniani v. Italy (No.2) (Application No. 26740/02). Page two.

537 Again, the question is asked: 'how did they know that?'

538 For example, on 10th November 2009, Gordon Prentice MP complained that it

was a 'disgrace' that applicants for the judiciary could no longer be forced to declare whether or not they were Freemasons. See a report of this in *The Independent*: http://www.independent.co.uk/news/uk/politics/anger-at-cloak-of-secrecy-for-freemason-judges-1818043.html

[539] *The Guardian*, 5th November 2009.

[540] It would be folly to suggest that Freemasons *en masse* changed their voting habits.

[541] See http://www.equalities.gov.uk/equality_act_2010.aspx for comprehensive information on the act.

[542] The text of this can be downloaded from: http://www.grandlodgescotland.com/images/stories/holocaustdeclar.pdf

[543] The list of groups so recognised can be found on the Holocaust Memorial Day website at: http://www.hmd.org.uk/genocides/the-holocaust/victims-of-nazi-hatred

[544] Even the National Geographic television programme *World War II: The Apocalypse: The Fall of France* (broadcast a number of times and viewed by the author on 20th February 2010) acknowledges Freemasonry as a separate group targeted by the Nazis. The relevant extract follows:
'One of the first tasks of the German occupiers [of Paris] is to seize all the records of the abandoned ministries, lists of spies, of Jews, Freemasons and even the original copy of the Treaty of Versailles that so humiliated Germany in 1919.'

[545] Seven letters, several emails and telephone calls have been ignored.

[546] Holocaust studies now also include recent genocidal conflicts such as Rwanda.

[547] Such vows, in various forms, exist in most denominations of Christianity.

[548] I am aware that some churches in this situation have made amends as far as they are able, but that still does not mean that every single member of that church is involved in a conspiracy to protect the perpetrator.

[549] For example if one accesses the online edition of *The Times* (London) and types 'Freemasonry' in the search box one will be supplied with a list of articles which mention Freemasonry. Prominent is a 'Sponsored Link': *Do Not Join The Freemasons Until You've Seen This...* Other links invite one to buy Masonic artefacts or place those Masonophobic websites in the pecking order.

[550] See *The Rosslyn Hoax?* chapter six, pp.142-145 and 165-166.

[551] This is incorrect. See *The Rosslyn Hoax?* pp.142-154.

[552] I have heard the chapel guides describe them as such on numerous occasions, although they no longer do so.

[553] The guidebook and signage in the chapel have now been corrected.

[554] The first reference to lodges of stonemasons which evolved into modern Masonic Lodges took place in Scotland. The first recorded reference was in 1491.

[555] Oswald was murdered by Jack Ruby (1911–1965), who claimed he had been distraught and acted out of a need for retribution. Ruby became ill soon after and died just two years later, before other possible motives could be obtained from him.

[556] There is a widespread belief that Kennedy's assassination was a conspiracy of some kind. See: http://www.foxnews.com/story/0,2933,102511,00.html

[557] One of the more notorious instances (although not involving Freemasonry) that

the author can vividly recall was that of Miss Jo Moore, an aide who worked for Stephen Byers, the then Secretary of State for Transport, Local Government and the Regions. She suggested, during the attack on the Twin Towers in New York (11th September 2001), that it was a good time to bury bad news about local councillors' expenses.

[558] It would be cynical indeed to suggest that the leaders of any religious group would consciously select Freemasonry as an 'enemy' in the knowledge that it posed no threat to them.

[559] Only vague suggestions were made that this would 'do the Freemasons a favour' by countering the prevailing public perception of Freemasonry!

[560] Used as a disparaging term for one who is not a Jew.

INDEX